FROM AKBAR TO AURANGZEB

FROM AKBAR TO AURANGZEB

A Study in Indian Economic History

by

W. H. MORELAND

GYAN

Published by

GYAN

Gyan Publishing House
5, Ansari Road
Daryaganj, New Delhi-110002
Phone: 011-47034999, 9811692060
E-mail: books@gyanbooks.com

Distribution Network
gyanbooks.com
India, USA, Canada, UK, Australia, France

ISBN : 978-81-212-9978-7 (PB)
First Published, 1923

2nd Impression 2021

Printed at: Gyan Press, Delhi.

From Akbar to Aurangzeb
Author: W. H. Moreland

FROM AKBAR TO AURANGZEB

A STUDY IN INDIAN ECONOMIC HISTORY

BY

W. H. MORELAND

C.S.I., C.I.E.

LATE OF THE INDIAN CIVIL SERVICE

AUTHOR OF

"INDIA AT THE DEATH OF AKBAR"

AND "AN INTRODUCTION TO ECONOMICS FOR INDIAN STUDENTS"

MACMILLAN AND CO., LIMITED

ST. MARTIN'S STREET, LONDON

1923

PREFACE

In this book I have carried a stage further the study in Indian economic history of which the first portion was offered to the public in *India at the Death of Akbar*. I there sketched the economic position at the opening of the seventeenth century: I now examine the changes in that position which took place in the course of the next fifty or sixty years, the period covered by the reigns of the Mogul Emperors Jahangir and Shahjahan. Apart from chronological or dynastic considerations, this period has a unity of its own. In the region of commerce it is marked by the practical elimination of the Portuguese, the establishment of Dutch and English merchants in the country, and the first experimental phases of the new-comers' activities; while in the wider economic sphere it covers the most significant stages in the deterioration of Akbar's administrative institutions. These topics call for somewhat detailed examination, and it is convenient to treat them by themselves, without extending our survey to the new conditions which marked the reign of Aurangzeb—the further administrative changes, the rise of the Maratha power, and the increasing interest of foreign merchants in territorial questions, evidenced by the settlements of the Dutch in Malabar, the English in Bombay, and the French in Pondicherry.

The order of study has been determined mainly by the nature of the materials which are available. The Dutch and English records of the period, while they are incomplete, are sufficiently copious to render possible a tolerably precise treatment of the commerce with which they are primarily concerned, while their examination for this purpose furnishes a large mass of incidental observations, which enable us to interpret with some degree of confidence the fragmentary information supplied by Indian sources regarding the economic life of the country as a whole, and its domination by the activities of the various administrations. I have thus found it convenient to begin with the subject of external commerce, and then to use the knowledge so obtained to throw light on topics of greater internal interest. From the outset I have attempted to exhibit the activities of the English commercial pioneers in what I take to be their true relation to the earlier, more extensive, and more profitable operations of the Dutch, operations which are almost ignored in some current textbooks of Indian history. It was the Dutch, not the English, who succeeded to the Portuguese mastery of the Asiatic seas, and for the greater part of a century it was the Dutch who took the largest share in the external commerce of India. That few students have hitherto given their attention to influences of such importance is in my opinion unfortunate, but the omission finds adequate explanation in the inaccessibility of the sources from which information regarding them must be drawn. In the first place, Dutch scholars have very naturally devoted their energies to the history of their great island-empire rather than to the affairs of a mainland on which their nation has retained no footing, and, apart from Dr. Terpstra's two volumes, which I have quoted so frequently, I know of no attempt to utilise the materials at their disposal for a study of any definitely Indian question. In the second place, ignorance of the language has prevented most Englishmen, and nearly all Indians, from making use of even the published materials available in Dutch; and the result may be seen in various popular works, which praise, or censure, the English pioneers for their daring initiative, or their brutal misconduct, as the case may be, when, in fact, they were merely following a road already worn by their predecessors' feet. The neglect of Dutch sources for this period is all the more to be regretted, because in some respects they are definitely superior to the English. The Dutch merchants were careful to set down in black and white many things which the English were content to take for granted: their more extensive operations gave them wider views; and the discipline enforced by the authorities at Batavia produced detailed and precise records of transactions carried out in distant places. English-reading students will naturally continue to rely mainly on the English sources, but they are likely to form inaccurate or distorted views on many important questions if they fail to take account also of the information furnished by the Dutch.

Regarding unpublished sources of information for the period, it may be said at once that there is now little to be found in the records of the India Office. The calendars prepared by Mr. William Foster, or issued under his supervision, are sufficiently detailed to meet all the needs of ordinary students; I have gleaned among the original records, but have gathered very little indeed that was not already in print—some figures from commercial documents, and occasionally a few phrases throwing additional light on some minute point—so that Indians unable to visit England may be confident that the printed calendars tell practically the whole story. No similar calendars exist for the voluminous Dutch records, and it is not possible to speak of their contents with certainty. I have not been able to undertake their systematic examination, and, so far as I know, the only study of them from the Indian point of view has been that which resulted in the preparation of the Transcripts from Archives at The Hague, which are available at the India Office. This series is invaluable to students working in England, but it is very far from being complete on the economic side. When I have applied to the Dutch Public Record Office for information on specific points, I have usually been furnished with photographs of important documents not included in the Transcripts, or hitherto quoted in English; and the existence of this large store of unexplored materials should be borne in mind by all students of the period. Its complete exploration would probably be a task too great for any individual, but the undertaking deserves the attention of societies or organisations interested in Indian historical research.

As to Indian sources, I have not had an opportunity of examining contemporary MSS. other than those which are available in this country, and I have little doubt that much additional information on the subjects dealt with in the later chapters of this volume could be obtained by study of the collections in Indian libraries. The present volume therefore is, like the former, a sketch rather than a definitive treatise; it reviews all, or almost all, the evidence which is now in print, but scattered through a large number of works, not all of which are readily accessible to students in India; and it takes account of some sources not yet published, but it does not claim to exhaust them. There is still a wide scope for research in the history of this period, not only among the Dutch records, but in literature which is within the reach of Indian students, and which they are in the best position to interpret.

I have tried to arrange the book in such a way that, while it should be intelligible to ordinary readers, it should serve serious students as an introduction to the original literature. Authority for, I hope, every assertion of fact will be found in the notes at the end of each chapter, while in the Appendices I have brought together a large amount of detail, some of it not very readily accessible, regarding the course of Asiatic commerce, which may help students in the early stages of their reading before the technical language of the literature has become familiar through experience. In making quotations from old writers and documents, I have usually modernised the spelling and punctuation. In regard to Indian words, I have as a rule followed the system of transliteration adopted in the *Imperial Gazetteer*, but an exception has been necessary in the case of the descriptions applied to Indian cotton goods. The nomenclature of these offers a wide field of study; the derivation of many commercial terms is still an open question; and precise transliteration is impossible so long as the derivation remains obscure. In such cases I have thought it best to select common contemporary forms of the names, and thus avoid the appearance of prejudging linguistic questions on which I am not qualified to pronounce.

It remains only to acknowledge the generous assistance which I have received from scholars in this country and in India. For information or help on particular points I have to express my thanks to Miss L. M. Anstey, Dr. W. R. Bisschop, Mr. R. Burn, Mr. C. E. Carrington, Sir Robert Gillan, Sir Wolseley Haig, Professor Jadu Nath Sarkar, Professor Shafaat Ahmad Khan, Professor G. W. Daniels, and the officers of the Departments of Coins and Medals, and of Oriental Manuscripts, at the British Museum. Profesor P. Geyl, of the University of London, has given me most valuable assistance in getting at the full meaning of some of the Dutch records; Dr. J. de Hullu, of the Rijksarchief, has been most generous in searching for, and supplying me with information from the records in his charge; and finally, Mr. W. Foster, of the India Office, has again allowed me to draw continually on his unique knowledge of the period.

April 1923.

CONTENTS

CHAPTER I

CHAPTER II

CHAPTER III

CHAPTER IV

CHAPTER V

CHAPTER VI

CHAPTER VII

CHAPTER VIII

CHAPTER IX

CHAPTER X

APPENDICES

MAPS

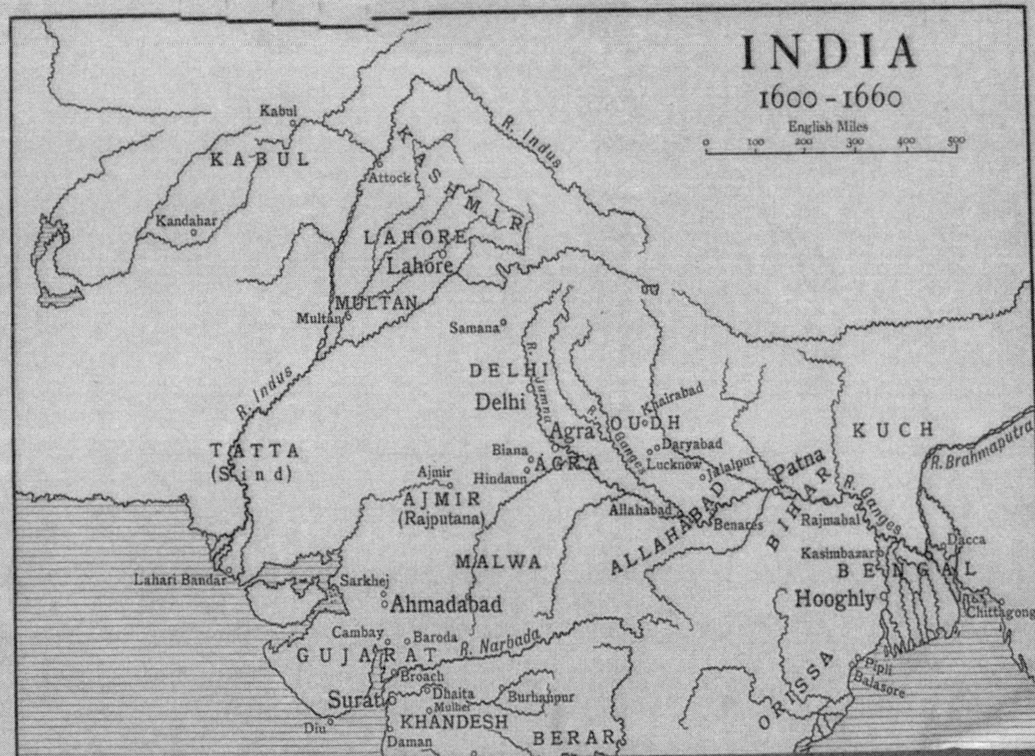
INDIA
1600-1660
English Miles
0
100
200
300
400
500
KABUL
Kabul
Kandahar
Attock
KASHMIR
LAHORE
Lahore
MULTAN
Multan
R. Indus
Samana
DELHI
Delhi
R. Jumna
Agra
AGRA
Biana
Hindaun
Ajmir
AJMIR
(Rajputana)
TATTA
(Sind)
Lahari Bandar
Sarkhej
Ahmadabad
MALWA
Cambay
Baroda
GUJARAT
R. Narbada
Broach
Dhaita
Mulher
Burhanpur
Surat
Diu
Daman
KHANDESH
BERAR
R. Ganges
Khairabad
OUDH
Daryabad
Lucknow
Jalalpur
Allahabad
ALLAHABAD
Benares
Patna
BIHAR
Rajmahal
KUCH
R. Brahmaputra
Dacca
Kasimbazar
BENGAL
Hooghly
Chittagong
ORISSA
Pipli
Balasore

CHAPTER I

THE ASIATIC ENVIRONMENT

1. The Political Situation

The subject of this book is an examination of the economic movements which affected India during the first half of the seventeenth century, but it is desirable to say a few words by way of introduction about the political situation in India itself, and in the countries with which India then maintained commercial relations. In this volume, as in *India at the Death of Akbar*, I mean by " India " the area now occupied by the Indian Empire and the Indian States, but exclusive of the province of Burma, the political union of which with India dates from a much later period.

The bulk of this area falls into three main divisions, the Mogul Empire in the north, the Deccan kingdoms in the centre, and the territories held by Hindu chiefs in the south. So far as the Mogul Empire is concerned, the period I have chosen coincides with the reigns of Jahangir and Shahjahan, and during these reigns the political history of the Empire possesses but little interest for the economist. Occasional rebellions, struggles for the succession to the throne, an endless series of Court intrigues,—such matters as these will not concern us greatly, apart from the obvious facts that recurring outbreaks of disturbances involved not only loss at the moment but discouragement of enterprise for the future, and that the growth of public expenditure meant a progressive increase in the administrative pressure on producers. As regards the frontiers, no events of importance occurred on the north, while on the west it is sufficient to mention the struggle with Persia for the possession of Kandahar, which affected not only the land trade between the two countries but also the commerce of the Gulf of Cambay. On the east, the effective rule of the Moguls stopped short at or near the estuary of the Meghna, and portions of eastern Bengal were ruled by the king of Arakan until the year 1666, when Chittagong was captured, and, with the intervening country, brought under the administration of the Empire. More important changes occurred on the southern frontier, where the subjugation of the Deccan kingdoms had already begun. Of the five states usually included under this expression, Bidar was absorbed by its neighbours and disappears from history, while Khandesh was already a Mogul province. The conquest of Ahmadnagar had been attempted by Akbar, but was not finally effected until the year 1635, when most of its territory was incorporated in the Empire, and about the same time the two remaining kingdoms, Bijapur and Golconda, were reduced to the position of vassals, though their internal organisation remained practically intact.

Of the Hindu territories in the south no detailed history is required. After the destruction of the power of Vijayanagar in 1565, the country was left in the hands of chiefs, who were known as Nāyaks, and who recognised in theory, and occasionally in practice, the overlordship of a representative of the Vijayanagar dynasty, styled king of Chandragiri, or popularly king of the Carnatic. Such glimpses as we obtain through the Dutch and English records show these nayaks constantly fighting among themselves, with the king sometimes as a puppet and sometimes as an active partner; the grouping changes rapidly, and all that need be said is that peace was rarely enjoyed, and could never be expected to continue. Meanwhile Golconda and Bijapur were extending their territories in this direction, sometimes in alliance with one nayak or another; I can find no suggestion of anything that would nowadays be regarded as a reasonable *casus belli*, but at this period the prospect of obtaining revenue or treasure was commonly a sufficient motive for hostilities.

Of the lesser territorial units in India, the position of the Portuguese will be discussed in subsequent sections; the remainder are of little economic interest, and the only one which requires mention is the small state of Calicut, still practically independent, and, from its situation on the pepper-yielding coast of Malabar, a place of some importance in the commercial politics of the time.

The description which has just been given of Southern India might almost be applied to the greater part of Asia. Throughout the countries with which India maintained relations, war was, if not the normal condition of affairs, at least sufficiently probable to dominate the minds of merchants and producers, while the slightness of the pretexts on which it might be undertaken made a reasoned forecast impossible, and there was nothing for it but to accommodate oneself to circumstances as they arose. The most important countries on the western side of India were Persia and Turkey; they were frequently at war, and their hostilities had marked effects on the course of trade, while Turkey had in addition occasional troubles with the Arab tribesmen on the shores of the Red Sea. To the east of India, the countries of Arakan, Pegu, Ava, and Siam form a group of which it can be said only that war might break out among them at any moment, and Siam might also be expected to interfere in what is now Indo-China, where local wars were not less frequent. China was being conquered during this period by invaders, while Japan had recently attempted to seize Korea, and had been the scene of prolonged civil wars.

The situation in the southern islands was perhaps worse than on the continent, for kingdoms were smaller, and sources of dispute were accordingly more numerous. The chief power in Sumatra was the tyrant of Achin, a dynasty founded in the sixteenth century on the destruction of some older kingdoms. Achin controlled most of the pepper-yielding country on the West Coast, and attempted from time to time to extend his dominions over the minor kings farther to the east, but his hostility was directed primarily against the Portuguese at Malacca, a place to which he had no particular claim, but to which he was attracted by its commercial advantages. In western Java the adjacent maritime kingdoms of Bantam and Jakatra might be at war at any time, either with each other or with their neighbours, and the establishment of the Dutch at Batavia did not at first make for peace. The king of Macassar, the chief place on the island of Celebes, had ambitions towards the conquest of eastern Java, while his commercial policy involved occasional hostilities with the Dutch. The position in the Spice Islands [1] at the end of the sixteenth century was nearly desperate. The inhabitants of the Banda Islands had then ousted the Portuguese, and were for the moment in enjoyment of a precarious independence. In Amboina the Portuguese still held out, owing mainly to dissensions among their local enemies. In the Molucca Islands proper there were nearly as many parties as islands ; and since the control of exports from these islands was essential to the successful prosecution of the Eastern trade, the advent of the Dutch and the English served at first to increase the confusion. Eventually the Dutch secured the mastery, but in spite of their drastic methods of pacification it was long before tranquillity was established.

The economist can pass lightly over the details of such conflicts, but it is important for him to realise that, with the exception of China, none of the Asiatic powers had developed anything which could properly be described as naval force. We read indeed of "fleets" set out by Pegu, or Achin, or Macassar, but the descriptions of their activities show that the vessels must be regarded as transports rather than as fighting units. When Achin, for example, sent an expedition against Malacca, it meant that an army was embarked on some hundreds of craft of different types, to be ferried across the intervening

[1] The nomenclature of the islands varies in the literature of the period. I use the term Spice Islands in a wide sense, to include the Moluccas, Ceram, Amboina, and the Banda Islands ; the balance of convenience appears to lie in confining the term Moluccas to the small islands lying to the west of Gilolo. The Moluccas and Amboina yielded cloves, while mace and nutmegs came only from the Banda Islands. There were cloves also on Ceram, but this island does not come into prominence during our period. The position of the islands is shown on the map facing p. 16.

waters and landed on the enemy's coast; and if such an expedition met with a Portuguese fleet in the strict sense, the transports were simply swept off the sea. The Mogul Empire had no navy, and it is almost pathetic to read the demands of the Surat authorities for the help of one or two Dutch or English ships to protect their harbours against attack.[1] A few Dutch gunboats sufficed, as we shall see, to force Golconda to sue for peace. On one occasion the steward of the king of Persia declared with perfect truth that his master was king of the land but not of the sea. We shall refer later on to the "fleet" maintained by the Turks at Mocha; here it is enough to say that in the closing years of the sixteenth century the Portuguese were indisputably masters of the Indian seas, not so much from their own strength as from the failure of the Asiatic nations to realise the nature of sea-power. The history of Indian commerce during our period is bound up indissolubly with the transfer from the Portuguese to the Dutch of sea-power in the region between Mozambique and the Moluccas, and it is necessary therefore to describe this change in some detail.

2. The Portuguese Maritime Empire

The first Portuguese vessels appeared in Indian waters at the end of the fifteenth century, and within a very few years the conception was formed of a type of Empire of which Asia had no recent experience. The design was to hold the seas in strength, and control sea-borne commerce for the benefit of the ruling power: it was an enormous enterprise for a small nation seated some thousands of miles away, and its realisation was rendered possible only by the attitude of the Asiatic powers which has just been described. The essentials

[1] See, for an instance, the entries in Methwold's diary, in *English Factories*, v. 310 ff. When the harbour at Surat was threatened by pirates from Malabar, and the English were not disposed to provide for its defence, the Mogul Governor "fitted up three frigates, and pressed a crew of poor, unexperienced cotton-beaters, etc., who had never seen the sea, and therefore could be of no great use unto him; yet sometimes they would row out of the river, and then, riding under the security of our ship, or rather on board her, they would return into the river again at night."

for success were two: fleets strong enough to overcome opposition on the water, and a small number of naval stations, defensible both by land and by sea, to afford shelter and supplies for the fleets, and—as time went on—to furnish reinforcements of sailors and fighting men. The absence of any serious opposition made it possible to control the seas by means of fleets of very moderate strength, so that at the outset the real problem for the Portuguese was the acquisition and fortification of the naval bases. The primary bases were three in number: Goa on the western coast of India, Malacca at the gateway of the Farther East, and Ormuz at the entrance to the Persian Gulf. The original design had included also the harbour of Aden, to control traffic with the Red Sea; the spread of the Turkish power along the Arabian coast prevented its acquisition, but the three places named proved sufficient for nearly a century. Apart from them, the Portuguese held various forts designed for special purposes, the chief of which were Mozambique, Diu, Damān, Cochin, and Colombo. Mozambique on the eastern coast of Africa served as a halting-place for the annual fleets from Europe, and also as a trading centre; Diu and Damān watched the Gulf of Cambay, the most important of the various outlets of Indian trade; Cochin was the chief port for the pepper of Malabar, which formed the largest single item of the cargoes sent to Europe; and in the same way Colombo controlled the principal source of marketable cinnamon. There were also smaller forts scattered among the hostile populations of the Spice Islands, to secure the trade in cloves, mace, and nutmegs, and at carefully chosen points on the East African coast; while at or near some of the stations, particularly on the west of India, small areas of territory came from time to time under Portuguese rule.

As the century went on, Portuguese communities of a somewhat different type came into existence. Some of them were provided with forts to which commanders were appointed from Goa, others were merely settlements in foreign territory, but all were distinguished by being primarily places of trade rather than centres of power. On the eastern side of India, such settlements existed at S. Thomé and Negapatam in the south, and at Hooghly and Chittagong in Bengal. Farther east there was Macao, at the entrance to the harbour of Canton, whence merchants were admitted under severe restrictions to a share in the trade of the mainland of China; there was a small colony on the distant island of Timor, engaged in supplying the white sandalwood procurable in those parts, and at a later period there was an extensive settlement in Macassar; but these and various places of less importance did not add materially to Portuguese power, though they made important contributions to the wealth of the community. The centre of power was Goa, on which the chief fleets were based, and whence reinforcements were despatched East or West in case of need. The smaller vessels, and some of the larger, were built in India, either at Goa itself or at Bassein, and the dockyard at the former city was probably the most highly organised industrial enterprise in the country.

The methods adopted for the control of sea-borne commerce were briefly as follows. In the first place, certain trade routes were declared a monopoly of the king of Portugal, and on these routes no vessels of other nationalities were allowed to ply. The reserved routes varied from time to time, but at the end of the sixteenth century it may be said that no Indian ship could venture to East Africa, to China, to Japan, or to the Spice Islands without risking capture or destruction by the Portuguese; commerce to these countries was either conducted as a State enterprise, granted to individuals by way of reward, or farmed for the benefit of the treasury. In the second place, the carriage of certain goods, notably munitions and pepper, was prohibited to all foreign vessels, and a breach of this rule involved destruction or confiscation. In the third place, no Asiatic vessel could ply to any port, or carry any cargo, until fees had been paid and a licence (*cartaz*) obtained; while, apart from licence-fees, customs duties were levied at such ports as Ormuz or Malacca. In theory, then, the official control of sea-borne commerce was complete, but in order to understand the actual position allowance must be made for the fact that the Portuguese administration was exceedingly corrupt. The income of the commanders appointed to the various stations was popularly estimated not in terms of the official salaries, but on the basis of their illicit gains, and, as Pyrard wrote of Ormuz, the authorities "for money let everything pass." The same writer tells us that Portuguese merchants frequently joined with Indians as partners in their ventures, an arrangement of obvious convenience for evading control; free licences given for political reasons to various Indian rulers were employed for the same purpose; and the final result of the system was that, while commerce was active throughout the Indian seas, a large part of the profits came into Portuguese hands, the sum total of charges, legitimate and other, tending to approximate to "what the traffic would bear." It would not pay a commander to discourage trade with his port, but there was no other limit to his rapacity.

The question may perhaps be asked, By what right did the Portuguese assume sovereignty over the Indian seas? There are two possible answers, either of which is conclusive within the limited sphere of its validity. To the Portuguese themselves it was sufficient that their enterprise had the sanction, and the blessing, of the Pope. It will be remembered that in temporal affairs the position of the Pope was at that time supra-national, and that his "mandates" (as we might now term them) were accepted as valid throughout Latin Christendom; the Portuguese title was therefore beyond question among those nations which adhered to this view of the Pope's authority. On the other hand, the papal sanction had no validity whatever in the eyes of nations like the Dutch and English, who at the close of the sixteenth century had definitely rejected this view of the Pope's position, and of course it was entirely irrelevant in the case of Asiatic powers. From the Asiatic standpoint, however, the Empire of the Portuguese was equally beyond question, because it rested on force, the only origin of public right then recognised in practice on that continent. The king of Portugal was Emperor of the Indian seas because he had been strong enough to seize on them, and because no other power was strong enough to take them from him ; Akbar was Emperor of the Indian plains for precisely the same reasons. Had Asia paid any regard to prescription or lapse of time, it must have recognised the Portuguese Empire as the more legitimate of the two, for the Portuguese were already firmly established in India when Babur started on his great adventure, but length of possession was not regarded in practice as an obstacle in the way of other claims.

Akbar tacitly recognised the position of Portugal by taking out licences for ships sent by him to the Red Sea, and the Moguls made no attempt either to free or to command the water. Bijapur more than once attacked Goa, and the concerted action taken about the year 1571 by various Moslem powers may be regarded as a threat to the Portuguese Empire as a whole, but as such it was ineffective. Some years later, the Turks renewed the efforts made earlier in the century to capture the Indian seas for themselves, and, conscious of the want of timber for shipbuilding in their dominions in Arabia, established themselves on the wooded coasts of East Africa ; but their " fleet " of two galleys, one of them unseaworthy, and supported by small craft of low fighting value, was altogether inadequate for the purpose, and the Portuguese had little difficulty in recovering the lost territory ; and the only other challenge to the Empire was that of " Cunnale," the pirate-king of Malabar.[1] The story of his rise to power is curious rather than important. Enjoying the secret protection of Calicut, he gradually became a serious danger to Portuguese shipping, and towards the close of the sixteenth century he assumed the title of " Lord of the Indian Seas," and granted licences for shipping on the lines adopted by his enemies. A Portuguese expedition sent against him was defeated, and he then styled himself " Defender of Islam, and Expeller of the Portuguese " ; but his enjoyment of these titles was short,

[1] The name of the pirate-king appears in various forms, and I am not certain of the correct transliteration ; presumably it is Kunhi Ali. A Dutch narrative says he was sent to the galleys (*Renneville*, iii. 451) ; the statement that he was executed comes from Portuguese sources (*Calendar S.P.*, 1513–1616, No. 280).

for a second expedition was completely successful, and it is said that the "Lord of the Indian Seas" was eventually executed at Goa. Thus the Portuguese had up to the end of the century held their own against all challengers, and there were not many powers in Asia which could show any better cause for their existence.

To all appearance, then, the Empire stood firm, but its foundations had been shaken, and it was in no condition to resist a determined attack. The story of its decay must be left to the political historian; there were many grave errors of policy and administration, but the central fact is that the strength of Portugal had been overtaxed by the enterprises carried on simultaneously in Asia, Africa, and Brazil. The population of the country declined seriously during the sixteenth century, and at its end was perhaps about the same as that of the modern city of Calcutta; a time had come when it was no longer possible to send out year by year the men needed for these enterprises, men of whom very few returned, and the manning of the fleets, together with the defence of the Asiatic possessions, was left more and more to the mixed race which had grown up in the various settlements. It is no slur on the men of this race to say that they were not the equals of their ancestors; on occasion they could fight well, but they fell short in the extraordinary qualities which in the earlier days had gained for the Portuguese in Asia the reputation of invincibility on land and sea. The men of mixed race were not invincible, and even of them the number was inadequate for the continuous wars of attack and defence; Goa was still able to build ships, but not always to provide the necessary crews and soldiers.[1]

[1] It is of course impossible to speak precisely regarding the population of Portugal at this period. I have seen an estimate that the number of Portuguese fell from two millions in 1500 to half that number a century later, but I do not know the basis of the calculation. The insufficiency of "man-power" during our period is evident from numerous incidental notices, *e.g. Lisbon Transcripts*, i. 126; *Hague Transcripts*, I. 318; *Calendar S.P.*, 1513–16, Nos. 408, 432; *Dagh Register*, June 20, 1633. *Linschoten* (c. 93) noted that while 1500 or more soldiers reached Goa yearly about the year 1590, the number returning was rarely as large as 100.

This fundamental weakness was aggravated by the diversion of Portuguese resources to meet the needs of Spain, when the sovereignty of the two countries was united at the end of the year 1580. The union was purely personal. Portugal remained a separate nation, but for a period of sixty years the policy of the country was directed by the king of Spain, and such power as the smaller nation still possessed was squandered in the attempt to establish Spanish supremacy in Europe. When Portuguese independence was regained in 1641, the position in Asia was already desperate. The diversion of material resources was, however, not the only result of this period of "subjection to slavery," as the union was regarded by patriotic Portuguese. The national spirit, which had counted for so much in the Asiatic enterprise, was almost crushed, and a tone of fatalistic resignation replaces confident aspiration in the literature of the time. The Portuguese in Asia quickly realised that they could expect little help from Europe in their struggles with their neighbours, but they had also to learn that their connection with Spain had brought them new enemies, and that their supremacy at sea was to be challenged successfully by the Dutch, the inveterate opponents of the Spanish power.

3. The Advent of the Dutch and English

The enmity between Spain and Holland is one of the outstanding facts of European politics in the latter portion of the sixteenth century. The country which we know as Holland has grown out of those United Provinces of the Netherlands which revolted from the sovereignty of the king of Spain, and engaged in a struggle for national independence. It was a small country, and its internal resources were scanty. A large proportion of the national income was derived from the fisheries and the sea-borne carrying trade, and Dutch vessels plied in large numbers throughout the waters of Western Europe; but the shipping industry was more than a source of income, for its maintenance was essential to the security of the national existence. Holland could hope to withstand Spain only with the aid of strength at sea, and the success of her efforts depended on sea-power in the full meaning of the term, not merely a fleet on the water, but adequate numbers of vessels of all kinds, dockyards equipped for construction and repair, a steady supply of expert sailors and navigators, and the wealth necessary to employ these resources to the best advantage. The efficiency of the mercantile marine was thus a primary national interest.

This national interest was threatened by the succession of the king of Spain to the Portuguese throne, because at this period Lisbon and the neighbouring seaports formed the principal market for the goods carried southwards by the Dutch. It was here that they sold most of the grain, timber, and materials for building and equipping ships which they brought from the Baltic, as well as the salted fish and other produce of their own country; and it was here that they obtained goods to carry northwards on the return voyage, in particular the salt which was required for curing fish, and the spices and other Eastern goods for which Antwerp, and subsequently Amsterdam, were the principal distributing centres. The effective closure of the Portuguese seaports would therefore have entirely disorganised the fishing and shipping industries on which the existence of Holland depended, and it is at least doubtful whether in the conditions of the period their vessels could have found adequate employment elsewhere in European waters. The common statement that the Dutch trade with Portugal was in fact closed is so far true that orders to that effect were issued from time to time; but the Portuguese were not enthusiastic in the Spanish cause, and in spite of prohibitions they continued to trade with the Dutch, who on their side considered it sound policy to draw from the enemy's country the money which they needed in order to fight him. The trade therefore continued, but it was subject to frequent interference: Dutch vessels in Portuguese waters were seized and impressed for naval service; merchants and seamen were arrested and handed over to the Inquisition; goods were confiscated; and the danger increased as time went on. The Dutch were thus compelled to face the possibility that their trade with Portugal might cease, and among the alternatives open to them that which offered the most hopeful prospect was the extension of their business to a wider area, and the establishment of direct commercial relations with countries where Spain and Portugal still enjoyed a practical monopoly. Such a project was in harmony with the new ideas which were spreading rapidly in Holland. The material resources of the country were increased very greatly by the transfer of trade from Antwerp to Amsterdam, while a strong national spirit was developing, and enterprises which ten years earlier would have seemed to be impracticable quickly came to be regarded as reasonable commercial propositions.

About the same time English merchants also were becoming eager to secure a share in the Eastern trade, and were studying in particular the possibilities of the Mediterranean route, because the voyage round the Cape of Good Hope was barred to them by the Spanish or Portuguese claim to a monopoly. The main result of their efforts at this time was the increase of knowledge furnished by the reports of John Newbery, who, along with Ralph Fitch, reached India overland. The prospects of the Mediterranean route were found to be unattractive, but the Cape voyage became practicable after the defeat of the Spanish Armada in 1588, which relieved the Dutch, no less than the English, from their most immediate political anxieties. Three years later an English expedition under George Raymond started for the East, but it led to nothing, and the Dutch were probably wise in waiting until they had procured more detailed information regarding the conditions of the enterprise. The data upon which they acted came mainly from two sources; in the year 1592 van Linschoten arrived in Holland after more than five years' residence in Goa, while about the same time Cornelis Houtman was sent by a group of merchants to collect secret information in Lisbon; and on his return two years later the Dutch were in a position to make a definite attempt to enter the Eastern trade.[1]

[1] Some of van Linschoten's results were not actually published until 1596, but it is clear that the information he brought was available to Houtman

Their earliest ventures were strictly commercial: it is true that from about 1603 onwards, the Dutch fleets went out prepared to fight as well as trade, but for nearly ten years previously their ruling policy had been to reach the East without encountering Spanish or Portuguese, and to establish commercial relations with those Asiatic countries which were not under direct Portuguese influence or control. In theory three routes to the East were available, round the north of Asia, round the south of America, and round the Cape of Good Hope. The first of these appeared to offer exceptional attractions, mainly owing to the fact that neither Spain nor Portugal was established in the Northern seas, and ships were despatched northwards in 1594 and 1595, but the difficulties of navigation proved to be insuperable. The route by the south of America was also tried, and in the year 1600 Dutch ships succeeded in reaching the intended markets by this course, but it was unsuitable for trade, mainly because the Spaniards were established in strength on the west coast of South America, and also in the Philippines, where it was necessary for ships to refresh after crossing the Pacific. There remained the route round Africa, and this was attempted for the first time in the year 1595, when four vessels were despatched from Amsterdam with the object of bringing direct to Western Europe supplies of the spices, drugs, and other goods available in the East. In view of the vast political changes which eventually resulted from this small beginning, it may be well to insist on the fact that at the outset there is no trace of any design to acquire territory, or establish what are now called colonies. The projectors of this first voyage did not even provide for the establishment of "factories" or agencies in the Eastern markets: their intention was merely that their ships should visit Eastern ports,

---

on the first voyage round the Cape; vide *Houtman*, i. xxxii, 62, and *passim*. As he was a member of the Northern expeditions of 1594 and 1595, his knowledge was obviously at the disposal of their promoters. The details of Houtman's proceedings in Lisbon are obscure (*van der Chijs*, 29), as might be expected from the fact that he was in search of information which the Portuguese endeavoured to keep absolutely secret; but the fact of his visit is clear (*Houtman*, i. xxxi, *n.*).

sell their goods, and return as soon as suitable cargo had been procured. The gradual change of organisation, from trading voyage to factory, from factory to fort, and from fort to territorial sovereignty, resulted mainly from the conditions prevailing in the Eastern markets, conditions which, as events proved, were imperfectly realised by the first projectors.

Experience quickly showed that the difficulties of the African route were not insuperable. For the first part of the voyage there was indeed a risk of meeting hostile ships, but the Dutch fleets were equipped for such casual encounters, and, once past the Cape of Good Hope, it was possible to find a safe course, provided that the objective was rightly chosen. India had no attractions for the promoters of the earliest voyages. Of the goods most in demand, India furnished nothing but pepper, and to sail to the Malabar coast for pepper would have been to challenge the Portuguese at the chief centre of their power. The information available at the outset indicated that the most suitable objectives were western Java, and Achin in Sumatra, and both these localities possessed great attractions for the Dutch adventurers.[1] Achin controlled the large supply of pepper on the west coast of Sumatra; it was within reach of the east coast of Ceylon, whence a supply of cinnamon might be anticipated; and it was a commercial centre where a variety of other Eastern goods could be procured. The king was notoriously faithless, but the dominant feature of his policy was hostility to the Portuguese, and there were thus grounds for the hope, which was not entirely realised, that he would welcome their declared enemies. The attractions of Bantam and Jakatra in western Java were still greater. The Portuguese were represented only by a few merchants; pepper and various Eastern goods were available; and, assuming that trade could be established in one of these harbours, the road onwards to the Spice Islands lay open. The route to Bantam by way of the Straits of Malacca was of

[1] The advantages of these objectives were brought out clearly by *Linschoten*: in c. 19 he pointed out that the Portuguese had no settlements in Sumatra, and that the king of Achin was their great enemy, while in c. 20 he entered into details of the pepper trade of western Java, which could be enjoyed without interference from the Portuguese.

course to be avoided owing to the existence of the Portuguese naval station in the narrow waters, but this obstacle could be turned by sailing outside Sumatra, and passing through the Strait of Sunda, the navigability of which had by this time become known. The course marked out for the earliest voyages after rounding the Cape was thus to avoid Mozambique, to refresh if necessary at the south end of Madagascar, or preferably at Mauritius,[1] and then strike across the open sea in the direction of Sumatra.

The early voyages directed on these lines were, on the whole, profitable. Particular ventures had disastrous endings, but others, notably that conducted by van Neck in 1598, were highly successful; the great possibilities of the enterprise were generally recognised; and by the year 1602 Dutch merchants were known not only in Bantam and Achin, but also on the east coast of Ceylon, in the Spice Islands, and at the important Siamese mart of Patani. Success, however, brought fresh anxieties. The various expeditions, sent out independently from nearly every port in Holland, came into competition in the East, and quickly raised prices against each other, while the large supplies of spices brought to Europe threatened to glut the consuming markets. The national importance of the new trade was too great to allow of the continuance of such injurious competition, and through the intervention of the States General, the supreme political authority in Holland, the competitors were eventually united in a single powerful Company, with exclusive privileges for the Eastern trade, an exceedingly wide charter, and a constitution which may almost be described as national. The first fleet of the new chartered Company, which sailed in June, 1602, consisted of 15 ships, aggregating nearly 7000 tuns' burden,[2] and the rapidity of the Dutch progress may be

[1] The idea of refreshing at the Cape does not appear to have been suggested at this time; the Dutch were well established in Java before the founding of their settlement there.

[2] For reasons explained in *India at the Death of Akbar* (p. 230 and Appendix D), I use the spelling "tun" to indicate that the unit of ship-measurement at this time was substantially different from the modern registered ton. A "tun" represented approximately 60 cubic feet of cargo space.

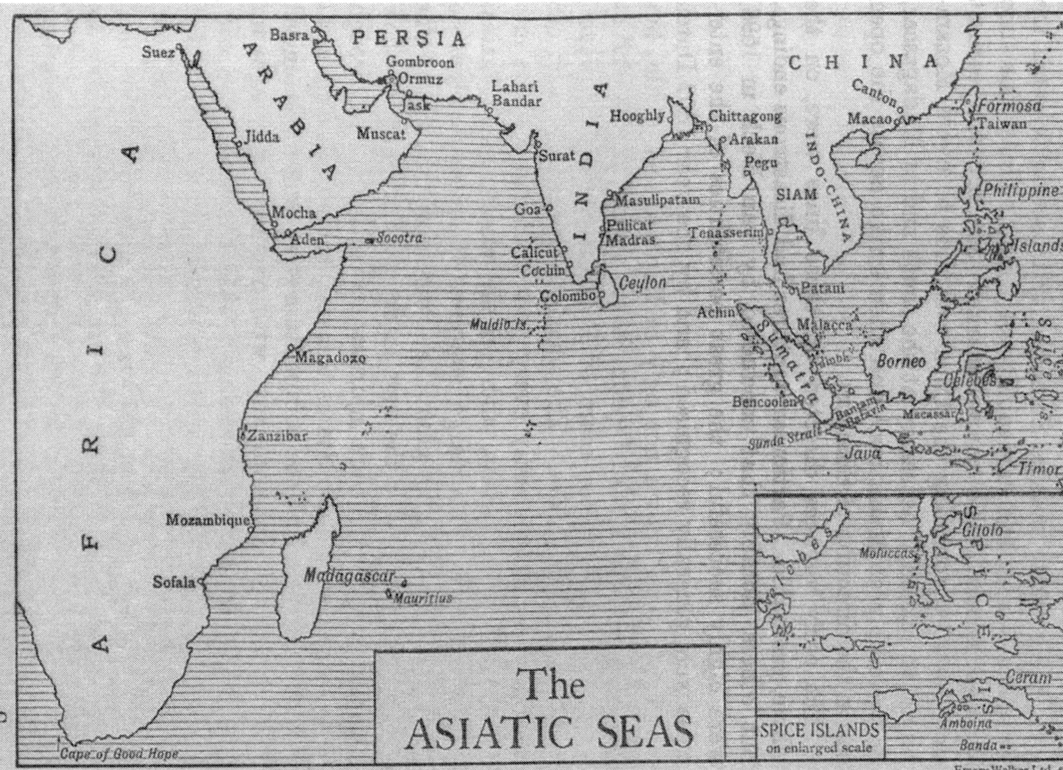
The ASIATIC SEAS
AFRICA
ARABIA
PERSIA
INDIA
CHINA
SIAM
INDO-CHINA
Suez
Basra
Gombroon
Ormuz
Jask
Muscat
Jidda
Mocha
Aden
Socotra
Lahari Bandar
Surat
Goa
Calicut
Cochin
Colombo
Ceylon
Hooghly
Masulipatam
Pulicat
Madras
Maldiv Is.
Chittagong
Arakan
Pegu
Tenasserim
Patani
Malacca
Achin
Sumatra
Bencoolen
Sunda Strait
Bantam
Batavia
Java
Borneo
Celebes
Macassar
Timor
Canton
Macao
Formosa
Taiwan
Philippine
Islands
Magadoxo
Zanzibar
Mozambique
Sofala
Madagascar
Mauritius
Cape of Good Hope
SPICE ISLANDS
on enlarged scale
Moluccas
Gilolo
Ceram
Amboina
Banda
Emery Walker Ltd. sc.

gauged by comparing this fleet with the four vessels, of about 1000 tuns in all, which had started in the year 1595.[1]

Internal competition was not the sole danger threatening the Dutch enterprise, for other European nations were realising the possibilities of Eastern trade, and, stimulated by the high prices charged at first by the Dutch, were preparing to follow their example, and fetch for themselves the spices which they needed. From England a second attempt to reach the East was made in 1596, but the fleet was wholly lost. Three years later the project was revived, and " divers merchants, induced by the success of the voyage performed by the Dutch nation, were stirred up with no less affection to advance the trade of their native country." The result was the establishment of the English Company.

> The Merchants of London, in the year of our Lord 1600 joined together, and made a stock of seventy-two thousand pounds, to be employed in Ships and Merchandises, for the discovery of a Trade in the East-India, to bring into this Realm Spices and other Commodities. They bought four great Ships to be employed in this Voyage. . . . These ships they furnished with men, victuals and munition for twenty months, and sent in them, in Merchandise and Spanish money, to the value of seven and twenty thousand pounds: all the rest of their stock was spent and consumed about the ships and other necessaries appertaining to them.[2]

This fleet sailed in February 1601, under the command of James Lancaster, reached Achin in the following year, and returned after a successful voyage in August 1603, but it was a small venture compared with that of the Dutch Company;

[1] Some particulars regarding the constitution and operations of the Dutch and English Companies will be found in Appendix A.

[2] What little is known of " the miserable disastrous successe " of the voyage of 1596 will be found in *Purchas*, I. iii. 110 ff. The first quotation in the text is taken from the Petition of the Adventurers for the voyage to the East Indies, presented in September 1599 (*Calendar S.P.*, 1513-1616, No. 258); the Dutch voyage alluded to is presumably that of van Neck, who had returned to Holland in the previous June, and had received a spectacular welcome at Amsterdam (*van der Chijs*, 85). The second quotation is from the opening paragraph of *Purchas*' account of Lancaster's voyage (I. iii. 147); the figures given for the capital are said to be exaggerated, but the difference is not very material.

the capacity of the ships aggregated less than 1500 tuns, while the cargo carried out proved to be insufficient to procure a return lading, and Lancaster found it necessary to cruise for a Portuguese prize in order to put himself in funds. The English Company sent out ships regularly from this time forward, but its resources were limited, and in these early years the leadership was unquestionably with the Dutch.

The formation of the Dutch Company coincided with a fundamental change in policy. We have seen that the early voyages were planned so as to avoid the Portuguese, but the experience gained in them yielded two lessons, the ubiquitous hostility of that nation, and its weakness on the sea. Portuguese traders or missionaries were to be found in every seaport, and they exerted all their skill in diplomacy to render the Dutch unpopular in the markets and at the Courts: the idea of trading at places where the Portuguese had no influence had therefore to be abandoned, and at the same time various encounters with their ships had demonstrated their weakness in action. Accordingly, we now find the Dutch determined to oust the Portuguese from those seas which at first they had aspired only to share, and for some years from 1603 onwards each of the fleets sent out attempted some definite act of aggression.[1] Success was not quickly attained on land: some small forts were captured in the Spice Islands, but Mozambique, Malacca, and Macao in turn resisted attack, and the Dutch soon realised the need for a base in Eastern waters if they were to bring such enterprises to the desired conclusion. In purely naval actions they were much more successful: Portuguese fleets were defeated, merchant vessels were captured in large numbers, and the enemy was rapidly

[1] A note in *van der Chijs* (p. 84) suggests that van der Hagen, who sailed in the year 1599, had orders to conquer Amboina. If this is correct, the aggressive policy began slightly earlier than is stated in the text. As a matter of fact the Dutch attempted to capture a fort in Amboina in 1600, but the account in *Begin ende Voortgangh* (p. 11 of the narrative of Verhagen's voyage) shows that on that occasion the initiative was taken by the native inhabitants; the Dutch refused repeated requests for aid, but at last yielded to the importunity of the native leaders. In any case, an attack on an outlying post, where the Portuguese position was already weakened, would not be on the same footing as the attempts to capture strongholds like Mozambique or Malacca.

reduced to the defensive ; the Portuguese supremacy on the water had already passed away.

The Dutch were not slow to develop a commercial policy based on the position they had won. The first sketch which I have found on such a policy is contained in a memorandum written apparently by order of Admiral Matelieff, who commanded the Dutch fleet of 1605.[1] After insisting on the need for a base in Eastern waters, the writer took a general survey of Asiatic trade, which he considered under five principal heads, (1) pepper, (2) other spices, (3) Gujarat, (4) Coromandel, (5) China and Japan. The basis of his policy is found in the proposition that the trade in cloves, mace, and nutmegs must be monopolised, since competition would ensure the ruin of all competitors, and consequently the English must at all costs be kept out of the Spice Islands. Entire exclusion from the pepper trade was not immediately practicable, seeing that England had already secured a footing in the markets of Java and Sumatra, but he suggested that this difficulty could be surmounted if the Dutch Company would content itself for a few years with the profits arising from other spices, and sell pepper so cheaply in Europe that the English should be driven out of Asia ; this being accomplished, victory over the Portuguese would ensure a monopoly of all spices, as well as of the trade to China and Japan. The Indian trade he regarded as purely subsidiary : Gujarat, he thought, could wait, but Coromandel must be developed, because its cotton goods were the chief medium of trade in the markets farther East. Such was the early design : monopoly from Java eastwards, and if possible in Java and Sumatra, with the Indian trade developed as subsidiary to the main business of the Company. The history of the period can be told most conveniently on these lines, and I shall attempt first to sketch briefly the events in the Farther East, the principal theatre of the Dutch effort, and then to trace the development of Indian trade together with

[1] The memorandum is given on pp. 72 ff. of the journal of Matelieff's voyage in *Begin ende Voortgangh* ; a French translation will be found in *Renneville*, vi. 35-47. From its position in the journal, it may perhaps be inferred to date from the year 1607.

the associated enterprises in Persia and Arabia, countries with which the earliest schemes were not concerned.

To modern readers the most surprising feature of this policy is the importance attached to the trade in spices, a trade which is so little heard of in Asia at the present day. In our period, however, spices were the main commercial link between Asia and Western Europe. The insistent demand for pepper and cinnamon, cloves, mace, and nutmegs, arose partly from their use in preserving meat for winter consumption, and partly from the taste of the time; while its gradual reduction was due on the one hand to changes in Western agriculture, which ensured supplies of fresh meat throughout the winter, on the other hand to changes in the art of cooking, and in particular to the substitution of sweet for spiced dishes. Writers of the eighteenth century usually attributed the declining profits of the Dutch Company to this change in fashion, which steadily depreciated the value of the monopoly of spices; but throughout our period, and for some time after, the monopoly was one of the most important facts of the world's commerce, and the large expenditure incurred on its acquisition could be regarded as a thoroughly sound investment. In later chapters we shall see that spices were almost equally important for some branches of Asiatic trade, in which the Dutch took so large a share; and looking at the commercial situation as a whole, there is no doubt that the policy outlined in the memorandum was justified.

4. Dutch Progress and Portuguese Decay

The first Dutch objective, a monopoly of the trade in the Farther East, was attained as a result of events which took place mainly in the second decade of the seventeenth century. In the year 1610 Dutch interests were already predominant in the spice trade, while in India their factors were established on the Coromandel coast; but it cannot be said that their position in Asia was assured, for the Portuguese were their open enemies, while the English were dangerous commercial rivals. The sea-power of the former nation had been weakened, but its framework was still intact; the small forts in the Spice Islands, which had been lost, were in any case at the mercy of the strongest fleet; and, so long as Goa and Malacca stood firm, nothing but adequate reinforcement was required to re-establish the maritime Empire of the previous century. The English competition was vigorous, and, had greater resources been available, it might finally have prevailed; but Portugal was not reinforced, while the English effort was hindered partly by lack of capital, partly by the attitude of the home government; and thus the general situation turned definitely in favour of the Dutch.

The story of the critical years is complicated by the fact that the official relations subsisting between the various nations in Europe did not correspond with the hard facts of Asiatic waters. England had no quarrel in Europe with Portugal, and was at peace with Spain from the year 1604 onwards, but Portuguese fleets attacked the English ships off Surat in successive years, and in 1614 the king of Spain ordered the Viceroy of Goa to drive the English out of India by force; subsequently there were occasional naval actions in the Indian seas, while in 1622 we find the English joining Persia in the capture of Ormuz; and it was not, in fact, until 1635 that friendly relations were established with the Portuguese authorities in Goa by the convention negotiated there by William Methwold. Nor was England openly at war with Holland until the year 1652, but about 1617 the ships of the Dutch and English Companies were fighting over the seas from Bantam eastwards. The war between Spain and Holland was suspended by the twelve years' truce arranged in 1609, which in theory became effective in the East in the following year, but hostilities between Dutch and Portuguese in Asia were not prevented; and thus we find that each of the three nations concerned in the struggle for the spice trade might at any time be called on to fight either of its two competitors. Except, however, on the western side of India, the activities of the Portuguese were of comparatively small importance, and the real contest lay between the English and the Dutch. A description of its incidents is unnecessary for the present purpose: the agents of the two Companies were active in the attempt to secure the trade of the Spice Islands and the Farther East; the markets of Siam, Indo-China, and Japan were explored with feverish energy; and, as has just been said, the competition developed into war. Hostilities were terminated by an agreement negotiated in Europe in 1619, by the terms of which the disputed trade was to be shared between the two Companies, whose merchants were to live in harmony, and conduct their business in the common interest; but the relations which seemed so desirable to the diplomatists at home proved incapable of realisation in the East, and the events of the next few years served only to emphasise the fundamental divergence of aim, the English seeking a share of the trade which the Dutch aspired to monopolise. The English Company was already contracting its operations when the tragic affair at Amboina in the year 1623 brought matters to a head;[1] the Company then abandoned the attempt to enforce its claim to a share in the trade of the Spice Islands and the Farther East, and all its agencies lying to the eastward of Macassar were closed. Meanwhile the Dutch had realised their project of establishing a permanent base in Eastern waters. The port of Jakatra in Java had fallen into their hands, and in 1619 they founded there the new city of Batavia, which remains the capital of their Asiatic possessions.

The Dutch had now succeeded in eliminating English competition from the commerce to which they attached the highest value, and shortly afterwards they completed the framework of their far-Eastern organisation by the establishment of a settlement at Taiwan on the coast of Formosa, as a base for

[1] A misleading idea of the affair in question is given by the phrase "the massacre of Amboina," which became classical in England. The English merchants, who were resident in the Dutch fort under the agreement of 1619, were charged with conspiracy to seize it; they were convicted on confessions obtained by torture, and most of them were executed. The Dutch admitted that the proceedings were in some respects irregular, and the "massacre" may be regarded either as a judicial murder or a tragic failure of justice according to the view formed of the intentions of the judges. The literature relating to the affair is extensive; the important contemporary documents can be traced through the *Calendar S.P.*, 1622–1624.

the trade with China.[1] Their next task was to destroy the remaining power of the Portuguese, and thus consolidate their monopoly in this region. For some years they relied for this purpose mainly on a policy of blockade, but at last in 1641 they became masters of Malacca, and the possession of this naval base secured to them undisputed control of the trade with all the countries to the East: Portugal retained the settlements of Macao and Timor, but without Malacca they were of little use, while her commercial settlement in Macassar, which was for some years a source of annoyance to the Dutch, was eventually dispersed in 1661.

The second objective of the Dutch, the elimination of English competition from the pepper-markets in Java and Sumatra, was not destined to be realised. After the failure of the attempt to live in harmony, the English Company established its Eastern headquarters at Bantam, and maintained a factory at Jambi on the coast of Sumatra, while its agents traded with other parts of the two islands from time to time. When war broke out between England and Holland in 1652, the Dutch strength in the East was very much the greater: the English merchants left Bantam for Madras, many of the English ships were captured, and it must have seemed to the Dutchmen on the spot that the monopoly of pepper, and also of the Indian trade, was within their grasp. The questions at issue were, however, decided in the North Sea, not in the Indian Ocean, and the success of the English was followed by the restoration of their Eastern trade. But by this time their position in the islands was being weakened

[1] The Dutch, like most other nations, were strongly attracted by the commercial possibilities of China, and ships were sent on from Java in that direction as early as the year 1601. Three years later, a Dutch admiral was negotiating for admission to a port on the Chinese coast, and was advised unofficially to occupy some island not belonging to China but sufficiently near to facilitate regular trade. The advice was not acted on at once, but some years afterwards the Dutch established a post on one of the Pescadores Islands lying between Canton and Formosa. The Chinese objected to this settlement, and suggested in its place Taiwan in Formosa itself; their strength at sea was sufficient to convince the Dutch, and the change was promptly effected. See the voyages of van Neck, de Veen, Spilberg, Warwyk, and Matelieff, and the Account of China, in *Begin ende Voortgangh* (*Renneville*, iii. 229, 480; iv. 146, 381; vi. 48; ix. 199).

by other causes, for the Dutch were securing political predominance in Achin, while in western Java pepper was giving way to sugar-cane ; without pepper, factories in these islands would have been unprofitable concerns, and at the close of our period their abandonment by the English was foreshadowed.[1]

Apart from the war with England, the period from 1624 to 1660 was for the Dutch one of commercial and administrative success. Their capital, Batavia, was occasionally threatened by their local enemies, but it prospered and extended steadily. The population of the Spice Islands yielded gradually to the drastic discipline which was enforced, and it became possible to regulate production on strictly monopolistic lines. Political difficulties in Japan were overcome, and trade with that country was developed as a profitable branch of the main undertaking ; while Taiwan was perhaps the most hopeful of all the Dutch possessions, and we read not only of its extensive commerce with the mainland, but of important agricultural developments carried out under the guidance of the merchants. The loss of this settlement in the year 1661 was the first serious blow to the progress of the Dutch enterprise, but its effects lie outside the period of which I am writing, which begins with their appearance in Eastern waters, and ends with their supremacy in Eastern commerce.

A few words must be said of the position occupied by Macassar during this period. This seaport was of very little importance in the sixteenth century, but as the Portuguese hold over the Spice Islands grew weaker, it came into prominence as a market for cloves, mace, and nutmegs. The voyage to the islands was well within the power of the local vessels, large numbers of which sailed every season to gather up whatever spices they could procure ; the king actively supported the trade ; and some of the Portuguese who were driven from the islands settled under his protection,

[1] The factory at Bantam was closed in 1683, when the Dutch became masters of the town, but the establishment of a fortified post at Bencoolen on the west coast of Sumatra enabled the English Company to retain a footing in the pepper trade.

and thus retained at least a portion of their former commerce. The Dutch regarded this trade with the utmost disfavour, because it infringed the monopoly which they sought to establish. The Portuguese at Macassar distributed spices in some of the Eastern markets; the English maintained a factory there to procure supplies for Europe; and the Danes from Tranquebar made the trade a speciality. Various measures were therefore taken to cut off the supplies which reached Macassar. The most important sources were policed by resident garrisons, while the spice-trees on the outlying islands were systematically destroyed. Fleets were posted off the islands to intercept the Macassar vessels; Macassar itself was occasionally blockaded; and the Danes were driven out of the Indian market by the offer of spices below cost. Eventually friendly relations were established with the king of Macassar, who expelled the Portuguese settlement from his dominions, and the trade was reduced to meagre limits, though small quantities of spices continued to find a market throughout our period.[1]

Mention of the Danes recalls the fact that the Dutch and English were not left to dispute the Eastern markets entirely alone. The other competitors proved, however, to be unimportant. The Danes did little during our period, and, apart from their connection with Macassar, their energies were devoted mainly to local activities in the Bay of Bengal. French vessels appeared from time to time off Java and Sumatra, and more rarely in other parts of the Eastern seas, but the part played by them was small, and the story of their enterprise in India lies outside the limits of our period. For a few years early in the century it looked as if the Spaniards, from their settlements in the Philippine Islands, might play an important part in the spice trade, but their effort was not sustained.[2] In order, therefore, to complete the outline of the

[1] These friendly relations did not last for long; by 1668 the Dutch were supreme in Macassar.

[2] It will be recollected that the union of 1580 did not destroy the separate existence of Portugal, and in the East the distinction between the two kingdoms was punctiliously observed. Spaniards from the Philippine Islands had secured a fort in Ternate, one of the Moluccas, whence they

history of this period, it remains only to record the territorial losses of the Portuguese. As we have seen already, their possessions in the Spice Islands went first. The next loss was Ormuz, which surrendered to the allied Persian and English forces in the year 1622; the neighbouring fort of Muscat was retained for a quarter of a century longer, but did not suffice to support Portuguese authority in the Persian Gulf, and when it was taken by the Arabs the story of the Portuguese in those waters was closed. The next loss after Ormuz was the trading settlement at Hooghly, which was destroyed by Shahjahan's forces in 1632, and though some Portuguese were allowed to return to the vicinity, their predominant position in the trade was not recovered. Their hold over Chittagong lasted longer, but shortly after the close of our period that port also passed definitely under the jurisdiction of the Moguls. Nine years after the loss of Hooghly, Malacca fell to the Dutch. A truce followed, but in the 'fifties the Portuguese were driven gradually out of Ceylon, and subsequently the Dutch occupied first Negapatam on the east coast of India, and then Cochin and the minor fortresses in Malabar. When therefore a stable peace was at last framed, the Portuguese possessions in the East had been reduced practically to the list as it stands to-day.[1] Their sea-power had vanished, and their commerce was almost negligible. In the Far East there remained to them only Macao and part of Timor; in India, the metropolis of Goa, and the ports of Damān and Diu, which still watched the shipping of Gujarat, but had lost the power of interfering with its course.

---

occupied other forts which the Portuguese had abandoned under Dutch pressure, but they were unable to hold all of these. They retained a footing in the islands for many years, and they also possessed a fort in Formosa, but they made little use of these opportunities (*Renneville*, v. 235; vi. 5, 424; vii. 114, 308, etc. *Dagh Register*, June 11, 1645).

[1] The harbour and islands of Bombay were ceded to England under the terms of the treaty of marriage between Charles II. and the Princess of Portugal. The territories of Bassein remained in Portuguese hands until their seizure by the Marathas in the eighteenth century.

AUTHORITIES FOR CHAPTER I

In these notes on Authorities, reference is made by means of abbreviated titles or key-words, which are printed in italics, and are explained in alphabetical order in Appendix E.

SECTION 1.—The account of the political situation in India is based on standard authorities such as *Elliot* and *Tuzuk*; detailed references would be superfluous. The position in the south can be realised by studying the Dutch reports contained in the *Dagh Register*. The remarks on conditions in other Asiatic countries are drawn from a wide field. The relations between Turkey and Persia are mentioned frequently in *English Factories* and the *Dagh Register*, which also throw occasional light on the countries east of India; further information regarding Pegu, etc., will be found in *Faria y Sousa*, *Begin ende Voortgangh*, and other general works; the state of the islands can best be gathered from the Dutch authorities just named.

The attitude of the Moguls towards sea-power is brought out in *Terpstra's Surat*, especially App. V., VI., VIII., XIII., but it is obvious throughout the English correspondence (*Letters Received* and *English Factories*); see also *Jourdain*, 223. *Manucci* (ii. 45) tells an illuminating, and possibly authentic, story of Aurangzeb's decision that naval warfare was only fit for Europeans. For the attitude of Persia, see *English Factories*, ix. 226.

SECTION 2.—The Portuguese maritime Empire can be studied in *Whiteway* and *Danvers*, and more fully in the voluminous works of *Barros*, *Couto*, *Castanheda*, *Correa*, and *Alboquerque*. For the European aspect of their enterprise, it is perhaps sufficient to refer to the *Cambridge Modern History* (especially I. i.; III. xv.), where full bibliographies will be found. *Pyrard* gives a clear account of the working of their maritime control; his reference to the prevailing corruption is ii. 240. For the recognition of their Empire by Akbar, see *Couto*, ix. 246 and x. 441; and *Elliot*, v. 403. The Turkish attempts to capture the Indian seas were described in an article by the late Mr. Longworth Dames in *Journal R.A.S.*, January, 1921; their enterprise in East Africa is recounted in *Couto*, x. For the exploits of "Cunnale" see *Faria y Sousa*, iii. 99 ff., *Hay*, 831 ff., *Renneville*, iii. 453, *Calendar S.P.*, 1513–1616, No. 280. The courage of the Portuguese forces as late as 1625 is attested by *della Valle* (ii. 290), as well as by various narratives of naval actions.

SECTION 3.—The position of Holland in Europe at this period is dealt with in the *Cambridge Modern History* (Vols. I.-IV.); *Edmundson* also gives the facts in a convenient form. Dutch materials for the Eastern enterprise are voluminous; what I have written is based on *van der Chijs*, *de Jonge*, *Elias*, *Linschoten*, *Houtman*, and the early voyages narrated in *Begin ende Voortgangh* (*Renneville*, i.-iv.). For the first English voyages, see *Early Travels*, 1 ff., *Letters Received* (Introduction to vol. i.), *Purchas*, Book I., and *Calendar S.P.*, 1513–1616 (Nos. 258, 268, 281, etc.).

The maintenance of Dutch trade with Lisbon is dealt with in *van der Chijs*, c. I.; its difficulties are stated in *Houtman*, i. xxxi; *Linschoten* (c. 99) gives instances of impressment of shipping. The original policy of avoiding the Portuguese is brought out in various authorities, *e.g. Houtman*, i. xxxii. A passage in the *Cambridge Modern History* (IV. 729) suggests that the aggressive policy of the Dutch Company dates only from 1608, but the narratives in *Begin ende Voortgangh* show that the fleet of 1603 threatened Mozambique and Goa, while the fleet of 1605 carried secret instructions directing an attempt to seize Malacca (*Renneville*, v. 1 ff., 264 ff.). That the necessity of monopolising the Spice Islands was generally accepted is shown by the whole course of Dutch action: the first direct orders I have seen on this subject are in the instructions issued in 1609 to the first Governor General (*de Jonge*, III. 133), one of whose earliest acts was to improve the fortifications in Banda in order to secure the entire produce of the islands for the Company (*van Dijk*, 10). The importance of spices in Europe is discussed more fully in *India at the Death of Akbar*, 221 ff.

Section 4.—The English side of the struggle for the Farther East can be studied in *Letters Received*, *English Factories*, i. ii., *Calendar S.P.*, from 1611 onwards, *Purchas*, Book I., and *Jourdain* (especially 318 ff.). The *Hague Transcripts* throw light on the Dutch attitude, and the *Lisbon Transcripts* help us to appreciate the situation of the Portuguese. The concentration of the Dutch on essentials is well brought out in *Hague Transcripts*, Series II. Nos. 1, 2, 5, 9, 12, 26, etc., and Series III., B, and T3. The difficulties of Portugal are seen in such records as *Lisbon Transcripts*, 126 (want of men, ships, and money), 371 (want of timber), 409 (want of guns), 931 (want of saltpetre), and so on. The order to drive the English out of Surat is in *idem*, 444. The establishment of peace between the English and Portuguese is dealt with in *English Factories*, v. p. ix and *passim*.

There are various references to hostilities between Portuguese and Dutch during the Twelve Years' Truce, *e.g. Hague Transcripts*, I. 69, and *Renneville*, vii. 256. The abortive agreement between Dutch and English bulks largely in the *Calendar S.P.*, 1617–21 (*e.g.* Nos. 115, 351, 425, 666, etc.), and its working can be appreciated from various details in *English Factories*, i. and ii. The subsequent action taken by the Dutch against the Portuguese can be traced in the *Dagh Register* from 1624 onwards.

The events of the Anglo-Dutch war in the East are detailed in *English Factories*, ix.; the relevant volume of the *Dagh Register* is unfortunately too concise to be of much value. For the war in European waters, see *Cambridge Modern History*, IV. xvi.; and for the loss of British trade in Java and Sumatra, see *English Factories*, x. 255, and *Elias*, ii. 46. For the Dutch progress during the intervening years, the *Dagh Register* is the most important authority, but it is reflected in the envious comments scattered through *English Factories*. The affairs of Macassar can best be studied in the *Dagh Register*; there are occasional references in the *Hague Transcripts* (*e.g.* I. 233, 264; II. 94, 100; III. R5). For its importance about 1612, see *Jourdain*, 294.

I know of no contemporary Danish sources for the enterprise undertaken by that nation. Scattered notices of their activities will be found in the *Dagh Register* and *English Factories*. For the capture of Ormuz, see *English Factories*, ii. (Introduction, and *passim*); its effect on the affairs of the English Company is recorded in *Calendar S.P.*, 1622–24, Nos. 418, 448, etc. For the fall of Muscat, see *English Factories*, viii. 311; for Hooghly, *Elliot*, vii. 31, 211; for Chittagong, *Sarkar's Studies*, 131; for Ceylon and Cochin, *The Dutch in Malabar* (Introduction, 7 ff.).

CHAPTER II

THE DEVELOPMENT OF DUTCH AND ENGLISH COMMERCE IN INDIA

1. First Attempts, and the Factories on the Coromandel Coast

We must now turn to the development of the relations of the Dutch and English Companies with India and the countries farther to the West. The design of the earliest voyages was, as we have seen, in no way concerned with India, but Dutch merchants had not been long in the East before they were forced by experience to realise that, in order to trade profitably, India must be included in their scheme of operations. The necessity arose from the fact that pepper and the other spices which they sought were ordinarily obtained from the producers by bartering Indian-made cotton cloth. The first Dutch ventures were organised on the basis of the information which had been collected regarding the commercial methods of the Portuguese. The Lisbon practice was to send out chiefly silver, and accordingly the Dutch carried their capital mainly in money, together with a miscellaneous assortment of merchandise; but the precedent was not really applicable, for the silver from Lisbon went to India, while the Dutch carried silver to Java, and experience soon showed that while they could procure a cargo of pepper in this way, the transaction was commercially unsound. The trade at Bantam was in the hands of Chinese dealers, who bought up pepper from the producers at the harvest, and stored it until the arrival of ships to carry it to China: being sure of this old-established market, they were not particularly eager to sell elsewhere, and consequently the Dutch had to pay whatever price was asked, or in the alternative risk the success of their voyage by waiting in harbour until the next crop should come forward. The risk was very great: the mere running cost of maintenance was by no means negligible, but of much more importance was the injury to the ships from the worms with which the harbours were infested, and, most of all, the appalling mortality among the crews, aggravated as it was by the disorderly living for which the seaports offered every facility. A prolonged stay in port might render a ship unfit to return to Europe, or might lead to its loss on the homeward voyage for want of men; and the Dutch quickly realised that, in order to establish a profitable business, they must adapt themselves to the methods of the country, leaving factors or agents on the spot to buy direct from the producers at harvest-time, and supplying the factors in advance with the cotton cloth required for their transactions, so that the ships might remain in port only for the time required to take on board the cargo which had been provided. The conditions in Achin were generally similar to those which prevailed in Bantam, with the additional risk of outbursts of lawlessness among the people, or of greed or tyranny on the part of the king. In the Spice Islands the position was even more difficult, for money was not yet generally current, though such of the inhabitants as knew its use were willing to take it in payment; and here, too, it was necessary for successful business to be in the market at harvest-time with a stock of Indian cloth. Such cloth could be bought from middlemen in Achin or Bantam, but only at exorbitant prices, and we need not be surprised that such keen merchants as the Dutch should have determined after very little experience to buy at firsthand, and save the large profits of the middlemen.

The first recorded attempt to enter the cloth markets in India was made at the end of the year 1601, when two Dutch factors took passage on a ship which was returning to Gujarat from Achin. They were welcomed in Surat and wrote encouraging reports, but they were tempted, or perhaps decoyed, to Calicut by promises of trade, and at Calicut they were handed over to the Portuguese, carried to Goa, and there executed. The story of the next few years is not on record, but apparently other factors were sent to Gujarat, and it is clear that a Dutch agency was in existence at Surat in 1606; it came to an end in the following year when van Deynsen, the only survivor of the party, was driven to suicide by the intrigues and persecution of the Portuguese. After this, the Dutch left Gujarat alone for some years; the potential value of its trade was recognised, but the authorities were now intent on concentrating their resources on the struggle for the Spice Islands, and for the time they bought Gujarat goods in the market at Achin.

Gujarat was, in fact, less important than the Coromandel coast for the supply of cotton goods to the spice markets, and by this time the Dutch had secured a footing at Masulipatam. A junior merchant was already resident there in 1605, but the formal establishment of factories dates from the following year, when an agreement was concluded with the king of Golconda, and the merchants set to work at Masulipatam itself and at the neighbouring town of Nizampatam, then more generally known as Petapoli. Here they quickly learned that the delta of the Kistna was not the best place to provide all the requirements of their trade. The local produce consisted chiefly of plain cloth or calico, bleached or dyed, but some markets, the Molucca Islands in particular, required what are spoken of in contemporary records as *pintados*, or "painted" goods, and the chief seat of this specialised industry lay farther south, in the vicinity of Pulicat and S. Thomé.[1] Extensions to the

[1] The Kistna delta was well supplied with the principal dyes, for indigo was grown in the neighbourhood, and Petapoli itself was noted for the high quality of its Indian madder, or chay-root; see for these the Account of Golconda inserted in van den Broecke's journal in *Begin ende Voortgangh*. *Renneville* (vii. 512 ff.) evidently did not understand the word *saye*, or *zaaie*, Dutch forms of chay, and rendered "serge," thus obscuring the significance of these passages. The Portuguese word *pintado* (painted) is a reasonably accurate name for the goods to which it was primarily applied, for the production of which see *First Letter Book*, 59 *n.*; the English adopted the word, while the Dutch translated it as *geschilderd*. Its meaning was soon extended to printed goods, on which the pattern is produced not by a brush but by means of blocks; many of the *pintados* mentioned in English

southward were consequently found to be desirable, and in the next two or three years we hear of factories near Tegnapatam, which appears on modern maps as Fort St. David; but the most important development was the grant by the king of Chandragiri of a site in Pulicat itself. The Dutch established themselves here in 1610, and the factory was made the headquarters of all their business on the coast; it was taken from them by the Portuguese of S. Thomé in 1612, but was recovered shortly afterwards, and was made sufficiently strong to resist further attack by land.[1] Henceforward trade on the coast progressed steadily. The requirements of Eastern commerce were supplied; such goods as could be sold were imported; and in time direct trade was opened up with Persia and with Europe.

The English settled at Masulipatam and Petapoli in the year 1611, but their trade did not develop to the same extent as that of the Dutch, probably because they had not an equally extensive market in the Farther East. Coromandel supplied goods which they bartered for pepper in Java and Sumatra, or could dispose of at Macassar, and in time it contributed to their trade with Europe and Persia; but throughout our period the larger business of the Dutch gave them a definite predominance in the markets, and as a rule the English merchants were content to follow. Masulipatam remained their headquarters in the north. In the south they were admitted to the Pulicat settlement in 1621 under the agreement made between the Companies in Europe; but here, as elsewhere, the conditions of residence in a Dutch fortress proved to be intolerable, and in 1626 they moved to Armagon at the northern end of the Pulicat lagoon, having been granted favourable terms by the local nayak or chief. Armagon served its purpose for a time, but as a centre of commerce it had many drawbacks, and in 1640 the factors established themselves in what is now Madras, where a fort was built

letters from Surat were probably printed goods, or chintz, and the two words are used as synonyms in an early letter from Agra (*English Factories*, i. 46).

[1] The fortification of Pulicat is discussed in Chapter VIII.

under an agreement with the nayak in possession of this part of the coast. These arrangements continued for the remainder of our period, the Dutch having their headquarters at Pulicat and the English at Madras, while both Companies maintained factories at Masulipatam and other places in the neighbourhood, and also traded in the various markets along the coast.

2. The Factories in Western India

We have seen that the early efforts of the Dutch to establish themselves on the West Coast terminated on the death of van Deynsen in 1607 : a year later, an English ship arrived off Surat, and, when the preliminary negotiations had been completed, the development of commerce with Gujarat began in earnest. At this point we meet with a new motive. The English intended, as the Dutch had intended, to obtain cotton goods from Gujarat for employment in the Eastern trade, but they hoped also to extend the scope of the Company's operations by establishing direct commerce between India and England. The need for extension was being felt as early as the year 1603 ; the European demand for pepper was urgent but not insatiable, and when English and Dutch supplies arrived in quantity there was something like a glut. A few years later the English merchants at Bantam were instructed to send any commodities rather than pepper, though pepper would be preferable to an empty ship ; and it was obviously to the interest of the Company to find new Asiatic markets, where English manufactures could be sold and goods suitable for England could be procured. How little was at that time known of the potentialities of India may be gathered from the instructions issued with this object to the commander of the Third Voyage in the year 1607. The markets of the Red Sea were thought to be more hopeful than those of India, and, if the season served, the fleet was to try for trade at Aden, and, on its way thence to Bantam, make inquiries regarding the Gulf of Cambay. If, however, Aden could not be reached in the trading season, the fleet was ordered to make for Gujarat, and if possible open trade : India, in fact, was regarded as a "second string." The fleet was too late to attempt the Red Sea trade, and it was owing to this fact that Hawkins in the *Hector* anchored off Surat in August, 1608.

In order to understand his reception by the local authorities, it is necessary to take into account the position occupied in Surat by the Portuguese. They had no territorial settlement in the town, but for nearly a century they had dominated its sea-borne trade: they were established in strength at Diu and Damān, from which stations they collected licence-fees on the ships leaving all the ports of Gujarat; their coasting-fleets (*kafila*) carried a large proportion of the merchandise exported from the province; and their fighting craft policed the coastal waters, which were not protected by the Moguls. The local officials lived in terror of the Portuguese commanders who visited the port from time to time, and who could threaten to burn the shipping if their wishes were disregarded. The Dutch had just been deprived of the foothold they had obtained in Surat; and when Hawkins arrived, the local prestige of the Portuguese was probably at its highest point, while their determination to maintain their position was uncompromising. The English were, however, by no means daunted by the hostility they experienced, and when the local officials declared that the settlement of a factory required the sanction of the Emperor, Hawkins promptly set out for the Court of Jahangir at Agra in order to negotiate an agreement for regular trade. His reception was favourable, but his somewhat boisterous diplomacy proved to be ineffective against Portuguese intrigue, and after prolonged negotiations he left Agra without having achieved his object.

The English Company continued to send ships to Surat while waiting for news of the results obtained by Hawkins. In 1609 the *Ascension* arrived off the coast, but was wrecked on a shoal, and this loss, together with the misconduct of some of the survivors on land, probably injured the prospects of the English already in the country. In 1611 Sir Henry Middleton reached Surat, but found the Portuguese influence still too strong; in the following year Best had a more favourable reception, and concluded an agreement under which the

English were permitted to establish factories in Gujarat. The motives which led to this change of front are not on record, and it is dangerous to speculate regarding the course of Oriental diplomacy, but apparently one of the contributory factors was the injury to Portuguese prestige which resulted from the failure of their attacks on Best's ships. The Moguls, having themselves no strength on the water, had come to regard the Portuguese naval forces as invincible, and the successful defence of the English against a greatly superior fleet, in actions some of which were witnessed from the land, probably suggested the idea of playing off one nation against the other, and thus loosening the Portuguese grip on the commerce of the country. Middleton's activities in the Red Sea, which had involved interference with Gujarat shipping, had already shown that the English were formidable on the water: probably also the news of Dutch successes in the Eastern seas was by this time opening the eyes of the Mogul authorities to the fact that the Portuguese supremacy was no longer unchallenged; but, whatever the motives at work, the fact is clear that Best's defence was followed by the formal delivery to him of what purported to be an Imperial *farmān* or rescript, confirming the terms of agreement which had been settled provisionally with the Mogul officers in Gujarat.

The issue of this rescript was considered by the English to justify them in establishing factories in Gujarat, and action was taken accordingly, but it is clear that the Mogul diplomatists, who presumably desired English trade but did not wish to commit themselves for the future, had the best of the negotiations, for the supposed farmān proved to be a document of little value; for the moment, however, it served, and regular English trade at Surat may be said to date from the beginning of the year 1613.[1] The precarious footing so secured was improved, at least temporarily, by the outbreak

[1] The defects of the farmān are clearly brought out in *Letters Received*, II. xxix. 103, 180; IV. xxix. 311. The credit of establishing the factory at Surat was generally given to Best, but contemporary documents show, as Mr. Foster has pointed out, that the result was due largely to the firm stand taken by a merchant named Thomas Aldworth (*Letters Received*, ii. 137, 157).

of war between the Moguls and the Portuguese. Hostilities continued for two years, the Moguls besieging Damān by land, while the Portuguese caused much injury to Gujarat shipping, and eventually an inconclusive peace was arranged; but this very fact tended to emphasise the rapid decline of Portuguese prestige, while, so long as hostilities lasted, merchants of other European nations were obviously more likely to be welcomed than when Portuguese agents were active throughout the country.

The reappearance of the Dutch at Surat is probably to be explained by this cause. In the year 1614 the local authorities at that port wrote to the Dutch factory at Masulipatam to say that the merchandise left by van Deynsen was still in their possession; they suggested that the Dutch should reclaim it, and hinted at the same time that they might care to take Diu or Damān from the Portuguese. This letter was, I have no doubt, meant as a semi-official invitation to the Dutch to send a fleet against the Portuguese, the offer of the abandoned property being a mere formality;[1] but the Dutch took it literally, and in the following year a factor named van Ravesteyn came to Surat with a small party overland. As was only to be expected, he recovered very little of the property which he sought, but he learned much of politics as well as commerce, notably the Mogul's fear of the Portuguese sea-power. They might hope to capture Damān by assault from the landward side, but they could not starve out the garrison so long as provisions could arrive by sea, and in the meantime their own seaports lay open and unprotected: the Moguls, he was told, did not fight upon the sea; the Imperial Court knew nothing of maritime affairs; and since a truce with Portugal had just been made, the priests were likely to regain their former influence at the Court. Van Ravesteyn recognised the great possibilities of the commerce of Gujarat, but he realised also the drawbacks, and he insisted that a

[1] This view of the real intention of the Mogul officials is borne out by a letter written by Nicholas Downton from Surat in November, 1614, in the course of which he says that the Governor "hath sent to Masulipatam for the Hollanders to come hither, promising them Damān when it is taken from the Portuguese" (*Letters Received*, ii. 171).

very comprehensive agreement would be necessary before the Dutch could open business with any hope of success.

Van Ravesteyn argued at length from the experience of the English, which in the later months of 1615 was certainly discouraging. The position is described fully in the Journal of Sir Thomas Roe, who arrived while van Ravesteyn was at Surat; the attitude of the local authorities was very nearly intolerable, and unless it could be altered, there was no hope of establishing regular commerce. Roe's diplomatic efforts at the Court of Jahangir were not entirely successful, but his influence brought about a decided improvement; the English factors settled down to buy and sell; in spite of some unpleasant experiences, their objects were attained; and, while Bantam was supplied with its requirements, the direct trade between Surat and London increased rapidly in importance.

Shortly after van Ravesteyn's mission, the Dutch arrived in earnest. Their plan of buying Gujarat goods in Achin broke down in the year 1616 when their factory there was closed, and the Governor General in Java decided, against the advice of the factors on the Coromandel coast, that direct trade with Surat must be established. With this object he deputed Pieter van den Broecke to conduct the necessary negotiations. The growing prestige of the Dutch in Eastern waters facilitated his efforts, reasonable terms settled with the Gujarat officials were confirmed in due course by the Court, and a factory was opened in 1617; but at first the available capital was scanty, and the factory became important only in 1621, when van den Broecke returned as resident Director, and began to push the Dutch trade with vigour and success. For the remainder of our period, English and Dutch traded side by side in Surat and throughout the towns of Gujarat. In this region neither Company had any possessions such as the fortresses on the Coromandel coast; the factors lived merely as foreign merchants, on the strength of the terms which they obtained from the Imperial Court.

Van den Broecke's charge extended to the commerce with Persia and the Red Sea, regions which were intimately connected with the markets of Gujarat. At this period the trade of the Red Sea was concentrated at the port of Mocha, where goods from India and other Eastern countries were sold for transport to Egypt and the Mediterranean markets. Both Dutch and English were tempted to obtain a share of this trade by the fact that most of the goods sold were paid for in gold and silver, the commodities in most demand in India; but it cannot be said that the results answered their expectations. Political and administrative difficulties arose occasionally at Mocha, leading to temporary suspensions of business, while the market proved to be very uncertain; the trade was maintained with some interruptions throughout the greater portion of our period, but it cannot be classed among the most profitable ventures of either Company.

The story of their enterprises in the Persian Gulf is different. At the beginning of the century, the Gulf trade with India was closely controlled by the Portuguese, by whom it was regarded as most remunerative. Persia sent out horses, dried fruits, rosewater, and a variety of luxury goods, while the imports consisted mainly of spices and cotton cloth, and the balance of trade was settled by remittances of silver to India. Silk, however, the outstanding commercial product of Persia, scarcely entered into this trade, as practically the whole surplus production was carried by land to the Mediterranean, and the developments during our period resulted mainly from the transfer of this commerce from land to sea. Shah Abbas objected to his enemies, the Turks, profiting by the transit of his silk through their territory, and he was at some pains to persuade various European nations to send shipping to the Gulf; the English merchants eventually took the matter up, and the first consignment of silk was shipped from Jask at the end of the year 1618. The Portuguese naturally resented the appearance of the English in what they regarded as their particular domain, and they sent out a war-fleet to assert their claims, but it failed to do so effectively, and in 1622 the English joined with the Persian forces in a successful attack on the Portuguese fort of Ormuz; as the result of this action, Ormuz ceased to exist as a seaport or market, and its commerce was transferred to the Persian mainland at the port of Gombroon, known also as Bandar Abbas. The Dutch had declined to take part in the attack on Ormuz, but, when the fortress had fallen, they were quick to claim a share in the silk trade, and from about 1623 onwards both nations were actively engaged in exporting to Europe. In one way the trade was simple, for silk was a royal monopoly, and merchants could expect reasonable treatment so long as their position at Court was maintained. I think the Dutch were on the whole better served by their agents at the Court, but in any case they had a very great commercial advantage over the English in their ability to supply the Persian market with spices, the commodities in most demand; the English, being unable to offer spices, were frequently in difficulties as to laying down saleable goods in adequate quantities, and the Dutch certainly secured the larger proportion of the silk trade. For a time it was highly remunerative, but at the close of our period the European demand was falling, while the produce of Bengal was beginning to compete in the market, and by the year 1655 the English Company had ceased to buy silk in Persia.

Surat was the centre for extension of trade to a large portion of India as well as to the countries farther West. The production of the town itself was not of very great importance, and almost as soon as the merchants had settled there they established factories throughout Gujarat, at Ahmadabad, Broach, Baroda, and occasionally elsewhere, in order to maintain close touch with the producers of indigo and cotton goods. Indigo was at first regarded as the "prime commodity" for the trade with Europe, and English buyers were promptly sent northwards to Agra to secure supplies from the neighbourhood of Biana, the produce of which was familiar in distant markets, and was superior in point of purity to that of Gujarat. The Dutch in their turn established themselves at Agra as soon as their organisation in Surat had become effective, and at once took the leading position in the indigo trade. The buyers did not, however, confine their attention to a single commodity, and when it was found that Europe would buy cotton cloth, they explored the possibilities of

Northern India, so that as early as the year 1620 we hear of English factors at Samana (now in the Patiala State), and at Patna in Bihar. These particular factories were not maintained for long, because experience showed that Gujarat could supply the European demand; but when its productive resources were temporarily destroyed by the famine of 1630, which will be described in a subsequent chapter, extensions northward became necessary, and large purchases of cloth were made in the neighbourhood of Agra, while an English factory was established at Lucknow as a collecting depot for the products of Oudh. The country between Surat and Agra was of course well known to the factors who traversed it with frequent consignments of goods, and the fact that they did practically no business in it must be taken to show that it had no attractions for them. The only intermediate factory was at Burhanpur, which was maintained for some time for the sale of imported goods to the large Mogul army concentrated there for the conquest of the kingdom of Ahmadnagar, but the business was not of sufficient importance to justify a permanent establishment.

A share in the trade of Sind was one of the earliest objectives of the English merchants. This trade centred in the town of Tatta and its port of Lahari Bandar, whence goods were exported mainly to the Persian Gulf, or sent southwards along the coast to Gujarat and Goa; Basra was the chief foreign market for the cotton cloth which formed the bulk of the exports. The port of Lahari Bandar, which has now disappeared, could not at this period accommodate large ships owing to lack of depth in the channel: local ship-owners were few, and most of the trade was carried in Portuguese coasting vessels, known at this time as frigates. At the beginning of our period, the Portuguese dominated the commerce of the region, and their influence with the Mogul authorities sufficed to defeat the first English attempt, made in the year 1613, to obtain a footing in the port; their arguments were not in this case based on their naval or military power, but they threatened to desert the port if the English were admitted, and the Governor, who held the farm of the customs, could not face the risk of the resulting loss. The volume of commerce at this time had apparently been exaggerated: Sir Thomas Roe reported in 1618 that "it is not so great as pretended, nor the profit to the Portugals a tenth part," and he added that the trade had suffered greatly owing to the exactions of the Portuguese, while in a subsequent letter he said the market would take nothing but ivory, and supply only "good cloth and many toys." There were thus few attractions for foreign merchants. The Dutch attempted trade in the year 1631, but did not continue the venture, and the practical monopoly of the Portuguese lasted until 1635. The arrangement negotiated by Methwold for peace between the English and the Portuguese in India resulted in the termination of this monopoly; an English ship anchored off Lahari Bandar in November of that year, the merchants were favourably received by the authorities, a factory was established, and trade continued throughout the remainder of our period. The Dutch returned to Sind some years later, and from about 1652 were engaged regularly in the trade, but not, so far as I can discover, on a considerable scale. Sind was, in fact, more important for the English than for the Dutch, because its trade with the Gulf provided a method of laying down goods in Persia, and so helping to finance the export of silk. The Dutch could, as we have seen, obtain purchasing power in Persia by the sale of spices, but the English, having no access to the principal spice markets, were forced to develop other lines of trade, and among these the sale of Sind calico took a prominent place, whether it was marketed in Persia itself or sold for cash at Basra. At the same time, the English devoted much energy to placing Sind goods on the London market, which after 1630 could not, as has just been said, be fully supplied from Gujarat, and calico was sold there in substantial quantities; but, taken as a whole, the trade of this region cannot be said to have assumed really important dimensions. The country was poor, and suffered severely from oppressive administration: the difficulties of navigation increased as time went on; and the most that can be said is that Sind formed a useful subsidiary to the main establishment at Surat.

The attempts to extend trade to the southward along the Konkan coast were even less successful than this venture on the west. The possibilities of the coast were thoroughly tested, and we hear of the English Company's factors residing for various periods at the ports of Danda Rajpur, Dabhol, and Rajapur, while Bhatkal, further south, was for a time the Indian headquarters of Courteen's Association, the rival English company founded in 1636.[1] A factory at Vengurla was established by the Dutch, primarily in order to obtain provisions for their fleets during the seasonal blockade of Goa, and a substantial amount of trade was at times put through; but the truth seems to be that during most of our period the kingdom of Bijapur, which was served by all these ports, was an unsatisfactory market, demanding little but the precious metals, and having few goods to offer in exchange. This section of the coast received further attention about the year 1659, when the English Company made a vigorous attempt to develop its trade, but the results lie outside our period. The chief commercial attraction was the supply of pepper, which became important at this time owing to difficulties in procuring it at Bantam or Achin; but when Indian pepper was wanted, merchants naturally looked for it farther south in the neighbourhood of Cochin and Calicut. The latter place was indeed one of the first objectives of the Dutch after they had decided to confront the Portuguese. In 1604 they entered into an alliance with the Zamorin for the expulsion of the Portuguese from India, and further agreements were subsequently made, but no regular trade resulted at this time; while the experience of the English about the year 1620 led to the decision not to attempt further business. Some years later, however, the merchants of both nations obtained admission to the trade of this coast, as will be explained in

[1] The activities of Courteen's Association from about 1636 to 1646 bulk largely in the English correspondence, but they made no particular difference to the trade of India, except in so far as their competition discouraged the members of the older Company from providing the capital required to develop its business on profitable lines. The story of the Association can be read in *English Factories* (v. xxx ff.; vi. xxi; vii. xx ff.: viii. x ff.); and in occasional references in the *Court Minutes*.

Chapter III. The reorganisation of the pepper trade, which followed on the Dutch conquest of Cochin, lies beyond the limit of our period.

3. The Extension to Bengal

We must now return to the East Coast, where, as we have seen, the original settlements extended from Masulipatam to the vicinity of Tegnapatam. A few years after the arrival of the English, another nation, the Danes, appeared upon the scene, and obtained a grant of the port of Tranquebar, which remained their headquarters throughout the rest of our period. I have found no regular records of their commercial activities, but from what may be read in the reports of the Dutch and English merchants it is clear that they suffered from a chronic shortage of capital, and that their share in the trade of India was small. The activities of the Dutch and English were not confined to the factories already named, but extended along the coast to any town where goods could be had on reasonable terms: the Dutch also made purchases inland in the neighbourhood of Golconda, and the English followed the same practice, but farther south the continual disturbances made it hopeless to attempt business in the interior, and even on the coast contracts were liable to be interfered with by outbreaks of war or lawlessness. The extreme south was left alone for the greater portion of our period, but in 1645 the Dutch established a factory at Kayal, to the south of Tuticorin, and about the same time the English were buying cotton goods and pepper in that neighbourhood, while an English factory was subsequently established at Kayal, designed apparently to compete with the Dutch. A little later the Dutch captured from the Portuguese the more important town of Negapatam.

The trade of the coast was thus fairly well developed from Masulipatam southward, but the chief interest of the story lies farther north. From the outset the Dutch had hoped for remunerative intercourse with Pegu, Arakan, and Bengal. It may be said at once that Pegu was a disappointment, the commercial and administrative conditions being almost intolerable, and neither Dutch nor English succeeded in establishing an extensive trade; the English factory there sent more or less encouraging reports from time to time, but in 1655 it was described as "needless," and in the following year it was dissolved, while about the same time a Dutch report described the trade as dead.

The Dutch maintained relations with Arakan throughout most of our period, though commerce was interrupted by occasional wars. The trade was of small value, but it furnished two commodities in particular, rice and slaves, which, as we shall see later on, were urgently required in Batavia, and such interest as it possesses for us arises from the fact that these commodities were obtained to a great extent from Chittagong.

Bengal offered such obvious attractions to merchants that it is at first sight difficult to understand why it was neglected alike by Dutch and English for so many years after their arrival on the coast. The explanation is to be found in the conditions which prevailed locally: the country itself was too unsettled for peaceable trade, while the seaports were difficult of access, and were dominated by the Portuguese. Indian chroniclers tell us little of the internal condition of Bengal during the reign of Jahangir, and the English correspondence discloses only projects which were not put into execution, but the Dutch records show that, while the merchants at Pulicat and Masulipatam were alive to the possibilities, they were deterred from action by the news which reached them, and which may be summed up in the judgment passed by the Governor General at Batavia in 1627, that there was no hope of profitable trade because of the constant wars and rebellions, and the frequent changes in the administration. That the commercial life of Bengal was in fact depressed at this period seems to be proved by the attitude of the Indian traders on the Coromandel coast: from time to time we read of the Dutch relying on them to bring Bengal goods to Masulipatam, but their expectations were not fulfilled, and we may reasonably accept the inference that Indian merchants did not consider the venture worth their while.

The conditions prevailing in the principal seaports afforded ample grounds for hesitation. Bengal is served by two estuaries, the Meghna and the Hooghly.[1] Of these, the Meghna was dominated by the pirates of Chittagong, some of them natives of the country, others Portuguese settlers, who lived by depredations on commerce, and were (subject to temporary disagreements) protected by their sovereign, the king of Arakan, to whom they are said to have paid a percentage on the gross produce of their industry.[2] It is obvious that legitimate commerce must have suffered from their operations, the more so that persons as well as goods were treated as booty, the prisoners taken being sold into slavery; and I have found no evidence of the existence of any considerable direct trade between the Meghna and foreign countries at this period. The other estuary, the Hooghly, was also threatened by pirates, though to a less extent; in addition, the dangers attending its navigation were notorious,[3] and there can have been little temptation to incur these risks in order to reach a port the business of which was almost entirely in the hands of the Portuguese. The extent of their domination was fully realised by the English. In 1618 Sir Thomas Roe, who wrote " upon searching the bottom of all the secrets

[1] In Appendix C of *India at the Death of Akbar* I stated some reasons for rendering the Portuguese word *porto* as estuary, not seaport, in references to Bengal during the sixteenth century. A good instance of this use of the word is contained in a Dutch report made in the year 1608 by a factor who had visited Arakan, and who speaks of Chittagong as the *hoofstadt*, or chief town, of Portogrande, an expression which indicates that by Portogrande he meant the Meghna estuary (*de Jonge*, III. 287). It may be added that the Dutch sometimes speak of Chittagong itself as " Little Bengala," so that they at least did not regard it as the " great city of Bengala " (*Dagh Register* (Coromandel), March 19, 1644, and January 6, 1645).

[2] In his interesting account of the Portuguese in Bengal, Mr. Campos takes the year 1607 as marking the beginning of Portuguese piracy. I think there were individual pirates earlier than this, but there is no doubt that the menace to trade increased greatly in the first years of the seventeenth century, and lasted until the capture of Chittagong by the Mogul forces (*Campos*, 81-87, and 155-167.) The statement that the pirates paid a share of their plunder to the king of Arakan is taken from Shihabuddin's account, translated in *Sarkar's Studies*, 128.

[3] Methwold, writing of the years about 1620, says that in Bengal " we are mere strangers; the coast is too dangerous, and our shipping too great, to adventure them among so many shelves and sands " (*Methwold*, 1004).

of India," declared that Bengal had no ports but such as the Portuguese possessed for small shipping; and two years later the English factors who had penetrated from Agra to Patna reported that "The Portugals of late years have had a trade here in Patna, coming up with their frigates from the bottom of Bengal, where they have two ports, the one called Gollye [Hooghly] [1] and the other Pipli, and therein are licensed by this king to inhabit. Gollye is their chiefest port, where they are in great multitudes."

The obstacles to trade on the Meghna continued throughout our period; Chittagong was visited occasionally by Dutch merchants from Arakan, and their incidental remarks show that piracy rather than commerce was the chief occupation of the inhabitants, while the lists of the cargoes which they obtained indicate no signs of commercial progress. On the Hooghly an abrupt change in the situation followed on the destruction of the Portuguese settlement in 1632, and Indian merchants on the Coromandel coast set out to reopen trade as soon as they were relieved of the fear of the Portuguese, while both Dutch and English vessels started northwards.

The extension was gradual. The first ventures we read of were to roadsteads in the vicinity of Cuttack; later on, ships were taken farther north to the ports of Pipli and Balasore; while in the year 1634 instructions were sent from Batavia to attempt trade with Hooghly itself. The early experiences of the Dutch at this port were, however, not encouraging. A monopoly of all trade had been granted to two local merchants; the authorities were not friendly; a fairly favourable agreement was settled with the Viceroy of Bengal at Dacca, but it did not prevail against the local obstacles; and in 1636 the factors decided to move down to Pipli, where Bengal goods could be obtained without the oppression and extortion met with at Hooghly. For some years both Dutch and English followed this policy, remaining off the mouth of the river at Pipli and Balasore, and sending buyers up the country from these bases; information regarding the English

[1] The name Hooghly takes a variety of forms in contemporary literature. An account of discussions on its derivation is given by *Campos* (63-65).

activities is scanty, but it suffices to show that the merchants preferred their own interests to those of the Company, and the real pioneering in this region was done mainly by the Dutch, whose factors were at Patna and Kasimbazar early in the next decade. I have not ascertained the precise date when the Dutch returned to Hooghly, but it lies between 1645 and 1650;[1] in the former year their business was still being transacted at Pipli, while in December, 1650, the English factors who were sent to settle at Hooghly were instructed to follow the Dutch example, and to obtain land adjoining their settlement. This English factory was established early in 1651, and the two Companies traded side by side, but for the remainder of our period the Dutch predominated in the markets; the staples purchased by them were raw silk from Kasimbazar and saltpetre from Patna, and the development of the former trade was their most conspicuous achievement. Cotton goods of relatively fine texture were also exported in small quantities, but the fame of the Bengal muslins was not yet established in the Western markets. The difficulties of navigation on the Hooghly have already been mentioned, and up to the close of our period goods were usually brought down in small vessels and transhipped at Pipli or Balasore. This course, however, involved heavy expense, and in the year 1660 the English Company authorised experimental trips up the river by seagoing ships; the story of this development lies outside our period.

It was said in the previous chapter that the Danes were active chiefly in the Bay of Bengal. I have not found any contemporary account of their activities, but according to Thomas Bowrey, who was in these waters from 1669 onwards, they were at war with Bengal for over thirty years, and they must consequently be regarded as obstacles to the progress of its commerce. Bowrey's story is to the effect that the Danes had obtained a settlement at Balasore, but that about the year 1642, when ships failed to arrive from Denmark, the local

[1] The series of the *Dagh Register* is unfortunately incomplete. Between 1645 and 1653 the only volume extant is a very brief summary for 1648, which does not include abstracts of the news received from India. The gap is not covered by any documents which have come to my notice.

Governor had the residents poisoned, seized on their goods, and demolished their factory. The next Danish fleet found the settlement desolate, and the commander was forced to declare war in a just cause; but the operations, which could have ruined the sea-borne commerce of the country, were not effectively prosecuted. Negotiations for peace were in progress in the year 1674, and shortly afterwards the Danes were admitted to a settlement at Serampur on the Hooghly. I have found no other account of the origin of the trouble, and the story of poisoning is in itself improbable; but whatever the facts may have been, the existence of a state of war is borne out by various incidental records of Danish attacks on Bengal shipping, and the conclusion appears to be justified that local ship-owners were in this way prevented from enjoying their full share of the revival of commerce which followed on the destruction of Portuguese domination.

The facts which have been summarised in this chapter show that by the close of our period the influence of the European merchants had extended over the greater part of India. On the coast, from Sind to Bengal, Dutchmen and Englishmen were to be found wherever there was trade worth having, while in the north they were active over large portions of the areas now known as Bihar and the United Provinces, and their presence was familiar on the roads leading from Agra to the seaports. In the south they had not penetrated inland to any great extent, but in this region the internal markets were not too distant to experience the influence of transactions on the sea-board; and it may fairly be said that, with the exception of the Punjab, every important part of India was affected by the new conditions which had come into existence. The next step in our inquiry is to attempt to determine the nature and magnitude of the commercial changes which resulted.

AUTHORITIES FOR CHAPTER II

SECTION 1.—The working of the various spice markets, and their dependence on Indian-made cotton goods must be studied chiefly in the narratives of the earliest Dutch and English visits; after the first voyage or two, such matters were usually taken for granted by the narrators. The following passages may be cited: *Houtman*, i. 72-122; *Renneville*, i. 3, 369 ff. (Bantam), ii. 1 (Java), ii. 220 ff. (Moluccas), ii. 158 ff. (Achin), ii. 371 ff. (Amboina); *de Jonge*, II. 448, III. 149; *Terpstra's Koromandel*, 1 ff.; *Terpstra's Surat*, 3, 35; *Purchas*, I. iii. 153 ff. (Achin), 161 ff. (Bantam), 194 ff. (Priaman); *First Letter Book*, 73, 74, 77, 84, 131, 148, 427; *Letters Received*, i. 18, 68 ff. 77 ff.; ii. 275, 314, 336; iii. 139. The danger to ships in Eastern harbours is a common topic; see, *e.g.*, *Purchas*, I. iii. 179, 180; iv. 522; *Letters Received*, iii. 22; *Jourdain*, 234, 236, 303, 311 *n.*; and for losses by disease or disorder, see *Renneville*, i. 101; Scott's Discourse, in *Purchas*, I. iii., and *idem*, I. iii. 186; *Middleton*, 19 ff.

The first Dutch visits to Surat are recounted in *Terpstra's Surat*, 17 ff.; some of the relevant documents are also in *de Jonge*, II. 491 ff. The concentration of the Dutch on essentials, and the consequent temporary neglect of Gujarat trade, are obvious in many passages in the *Hague Transcripts*, *e.g.*, II. 1, 5; see also *van Dijk*, 29. The early settlements on the East Coast are described in *Terpstra's Koromandel*, 34 ff. For the capture of Pulicat by the Portuguese, see *Hague Transcripts*, I. 69; *Lisbon Transcripts*, I. 424; and *van Dijk*, 20 ff. The arrival of the English on the East Coast is in *Purchas*, I. iii. 315, 320 ff.; for the English at Pulicat, see *English Factories*, i. p. xliii; at Armagon, *idem*, iii. p. xlii ff., and *passim*; at Madras, *idem*, vi. pp. xxxvii, 153 ff.

SECTION 2.—The motives of the first English voyage to Surat can be traced in *First Letter Book*, 38, 114 ff., 291; that the Dutch also experienced a glut of pepper appears from *de Jonge*, III. 120. The determination of the Portuguese to exclude other European nations from Surat is well brought out in *Lisbon Transcripts*, I. 58, 444. Hawkins' narrative is in *Purchas*, I. iii. 206 ff., and also *Early Travels*, 70 ff. For the wreck of the *Ascension*, see *Purchas*, I. iii. 230, and *Jourdain*, 124 ff.; for Middleton's visit, *Purchas*, I. iii. 267 ff.; and for Best, *idem*, I. iv. 458 ff. The Mogul-Portuguese war is frequently referred to in the English records, *e.g.*, *Letters Received*, iii. p. xxxvii; the Portuguese view will be found in *Faria y Sousa*, iii. 195 ff. For the reappearance of the Dutch in Gujarat, see *Terpstra's Surat*, especially Appendices V. and VI. *Roe* is the chief authority for the English position at this time. Van den Broecke's narrative is in *Begin ende Voortgangh* (*Renneville*, vii. 380 ff.).

The conditions prevailing in the Red Sea trade are explained in *Jourdain*, 77, 103, and in the narratives of Middleton and Downton in *Purchas*, I. iii. The English activities can be followed in *English Factories*, beginning with i. p. xi ff.; those of the Dutch in *Terpstra's Surat*, 106 ff., and from 1624 onwards in the *Dagh Register*. For the unsatisfactory nature of the trade, see, *e.g.*, *English Factories*, vi. 59. The Persian attempts to divert the silk-trade are mentioned from time to time in the *Calendar S.P.*, *e.g.*, No. 486 of 1513–1616, and 16, 210 of 1617–21. For the beginnings of the English enterprise in Persia, see *Roe*, *passim*, *English Factories*, i. p. xxv, and ii. pp. vii ff.; for the Dutch, *Terpstra's Surat*, 137 ff. The cessation of English trade in silk is recorded in *English Factories*, x. 24, 46, 119.

For extensions in Northern India, see *Letters Received*, *English Factories*, and *Dagh Register*, *passim*, and also *Terpstra's Surat*, 74, 75, etc. The first English attempt in Sind is in *Purchas*, I. iv. 497 ff.; the volume of the trade is discussed in *English Factories*, i. 12, 14; the Dutch voyage of 1631 is mentioned in *idem*, iv. 207, and *Hague Transcripts*, I. 318; and the

English establishment of 1635 in *English Factories*, v. 117 ff. The drawbacks of the country appear frequently in subsequent volumes of *English Factories*; the settlement of the Dutch is in *idem*, ix. 116, and is mentioned in *Tavernier*, i. 313, and *Manucci*, i. 57. For sales of Sind goods in London, see *Court Minutes, passim, e.g.*, May 19, 1643, and June 8, 1658. As regards the West Coast, the English Company's enterprises can be followed in *English Factories* from vol. i. onwards, while those of Courteen's Association commence in vol. v.: for the Dutch at Vengurla, see *Dagh Register* from 1637 onwards. The renewed English efforts are noticed in *English Factories*, x. 233 ff., 352 ff. The early Dutch negotiations with Calicut are related in *Begin ende Voortgangh* (*Renneville*, v. 20; vii. 57 ff.): the treaties are in *de Jonge*, III. 204, 278; for later intercourse from the East Coast, see *Terpstra's Koromandel*, 146. For the English at Calicut, see *Letters Received*, vols. iv.-vi., and *English Factories*, i. 76.

Section 3.—The Danish activities at this period are noticed occasionally in *English Factories* and the *Dagh Register*; see especially *English Factories*, i. pp. xliv ff. For Kayal and Tuticorin, see *Dagh Register* (Coromandel), September 17, 1645, and *English Factories*, vii. 252, viii. 15, and x. 218, etc. Pegu is referred to frequently in both Dutch and English records; see especially *English Factories*, ix. 19, x. 40, and *Dagh Register*, May 16, 1661. The first Dutch account of Arakan is given in *de Jonge*, III. 287; there are frequent later reports in the *Dagh Register*.

For the early Dutch investigations of Bengal, see *Hague Transcripts*, I. 63, 139, 246, 270, and III. L3, P4; for the English projects, *Letters Received*, iv.-vi., and *English Factories*, i. 116. The Chittagong pirates are common topics; an interesting account of them is given in *Sarkar's Studies*, 118-152, while the *Dagh Register* has some incidental notices. For the Portuguese domination of Hooghly, see *English Factories*, i. 14, 213. Indian enterprise after the fall of Hooghly is recorded in *Hague Transcripts*, I. 318; the first English ventures, in *English Factories*, iv. p. xxx, and *passim*, v. p. xxxvi, vi. p. xliv; and those of the Dutch in the *Dagh Register* from 1634 (see especially February 8 and July 12, 1634, June 10, 1636, and March 14, 1637). The English establishment at Hooghly is in *English Factories*, viii. 334, and ix. p. xxvi. For seagoing vessels on the river, see *idem*, x. 408.

For the war between the Danes and Bengal, see *Bowrey*, 181 ff., also *Master*, i. 318. Traces of it will be found in *English Factories*, vii. 156 and viii. 174, and in *Dagh Register* (Coromandel), May 6 and December 29, 1645.

CHAPTER III

CHANGES IN THE FOREIGN COMMERCE OF INDIA

1. The Commercial Position of India at the Opening of the Seventeenth Century

In order to understand the commercial operations of the Dutch and English, whose gradual extension over India has been recounted in the last chapter, it is necessary to possess a general idea of the main lines of the trade into which they sought an entry. At the opening of our period, Indian goods were not in great demand in Western Europe. The principal item of the direct trade was Malabar pepper, the produce of a very small part of the country; Europe wanted pepper, but not necessarily the pepper of Malabar, and the extensive export from this region depended rather on the nature of the Portuguese organisation than on the slight differential advantage enjoyed by Indian producers.[1] Indigo was used in the Mediterranean area, but only to a small extent in Western Europe; the trade in cotton goods was, at the most, retail, and the same description may be applied to such other merchandise as was carried westwards. The Indian demand for European goods was of still less importance, and, speaking generally, Western Europe and India were not employed to

[1] Records of sales in London show that Malabar pepper usually brought 1*d.* or 2*d.* a pound more than the produce of Sumatra; *vide Court Minutes*, December 18, 1646, September 20, 1648, and *passim*. The transit of pepper to Portugal was a royal monopoly, which towards the close of the sixteenth century was farmed. The farmers had their agents in Goa, and pepper from Java or Sumatra would have had to be carried to Goa and sold to these agents at their monopoly price; the extra expense involved was sufficient to render business unprofitable (*Houtman*, i. 105).

any great extent in satisfying each other's needs. The position in Asia was very different, for there Indian cotton goods were indispensable; the clothing demand of Southern Asia kept the weavers of Gujarat and the East Coast busily employed; and Indian connections were necessary for profitable commerce in Eastern waters.

The most conspicuous feature of Indian foreign commerce was the absorption of the precious metals. This was no transient phenomenon: it had disturbed the minds of the financiers of the Roman Empire, much as it arouses anxiety in some quarters at the present day; and Sir Thomas Roe's epigram that Europe "bleedeth to enrich Asia" undoubtedly represented the contemporary Western view. The absorption of gold and silver was favoured by the laws in force in India, but in any case it must have resulted from the economic conditions which prevailed. Indian producers were eager to sell their wares, and, except in a few special cases, there were no official restrictions on exporters. On the other hand, the masses of Indian consumers were too poor to buy imported goods, the market for which was limited to the wealthy, but numerically unimportant, upper classes; the demand for foreign commodities, though it was not altogether negligible, was very far from being equivalent to the goods exported, and so it came to pass that, in the words of William Hawkins, "India is rich in silver, for all nations bring coin, and carry away commodities for the same; and this coin is buried in India, and goeth not out."

An enumeration of the principal imports is sufficient to indicate the narrow limits of the Indian markets. Spices and dye-woods, horses and elephants, raw silk, ivory, coral, and a few other materials, copper, lead, tin, zinc, and quicksilver in quantities which nowadays seem absurdly small, together with luxury goods and miscellaneous articles valued mainly for their novelty,—these were the commodities chiefly in demand, and merchants who were not in a position to provide them had to offer silver or gold if they desired to purchase Indian produce. It is important for our present purpose to note that Europe supplied few of these goods. Some quicksilver reached India from Lisbon and by way of the Red Sea, though China also sent supplies; lead was brought from Europe, and also coral, superior woollen cloth, silks, velvets, and other fabrics, wines and spirits, glass and mirrors, delicacies for the Portuguese residents, and a variety of miscellaneous goods; but the bulk of the imports came from Asia, so that European merchants who desired to trade with India were faced by the initial difficulty of providing remunerative outward cargoes.

As regards exports, if we look at India as a whole, the quantity of cotton goods stands out as by far the most conspicuous feature of the trade, though particular seaports depended in part on certain other articles. The Malabar ports, for instance, exported large quantities of pepper, and very little else: Cambay [1] and the adjacent seaports shipped indigo and much other merchandise; rice and sugar were sent out from Bengal; Pegu took quantities of dyed yarn from Coromandel; and among other articles exported may be mentioned the minor spices, such as ginger, cardamoms, and turmeric, various drugs, lac, pearls, and diamonds. In the case, however, of all the exporting regions except Malabar and Bengal, cotton goods were the foundation of the trade, and a few details are necessary to enable us to appreciate the conditions in which this business was carried on. Most of the consuming markets may be described as conservative, demanding goods of recognised kinds, and refusing to purchase unfamiliar products; and the producing regions in India had specialised to meet the needs of those markets with which they were in communication. The goods exported were thus highly diversified, and, since the descriptions in current use were drawn from several languages, the nomenclature employed in the trade is extraordinarily confusing to modern readers. It is possible, however, to reduce the multiplicity of names to a very simple classification, and I shall speak of the exports as calicoes, muslins, and dress or fancy goods.

[1] Strictly speaking, Cambay was not a seaport, because sea-going vessels could not approach it. Its exports were either carried to Goa by coasting boats, or else taken in harbour-craft to Gogha or Diu, and there loaded on the ships.

Calicoes were produced in almost all parts of the country, and were designed primarily for Indian wear, but they were also exported in considerable quantities. They consisted of plain cotton cloth, and could be obtained unbleached, bleached, or dyed in various colours. As a rule they were made in pieces of from 12 to 15 yards long by less than ¾-yard broad, and these were known in the Gujarat market as dutties or baftas,[1] but wider pieces, spoken of by the merchants as broad baftas, could be obtained from some centres of the industry. Sales were ordinarily made by the piece, or by the "corge" of twenty pieces, but in a few localities calico was woven in much longer pieces, and sold by length; the longcloth of the Coromandel coast was the best known, but long pieces were also produced in Northern India, where they were known to the merchants as guzzees (doubtless from *gaz*, an Indian yard). The export of calico to various parts of Asia was of old standing, but during the sixteenth century the Portuguese had developed an extension of the trade to West Africa, and also to their possessions in Brazil. The demand of these two markets was nearly identical, because the settlements on the coast of Brazil were populated largely by African slaves; the calico exported to them was usually described as Guinea cloth, but they consumed also some fancy goods, which appear in the commercial correspondence under such names as Guinea stuffs, slave-clouts, or negro cloth.

The distinction between calico and muslin is one of degree, and in a few cases it is doubtful whether a particular textile should be classed as a fine calico or a coarse muslin. Speaking generally, muslins were thinner in texture and lighter in weight than calicoes; they were suitable for wear in hot countries, and they appear to have been exported chiefly to Persia, Arabia, and Egypt. The Portuguese developed a trade in these goods to North-West Africa, where they were in demand as girdles and turbans, but it is not clear to me how far this development represented new business for India, and how far

[1] "Dutties" doubtless represents *dhoti*, the Hindi name for a loin-cloth; *bafta* is a Persian word meaning "woven," but in the markets of Gujarat it had acquired the specific signification of calico of rather better texture than dutties.

it was merely a diversion of trade from the older route by way of Egypt. The manufacture of muslin was to some extent localised, notably in Bengal and in the Deccan, though thin cloths could also be obtained in some other regions.

Dress and fancy goods, including *pintados*,[1] chintzes, handkerchiefs, short dyed pieces of calico, goods woven with patterns, and cloths with an intermixture of silk, were in great demand in the Eastern markets, each of which had its peculiar tastes or fashions. As William Finch wrote in the first commercial report sent to England from Surat,[2] "To write of clothing for Priaman [Sumatra] and Bantam with the Maluccos, etc., were infinite, they being of so many sorts and of such different prices": Dr. Terpstra enumerates 42 descriptions of goods handled by the Dutch in their earliest years on the Coromandel coast; about 30 distinct entries appear in the invoice of an English ship which sailed from Surat for Java in the year 1619; and about 150 titles are indexed as cotton goods in the first ten volumes of *English Factories*. For our present purpose, however, it is unnecessary to attempt the identification of all these goods: it is sufficient to know that the varying tastes of different markets were met, some from Gujarat, others from Coromandel, and others from both sides of India; and that, while the demand for particular descriptions may have been small, the aggregate trade in dress and fancy goods was of very great importance to the country.

The partial specialisation of the export trade can best be shown in tabular form, and I have set out in the following statement the names of the chief ports in each of the recognised coastal regions, the staple goods which they exported, and the directions in which those goods were carried. The information given in this table is, of course, far from complete; it is probable that nearly every ship carried a variety of goods other than those which I have specified, and that many of the seaports despatched occasional ships in other directions, but the general course of ordinary trade was that which I have

[1] For *pintados*, see above, p. 32.

[2] The report, which is given in *Letters Received*, i. 28, bears no signature, but Mr. W. Foster is undoubtedly correct in attributing it to Finch (*Early Travels*, 123 *n.*).

shown, up to the time when alterations were brought about by the activities of the Dutch and English merchants :

CONSPECTUS OF THE INDIAN EXPORT TRADE AT THE OPENING OF THE SEVENTEENTH CENTURY

Coastal Regions and Chief Seaports.	Principal Exports.	Destination.
SIND— Lahari Bandar.	Calico.	Persian Gulf; coastwise to Goa.
GUJARAT— Cambay, Gogha, Diu, Surat.	Cotton goods, yarn, indigo. (Also pilgrim traffic.)	Red Sea; Persian Gulf; Achin; coastwise to Goa.
KONKAN— Chaul, Dabhol, Rajapur.	Chiefly calico and fancy goods; some pepper. (Also pilgrim traffic.)	Red Sea; Persian Gulf; coastwise to Goa.
GOA— Goa (Bhatkal, decayed).	Transhipment; few local exports.	Persian Gulf; East Africa; Lisbon; Malacca and beyond; Ceylon.
MALABAR— Calicut, Cochin; several minor ports.	Pepper.	Cochin to Lisbon, and to Ceylon and Malacca. Calicut and minor ports to Red Sea.
SOUTH COAST— Quilon, Tuticorin, Negapatam.	Calico, pepper.	Mainly coastwise; Negapatam to Malacca and beyond.
COROMANDEL COAST— *South*— S. Thomé, Pulicat.	Fancy goods, calico and muslin, yarn.	Malacca and beyond; Achin; Pegu and Tenasserim; coastwise to Goa and Malabar.
North— Masulipatam.	Calico and muslin, fancy goods, yarn.	Malacca and beyond; Achin; Pegu and Tenasserim; Persian Gulf; coastwise, north and south.
GINGELLY COAST— Vizagapatam, Bimlipatam.	Provisions (rice and oilseeds).	Chiefly coastwise.
BENGAL— Hooghly, Pipli, Balasore, Chittagong.	Provisions (rice and sugar), muslin.	Pegu and Tenasserim; Malacca and beyond; Achin; extensive coastwise trade.

In addition to the exports by sea, a small amount of traffic existed on the two land routes leading westwards by way of

Kabul and Kandahar. The European merchants did not enter directly into this commerce, but it was probably affected to some extent by the competition of their shipping. Thus the indigo carried to the Levant by land from Agra, or by sea and land from Gujarat, came into competition in Mediterranean markets with the same commodity carried by way of Surat and London or Amsterdam, and it is probable that the volume of the land trade was reduced, though it was certainly not extinguished, during our period. The route to Kandahar was affected from time to time by political conditions. Early in the century the number of camels passing annually was said to be about 3000, representing a total export of 500 tons or a little more, but the number increased fourfold about the year 1615, when the hostilities between the Portuguese and the Moguls interrupted the traffic by sea from Gujarat to Persia. About thirty years later we find trade diverted from land to sea by the Mogul-Persian war over the possession of Kandahar, while some incidental remarks in letters from the factors in Persia suggest that the two routes were more or less in competition for the markets in the interior of that country, and that, apart from temporary fluctuations due to hostilities, the English and Dutch activities may have resulted in the transfer of some portion of the northern trade to the sea-route. The question is, however, obscure, and the volume of trade concerned is in any case too small to make it worth while to go into the matter in detail; the important developments of Indian commerce took place on the sea, and we may confine our attention to the business transacted on the coast.

2. The Provision of Purchasing Power

The sketch of Indian foreign commerce which has just been given makes it easy to understand that European merchants who wished to buy Indian produce were confronted at the outset with the problem of providing purchasing power in the markets of Gujarat and Coromandel. The Dutch quickly learned, as we have seen, that Indian cotton goods were needed for the spice trade which they had come to the East to develop, but they had still to discover how to pay for the Indian goods which they required. When the English came to Surat to buy indigo and calico for Europe, the same question arose. The establishment of the trade in Persian silk raised it again, for the silk had to be paid for either in Indian produce, or in goods, such as spices, which Indian produce was needed to procure. Commodities of minor importance, which Europe required from the Far East, had likewise to be bought mainly with Indian goods; and, speaking generally, Europe had to provide purchasing power in India for practically all the goods required, not merely from India itself, but from all quarters of the Asiatic seas. The obvious course was to carry out European goods for sale in India; but when it was found that the Indian demand for commodities was far too small to meet the cost of Europe's needs, three other expedients presented themselves—to carry out the precious metals, to raise funds by borrowing in the Indian market, or to employ capital in Asiatic trade and remit the profits to Europe in the form of spices or other Eastern produce. These different courses were tried with varying success, and the commerce which developed during our period was the result of their combination.

The lesson that the Indian demand for commodities was insufficient was quickly learned. Dutch and English merchants carried out consignments of almost every article produced in quantity in Western Europe, but disappointments were numerous, and after a short experience many items disappeared from the outward cargoes, while of those which were saleable the quantities were strictly limited. Iron, for instance, could not yield a profit except by accident, tin could not ordinarily compete with the produce of the Malay Peninsula, while to offer linen in the centres of cotton-production was evidently a hopeless business. When experience had once been gained, the cargoes sent out from Europe became for a long time almost stereotyped, with variations only in the quantities of particular items: apart from stores and treasure, the ships carried merely some pieces of woollen cloth, some lead, some quicksilver and vermilion, coral brought from the Mediterranean and ivory from the coast of Africa, some sword-blades or cutlery, and any fancy goods which were considered to be saleable, the total value being, as has been said, altogether insufficient to purchase the spices, calico, indigo, silk, and other merchandise which Europe required from Asia.

The initial experience which established the impossibility of selling European goods in sufficient quantities demonstrated also that an adequate supply of the precious metals would overcome all difficulties, since India was always ready to sell goods for cash. Export of gold and silver was, however, condemned by the theories which prevailed among the statesmen and financiers of Western Europe, theories which had a solid basis in the conditions of the time, and which were reinforced by a large mass of popular prejudice. Merchants who desired to export treasure could indeed argue with Thomas Mun that such exports would be advantageous if they resulted in a subsequent influx of greater amount; but the popular prejudice was not removed by such contentions, and its existence had to be taken seriously into account. The English Company could export gold or silver only up to the limit authorised by its charter or sanctioned by the Privy Council from time to time, and it was bound to conduct its business in such a way as to make good the export by sales of Eastern produce in other European countries, but the existence of these restrictions did not suffice to protect it from criticism. In 1618 the Moneyers of the Tower petitioned regarding the scarcity of silver, which they alleged to be due to the exports of the Company; in 1620 complaints on the subject were examined by the Privy Council; next year the Company was ordered to consider how silver might be brought more plentifully into the kingdom; in 1622 there was a war of pamphlets on the subject; and in 1624 the outward-bound ships were detained owing to a debate in the House of Commons, when the feelings of the members were sufficiently intense to produce what would now be called a "scene." In view of such experiences, no surprise will be felt that the Company should have taken all possible steps to minimise the need for exporting treasure, and in fact a considerable chapter of its early history relates to its efforts to sell English goods in other parts of Asia, since the Indian market would not take them. The instructions issued to the factors in Java in 1609–10 urged the need for pressing sales, especially of woollen goods and other English products, "whereby we may be able to drive a trade without the transportation of money, which is the chief scope of our desires"; while in 1628 the profit brought by ivory was described by the Surat factors as inadequate, "if your continued desire to lessen the transportation of coin did not occasion our advice for all commodities that will yield their prime cost." These attempts, however, met with little success, and all that could be done was to make the best possible use of so much gold and silver as could lawfully be sent out.

In this matter the Dutch Company appears to have been situated on the whole somewhat more favourably: at least, the English merchants urged in a representation to the Commons that "neither the Hollander, Venetian, nor Genoese are so curious to forbid exportation of money," and it is improbable that the memorialists would have ventured on this statement if it had not possessed a substantial basis of fact. The Dutch Company probably benefited in this matter from its wide basis; the merchants who composed it were the dominant power in the State, and could hope to carry their projects through, while at this period the Parliament in London was but little subject to the influence of the English adventurers. The difference was, however, one of degree, and the influence of monetary theory, or prejudice, on the transactions of the Dutch Company is apparent in the records of the period, as when a merchant at Surat urged that trade should be pushed at Agra on the specific ground that no money would be required, or insisted that the money to be obtained by trading to Mocha was essential to the prosperity of their business in India. The practical result was to limit the operations of both Companies, and, as in the case of Mocha, to set them seeking for means of expansion outside the limits so imposed.

One of these expedients, the borrowing of capital in India, was practised at times by the Dutch, and more frequently by the English; but the amount available was limited, and consequently the rate of interest was high.[1] Between 1625 and 1650 the rate paid in Surat ranged about 12 per cent; in the next decade it fell, and we read of transactions as low as 6 per cent, but the fall was temporary, and in 1659 offers of 9 per cent brought out very little capital. On the East Coast the ruling rate was probably nearer 18 per cent, but from about 1630 to 1640, when the English merchants' credit was low, they were charged from 24 to 36 per cent: at Agra we read of rates between 9 and 24, in Sind 15, in Bengal 36, and on the Konkan coast 13½ per cent. Such rates were crippling to enterprise, and we need not wonder that both Companies, after experience had been gained, decided against trading with funds borrowed in India; the large resources of the Dutch enabled them for a long time to dispense with the practice altogether, but the recurring difficulties in raising capital in London made it necessary for the English Company to authorise borrowing in India under strict limitations, and for their factors to exceed these limitations occasionally, in order to keep their trade alive. The necessity was, however, always irksome, and this method of providing purchasing power was in fact too costly to be used except in emergency.

3. The Companies' Asiatic Trade

One course remained to supplement the inadequate cargoes of European goods and treasure, and that was to employ part of the available capital regularly in Asiatic trade, conducting operations so as to provide the purchasing power required in India, and remitting to Europe the profits earned but not the capital itself. The advantages to be gained in this way were

[1] The figures quoted in the text are annual rates calculated from the monthly rates given in *English Factories* and the *Dagh Register*. That they were not above the ordinary market rate may be inferred from the statement of a Dutch factor that the high officials in Golconda lent money at four per cent per mensem, but charged five per cent to people known to be in difficulties (Account of Golconda in *Begin ende Voortgangh, Renneville*, vii. 510). The writer of the Batavia Journal for 1641, when recording that no debts carrying interest remained due on the Coromandel coast, added the pious aspiration, "God grant that the Company may in future trade on its own capital!" (*Dagh Register*, December 26, 1641, Coromandel).

stated forcibly by Sir Thomas Roe, who told the Directors in London that the cargoes they were then sending out would "never drive this trade: you must succour it by change"; and who shortly afterwards urged that trade to the Red Sea would suffice to finance the whole of the Company's Indian business. This course was followed largely by the Dutch, and to the extent of their smaller opportunities and resources by the English; and it accounts for what is at first sight a puzzling phenomenon—that merchants who came to buy Eastern goods for Europe should devote so much of their energies to the conduct of purely Asiatic trade, carrying all sorts of merchandise from one Asiatic port to another, and dealing largely in markets which had little to offer for shipment to Europe.

It will be observed that this expedient contained the germ of what came to be known as the "colonial system," but if effect had been given to the views of Coen, the great Dutch Governor General, that system would have been introduced in its fullest development almost from the outset. In the memorandum of instructions which he left for his successor in the year 1623, Coen urged not merely the prosecution of Asiatic trade, but the investment of all the available capital in the principal means of production ("many thousands" of slaves), and the development of the Company's possessions, "so that the returns for our native country be made out of the gains of the inland trade and the ordinary revenues," and the need for annual importations of capital might finally disappear.[1] Some development of production on these lines was in fact carried out by the Dutch in the Moluccas, Java, and Formosa, but the Company in Holland vetoed Coen's more ambitious projects, and during our period their agents in the East depended mainly on the profits of Asiatic trade. The English had at this time no territorial possessions in Asiatic

[1] The quotation is taken from the English abstract of the instructions given in *Calendar S.P.*, 1622–24, No. 243; the Dutch word here rendered "inland" is frequently used in contemporary records to denote what I have called Asiatic trade as distinct from the Company's original business of carrying goods to Europe. Coen's presentation of the case for a colonial policy can be read in *de Jonge*, III. 269 ff.

waters, so that in their case the question of a definite colonial policy did not arise.

Seeing that the main object of entering the Asiatic trade was to increase the quantity of gold and silver available for disbursal in India, the lines chosen by both Dutch and English were naturally those by which these metals could be most readily obtained. Some of the islands, such as Sumatra and Borneo, yielded small quantities of gold, and in them we find the factors buying gold with Indian goods, the gold on arrival in India exceeding the original cost of the goods by the profits of two voyages. The supplies of treasure obtained in this way were not negligible, but they counted for little compared with what could be obtained from the Red Sea, and from China and Japan. We have seen already that the European merchants were drawn to the Red Sea trade by the fact that it was conducted largely for cash; spices and Indian goods sold at Mocha returned ducats and other coins for employment in India; and the persistence of the merchants in face of the serious obstacles they encountered is the best evidence of the importance attached by them to this branch of their undertaking. It was, however, from Japan and China that the largest supplies were drawn, and the practical monopoly of trade with these countries enjoyed by the Dutch was, next to their control over the Spice Islands, the most important commercial factor in their success.

Japan at this period produced large quantities of silver, which was willingly paid away for those commodities which the country required. The Portuguese had become familiar with the fact during the sixteenth century, and it was emphasised in the letter which William Adams addressed to his "unknown friends and countrymen" in the year 1611, in the course of which he wrote: "You shall understand that the Hollanders have, here, an Indies of money; for they need not to bring silver out of Holland into the East Indies. For in Japan there is much silver and gold to serve their turns in other places where need requireth in the East Indies."[1]

[1] Adams is a striking figure of the period. According to his own account, after he had served in the Mediterranean trade for several years, he became

Experience furnished abundant proof of the truth of this statement, so far at least as silver was concerned,[1] and the Dutch learned that they could supply their requirements, provided that they could find suitable goods for sale in the Japanese markets. The taste of these markets was, however, distinctive. European goods sold only in small quantities, and Indian cotton goods were bought merely as curiosities, while the demand for spices was not extensive; the way to obtain silver from Japan was to bring raw silk, hides, and skins. The latter goods were to be had mainly in Siam, where Indian cotton goods were readily vendible, and a large business was developed on these lines—cotton goods from India to Siam; skins and some hides, thence to Japan; and silver from Japan to India. Later in our period, Indian skins also were handled, as will be shown in a subsequent section, but the main supply for Japan continued to be obtained in the Siamese markets.

The chief demand of Japan was, however, for raw silk. The supply of this commodity was at first in the hands of Chinese merchants, and the Dutch soon learned that the direct China trade was protected by the Emperor for political reasons: they could not therefore openly bring silk from China itself, but they could, and did, bring it from Indo-China, where they obtained it in exchange for Indian cotton goods, and for spices or other articles previously bought with the same

desirous to study the Dutch traffic to the East, and in 1598 entered Dutch service as steersman on a fleet which set out for the Indies by the South American route. The voyage was disastrous, and eventually Adams landed in Japan; he was for a time in prison, but won the Emperor's favour, received an allowance, and settled down in the country. When Dutch merchants reached Japan about the year 1610, it was Adams who conducted their business at the Court, and later on he acted for the English merchants, eventually entering the service of the East India Company. The letter quoted in the text is printed in *Purchas*, I. iii. 125, and also in *Letters Received*, i. 42; for his assistance to the Dutch, see *Renneville*, vii. 149.

[1] I have found no record of gold coming from Japan to India in large quantities during our period. Export seems to have begun in the year 1665, after the supply from the mainland had been disorganised through the loss of Taiwan; an entry in the *Dagh Register* for 25th April of that year mentions that the export of gold had been sanctioned by the Emperor of Japan, and from this time on we read of more or less regular consignments to the Coromandel coast. Writing at the end of 1640, the English factors at Surat referred to the "Japan silver and China gold" of the Dutch (*English Factories*, vi. 279).

commodities. Persian silk was also offered, but this trade did not develop, and the greatest success of Dutch enterprise in this direction was the opening of the Japanese market to the raw silk of Bengal. I have not been able to trace the details of this achievement, because the Batavia Journals are missing for the important years. A sample appears to have been sent as early as 1641, for in that year the factors reported that Bengal silk was found to be unsuitable for the Japanese market, being too coarse and uneven, and also too dear. No further mention of a trade is made in the Journals up to 1646, but when the series is resumed in 1653, the trade is found to be in full swing, a cargo sent to Japan in that year consisting mainly of Bengal silk, and subsequent entries tell the same story. There is no trace of any such trade in the sixteenth century, and the opening of this new market for Bengal must be attributed definitely to Dutch enterprise.

While Japan thus furnished silver, China and Indo-China contributed gold, which merchants were able and willing to give in exchange for pepper, sandalwood, dyewoods, and other Asiatic commodities, practically all of them bought with Indian cotton goods. The Dutch settlement at Taiwan in Formosa was the centre of this trade, and the factory in Japan was under the control of its Governor, who thus became responsible for the main supply of treasure, both gold and silver, to the Indian markets. In the latter half of our period, a large proportion of the requirements of the Dutch in India was supplied by direct shipments from Taiwan, gold being taken to the Coromandel coast, silver to Gujarat and Bengal, and their demand for remittances from Europe was correspondingly reduced.[1] Their business had thus been transformed; beginning by the direct purchase of spices for Europe, they were led gradually to engage in nearly every important line of commerce throughout Asiatic waters, and their operations

[1] In 1640, for instance, the indent on Taiwan for Surat and Coromandel was 2,000,000 guilders, while in the following year Surat alone asked for 1,000,000 guilders (*Dagh Register*, December 6, 1640, July 31, 1641). About this time the indent on Holland for all the Dutch needs in the East was about the same sum as Surat alone asked from Taiwan (*Realia*, iii. "Vaderlandse Geld Eysch").

were directed to pouring treasure into India, because Indian goods were obtainable in sufficient quantities only in exchange for gold and silver. The English merchants pursued the same course as far as possible, but their exclusion from the Farther East deprived them of the opportunities which the Dutch turned to such good advantage, and throughout our period their share in Asiatic trade was much less important; their principal business was the development of the direct trade between India and Europe, while their rivals were at least equally successful in this trade, and at the same time were able to undertake a much larger proportion of the distribution of Indian goods, and thereby penetrate the commerce of the whole of Southern Asia.[1]

4. Changes in the Course of the Import Trade

Regarded from the Indian standpoint, the results of the activities which we are examining fall into two classes: on the one hand, the Dutch and English merchants established a new direct trade between India and Western Europe, while on the other they produced certain modifications in the course of the old-established commerce of India with other parts of Asia and the East Coast of Africa. In the remaining sections of this chapter, I shall examine firstly the changes in the import trade from all sources, secondly the changes in the export trade to other Asiatic countries, and thirdly the effect of these changes on the Indian shipping industry; the establishment of the export trade to Western Europe is a development of sufficient importance to require a separate chapter.

So far as imports are concerned the changes to be recorded are very slight. There is no evidence that any important new want was brought into existence, or that any large increase occurred in the consumption of foreign goods, while it is doubtful whether, on balance, Indian consumers in the

[1] In 1658 the English Company broke new ground in regard to the supply of the precious metals by buying up the Guinea Company, with a view to shipping African gold-dust, and also ivory, direct to India, but the story of this measure lies outside our period (*English Factories*, x. 141, 206, 398).

mass were better served than before.[1] Increased exports were paid for almost entirely in gold or silver, and the only new feature—the import of copper from Japan into Northern India—appears to represent not an increase in consumption, but an attempt to make good the failure of some of the local sources of supply. The chief interest of this change arises in connection with the currency, and its discussion may be postponed for the present: apart from it, the commercial correspondence of the period shows only that India's old needs continued to be met, in some cases rather more cheaply, in others at a somewhat higher cost, sometimes from new sources, but usually from the old, and that the upper classes enjoyed additional facilities for gratifying the prevailing taste for more or less costly novelties. The English merchants described these novelties as "toys," and the phrase is appropriate to this branch of their business.

This "toy" trade requires our attention, for, while it was neither extensive nor particularly remunerative, it was a commercial necessity of the period. Foreign merchants were helpless without the good will of the authorities; no request could be preferred without an appropriate present; and the fashion of the moment required that presents should consist largely of "toys." The Companies in Europe had therefore to keep their merchants supplied with articles suitable for this purpose; the far-Eastern markets had also to be ransacked; and the topic recurs constantly in the commercial correspondence of the time. Some of the "toys" imported were intended to be sold for use as presents, while others were to be offered by the merchants themselves, but in either case the source of the demand was the taste of Indian rulers and their courtiers. A few examples will suffice to illustrate the nature of this demand. The first English report regarding the trade of Mogul India, which was drawn up at Surat in the year 1609, after enumerating the regular imports—woollen goods, quick-

[1] Illustrations of this statement will be found in the examination of the course of markets in Chapter V. The prices of such goods as quicksilver or cloves show violent fluctuations; consumers benefited at some periods, but at others they suffered, and it is scarcely possible to strike the balance of loss and gain.

silver and vermilion, lead, tin, ivory, coral, and sword-blades—goes on as follows:

> Of new drinking glasses, trenchers for sweetmeats, but especially looking-glasses of all sorts and different prices (but not small baubles) some reasonable quantity would be sold to good profit, and I verily suppose that some fair large looking-glass would be highly accepted of this King [Jahangir], for he affects not the value of anything but rarity in everything, insomuch that some pretty newfangled toys would give him high content, though their value were small, for he wants no worldly wealth or riches, possessing an inestimable treasury.

Students of Jahangir's *Memoirs* will agree that this picture is substantially correct; the Emperor paid rather more attention to intrinsic value than the writer indicates, but it was novelty that he thought of most. The Dutch factor, van Ravesteyn, told the same story a few years later, reporting that all manner of curiosities should be sent, "particularly for the Great Mogul," pictures of landscapes and great personages, "mirrors as tall as a man with frames wrought with festoons," "fine greyhounds and some strong dogs which will tackle tigers," and so on; while he described the Emperor as "an amateur of all rarities and antiquities."

The merchants naturally did their best to gratify the taste of the Emperor, on whose favour they depended for the success of their enterprise, but they soon found that there were difficulties in the way. The Imperial Princes, and also the officials at Surat, were eager to obtain the credit of presenting any "toys" likely to prove specially acceptable to the Emperor; with this object they insisted on searching imported goods, and taking over what they wanted, at a price fixed by themselves; and not a little of the friction between the authorities and the merchants can be traced to this competition for the advantage of presenting an unusually attractive gift. Sir Thomas Roe tells at length how the presents sent to India in 1617 were seized by Prince Khurram (Shahjahan), and forwarded to the Emperor in his name. Two years later the English merchants succeeded in conveying a certain picture to Court without the knowledge of the Prince, in whose jurisdiction Surat then lay; when the matter became known, the Prince "enraged that he had received no notice in the roll from hence [Surat], chabacktt the haddee [horsewhipped the Imperial messenger] that went up with the goods," and "by express farman commanded the like as well to the Governor, Jumull Khan, as Isake Beg and the Customer, or, disliking the whip, are enjoined each 1000 rupees penalty." [1] The writer of the letter added that these authorities put the blame on the English, and threatened rigorous search to prevent such smuggling in future; and he anticipated that the resulting damage to business would exceed the benefits to be obtained by the sale or gift of twenty such pictures. In this case, Prince Khurram doubtless wanted the picture to present to the Emperor, but after he ascended the throne his own tastes became manifest: in his reign presents had to be costly as well as novel, and the Batavia Journal of 1643 has a curious tale of the Dutch efforts to convey unobserved to the Court a large copper lantern, of the outrageous conduct in regard to it of Prince Dara Shukoh, and of Shahjahan's delight when the lantern was at last exhibited. The immediate result was the grant of a distinctly favourable concession for trade, and a request from the Emperor for a few lacquered palankins from Japan.

In the Mogul Empire, then, a steady supply of "toys" was necessary throughout our period. The demands of the king of Golconda were not less insistent. The presents given by the English in order to obtain the concession known as the "Golden Farman," which was granted in 1634, were valued at over 6000 pagodas or say 20,000 rupees, and some versions of the farman indicate that the expectation of receiving "rarities" was part of the consideration for its grant.[2]

[1] "Haddee" is *āhadi*, the title borne by the Mogul corps of gentlemen-at-arms (*Ain*, translation, i. 249). "Chabacktt" is obviously derived from *chabuk*, a horsewhip, an implement in some favour with Mogul administrators, as may be seen from various records, *e.g.* *Fryer's* description of the Surat custom-house (i. 47).

[2] The text of the Golden Farman is not extant, and the three translations show some discrepancies. The contemporary version speaks of "rarities" being brought for the King; the version of 1670 also mentions "rarities," but that of 1676 has "goods" or "good things." The earliest

The Dutch were equally alive to the necessity, and in 1643 we are told that their present was worth 10,000 pieces of eight (say Rs. 20,000), consisting of elephants, horses, copper candelabra weighing nearly five hundredweight, and sandalwood and spices in abundance. The King's tastes were, however, wider than this list suggests, and in 1639 the English factors wrote that they might have anything in reason which they wanted in return for a present, which would not cost much money, consisting of "Persian horses, English mastiffs, Irish greyhounds and water spaniels; fair large looking-glasses; a piece of fine scarlet; crimson and violet satins; our King's Majesty's picture, large, in Parliament robes; a good buff coat; an excellent perspective and multiplying glass; a large pair of globes; and a suit of fine light armour, if possible musket-proof." The writers recognised that this proposal might sound unreasonable, but they urged that, whether the capital employed were large or small, presents must be given, "else no living among these people." The taste of the Hindu authorities in the south did not differ materially from that of the Moslems. The nayak who admitted the English to Armagon desired indeed the gift of so useful an article as a cannon, but this was to be supplemented "with some toys of worth," as velvet, damask, and taffeta, a Japanese writing-desk, and any "English toys" that might be available; while the liberal terms offered to the English at Madras were explained by the grantor as due in part to his desire for good horses from Persia, and in part to his hope of facilities for purchasing "hawks, apes, parrots and such like baubles" from Bengal. Throughout India, then, and indeed throughout the Eastern seas, this taste for novelties was a matter to be taken seriously into account, and the necessity must be allowed for in any estimate of the activities of foreign merchants; an ample provision of carefully selected "toys" was in the seventeenth century what judicious publicity is now, not a direct source of profit, but an indispensable preliminary to securing profitable business.

version suggests that the original text probably contained the word *tuhfa*, which at that period would bear the meaning of "rarities" or "toys." The three versions are printed in *English Factories*, v. 14 ff.

5. Changes in the Asiatic Export Trade

In regard to the export trade from India to other parts of Asia and to East Africa two distinct questions arise, relating respectively to the extension of existing commerce and to the opening of new lines of business: we have to inquire whether the activities of European merchants resulted, firstly, in an increase in sales in markets which were already open, and secondly, in a development of sales in regions to which Indian goods had not previously been exported in noticeable quantities. The first question is not easy to answer. A recent writer[1] dealing only with English activities, and examining them over a longer time, has suggested that more cotton goods must have been carried to Asiatic markets, but I have not been able to find positive evidence of such an increase during our period, and general considerations appear to me to indicate the necessity for caution in regard to this question.

Looking first at the most important aggregate of markets, those which were served through Malacca and the Java ports, there is no doubt that the quantity of cotton goods handled by the Dutch increased progressively. The statistics available are unfortunately incomplete, because, while the Batavia Journals purport to give the contents of each cargo despatched from India, there are in fact numerous blanks in the record, due in some cases to the disappearance of the Journals themselves, and in others to the neglect of individual compilers. Taking years for which most of the figures have been preserved, and making rough allowances for those items which are missing, the number of bales of cotton goods carried to Batavia by the Dutch was probably somewhat as follows:

Period.	Bales exported annually from			Total.
	Coromandel.	Gujarat.	Bengal.	
1625	1700	800	...	2500
1641–44	2500	1000	Samples only	3500
1657–61	4000	1200	500	5700

[1] C. J. Hamilton, *The Trade Relations between England and India*, p. 110.

Too much stress must not be laid on these figures, which include various conjectural elements, but they suggest in a general way that, starting from the time when merchants of other European nations were excluded from the Far East, the Dutch had by the close of our period doubled their exports from Coromandel, and increased their exports from Gujarat by one-half, while they had also begun to export from Bengal. There are no signs of a similar development of English trade in these markets, and the conditions which prevailed render any large expansion of their business improbable: the question therefore is whether the increased Dutch exports represent new business or merely a change in carrying agency. On this question direct evidence is wanting, but the following considerations are relevant. In the first place, the Dutch figures include a large proportion of the goods which they sent to Europe, America, and Africa by way of Batavia, and consequently the increase in Asiatic trade is at any rate substantially less than the figures suggest. In the second place, the Indian carrying trade was certainly declining during these years, if we regard as Indian the vessels owned by Portuguese;[1] it is certain, then, that the whole increase shown by the figures does not represent new business for India, and it is quite possible that the whole of it represents only a change in carrying agency. In the third place, it seems to me to be open to question whether the markets under consideration could have absorbed a large proportionate increase of cotton goods. We hear of no new developments in this direction, for the Dutch supplied markets which had previously been provided from India, and which had been adequately served first by the Arab traders and then by the Portuguese. These markets were by nature conservative; the bulk of the consumers were very poor, and in order to establish a large increase in consumption it would be necessary to prove either an increase in population or a rise in the prevailing standard of life. Whether such developments occurred during our period is a question which I have not attempted to study in detail, but until it has been investigated, it appears to me that it would

[1] The carrying trade is discussed in the next section of this chapter.

be unsafe to reckon on any large expansion in exports of cotton goods as the result of the far-Eastern activities of the Dutch: some expansion may have taken place, but the information which is available is consistent with stationary markets, in which nothing but the nationality of the carriers was changed. It would indeed be possible to argue that decrease is as probable as expansion. We have seen already that in some of the Eastern markets cotton goods served as the medium of exchange, and there is some evidence that in the sixteenth century they were employed also as a store of value, though they were obviously unsuitable for that purpose, and must have been liable to rapid deterioration.[1] The records of Dutch commerce show that during our period the use of coin was making headway in these markets, and the demand for cotton goods would tend to decline as the practice of hoarding gold or silver developed.

Turning to the other Asiatic markets for cotton goods, the disappointments, already mentioned, of the Dutch and the English in Pegu furnish fairly strong evidence that trade was not expanding in that region, while Arakan was certainly unprogressive. Nor can I find any evidence to show that the Red Sea trade developed materially during our period. It is possible that shipments to the Persian Gulf may have shown some increase in connection with the financing of the silk trade, but most of the English exports, if not all, probably represent merely a change in carrying agency or a transfer of business from the land route; and taking all the Asiatic markets together, the most that can be said in the present state of our knowledge is that, while there are no signs of a decline, there are no definite grounds for asserting that any proportionately large expansion occurred in the off-take of Indian cotton goods.

This provisional conclusion may be extended to the other goods which India ordinarily supplied to the rest of Asia, for in regard to none of them can I point to any evidence proving,

[1] *Barbosa* (ii. 199) recorded that in Amboina every man toiled to hold so great a pile of Cambay cloths that, when they were folded and laid on the ground one on the other, they formed a pile as high as himself.

or even suggesting, any considerable expansion. The position is different in regard to the opening of new lines of business, for here the activities of the Dutch produced definite results in the sale of Bengal silk, and probably of Coromandel skins, to Japan, as well as in the export of slaves, provisions, and other commodities required for their Asiatic settlements.

As has been explained in a previous section, the export of silk to Japan dates from somewhere about the year 1650, though the details of its establishment have not come to light. In May of 1653 there is a record of a consignment of 300 bales, while two months later a vessel left Batavia with a cargo consisting principally of Bengal silk. The Journals for the next three years are missing, but in 1657 we read of a consignment of 452 bales, and also of a small vessel laden entirely with silk; in 1659 a cargo was despatched of 662 bales, but part of it was the produce of Indo-China, while two other vessels carried mainly Bengal silk; and in 1661 a single consignment is recorded of 1010 bales. The bales of silk handled by the Dutch at this time averaged just under 150 lb., while the price approved by the English Company in 1659 was Rs. 90 to 100 per maund (probably of 74 lb.); on these figures, the value paid to the producers for 1000 bales would be about two lakhs of rupees yearly, a substantial figure when judged by contemporary standards of commerce. I have found no suggestion of any opposition to this export on the part of Indian dealers, and since opposition to export of raw materials was offered in the case of certain other goods,[1] it is reasonable to infer that production was extended to meet the new demand.

Up to the year 1643, I have found no record to show that skins from the Coromandel coast were carried to Japan, though small supplies were going to Batavia for local consumption. In 1644 samples of these skins, which had been forwarded to Siam, were reported on favourably by a Japanese merchant engaged in the trade of that country, and from this year onwards we find the Dutch exporting regularly to Japan. The importance of the trade during our period was much less

[1] The opposition to the export of yarn from Gujarat is referred to below (Ch. IV. sec. 6).

than that of silk; I have not found figures to indicate its extent, but probably it would be measured in thousands rather than lakhs of rupees.

Apart from silk and skins, the recorded developments in the Indian export trade to other Asiatic countries were connected chiefly with the activities of the Dutch in Java and the Spice Islands. The Dutch were engaged in establishing a new city at Batavia as their Asiatic capital, and at the same time they were reorganising the economic life of the Spice Islands; they drew largely on India for the material requirements of these enterprises, and we find the Coromandel ports in particular sending consignments of a large variety of goods, such as iron and steel, sacks and sacking, leather, salt, and even roofing-tiles, which were not readily obtainable in Java; but their main needs were two, population and foodstuffs, and it will be sufficient to examine the trade under these two headings.

At the outset, Batavia was a capital without a population. The Dutch themselves were few in numbers, and the hostility of their neighbours was sufficient to prevent any large influx of settlers from the vicinity; a letter written from Batavia in the year 1626 says that the natives had abandoned all parts previously inhabited, and that from paradise the country had become a wilderness. A supply of inhabitants had therefore to be organised, and, as might be expected from the conditions prevailing at the time, the skilled craftsmen, shopkeepers, market-gardeners and the like were obtained from China, while the East Coast of India furnished general labourers and domestic servants. The Chinese came of their own accord, and lived in Batavia as free men under a "captain" of their own nation; the Indians, on the other hand, were purchased on the coast from dealers of their own nation, and were imported as commodities in Dutch vessels.

The problem of the Spice Islands was also to a great extent one of population. Some of the islands had suffered terribly from a long period of disorder, and the drastic methods of pacification enforced by the ultimate conquerors, among them the wholesale deportation of the irreconcilable elements, contributed to reduce the population to an extent which hampered the supply of spices to the markets of the world. The necessary reorganisation was effected by settling a small number of Dutch families in the islands and providing them with sufficient slaves, mostly of Indian origin, to supply spices in the required quantities; and an idea of its thoroughness can be formed from the fact that in the year 1636, the population of the Banda Islands included only 560 natives out of a total of 3842; the balance was made up of 539 Dutch, 834 free foreigners, and 1912 imported slaves, the great majority of whom must have been Indians.

From about 1620, therefore, the Dutch requirements from India were, first, a large initial supply of slaves, and then a steady stream of reinforcements to make good the wastage, which may fairly be assumed to have been heavy; in fact the record of the census which has just been quoted states that, owing to the change of climate, imported slaves, "Bengalders, Arakanders, Malabars, etc.," were greatly affected by sickness on their arrival in the islands. The supply was obtained by ordinary commercial methods: there is nothing to suggest that the Dutch merchants practised either force or fraud, and we find them buying regularly from Indian dealers after obtaining the permission of the authorities.[1] The records of the numbers shipped are very incomplete, but it appears from the Batavia Journals that about the year 1625 the annual number might exceed 1000, by how much I cannot say, while from 1640 to 1660 it may have been somewhere about 500. Even if we take the value of an efficient slave at the high figure of fifty rupees, the transactions do not look very important from the commercial point of view, and the real interest of the trade lies in the light which it throws on fluctuations in economic conditions in India. Thus slaves were

[1] On this point reference may be made to an English letter from Pulicat in *English Factories*, ii. 102 ff. The writers were on bad terms with the Dutch, and they insist on the evils resulting from their trade in slaves, but they admit that steps were taken to minimise these evils. For the price of slaves, see *idem*, iii. 10, where an English factor was authorised to pay "20 rials and upward," or say Rs. 40 to 50, for ordinary labourers: the earlier reference shows that the Dutch demand had raised prices to about this level from the former standard of Rs. 15 to 20.

plentiful in Pulicat at the time of the famine of 1618, but by 1622 rice was cheap and slaves were for the moment hard to procure. The supply then revived, but shortly after the great famine of 1630 business was brought to a standstill, and the bulk of the trade was transferred to Arakan. In 1634 the factors at Pulicat reported that slaves were unprocurable owing to the great mortality which had occurred, while ten years later we hear from the same place that buyers still met with very limited success, the reason assigned being in substance that the surplus population had been disposed of by death and voluntary enslavement during the famine, so that no volunteers now came forward, and the Indian dealers could obtain slaves only by occasional kidnapping. At Arakan trade was more or less continuous from about 1635 to almost the end of our period. Bengal was afflicted by no serious famine during these years, and slaves, brought in from that region by dealers as well as by pirates, appear usually to have been available in moderate numbers, though the trade, like everything in Arakan, was hampered by the capricious interference of the King and his ministers: sometimes we hear of the sudden institution of a state monopoly, sometimes of a claim to pre-empt any slave skilled in handicraft, sometimes of an unexplained prohibition; but factors employed in Arakan must have expected such interruptions, and subject to them the trade was carried on, though not, I think, to the full extent of the demand. Towards the close of our period, there are signs of a revival of the Coromandel trade, for, after a gap in the series of the Batavia Journals, we hear in 1661 that the glut of slaves in Negapatam was beginning to diminish, and that a recent scarcity in the Tanjore country had affected the supply in that neighbourhood; on the other hand, the Arakan market was at this time unsatisfactory, owing partly to heavy mortality, and partly to the Bengal frontier being closed through hostilities.

Apart from the temporary prohibition in Arakan, which, whatever the cause, was certainly not due to humanitarian ideas, I have found only one instance of the refusal of Indian authorities to sanction the purchase of slaves. This was in the year 1643, when a nayak, or chief, rejected a Dutch request for leave to buy up to 1000 slaves yearly on the ground that the sale of human beings was not only a scandal but a sin. That this humane attitude was not universal is indicated by the fact, recorded in the same entry in the Batavia Journal, that the servants of another nayak were just then trying to sell two Dutch cabin-boys who had run away and fallen into their master's hands; in 1661 a ship belonging to the king of Golconda carried 300 slaves to Achin; and a perusal of the successive reports on the subject will show that the trade was regarded, by Indians as well as by Dutch, precisely as any other branch of commerce. The share taken in it by the English factors was naturally small, because their masters had no Asiatic territory to develop; Bantam occasionally asked for a few domestics from India, but as time went on the English needs appear to have been met chiefly from Madagascar or other islands. The Portuguese were more active, and we read of occasional consignments by them from both coasts of India, but this was not a new feature of our period, for the general trade was familiar in the sixteenth century; such development as occurred was due to the special needs of the Dutch in Batavia and the Spice Islands.

The same cause accounts for the development in the export of food-grains: the new populations had to be fed, and, in the absence of adequate local supplies, India was the most obvious source on which to draw. It is not clear to me whether in the sixteenth century the Spice Islands taken as a whole were self-supporting in the matter of food, but, if they were, it consisted largely of sago, and the reorganisation effected by the Dutch necessitated the provision of increased quantities of rice, together with some wheat and pulse, to meet the requirements of the settlers and imported slaves. These supplies were shipped regularly from Batavia, but owing to the hostility of its neighbours the city could at first count on little in the way of local produce, and thus it became a centre of the grain-trade, importing from India and elsewhere to provide for its own consumption as well as for the needs of its dependencies. The extent of the imports cannot be precisely stated, because, though the subject was sufficiently important for detailed record in the Journals, the arrivals are stated in terms of varying and uncertain units, a junk-load of rice, so many thousand baskets of paddy, and so on; but in the year 1632, the total imports cannot have been less than 2000 last, equivalent to about 3125 tons weight,[1] and representing a substantial fraction of the total tonnage leaving India. In this particular year, however, India's share in the trade was small, and speaking generally it may be said that the grain-trade, like the slave-trade, is an index to the economic condition of the country. In ordinary times the bulk of the supplies for Batavia came from the Coromandel coast and, by way of Arakan, from Bengal; but Siam, Indo-China, and even Japan also contributed, and since seasonal causes might affect one or other of these sources, the problem of supply was difficult, and in the early years there were occasional dangers of famine. The Coromandel coast furnished supplies regularly up to 1630, but the effect of the disastrous drought of that year was to cut off this source, and the trade was not re-opened until 1634. Meanwhile the supply from Arakan had been organised, and thenceforward Coromandel and Bengal shipped rice regularly, and occasionally sent smaller quantities of wheat and pulse. The trade must be regarded as beneficial to the eastern side of India, because it afforded an outlet for surplus produce, while the authorities were quick to prohibit export at times when no surplus was available. It may be added that from about 1660 Dutch exports to Ceylon come into some prominence, but this cannot be regarded as a new feature in Indian commerce, Ceylon having been traditionally dependent on the mainland for food.

Before leaving the Asiatic markets a few words may be said of the rise of the tobacco trade, the only development I have traced in which the impetus did not come from European merchants. The crop had been acclimatised in Gujarat towards the end of the sixteenth century, and in 1623 we find the commodity figuring among the exports from Surat; but

[1] For the weight of a last of rice, see Appendix D.

it was undesirable as freight, owing probably to the bulk of the bundles of dried leaves, and it appears to have been handled mainly by local merchants or by way of private trade. The crop had also reached the Coromandel coast, and Methwold, writing of his experiences about the year 1620, recorded exports to Mocha and to Arakan, while some years later we hear of the dried leaf being carried to Bengal and Pegu.

6. The Indian Shipping Industry

We have seen that, owing to the need experienced for taking an active share in the Asiatic trade, Dutch and English vessels were employed on the principal export routes from India, and that, while some new business was created for Indian producers, much of the additional cargo-space was devoted to established traffic; the inference is obvious that the existing carrying agencies must have been injuriously affected by the operations of the new competitors. So far as the Portuguese ship-owners are concerned, this inference is incontestable. After the fall of Hooghly, their commerce in Bengal practically disappeared, while from their other settlements in India we hear only of progressive impoverishment and decay. At the beginning of the century the Portuguese share of the export trade was certainly large, and, while it is not possible to speak definitely as regards quantity, it is probably correct to say that most of the Dutch and English business in the Asiatic carrying trade was acquired at their expense. On the West Coast, Surat prospered while Goa declined; in Coromandel, Pulicat and Madras superseded S. Thomé and Negapatam; while in Hooghly, the business lost by the Portuguese eventually passed mainly to the Dutch.

The position of Indian ship-owners, other than Portuguese, is not so simple, for in their case the effect was not uniform, and it is desirable to examine the question separately for Gujarat, Coromandel, and Bengal. In regard to Gujarat, the most striking change is the decay of the coasting trade to Goa, which was carried on largely by Indian vessels sailing under Portuguese protection. At the beginning of the century either two or three of the large coasting fleets (known as *kāfila*) sailed during each season, each fleet consisting of from 200 to 300 vessels, convoyed by war-frigates; the capacity of the cargo-boats averaged perhaps from 40 to 50 tuns, and their lading consisted partly of cotton goods, indigo, and other merchandise for export from Goa, partly of grain and other commodities for consumption on the West Coast. The decay of this trade was rapid. In 1621 van den Broecke wrote from Surat that the Portuguese coasting trade was already ruined, and that only two fleets, each of from 40 to 50 vessels, had sailed during that year, carrying nothing but provisions; a year later he put the total number of vessels at from 60 to 80 for the season; while Pelsart tells us that in 1626 only 40 vessels reached Cambay from Goa, and that their cargoes were of little value. After this, we hear little of these large regular coasting fleets; the Portuguese were at times unable to provide war-vessels for escort, while the seasonal blockade of Goa, maintained for several years by the Dutch, rendered a change in organisation necessary, and we read only of a few boats at a time evading the blockade, and slipping into Goa with the provisions of which the city often stood in urgent need. Gujarat business must have suffered through the enforced reduction of consumption on the West Coast, due partly to this blockade and partly to the impoverishment of the Portuguese, but so far as exports to foreign countries were concerned, the change was if anything advantageous, because the Dutch and English ships carried direct to Europe, or to the Eastern markets, the goods which had formerly been sent for transhipment at Goa. While, therefore, the owners of coasting boats were undoubtedly affected by the change, it was of little significance for producers or merchants, since the loss of business with Goa was more than compensated by the new direct trade.

Apart from the coasting trade, the routes in which Gujarat was most interested were those to Achin, Persia, and the Red Sea. Achin was important mainly as a distributing centre for cotton goods, and as such it came into competition with the Dutch at Batavia and the English at Bantam, while it was visited occasionally by the ships of both nations; unless, therefore, a large increase in the total off-take can be established, it is reasonable to infer that Gujarat ship-owners suffered by competition on this route. Their business was not, however, wholly lost, for we hear of their ships in the port throughout our period, and as late as 1661 the cargoes brought by them were sufficient to glut the market. For considerable periods also the Dutch were at a disadvantage in this trade. Before the year 1632 they were charged higher duties than the Indian traders, but in that year satisfactory terms were arranged, and equality secured. Friendly relations appear to have continued for the next decade, but after the Dutch had secured possession of Malacca they endeavoured to divert trade from Achin to their new settlement. The result of these endeavours is somewhat obscure, but they affected the relations between the Dutch and Achin, for in the 'fifties a state of war was in existence, and the trade was then chiefly in the hands of Indians; but at the close of our period the Dutch were at last realising their project of monopolising the local pepper trade, which would naturally enable them to dominate the whole commerce of Achin. So far, then, as our period is concerned, the facts which are on record suggest the inference that Gujarat ship-owners, though affected by competition, retained a substantial share of the trade on the route to Achin.

Turning to the sea-route to Persia, it is fairly clear that at the outset of our period most of the Gujarat goods were carried in Portuguese vessels, for the bulk of the arrivals at Ormuz from Western India came either from Goa itself or from ports such as Lahari Bandar, Chaul, and Diu, where most of the shipping was owned by Portuguese. After the fall of Ormuz there are indications that Indian owners were attracted to its successor Gombroon, for ships from Surat are recorded there from time to time. They were, however, placed at a disadvantage by the fact that the Portuguese at Muscat still endeavoured to collect from Indian vessels the tolls which had previously been levied at Ormuz; but the guard-vessels employed for this purpose were not in a position to interfere with Dutch or English ships, which were consequently preferred by Indian merchants sending goods to the Gulf. The fall of Muscat removed this difficulty, and it is probable that by the end of our period Indian shipping to Gombroon and beyond was at least as numerous as in the time of Portuguese domination.

The Red Sea route was, however, the most important of all, so far as Surat was concerned, and it was here that competition was most seriously felt, or at least most bitterly complained of. Opposition was excited by the mere suggestion that an English ship might be sent to Mocha; and when in the year 1618 the suggestion became a reality, the hostility aroused in Surat resulted in a boycott of the English merchants, and a petition to Prince Khurram, then in charge of the administration of Gujarat, urging that the Red Sea trade should be reserved for Indians, while all other routes might be open to the English. The Prince took the local view, and told the English that unless they were contented to have unrestricted trade with all places but Mocha, they might leave the country, an answer which closed the matter for the moment. By this time, however, the Dutch had become alive to the attractions of the trade, and under orders from Batavia began to press it energetically; while for the English the question was merged in a larger dispute with the Surat authorities, which came to a head in 1622, and was only settled in 1624.[1] The agreement which was then made contained no restriction on trade with the Red Sea, and I have not come across any later record of active opposition, but I do not think that we should be justified in inferring that the Surat ship-owners were satisfied; it is more probable that they realised the determination of the Dutch and English to pursue the trade, and decided to submit to the inevitable. However that may be, from about this time forward we meet European as well as Indian vessels on this route; I have found nothing to suggest that the volume of trade was expanding, and it is reasonable to infer that Indian ship-owners lost some portion of their former trade.

[1] The transactions in question are referred to below in Chapter VIII.

The facts appear then to establish some injury to Surat ship-owners on two out of the three principal export routes as well as in connection with the coasting trade to Goa, but it would be a mistake to regard this injury as progressive. The effects of competition were acutely felt between 1620 and 1630, and must have been intensified after the famine of the latter year, when the supply of goods for export was for a time almost cut off; but a recovery ensued, and in 1644 the English merchants reported that ships owned by Moslems had become so numerous "that for procury of employment they submit to any, however contemptible, freightments," a remark which indicates that cargo-space was increasing, though not necessarily profits. In 1660 again we are told that Indian ships were multiplying so fast that "whereas in Surat ten years past there were but 15 or so, there is now 80, and the most part of great burthen"; and, while some part of this increase may be accounted for by concentration at a single port, the evidence of recovery appears to be incontestable.

As regards the southern portion of the Coromandel coast, I have found nothing to show that Indian-owned shipping was important at the beginning of our period. The chief centres, Negapatam and S. Thomé, were definitely Portuguese, and in this region the principal change was the transfer of exports from these seaports to Pulicat and Madras. The coasting trade to Cochin and beyond was also in Portuguese hands until the reduction of their power caused by the activities of the Dutch, when it passed to Indian shippers, but the impoverishment of the consuming markets suggests that the resulting gain cannot have been very great. Farther north, the position is not altogether clear, but at Masulipatam at least the bulk of the shipping was at first in Indian hands, and while I have found no record of complaints such as were heard in Surat, I think it is probable that the local shippers suffered for a time. About the year 1640 the position was altered by the chief officials of Golconda, who insisted on preferential treatment for the ships which they owned. In due course preference was converted into monopoly, and about 1647 we hear that goods could be sent to Persia, Basra, Mocha, and (a little later) to Pegu only on these ships, most of which belonged to the famous Mir Jumla, at that time the Chief Minister of the kingdom. The monopoly appears to have been discontinued after the transfer of his allegiance to the Mogul Empire, for in 1661 we find that the Dutch and English were again competing for freight to Persia, but for the latter portion of our period Indian ships certainly secured the most profitable part of the export trade of this region.

In regard to Bengal, the evidence already summarised appears to justify the inference that up to about 1630 the bulk of the small export trade was in the hands of the Portuguese. It did not pass immediately to the Dutch and English, who at first handled few goods other than those intended for the new markets which they were developing, and for a time Indian ship-owners appear to have gained ground at Pipli and Balasore, from which ports as many as 26 foreign sailings were recorded in the season of 1643–44. After this year there was a sudden decline, due mainly to the attacks of the Danes in prosecution of their war with Bengal; while the establishment of the Dutch at Hooghly enabled them to handle exports for Asiatic markets in increasing quantities, and by the end of our period their share in the trade was certainly substantial.

Taking then the Indian-owned shipping as a whole, and excluding from that term the vessels owned by Portuguese inhabitants of India, we may say that during our period it lost ground definitely, but not progressively, in Gujarat, gained ground but failed to retain it in Bengal, and possibly lost on balance in the Coromandel ports. The Dutch handled all or nearly all of the new Asiatic trade which they had created, and the Dutch and English between them took over an undetermined but substantial portion of the trade which had existed before their arrival in India. It is safe to infer that those Indian merchants who were also ship-owners suffered by the change, but the inference cannot be extended to Indian merchants as a whole, or to any class of Indian producers with the exception of shipbuilders;[1] on the contrary, we are justified in concluding that Indian merchants benefited by a service at once cheaper and better, and it is possible that some portion of the advantage may have accrued indirectly to producers. The attitude of merchants in inland cities may be gathered from the fact that, at the time when Surat was actively opposing the admission of English ships to the Red Sea, Ahmadabad was asking the English to carry goods on freight to Mocha, Persia, and elsewhere; and after more than twenty years' experience of the business, the English at Surat reported that Indian merchants chose Dutch or English in preference to Indian vessels. That freights were lowered as the result of competition is shown in the same report; Indian owners were then not only quoting low rates but offering to bear a share of the customs duties or other incidental payments, and throughout our period the efforts of the Dutch to outbid the English furnished a guarantee against excessive charges. Indian merchants were frequently in a position to pick and choose, since cargo-space was available in excess of needs; in 1647, for instance, the English at Surat complained that they could not find employment for their ships owing to Dutch competition, while Dutch vessels were sailing half-laden or in ballast. The greater security offered by European vessels followed necessarily from the conditions which existed. The essence of Indian navigation was adaptation to stable seasons and avoidance of bad weather; the ships were weakly built, and their crews must often have been found wanting in experience during emergencies. The Dutch and English ships were built to stand bad weather, their crews were trained in the storms of the North Sea and the English

[1] It may be inferred from the facts given in the text that Indians built fewer vessels on the West Coast, though not on the East, during our period than at the close of the sixteenth century. The decline appears, however, to have affected mainly the Portuguese industry. Nearly all their trading vessels for Asiatic waters were built in India: the Dutch and English occasionally bought Indian vessels (see, *e.g.*, *English Factories*, v. 43 and viii. 91), but their larger ships came from Europe, and during our period they had scarcely begun to build in India as a regular practice. The developments in the delta of the Godavari recorded by *Bowrey* (p. 102) may have originated during our period, but I have found nothing to show that they had become important.

Channel, and men who had brought a ship safely round the Cape could be relied on to face the worst accidents of Indian waters.[1] Further, European ships were ordinarily better armed, and could defy attacks of pirates, against which Indian ships were almost helpless; while, as has been said already, the Portuguese customs boats left the Dutch and English alone. The preference shown by Indian merchants was therefore justified; and while those of them who owned ships must have suffered from reduced freights, and presumably from shortage of cargo, the larger number, whose business required only the transit of goods, found it possible to transact their business more cheaply and with a greater degree of security.

AUTHORITIES FOR CHAPTER III

SECTION 1.—Most of this section is condensed from the account of Indian foreign commerce given in Chapter VI. of *India at the Death of Akbar*, where detailed references will be found. The European demand for Indian goods is discussed more fully below in Chapter IV. The classification of cotton goods is drawn from the Dutch and English commercial records, but it is not, so far as I know, to be found set out in any of them. For names of fancy goods, see *Terpstra's Koromandel*, Appendix I., and *English Factories*, i. 62, 63; a long list of goods is given in *Hobson-Jobson* (*s.v.* Piece-goods), but it is compiled from later sources, and omits a large number of the names frequently used during our period. For changes in the land trade, see *Court Minutes*, April 7, 1624, and December 29, 1643; and *English Factories*, viii. 207, 261 ff.

SECTION 2.—The account of the import trade is based on a large number of isolated statements in the English and Dutch commercial records. The position in regard to export of the precious metals is discussed fully in *Cunningham* (The Mercantile System): Mun's treatise is in *Purchas*, I. v. 732; the limitations in force in England can be traced in the *Calendar S.P.*; and the hostility to the E.I. Company in *Court Minutes* (June 12, 1618; January 12, 1620; March 8, 1624, etc.). The instructions issued in 1609-10 are in *First Letter Book*, 319, and the report of 1628 in *English Factories*, iii. 196. The greater freedom of the Dutch is asserted in *Court Minutes*, April 16, 1624; chapter ix. of *van der Chijs* indicates the position in Holland in the early years; the instances of the Dutch merchants' consciousness of the limitations are taken from *Terpstra's Surat*, Appendices XI. and XIII.

[1] The best evidence of the superiority of European navigators is found in the frequency of their employment on Indian-owned vessels: Dutch steersmen in particular were in great demand, though Englishmen were also sought for (see, *e.g.*, *English Factories*, ix. 14).

SECTION 3.—*Roe's* views on Asiatic trade will be found on pp. 346, 348 of his Journal. Coen's Instructions are abstracted in *Calendar S.P.*, 1622–1624, No. 243; their significance is brought out by *Elias*, ii. 38, 74, 91. Agricultural development in the Dutch possessions is frequently mentioned in the *Dagh Register*. For the Sumatra gold-trade, see *Letters Received*, i. 74, 79; iv. 24; and for Borneo, *idem*, iv. 219.

The Japanese demand for goods is indicated by the abstracts of cargoes given regularly in the *Dagh Register*; the unsuitability of cotton goods for this market is emphasised in *Letters Received*, iii. 238 ff.; the offer of Persian silk is in *English Factories*, vi. 116. For Indian skins in Japan, see *Dagh Register* (Siam), November 14, 1644, and subsequent abstracts of cargoes sent to that country; for silks, *Letters Received*, iii. 242, 245, and *Dagh Register*, *passim*. The earliest mention of the silk-trade from Bengal to Japan is in *idem*, April 21, 1641.

SECTION 4.—The examples of the toy-trade given are taken from *Letters Received*, i. 33; *Terpstra's Surat*, 49, and Appendix VI.; *Roe*, 383; *English Factories*, i. 111; iii. 134; vi. 183, 184; and vii. 81; *Dagh Register* (Gujarat), April 27, 1643; the list could easily be amplified.

SECTION 5.—The cargoes of silk for Japan are compiled from the *Dagh Register*, beginning with an entry of May 21, 1653; the value is taken from *English Factories*, x. 276. The early references to the export of skins are *Dagh Register*, November 29, 1640, April 23, 1642 (Coromandel), and November 14, 1644 (Siam).

The Dutch requirements in Batavia and the Spice Islands are regular topics in the *Dagh Register*; the desolation of the country round Batavia is taken from *Calendar S.P.*, 1625–29, No. 255. For the pacification of the Islands, see *idem*, 1617–21, No. 1108, and 1622–24, Nos. 193, 243; *Hague Transcripts*, III. M4; as well as frequent references in the *Dagh Register*, where the census of Banda is given under the date October 6, 1636.

The facts regarding the slave-trade are taken from numerous entries in the *Dagh Register*, supplemented by *Hague Transcripts*, I. 162, and *English Factories*, ii. 85; v. 326; vi. 226; vii. 120; and viii. 54 *n*. The traffic in food-grains is also a regular topic in the *Dagh Register*; for an instance of prohibition, see the entry of January 6, 1645 (Arakan). The tobacco trade is referred to in *English Factories*, i. 211; iii. 286; iv. 105; etc.; *Methwold*, 1004; and *Dagh Register*, *e.g.* October 6, 1636, November 27, 1640, and April 26, 1643 (Coromandel).

SECTION 6.—The impoverishment of the Portuguese settlements is a common topic at this period; see, *e.g.*, *Pyrard* (translation), ii. 203; *della Valle*, i. 157; *English Factories*, v. 221, vi. 230, etc.; and, some years later, *Master*, ii. 84, and *Bowrey*, 191. The *kafila* is described by various writers, such as *Pyrard* (translation), ii. 245, or *Jourdain*, 173; for its decay, see the letters quoted in *Terpstra's Surat*, Appendices XI. and XIII., and *Pelsart*, 7, 8. Conditions of shipping in Achin can best be studied in the *Dagh Register*, from October 29, 1625, onwards. For shipping at Ormuz, see *Terpstra's Surat*, Appendix XXI., *Dagh Register*, *passim*, *e.g.* September 17, 1645 (Surat), and *English Factories*, v. 118, 126; vi. 276. The story of the Red Sea route is scattered through the Dutch and English records; the early opposition is narrated in *Letters Received*, vi. 227, and *English Factories*, i. pp. xi ff., 174 ff.; ii. pp. xviii ff.; xxix ff.; and iii. pp. i ff., 27 ff.; while the Dutch entry into the trade is recounted in *Terpstra's*

Surat, c. X. For the recovery of Surat shipping, see *English Factories*, vii. 142, 208 ; viii. 37 ; and x. 301.

The change in the Coromandel coasting trade is mentioned in *Renneville*, vii. 494 ; the early position at the northern ports is stated in *Schorer*, ff. 3-6 ; the later monopoly at Masulipatam, in *English Factories*, vii. 55 ; viii. 83 ; and ix. 12, 19 ; its disappearance is indicated in *Dagh Register*, May 11 and 16, 1661. For the volume of shipping at Pipli, see *idem*, April 3 and June 1, 1644 (Coromandel). For examples of the keen competition between Dutch and English shipping, see *English Factories*, viii. 173, 205. The Indian preference for European ships is indicated in *idem*, i. 301, vii. 142. *Van Twist* (c. xliv.) among other writers refers to the weakness of the Indian ships and the defects of their armament.

CHAPTER IV

THE ESTABLISHMENT OF NEW MARKETS IN WESTERN EUROPE

1. Trade with Western Europe at the Opening of the Seventeenth Century

We have now to examine the outstanding commercial development of our period—the establishment of new markets for Indian goods in England, France, and the Netherlands. In order to realise the position at the opening of the seventeenth century, it is convenient to think of Europe as consisting of three commercial regions, which for descriptive purposes may be called Russian, Mediterranean, and Atlantic. With the first of these regions we are scarcely concerned; a limited amount of Indian trade passed north-westwards by the Caspian and Black Sea routes, and we read occasionally of schemes for developing traffic on the Volga so as to bring Eastern goods to London from the Baltic seaports; but this traffic did not become practically important, while I have found no indications of any noteworthy variation in the volume of trade with Russia itself. The Mediterranean region had for long obtained Eastern goods by way of the Red Sea and the Persian Gulf; up to the close of the fifteenth century these routes served also the Atlantic region, but the high cost of transit imposed narrow limits on the trade, and the Eastern goods reaching the countries on the Atlantic seaboard were practically confined to spices, drugs, and curiosities. The opening of the route by sea to Lisbon necessarily resulted in a change of organisation. The Atlantic countries were served more cheaply and efficiently by the new route, which also competed in the Mediterranean markets, and while Eastern goods continued to be distributed from the Levant, the monopoly of the overland traders had passed away; during the sixteenth century distributors could look to Lisbon as well as to Aleppo or Alexandria, and the advantages of water-carriage were usually decisive in the case of those markets which were situated near the former centre.

The Portuguese did comparatively little to develop the commercial position they had thus secured. It is true that, as has been explained in the last chapter, they established trade to West Africa and Brazil in cotton goods brought from India, but there are no signs that they introduced any new Indian commodities into the wholesale markets of the Atlantic region of Europe; the vessels leaving Lisbon for the northern ports carried mainly spices and drugs, or the products of the Farther East, and during the sixteenth century we hear nothing of the extensive consumption of indigo, saltpetre, and calico which is the outstanding feature of our period. The Western markets benefited by larger and cheaper supplies of the goods already in demand, but, so far as the available records show, that was the total result of the intervention of the Portuguese. It is, however, impossible to speak with precision of the details of the Lisbon trade, because its secrets were jealously guarded, and I have not been able to find any official statistics of the quantity or value of the goods imported, or of their distribution among the various consuming markets; on the latter point we can only say in general terms that the bulk of the cotton goods went to Morocco, Brazil, or the Guinea coast of Africa, while most of the pepper and other spice was carried on Dutch vessels to Antwerp, Amsterdam, or other seaports in Northern Europe.

A rough idea of the volume of goods brought to Lisbon at the opening of the seventeenth century can be formed from two lists preserved in the Public Record Office in London, which purport to give the cargoes arriving in the years 1602 and 1603, or very shortly before the Dutch and English established factories in India.[1] The source of the figures

[1] These lists are classified as "State Papers, Foreign. Portugal: vol. 3; Nos. 7 and 10," and are noted as Nos. 309 and 327 in *Calendar S.P.*, 1513–1616; I am indebted to Miss E. Salisbury for their transcription.

given is not stated, but it is reasonable to assume that they were obtained surreptitiously, and they may contain substantial errors of detail; at the same time their contents agree generally with contemporary descriptions of the trade, and the following summary of them gives a view which on the whole is probably not far from the truth:

CARGOES FROM GOA TO LISBON

Article.	Unit.	1602. (2 carracks.)	1603. (4 carracks.)	
Spices	Quintal (=130 lb.)	9851½	25,582½	
Indigo	,,	17½	809	
Other goods detailed by weight . .	,,	889	nil	
Silks	Chests	303	931	In 1603 entered in one item as calico cloth, stuffs, silks, etc.
Calicoes	Chests	86	..	
,, ...	Large bales	273	959	
,, ...	Small bales	146	5,314	

Together with musk, ambergris, precious stones, and China dishes, enumerated by varying units.

These quantities represent in each case the total of the year's trade, and they include much that came from countries farther East than India. Excluding the goods of obviously foreign origin, the Indian merchandise may be shown as follows:

Article.	Unit.	1602.	1603.	Probable Source.
Pepper	Quintal	7598	21,349	Malabar coast.
Ginger *	,,	?	..	
Cardamoms . .	,,	82	..	South India.
Indigo	,,	17½	809	Gujarat or Agra.
Carnelians (*laqueca*)	,,	27	..	Gujarat.
Ebony	,,	? 55	..	Possibly South India: more probably East Africa.
Calicoes	Chests and bales	All	All	All coasts of India.
Precious stones .	..	?	?	Not identifiable: probably some diamonds and pearls from India.

* The origin of the 1277 quintals of ginger carried in 1602 cannot be determined. The European markets preferred Chinese to Indian ginger, and probably some, if not all, of this consignment was from the former country.

The chief difficulty in interpreting these figures is to form even a rough idea of the quantity of cotton goods which they represent. In the list for 1602 these goods are shown separately under the name calicoes, but there are no means of ascertaining the sizes of the bales or chests, and one can only conjecture that the bulk of the consignment consisted of coarse goods for Brazil or West Africa, while, despite the description, the chests probably contained articles of higher value, such as muslins or coloured goods, for Portuguese use or retail distribution.[1] The list for 1603 is hopeless in this respect, for the large number of chests and the very large number of bales are all lumped together as "calico cloth, stuffs, silks, etc.," and, assuming the figures to be correct, an indefinite proportion of the total may have consisted of silk goods from the Farther East, or of miscellaneous commodities packed in chests or bales. Taking these uncertainties into account, the most that can be said is that at this time Lisbon was receiving from India very large quantities of pepper, mainly for distribution to the northward, large quantities of cotton goods, the bulk being probably the coarse stuffs in demand in Africa and South America, and small quantities of indigo, carnelians, cardamoms, and perhaps ebony and ginger, along with some pearls and diamonds.

During our period the great bulk of the trade to Western Europe passed from the Portuguese to the Dutch and English, but, with the exception of one item, the transfer of agency did not affect the interests of India. The exception is the export of pepper from Malabar. In the sixteenth century practically all the pepper brought to Lisbon was the produce of this

[1] There are some grounds for thinking that, while the bales handled by the Portuguese were of varying sizes, they were on the whole smaller, perhaps much smaller, than the standard of later Dutch and English cargoes. The account given by *Linschoten* (c. 92) of the way the carracks were loaded shows a very large number of individual small consignments, in fact what might almost be called parcel traffic; while *della Valle* (p. 60), writing under Portuguese inspiration, commented on the great size, "as big as a Roman coach," of the bales handled by the Dutch and English. The bales carried in the carracks should not therefore be thought of in terms of the bales discussed in Appendix D, but their actual size is a matter of conjecture.

region, shipped at Cochin or neighbouring roadsteads under arrangements made by the Portuguese with the various local rulers. The pepper produced in Sumatra, Java, and other places farther East was not handled by the agents of the Portuguese royal monopoly, while, so long as the shipping was exclusively Portuguese, it could not be brought to Western Europe without their knowledge.[1] The Dutch and the English, as we have already seen, brought pepper mainly from Java and Sumatra; their attempts to enter the Malabar market were not at first successful, but the Portuguese export thence was hindered by their activities, and thus the trade to Western Europe was for a time partially lost to India. The adjustment could be rapidly effected, since a crop of pepper is secured in three or four years after planting; the yield in Java and Sumatra increased in response to the larger demand, and probably there was a corresponding decrease in Indian production, though no records exist in which the fact would naturally be mentioned.

The temporary decline in exports from Malabar was not due to any unwillingness on the part of the Dutch or English to handle its produce. The unsuccessful efforts of the Dutch to establish trade at Calicut have already been mentioned; and it is noteworthy that, when they found Calicut unsuitable, they attempted to export Malabar pepper from the East Coast, but the cost was excessive, and the trade did not develop. In the same way the English, after their early disappointments at Calicut, endeavoured to establish Surat as a pepper-market where they could obtain supplies for Europe, but many difficulties were experienced, and the cost proved to be twice as high as at Bantam, which in the year 1630 was

[1] There is a curious story in the journal of the first Dutch voyage (*Houtman*, i. 105), to the effect that the Portuguese had contemplated buying up the Java pepper, but that the Emperor of China had paid them to leave the trade open to his subjects. The editors of the journal treat this story as a joke, but there may be some substratum of fact; there was occasional friction between the Portuguese at Macao and the Chinese officials, and it is quite possible that a threat to cut off the supply of pepper by diverting the Java crop westwards may have been used as a diplomatic counter in negotiations with Canton. What is certain is that, until the Dutch reached Java, the produce of the island went chiefly to China.

definitely selected as the chief source of supply for England. Five years later, however, a large consignment was bought at Goa as a result of the friendly relations established with the Portuguese, and admission to the Malabar trade was by degrees secured; from 1640 onwards we find both Dutch and English buying on the Malabar coast and also in the Konkan seaports. Just at the end of our period, an English factory was established in Calicut, and a few years afterwards the Dutch secured possession of Cochin, so that the prospects of the trade were again favourable, but there can be little doubt that Indian producers had suffered for a time through the development of alternative sources of supply. Against this temporary loss to the income of the country must be set the gain resulting from the trade in indigo, saltpetre, calico, and other goods, which is described in the remaining sections of this chapter.

2. Volume of the Export Trade to Western Europe

It is by no means easy to arrive at an accurate idea of the volume of the new export trade to Western Europe. There are, as we shall see, occasional uncertainties regarding the extent of the English share, but the chief difficulty arises from the system of shipping adopted by the Dutch, and from the form in which the facts of it were placed on record. Speaking broadly, the Dutch preferred to centralise their trade, and goods from both sides of India, as well as from the Islands, China, and Japan, were assembled at Batavia, to be despatched thence to Europe by the annual fleets. During our period the cargoes of these fleets were not usually entered in the Batavia Journals, and unless their details have been preserved in records still unpublished, it is now impossible to calculate the quantity, or the value, of the Indian goods which they contained. The Journals give, it is true, most of the cargoes despatched from India to Batavia, and from these entries it is possible to arrive at the approximate quantities of such commodities as indigo or saltpetre, which were exported only to Europe; but this method fails us in the case of cotton goods, since it is impossible to distinguish the bales intended for Europe from the much larger quantity exported for the Asiatic trade. To take one example, a cargo despatched from Masulipatam for Batavia in November 1642 consisted of 597 bales of cotton goods, 297 bales of indigo, 498 bales of crude and 538 sacks of refined saltpetre, together with some yarn, wheat, iron, and gunpowder. The last three items were clearly destined for Batavia or other places in Asia. The yarn is doubtful, but from the word used in the description I think this particular consignment was intended for use in the Batavia dockyard; the indigo and saltpetre were certainly destined for Europe, but the attribution of the large consignment of cotton goods is purely a matter of conjecture. We can thus arrive at an idea of the quantities in which some particular commodities were exported, but not of the volume of the total trade.

There is, moreover, another complication. The practice of concentrating trade at Batavia, though it was usual, was not invariable; from time to time Dutch ships left both sides of India for Europe direct, and their cargoes were not, as a matter of fact, placed on record in the Batavia Journals. We know of direct sailings from the Coromandel coast at intervals from 1615 onwards, and from Surat from about 1623.[1] In 1620 the Company authorised direct sailings from the latter port; in 1626 the practice was prohibited so far as Coromandel ports were concerned; and two years later the prohibition was extended temporarily to Surat. Later on direct shipping from the latter port was resumed, but I have found no complete record of the extent; even, therefore, if we could calculate accurately the goods sent to Europe by way of Batavia, we should still be liable to underestimate the total by the amount of the unrecorded direct sailings. These considerations make it advisable to approach the subject by an examination of the English trade, where the complications are less serious; in this case direct shipping from the East

[1] In Appendix B I have given abstracts of some of the earliest cargoes carried to Europe from India, taken from the original invoices in the Dutch records.

Coast began late in our period,[1] and up to 1648 we can take the despatches from Surat to represent approximately the total volume of the English trade, though particular consignments may for one reason or another have been sent from Coromandel by way of Bantam.

In regard to this trade, it is important to realise that a large proportion of the goods reaching London were re-exported to other European markets. Judged by modern standards, the population of England was at this time very small, and consumption was accordingly limited; but neighbouring countries, and especially France, with a relatively large population, looked to London for their supplies, and for calico in particular the French demand went far to determine, as we shall see, the nature of the goods for which London indented on India. When, therefore, we speak of the English trade, the expression must be understood as referring to a large proportion of the consumption throughout Western Europe.

The English export trade from Surat passed through several phases. Up to about 1620 the cargoes can be described as indigo and miscellaneous goods. In the next decade the trade in calico developed with remarkable rapidity. From 1630 to 1637 the great famine left its mark on the cargoes despatched; but from 1638 to about 1653 exports were substantial, though not progressive, the principal articles being calico, indigo, and yarn, while saltpetre, pepper, sugar, ginger, shellac, and a few other items also appear. After 1653 the English Company was for a short time almost out of business; the trade was thrown open to private vessels, and no estimate of the goods carried by them appears to be possible. Finally, the years from 1657 onwards were marked by a great increase in the Company's activities, following on its success in raising new capital in London. The last decade of our period is also characterised by a rapid change in the relative importance of the East and West Coasts. The establishment

[1] The *Bonito*, which sailed in 1649, was "apparently the first ship to go home direct" from Madras (*English Factories*, viii. p. xxx). Direct sailings from the East Coast had been talked about before Madras was founded, but I cannot find that the project was ever put into execution.

of trade in Bengal, the discovery that Madras calicoes were better suited to European markets than those of Gujarat, the decay of the indigo trade for which Surat was the principal seaport, and the defects in the Gujarat administration—all these causes combined to bring the East Coast into the prominence which it was to retain for many years.

The first phase of the English trade may be illustrated by the exports of the season 1618–19 as set out in the invoice of the *Royal Anne*, which left Surat in February with a cargo valued at 720,000 mahmudis (Rs. 2,88,000), composed of the following goods :[1]

	Ma.	Ma.
Indigo : Sarkhej	351,600	
Biana	278,700	
		630,300
Calico		77,000
Fancy cotton goods and samples		7,600
Gumlac		3,000
Sealing wax		200
Turmeric		150
Precious stones and miscellaneous		1,750
		720,000

together with some indigo-dust, not valued, and some foreign goods captured from the Portuguese.

It will be noticed that the value of indigo was seven-eighths of the whole, and the quantity of this commodity was over 200 tons in weight.[2] The demand for indigo is in fact the outstanding feature of this phase of the trade, and that the

[1] The figures given in the text are compiled from the invoice printed in *English Factories*, i. 61 ; here and elsewhere I have rounded the figures, which in the original are detailed to fractions of a pice. The mahmudi was at this time worth ⅖ rupee. It is advisable to treat Indian trade by seasons rather than calendar years, because it was in fact seasonal ; the whole of a year's exports from Surat might be despatched either in December or in January according to circumstances. The lists of sailings given in *English Factories* (iii. p. xxxiv and vii. p. xix), being drawn up by calendar years, suggest that trade was more irregular than it really was ; thus three ships are shown in 1639, two in 1640, and none in 1641, whereas in fact two sailed in 1638–39, two in 1639–40, and one in 1640–41.

[2] The weight of three out of four consignments of indigo is given, but the fourth is shown only in terms of packages. I have calculated the weight of these on the assumption that the price paid per maund was about the same as for the corresponding consignment where the weight is given.

Dutch merchants agreed with the English is shown by the fact that they had already begun buying largely on the East Coast, while the Surat cargo sent by them to Batavia in 1622 consisted mainly of indigo, and earned the censure of the Governor General, who was at the moment more anxious for cotton goods to support the spice trade farther east. No other English ship was despatched in the season of 1618–19, and in 1619–20 again only one ship sailed with a similar cargo valued at 560,000 ma., or say 2¼ lakhs of rupees. We may take, therefore, 2½ lakhs of rupees as indicating roughly the standard of the English trade in this phase.

The primacy of indigo did not last for long. The discovery was quickly made that calicoes could be sold in large quantities in Western Europe, and by the middle of the next decade they had taken their place alongside of indigo as one of the two main foundations of the trade. No invoices of this decade appear to have survived, but in 1625 the merchants at Surat were arranging to provide Indian goods to the value of about 1,500,000 mahmudis (6 lakhs of rupees), or double the value of the cargo of the *Royal Anne*. The most striking feature of the list is the entry of over 200,000 pieces of calico, about fifteen times the quantity provided six years before, but it is marked also by the appearance of saltpetre, and by the attempt to secure pepper, to which reference has already been made. This larger scale of trading was maintained and further extended in the season of 1627–28, when four vessels carried goods of the value of £160,000, and the quantity of calico provided was greater than in any previous year; while the cargoes of six ships despatched in 1628–29 were valued at £104,500. The figures of these two seasons include the value of silk shipped from Persia and some other re-exports, so that it would not be correct to regard them as the measure of Indian trade, but we are, I think, justified in saying that during this decade a standard of 6 lakhs of rupees was attained.

This phase of the export trade was terminated abruptly by the famine of 1630, and, during the years of disorganisation which succeeded it in Gujarat, cargo was procured only with great difficulty by the extension of buying operations to other parts of India. The normal economic life of Gujarat was restored by about 1637, and the general course of trade in the years which followed can be learned from the invoices of cargoes sent in three successive seasons, which happen to have been preserved among the records at the India Office.[1] These documents, which are very lengthy, may be summarised as follows :

VALUE IN MAHMUDIS OF CARGOES FROM SURAT TO LONDON

	1638–39. (*Royal Mary* and *Swan*.)	1639–40. (*Discovery*.)	1640–41. (*Crispian*.)
Total value of cargo	1,405,200	816,200	1,189,100
Of which Indian goods	959,500	398,300	419,000
,, re-exports	445,700	417,900	770,100
Detail of Indian goods—			
Cotton goods	412,400	198,300	205,200
Cotton yarn	53,800	20,200	2,100
Indigo	362,300	118,900	206,200
Saltpetre	17,000	5,500	...
Pepper	101,200	...	...
Sugar	8,000	46,700	...
Ginger	3,300	8,700	...
Miscellaneous	1,500	...	5,500
Detail of re-exports—			
Persian silk	409,900	417,900	728,200
Bantam sugar	3,100	...	...
,, pepper	...	...	39,900
Aloes, myrrh, etc.	2,700	...	2,000
English goods returned unsold	30,000	...	...

The *Royal Mary* and the *Swan* carried all the exports of the season of 1638–39, and the *Crispian* was the only vessel despatched in 1640–41, but in the intervening season the *London* sailed in addition to the *Discovery*. The invoice of the *London* has not survived, and the figures showing the value of her cargo are not clear, but they have been read as

[1] These invoices are appended to Nos. 1656, 1725, and 1761 in the *Original Correspondence* at the India Office: I am indebted to Miss L. M. Anstey for their transcription. The figures given in the text have been rounded.

about 368,000 ma.; the quantity of Persian silk included was disappointingly small, and we may conjecturally add 250,000 ma. to the figure for Indian goods carried on the *Discovery*, giving about 650,000 ma. for the total Indian exports of this season. In these seasons, then, the trade may be put at 3¾, 2½, and 1¾ lakhs of rupees: the details in the invoice show that the cargoes of 1638–39 were bought at unusually high figures, and we cannot put the standard of these years at more than 2½ to 3 lakhs, or say half of that which had been reached before the famine. Even this reduced volume of trade was, as we shall see in a later section, drawn from a largely extended area; the economic life of Gujarat had been restored, but with a diminished population and a lower level of technical efficiency; and, while the local weaving industry was reviving, the bulk of the calico purchased for Europe was now the produce of Sind and Northern India.

For the next sixteen years I cannot trace any marked development in the Company's exports from Surat. In the seasons 1642–43 and 1643–44, the total cargoes were valued at about 1,200,000 and 920,000 ma. respectively, while in 1647–48 the value was 1,100,000 ma., and in 1648–49 almost the same figure was reported. Less Persian silk was now being carried, so it is probable that these figures represent a larger total of Indian goods than were carried in 1638–40; but this level was not maintained, the values in the following seasons to 1652–53 being only 574,000, 530,000, 740,000, and 507,000 ma. respectively, and these did not apparently include any large proportion of re-exports. From 1653–54 to 1657–58, the value of the Company's trade was greatly reduced, and figures for private vessels are not available, but there are good reasons for thinking that the total exports may have increased, because the Indian markets were temporarily disorganised by the competition of buyers. These conditions disappeared in the year 1658, when the Company was at last provided with adequate capital and had secured a renewal of its monopoly: the goods exported by it during the last three seasons of our period were valued at about 1,150,000, 1,400,000, and 450,000 ma. respectively; and since re-exports were still comparatively unimportant, it may be said that the standard of 1638–40 was by this time substantially exceeded, though that of the years before the famine of 1630 had not been fully recovered.

In order to complete the survey of English trade on the West Coast, it is necessary to mention the exports despatched by Courteen's Association between 1635 and 1647, but no very substantial addition need be made on its account to the figures already given for these years; comparatively few of the voyages undertaken were successful, much of the produce carried to England was obtained from sources outside India, and the Indian exports consisted mainly of pepper and saltpetre, which do not add largely to values, though they would make a material difference in regard to tonnage.

English exports to Europe from the East Coast and the Bay of Bengal become important only from the year 1649; the values for 1649–50 and the three following seasons may be put at Rs. 50,000, Rs. 96,000, Rs. 85,000, and Rs. 1,30,000, or say a standard of about a lakh of rupees yearly, only a small proportion of which represents re-exports. No estimate can be given for the years from 1654 to 1657, when trade was practically open, but there is no doubt that exports increased materially, the main efforts of the individual traders being directed to this side of India. I have found no complete figures of the trade for the few remaining years of our period, but the business of the Company was largely increased. The indent for 1658 amounted to £35,000, or about 3 lakhs of rupees, and those for subsequent seasons indicate that this scale was maintained, though the totals of the investments are not stated. Bringing together, then, the various estimates which have been offered, we get the following figures for the total value of Indian goods exported to Europe in English vessels; the estimates are very far from being precise, and they are put forward only to indicate in the most general terms the extent of the trade which came into existence during our period.

[TABLE

Annual Exports in English Vessels from India to Europe (in Lakhs of Rupees)

Period.	From West Coast.	From East Coast and Bengal.	Total.
About 1620 . .	2½	..	2½
„ 1628 . .	6	..	6
„ 1640 . .	2½–3	..	2½–3
„ 1643–48 . .	3½	..	3½
„ 1649–53 . .	2	1	3
„ 1658–60 . .	5	3	8

The volume of the Dutch trade cannot be estimated on similar lines, and the most that can be said with certainty is that, at any rate from about 1625 onwards, it was larger than the English. Produce from the East Coast was going to Holland, either direct or by way of Batavia, from about 1615, or for more than thirty years before this branch of trade was actively developed by the English : in Surat the Dutch soon caught up and surpassed the English, who were first in the field; while their despatches from Vengurla at any rate exceeded the exports carried by Courteen's Association, and in Bengal their predominance is indisputable from the outset. Their commercial supremacy may come as a surprise to readers familiar only with ordinary text-books of Indian history, but it is a commonplace to those who have studied the records of the period; and while the Dutch reports and journals are marked by frequent sneers at the poverty and inefficiency of their English competitors, the English correspondence is characterised by grudging and envious admiration of the Dutch. It will suffice for the present purpose to give a few illustrations from the latter sources, which obviously carry the greater weight. As early as the year 1622, the principal English factor at Pulicat wrote that "the Dutch in their glory laugh in their sleeves at our present miseries, and much disparaged the sufficiency [efficiency] of Mr. Duke, which is table talk amongst them, and of our small means at present in Masulipatam, as also in this place; which is very true, and not in a tenth part comparable to theirs; which is much noted among these people." Ten years later, similar views were being expressed from a much wider area, and, to borrow Mr. Foster's summary of the records of 1630–33, "we find the English merchants complaining of the competition of the Dutch, whose skill and prudence, backed by immense resources, had given them an indisputable supremacy in the Eastern trade. . . . We find them competing vigorously with the English Company's servants in India and Persia, outbidding them for silk, indigo, and piece goods, and beating them too in the sale of European and other commodities." Similarly, Mr. Foster says of the years 1637–41: "we have abundant evidence of the predominant position occupied by the Dutch; and this not only in respect of naval and military power, but also in ordinary commerce. Despite the vast sums spent in waging war against the Portuguese and garrisoning their many fortresses, they could still find money enough to outdistance their English rivals, even in Persia and India." The same story is told throughout the remainder of our period. In 1644 we hear from Surat that "the Dutch in these parts only prosper and flourish: who by their industry, patience, and infatigable pains and unalterable resolutions purchase [obtain] what they please"; and in the same year Madras reported that "the Dutch are grown so potent that they have almost gotten the whole Coast trade into their own possession." Ten years later Bengal tells the same story—the English short of capital, and unable to transact "any business which may be thought in the least proportionable to the great and vast trade of the Hollanders here"; and this remark is substantially applicable to the closing years of our period alike in Gujarat, on the Coromandel coast, and in Bengal.

A full discussion of the causes of Dutch predominance would take us too far,[1] but we can safely accept the English admissions as proof that their competitors excelled in commercial efficiency as well as in material resources. Their greater command of capital is beyond question: almost throughout our period the agents of the English Company were hampered seriously by lack of funds, while the Dutch were as a rule

[1] Some further particulars on this topic are given in Appendix A.

adequately provided, and were occasionally in a position to lend their balances on interest. Further, their monopoly of the spice trade and of the markets of China and Japan enabled them, as we have already seen, to employ their capital to the best advantage: they could meet the large Indian and Persian demand for cloves, mace, or nutmegs, and they could direct a stream of gold and silver from China and Japan to any part of India which offered a remunerative trade. In doing so, they derived great benefit from a sound system of commercial administration; the Governor General in his Council at Batavia exercised very wide powers throughout the East, and constituted the heart and the brain of the whole organisation, while for the greater part of our period the various English presidencies or agencies were more or less at loggerheads, differences of opinion might have to be referred home, and the decision might arrive long after the mischief was done. No student of the contemporary records can fail to be impressed by the ruthless efficiency of the Dutch commercial machine.

Some idea of the magnitude of the total Dutch investments in India can be formed from the figures recorded occasionally in the Batavia Journals of the value of cargoes (gold, silver, and goods) despatched to the country from Batavia and Taiwan. In the years about 1635, before Gujarat had recovered from the immediate effects of the famine, the annual investment exceeded one million guilders, equivalent to about 9¼ lakhs of rupees at the conventional rate of exchange. Between 1641 and 1645 the values were about doubled, ranging round 18 lakhs of rupees, while at the close of our period they had risen to about 30 lakhs. These figures represent the values of cargoes entered in the Batavia accounts, and are not directly comparable with figures for the English investment, which are given in terms of prices on the Indian coast; but they are worth citing as showing that Dutch business was not only large but progressive. It may be added that the detailed figures bring out the growing importance of Bengal and the East Coast: in the earlier years the investment was about equally distributed between Surat and Coromandel, but at the end of our period Surat received barely a quarter of the total.

These figures represent the total investment in Asiatic and European trade taken together. The indications which are available of the extent of the Dutch export trade to Europe are too vague to justify anything like a definite estimate of the proportions in which the total should be distributed; but taking into account the facts regarding particular commodities which are examined in subsequent sections, it is safe to say that at the close of our period the Dutch handled a larger volume of European trade than the English. If, then, English purchases for Europe are correctly represented by the figure of 8 lakhs of rupees annually, including all expenditure on putting the goods on board, then the total exports of both nations to Europe were probably worth at least from 18 to 20 lakhs in the currency of the period, or from 80 to 90 lakhs in terms of modern purchasing power.[1] No material addition to this figure need be made for the exports handled by the Danes or the Portuguese; the former did not attain large dimensions during our period, while the latter had become almost negligible by its close. Nor is any large allowance required for the value of what was known as private trade—that is, of goods belonging to individuals shipped on the Companies' vessels; it bulks largely in the English records, but probably an addition of from 5 to 10 per cent to these estimates would suffice to cover all classes of trade outside the figures on which they are based.

3. Indigo

From the development of the export traffic as a whole, we now pass to examine the trade in particular commodities, and among these indigo is fairly entitled to the first place. I have

[1] Here and in other passages where the term is used, "modern purchasing power" denotes the value of the rupee disclosed by official statistics for the quinquennial period 1910–14. The latter part of this period included times of scarcity, and for prices of agricultural produce I use the years 1910 to 1912 inclusive. It is too early yet to attempt a definitive estimate of the normal value of the post-war rupee; the process of adjustment was in any case bound to be slow, and the recurrence of bad seasons has prolonged the period of obscurity. The standard I use may be stated in concrete form as 12½ ser of wheat for a rupee in the country between Agra and Lahore.

not been able to find an account of the introduction of this product into Western Europe. A blue dye was required by the woollen industry, which occupied so prominent a position in that region, and originally the need was met by the use of woad; but towards the close of the sixteenth century woad was giving place to indigo, and the struggle between the two dyes resolved itself largely into a question of the price at which the Indian product could be obtained. The Portuguese carried indigo to Lisbon in moderate quantities, and the prospects of the trade were such as to induce the king of Spain to monopolise it in the year 1587; the result of this step does not appear to be on record, but the figures already quoted show that the export was only 20 cwt. in 1602 and 940 cwt. in the following year. I have found nothing to indicate the ultimate destination of these Portuguese exports; I suspect that they were mainly used in the western Mediterranean area; but even if they were carried northward, there is no doubt that at this time the standard of price and quality in the London market was set by Aleppo rather than Lisbon. The tendency to refer to the Aleppo standard is obvious in the early English correspondence: in 1609 a factor was chosen by the Company for his expert knowledge of "indigo, silk, and other Turkey goods"; a few years later another factor reported that his purchases in India were "as good as ever I saw in Aleppo"; and when Thomas Mun set out to calculate the value of the Company's trade with India, he took the Aleppo price as the basis of his estimates. The figure of 4*s.* 4*d.* a pound used by him would represent something like 8*s.* in London, and this price was in fact ruling for the produce of Northern India in the year 1609.[1]

Whatever the original source of supply, it is clear that indigo was the commodity chiefly sought by the first European

[1] I have been unable to trace any authority for the common statement that the use of indigo was prohibited in England during the first half of the seventeenth century, and it appears to be negatived by the fact that patents for processes involving its use were being granted at this time. Mr. William Foster conjectures that the statement may have arisen out of a confusion between indigo and another dye, logwood, the use of which was in fact prohibited by Parliament. (*Journal, Royal Society of Arts,* LXVI. 362.)

buyers in India. The Dutch factors who reached Surat in 1601 wrote of it as the most important local product; their successor van Deynsen was arranging to buy indigo in the year 1607; the report sent home from Surat by William Finch in 1609 gives indigo the place of honour among possible exports; and the instructions sent out from England by successive fleets furnish ample proof that at this time the Company relied more on indigo than on anything else for the development of the Indian trade. In Sir Thomas Roe's phrase, it was the "prime commodity."

At this period the crop was widely grown in India, and we hear of production at various places in the Gangetic plain, in Sind, in Gujarat, in the Deccan, and along the East Coast; but as a rule the product was intended for local consumption, and exporters at first recognised only two commercial descriptions—Sarkhej and Lahori. The town of Sarkhej, which lies a few miles from Ahmadabad, the chief market of Gujarat, was then an important centre of production, much of its produce being exported to the Persian Gulf. Some of the indigo known as Lahori came from the Gangetic *duāb*, but most of it was the produce of a small tract of country near Biāna, or Bayāna, lying about fifty miles south-west of Agra, and now within the limits of the Bharatpur State; it had for long been exported by the overland route, and had acquired the name of Lahori in the Aleppo market from the fact that the caravans were made up in Lahore. The indigo produced in the neighbourhood of Biana was adapted to overland transit, being comparatively pure, and it is often spoken of as "round" from the fact that it was made up in balls. The Sarkhej product was prepared in the form of cakes, and is spoken of as "flat"; its distinguishing feature was an admixture of sand, so that about three pounds of Sarkhej were equivalent to two of Lahori. The Court Minutes, however, contain some indications that the use of "round" indigo in England was in some cases attended by technical difficulties, and this fact, along with the distance of Biana from the coast, sufficed to put the two kinds on a footing of substantial equality so far as sea-transport was concerned; Lahori commanded the higher price in Europe, but it cost more to put on the market, and the variation in Indian prices was the principal factor in determining the quantity of each brand to be exported in any particular year.

Foreign buyers then looked in the first instance either to Ahmadabad or to Biana. We find Finch buying in the latter market in 1610, and Withington at the former three years later, while the Dutch, who arrived in Surat in 1616, were in 1618 seeking indigo in Agra, and thenceforward the two markets were familiar to the factors of both nations. The cargo sent to London in 1619 consisted, as we have seen, chiefly of indigo, and about three-fifths of it (by weight) came from Sarkhej, against two-fifths from Biana. Exports from both places continued throughout the rest of our period, but the dye was bought also at various other centres, the Dutch being especially active in the search for possible sources of supply. The English bought some quantities in Sind after the year 1636, while in 1645 the Dutch were buying in the Deccan country above Vengurla, and they attempted without much success to procure supplies in Chittagong, but their chief enterprise was the development of export from the East Coast. As early as 1613, before the Dutch had secured access to Gujarat or Biana, stress was laid on the importance of Masulipatam as a source of supply; the cargoes from this port enumerated in Appendix B include from 650 to 1000 cwt. of indigo, and exports on about this scale were maintained for many years; but throughout our period Surat remained the principal port of despatch. English exports from the East Coast were not important in these years.

It has been said above that the consumption of indigo in Western Europe was mainly a question of price: the following figures will give an idea of the change resulting from direct importation:[1]

[1] The figures in the text are taken from Mr. William Foster's paper in *Journal, Royal Society of Arts*, LXVI. 362-3. The very low price of Coromandel indigo is noteworthy; the fact that produce of such a low grade could be handled commercially may be explained by the absence of high charges for land transport, as it was grown in villages near the seaports on the East Coast.

Price of Indigo (per Pound) in the London Market

Period.	Biana.	Sarkhej.	Sind.	Coromandel.
	s. d.	s. d.	s. d.	s. d.
c. 1609 . .	8 0	5 0	Not on the market.	
1620–30 . .	5 6 to 6 0	4 0 to 4 6	”	”
c. 1646 . .	4 0	3 4	3 4	1 3
c. 1655 . .	6 0	4 0	..	1 5½

The drop about 1646 is attributable to the disturbance of the market caused by the civil war in England; excluding this period, it will be seen that the effect of the direct trade was to reduce the price of Biana indigo by 25 per cent or more, with a somewhat smaller proportionate reduction in the case of Sarkhej, and the difference sufficed to produce a large increase in consumption. The direct imports to Lisbon in 1602 and 1603 were, as we have seen, 20 and 940 cwt. respectively. In 1619 the imports to London exceeded 4300 cwt., while over 1000 cwt. reached Amsterdam in that year from the East Coast. In the next decade the English ships carried less, the standard of the years 1625–28 being from 2000 to 3000 cwt., but by this time the Dutch were busy at Surat as well as Masulipatam, and, though figures for their trade are not available, it is probable that on the whole there was an increase rather than a reduction in the total quantity exported. Passing over the years when the trade of Gujarat was disorganised owing to the famine, we find that at the end of the next decade English exports show a further fall, the invoices already summarised showing 1480 cwt. for 1638–39, and barely 1000 cwt. for 1640–41; but here again the fall in English trade was more than counterbalanced by the expansion of the Dutch. The figures of their trade during those particular seasons are not available, but their indent for 1639 was 3400 cwt.; in the calendar year 1641 they exported to Batavia over 4200 cwt.; and in 1642 they handled the remarkable quantity of over 8000 cwt., a figure which appears to mark the culmination of the trade.

A few figures extracted from the English invoices of this period may be given to illustrate the effect of variations in prices on the sources from which indigo was obtained:[1]

Source.	Exports in cwt.			Average Price in Rupees per cwt. paid on the spot.		
	1638–9.	1639–40.	1640–41.	1638–9.	1639–40.	1640–41.
Biana	385	70	927	106·3	93·3	76·4
Sarkhej	1060	661	75	90·6	58·1	56·6

It will be noticed that in the first year the price of Sarkhej indigo was abnormally high, very little below that of the superior quality: it would have been better to buy in Biana during this season, but the high level of prices in Gujarat seems to have taken the factors by surprise when it was too late to alter their arrangements. In the next year the price of Sarkhej fell heavily, and the bulk of the consignment was bought there; while in 1640 the fall in price extended to Biana, and the factors were thus enabled to comply with the Company's wishes by despatching a largely increased supply of the superior quality.

The last decade of our period is marked by a great decline in the quantity of indigo exported. I have not found complete figures for the Dutch trade in any of these years, but individual consignments were smaller than previously, the commodity is mentioned in fewer cargo-lists, and I think there can be no doubt that their exports were substantially reduced. As regards the English trade, we find that the commodity commanded "despicable rates" about 1649; the Company was discouraging supplies in 1651, and asked for only 200 bales in

[1] The exports of 1638–39 included about 35 cwt. from the East Coast, which, added to the figures in the table, give the total, quoted above, of 1480 cwt. for this season. No indigo from the East Coast was shipped in the two following seasons by the English.

1653; under the influence of a largely expanded capital, the indent for 1658 was raised to 800 bales; but in 1660 the quantity required was small and the price strictly limited.[1] The decline was not due to reduction in the European demand, but rather to the competition of supplies from America, which was destined eventually to bring the trade from India to an end. Indigo was reaching Spain from America at least as early as the year 1587, and a large consignment is recorded in 1628. Five years later we hear that a supply had reached London from Guatemala, while in 1645 we find the English Company issuing orders for a reduction of the export from Surat on the ground that the West Indies were producing large quantities of the dye, which, it is important to note, was better made than that which came from India. These competitors had an advantage in distance as well as in manufacture; the Indian trade, after fluctuating for a time, shrank to small dimensions, and came to an end in the year 1729, to be re-established subsequently in other parts of the country.[2]

Even in its best days the trade in indigo was not carried on without difficulties and drawbacks. In Europe there was the fall in prices to which reference has already been made, while in India accidents of season, interference by the authorities, and the tendency to adulteration all required to be taken into serious account. As to the accidents of season, it is sufficient to mention that in 1631 the Gujarat supply was entirely cut off as a result of the great famine, while the Biana crop was spoilt by excessive rain in 1621 and again in 1640, was destroyed by locusts for three seasons about 1625, and

[1] The usual net weight of a bale of indigo was about 220 lb. for Biana and 150 lb. for Sarkhej, so that the indent of 1653 would represent about 400 cwt. at most. Of the indent of 1658, half was Lahori and half Sarkhej, so the total would be a little over 1300 cwt.

[2] It is perhaps worth mentioning that the Dutch had already made efforts to supply indigo from other parts of Asia, from Siam, Formosa, and Java. Various entries in the *Dagh Register* (*e.g.*, May 20, 1641; November 14, 1644; December 1, 1645) show that the two former countries proved disappointing; I have found no record of positive results in Java during our period, but the dye was already manufactured in that island at the date of the first Dutch voyage (*Houtman*, i. 122).

was much damaged by drought in 1646. Official interference was a common source of complaint. In 1618 a Dutch factor reported that the Governor of Ahmadabad had demanded a lakh of rupees from the industry before he would give permission to start the annual manufacture. In 1632 Shahjahan granted a monopoly of the trade throughout the Empire, which brought business to a standstill for the time. In 1644 oppressive government in Sind had left the people "neither will nor means" to grow the crop. In 1647 we read of a "new custom" at Ahmadabad, under which the "indigo men ... bought their liberty to sell their commodity"; and various other instances could be cited to show that the production and sale of indigo was regarded as furnishing an opportunity for administrative exploitation. Lastly, the practice of adulteration was widely prevalent, particularly in Gujarat,[1] where the amount of sand added in manufacture appears to have varied with the demand for the commodity. In 1640 the factors at Surat wrote that a consignment had been "basely sophisticated," and that it was difficult to check the practice while competition among buyers was keen; the Governor of Ahmadabad had, however, taken the matter up, and had imposed the penalty of death on any one detected in adulterating. A temporary improvement was recorded, but fresh official action was required in 1645, and led to a serious decline in production, while in 1650 extended buying by the Dutch resulted in an unusual amount of fraud. The force of the objection in European markets to this practice can be realised if we remember that expenses of transit were more than double the prime cost; but official control was spasmodic, and there seems to be little doubt that adulteration was one of the factors which contributed to the eventual loss of this valuable trade.

In order to form an idea of the benefit derived by India from the increase in the consumption of indigo in Western Europe, it is desirable to arrive at an estimate of the pro-

[1] Adulteration was by no means unknown in Biana, for *Pelsart* (*f.* 4) enters into minute details regarding the precautions to be taken by buyers, but it does not seem to have been an open scandal, as it was in Gujarat.

portion borne by exports to the total production. A rough idea of the production in the chief exporting areas can be formed from estimates given from time to time by the factors engaged in the trade. The yield of the Sarkhej product was estimated at 8000 maunds (of 33 lb.) in 1628, which seems to have been a somewhat unfavourable year, while in 1634 the quantity expected was 9000 maunds. In 1638–39 a factor speaks of a general report of 40,000 maunds, but I take this to be loose and exaggerated;[1] in 1641 the Dutch estimated the yield as 12,000 maunds (37 lb.); and in 1644 the English estimate was 6000 maunds, of which one-sixth was required for local consumption, and the Dutch and English requirements were under 3500 maunds, the supply being described on this occasion as far from plentiful, owing to a bad market in the previous year. On these figures it appears reasonable to put the standard of production at somewhere about 10,000 Gujarat maunds, or say 3000 cwt., though high prices ruling in a favourable season might be expected to secure a larger crop. In Northern India the normal yield was estimated in 1626 as about 16,000 maunds (of 55 lb.), but at the moment it was 10,000 maunds or less,[2] owing to the effect of the calamities already mentioned. In 1633, when production had recovered, the yield was barely 15,000 maunds; of this quantity one-third was true Biana, while the rest came from Hindaun and other localities, but much of it was up to the standard required for export. Ten years later, a Dutch report says that the yield, which was then poor, used to be 3000 bales (approximately 12,000 maunds, or 6000 cwt.), so the produce of this region may be put at from 6000 to 8000 cwt., and, taking Gujarat and the north together, somewhere about 10,000 cwt.

[1] This estimate was put forward by a factor on his defence (*English Factories*, vi. 91); after excusing himself for certain past transactions, he winds up his letter by holding out better hopes for the future, with the "general report" that 40,000 maunds of indigo would be available. Such an estimate should not rank with the others quoted in the text, which were recorded in the ordinary course of business.

[2] These figures are taken from *Pelsart's* full and detailed account of the indigo trade. There are some discrepancies between the Dutch MS. and the printed translation; the former gives in all 2500 bales, while the figures in the latter total 2200 bales. The bale is given as 4 maunds (of 55 lb.).

were available when the export trade was at its height. Out of this the English and Dutch requirements cannot be placed above 5000 to 6000 cwt., or say something over one-half of the commercial crop, and the margin available for other buyers was substantial, though in the exceptional year 1642 the Dutch must have bought a much greater proportion. As regards the East Coast, an English estimate of the year 1640 puts the available supply at from 400 to 500 candies, or about 2000 cwt., while the Dutch exports were usually less than 1000, and those of the English were small. The yield of the principal area in Sind was 2000 maunds (probably 66 lb.); so that the total available for export from India was of the order of from 12,000 to 14,000 cwt., in addition to a large quantity suitable for local consumption. I have found no facts to indicate the yield per acre at this period; but if we may assume that it did not differ greatly from the figures (15-20 lb.) of the present century, we arrive at an area of from 75,000 to 100,000 acres in the exporting tracts.[1]

The figures which have just been given are important as showing that there was a wide scope for competition in the trade, and that it would be a mistake to regard the Dutch and English buyers as monopolising the markets; taken together, they were the most important purchasers, but as a rule they competed keenly with each other, and also with merchants from Persia and other countries, who bought for Asiatic consumption and for export to Eastern Europe overland. This latter trade was by no means extinguished, though its volume was probably reduced. The Dutch records mention that in 1641 indigo was still going by land from Agra, while the English Court Minutes of 1643 state that the quantity coming by way of Basra was reducing prices throughout Europe, so that we are justified

[1] The standards used by the Indian Statistical Department at the present time are 18 lb. per acre for the United Provinces and 20 lb. for Bihar. No standard is fixed for Bombay, where the crop is not now grown on an appreciable scale (*Estimates of Area and Yield of Principal Crops*, Table II.). There is nothing definite on record to show the yield per acre in Gujarat during our period; I suspect it was somewhat less than in Northern India, but the indications are too slight to justify any conclusion.

in regarding the trade as competitive throughout; much of what was brought to London was re-exported to the continent of Europe; and while Aleppo might be unable to compete in London, its effect must have been felt increasingly as indigo was carried from London farther East. From the nature of the case, it is impossible to calculate the quantity bought by Asiatic merchants, but various references in the commercial correspondence show that their activities had a pronounced effect upon the market. Pelsart has left a vivid description of the Armenian buyers, "racing over the country from village to village, with greedy eyes like guests who think there is not enough food on the table to go round, reaching for every dish, and jostling the other guests"; and he complained that their eagerness to buy forced up prices out of all proportion to the extent of their individual purchases. In 1644 the Surat factors reported a fall in the demand for Persia, Mocha, and Basra, the effect of which was such a decline in prices "that the planters[1] are almost beggared thereby, and therefore do annually more or less reduce the wonted quantities made by them." Again, in 1649, the factors explained that, though it would be more advantageous for them to buy at Biana in December or January, when the indigo would be thoroughly dried, they were forced to deal earlier in the season because the Asiatic merchants would not wait. While, therefore, the producers in Gujarat and in the Biana country looked primarily to foreign markets, they were not as a rule in the hands of a single group of customers: Dutch and English, Persians, Moguls and Armenians, were all in competition; and even when the European buyers combined for a season, they could not hope to dictate prices without reference to the Asiatic demand. The benefit available for producers was thus substantial while the trade retained its importance, but any attempt to measure it is rendered difficult by the fact that some of the indigo carried by sea to London or Amsterdam passed on to markets formerly served by the Aleppo route, and consequently does

[1] It may be advisable to point out that "planters" means here either the peasants who grew indigo, or the capitalists who financed them; the European indigo-planter had not yet appeared in India.

not represent a real addition to the former demand. The total of Dutch and English exports about the year 1640 would absorb the produce of from 30,000 to 40,000 acres, and after making a conjectural deduction for the proportion which would otherwise have come by way of Aleppo we may say that perhaps somewhere about 20,000 acres were cultivated to meet the new demand of Western Europe. On the basis furnished by Akbar's assessment rates, an acre of indigo in Northern India was worth about Rs. 20 in the currency of the time (equivalent to Rs. 140 in modern purchasing power), while an acre of ordinary food-grains was worth about Rs. 5 ; the Dutch and English purchases may, therefore, have increased the income of the manufacturers by some such figure as three lakhs of rupees, a trifle when spread over the whole country, but a very substantial sum for the limited areas in which it was expended. To this has to be added the expenditure on packing, handling, and carting, which, in the case of Biana indigo at least, was relatively considerable.

4. Saltpetre

The export of saltpetre may be definitely described as a new feature of Indian commerce. I have found no suggestion that the commodity entered into Asiatic trade during the sixteenth century: its bulk rendered its transit overland impracticable ; and if Portuguese vessels carried it to Europe, the quantity handled was, as we shall see, very small. The origin of the trade must be sought in the military history of Europe. Saltpetre was an essential constituent of the gunpowder of the period, and for a time the European demand was met by local supplies. The substance is a by-product of human and animal life under conditions which are now regarded as insanitary, but which prevailed widely during the seventeenth century, and indeed to a much later date ; and the necessary supplies were obtained by methods similar to those which are still practised in India, the product being washed out of the contaminated soil. By the beginning of our period, the progress of the art of war, and the prevalence of its practice in Europe, were outrunning these local supplies, and the discovery that practically unlimited quantities of saltpetre were available in India was a very great advantage to those belligerent nations which were in a position to obtain it by the ocean route.

The first reference I have found to the export of saltpetre occurs in a letter from the king of Spain, written in the year 1605, and directing the viceroy of Goa to send home ten or twelve casks of saltpetre yearly until further orders. The letter lays stress on the scarcity of saltpetre in Portugal, and says that for some years past it had been the custom to order its supply from India, so that export may have begun at the end of the sixteenth century; but the quantity spoken of is very small, and the requisition was official rather than commercial in its nature. About this time Spain was in serious difficulties over the supply of what are now known as munitions, and space on the homeward carracks was requisitioned without reference to the business aspect of the transaction; in 1613, and again a year later, Goa was ordered to make regular despatches of timber for shipbuilding, a commodity which no merchant would have handled on this route, and the demand for saltpetre must be regarded mainly as evidence of Spanish needs.

The commercial initiative was taken by the Dutch shortly after their settlement on the Coromandel coast. I have not traced the actual beginning of their trade, but a report written in the year 1617 indicates that the factors were already interested in saltpetre, and the invoice of the *Naerden*, which is given in Appendix B, shows that a substantial quantity was exported in 1621, after which year purchases become a normal topic of the commercial records. The English Company followed the lead given by the Dutch. The scarcity of saltpetre in England is reflected in various entries in the Court Minutes. As early as 1617, the Company had great difficulty in securing a supply of gunpowder owing to this cause: in 1624 the Commissioners of the Navy urged that saltpetre should be brought from India, as was already being done by the Dutch; and, later in the same year, the

Company were told that they must make their own powder and fetch their own supplies of saltpetre. The Company apparently ordered a supply from Surat in the year 1620, for an abstract of a report sent home in 1621 states that none was to be had in that neighbourhood; but four years later Captain Weddell reported that the Dutch were shipping it as ballast, and that the English were arranging to procure supplies, which were ordered in the first instance from Ahmadabad. These supplies reached London at the end of 1626, and the English trade may be regarded as established in that year.

Saltpetre was obtained from various parts of India. The Coromandel coast was, as we have seen, the first region to be exploited; a little later Gujarat and Agra come into the list, and then some of the Konkan ports; but these sources became of less importance when at last the buyers obtained easy access to Bihar, first from the Orissa ports, and then more effectively from Hooghly. Up to about 1650 the volume of the trade was moderate, and I have not found any instance of the English exports rising to 50 tons' weight in a season; we hear of 45 tons in 1625, of about 33 tons in 1639, of 300 to 400 bales (less than 40 tons) in 1643 and 1648, and of 20 to 25 tons in 1644. The quantities carried by the Dutch were certainly much larger, but it is difficult to calculate them with precision, because some of the cargoes are given in terms of units of uncertain size; assigning probable values to these, the exports between 1630 and 1650 would appear to have ranged between 200 and 300 tons, and perhaps the latter figure may be taken as the standard of the combined trade. Up to this time, indeed, saltpetre did not rank with indigo or calico as a primary object of commerce, because, at the prices paid for it on the coast, the profit to be gained was comparatively small, and the shipping space available was devoted by preference to goods which yielded a larger return: saltpetre could be profitably exported only because it could be stowed loose among the baled goods as "kintledge," to use the expression current at the time.[1]

[1] In the same way pepper was ordinarily carried loose among the bales, and raw cotton was sometimes stowed loose. Kintledge, or kintlage, is

The establishment of Dutch and English factories at Patna was followed by a remarkable expansion of the trade, increased facilities for supply coinciding apparently with an enhanced demand in Europe. In 1653 the English Company ordered 200 tons: figures for the following years are doubtful, but the commodity was much sought after by private ships; and on the restoration of the Company's monopoly the annual quantity to be shipped from Bengal was fixed at 800 tons. I take "tons" in these two cases to indicate measurement and not weight, so the figures are not directly comparable with those given above, but the expansion of the trade is obvious;[1] and it was shared by the Dutch, who in the year 1661 shipped the very large quantity of 1480 tons' weight. Thus, at the close of our period, saltpetre ranked definitely as a primary object of commerce, while less than twenty years before it had been a makeweight; and while formerly it had been obtained in small quantities from various sources, its production for export was now localised in Bihar. The explanation of these facts is to be found in the low prices prevailing in this region. The figures on record are too scanty to furnish the basis of an exact comparison between the costs in different centres of production, but occasional quotations scattered through the English correspondence and the Batavia Journals suggest that the cost of a maund of 74 lb. at Patna was about the same as for a maund of 37 lb. at Ahmadabad, or just half the price, while the greater distance of the former place from the port of shipment was more than neutralised by the fact that continuous water-carriage was available. Taking the cost price at Patna, it appears that at the close of our period the trade

---

defined in the *Oxford English Dictionary* as material used as permanent ballast, but the factors in India employed the word commonly in the sense of anything carried loose in the hold for a single voyage.

[1] As explained in Appendix D, it is often difficult to say whether "ton" indicates weight or measure, for the use of the word to denote 20 cwt. was not yet definitely established, though it was gaining ground at this period. From various figures given in the Dutch records it is possible to calculate the number of pounds taken as equivalent to a last; the different equations agree very closely, and give something between 1800 and 1900 pounds (avoirdupois) as the weight of a tun (half a last) of saltpetre; on this basis 800 tuns' measurement would represent between 600 and 700 tons' weight.

brought roughly somewhere about a lakh of rupees yearly to Bihar, while about the same amount was spent in charges between Patna and the ships, a substantial gain to the locality, though only a trifling addition to the income of India taken as a whole.

The trade was subject to frequent interference on the part of the authorities, but no objection could fairly be taken to the ostensible ground, that the available supply was required for local military purposes, while in practice the prohibition of export could usually be evaded by not unreasonable bribes, or by false declarations to the tax-collectors. A different ground of interference came up unexpectedly in the year 1646, when Prince Aurangzeb, then Viceroy of Gujarat, forbad export on the ground that gunpowder made from Indian saltpetre might be used against some Moslem power, but the transfer of the prince to another government quickly removed this obstacle; and in any case Christians of the period could have little right to object to his action in view of the fact that not very long before the Portuguese supply of horses to Bijapur had been challenged by ecclesiastics at Rome on precisely similar grounds. Apart from official interference, the only difficulty attending the trade seems to have been the supply of suitable vessels for the refineries. The commodity was in any case bulky, and needed refining in order to remove the impurities, but the Indian methods of evaporation, in which earthen vessels were used, were found to be unsatisfactory, and appliances made of copper could not be obtained locally. In 1641 the Dutch on the Coromandel coast wrote that their cauldrons were worn out, and requested Batavia to send sheet-copper for repairs and to order a new supply of cauldrons from Holland; while eleven years later the English found that suitable copper and pans could not be got in Hooghly or Balasore, and decided to divert to this purpose appliances which had been sent out for making sugar in connection with an abortive scheme for a colony in Madagascar. The obstacle was thus easily overcome, and at the present day its interest lies in the light which it throws on the supply of copper in India.

5. Cotton Goods

The trade in cotton goods between India and Western Europe has passed through several distinct phases in the course of the last three centuries, and it is important that students of the subject should concentrate their attention on the facts of that particular period in which they are interested. The period with which we are dealing does not cover the remarkable change in European fashions which occurred in the second half of the century. Up to the year 1660 there was practically no demand for muslin or prints as apparel: such dress-goods as were carried westwards were destined almost entirely for Africa or America, where the trade had been established by the Portuguese; and we are concerned in this section mainly with the adoption of Indian calico to meet European household needs—tablecloths, bed-linen, napkins, or towels—and to a very small extent with the use of Indian coloured or fancy goods as hangings or for decorative purposes.

Before our period opened, the nature of Indian cotton goods appears to have been known in Western Europe mainly through small quantities arriving by the overland route, and the high cost of transit is a sufficient explanation of the very limited consumption. Europe produced linen for domestic use, and tapestry for decoration; calico and chintz could not compete with these goods on their merits, and could secure a market only by offering an advantage in point of price; and this offer was not possible until they were brought all the way to Europe by sea. The Portuguese did not take advantage of their opportunities in this respect, and consequently at the beginning of the seventeenth century Western Europe constituted a large but wholly undeveloped market for cotton goods. The possibilities of the situation were realised mainly through the activities of the English Company, for, as we shall see further on, the Dutch took little share in opening up the new market, though they entered it when it was an established success. The main reason for this attitude is probably to be found in the conditions ruling in the European linen-industry. England did not produce linen on a large scale, so that imports of calico would not compete seriously with home industry, while sales of calico abroad "brought money into the country," and were therefore regarded with favour by the prevailing mercantilist opinion. Holland, on the other hand, possessed an important linen industry, and it is improbable that the merchants who constituted the Dutch Company should have pressed for imports which would enter into competition with a staple product of their country, and one which some of them must have handled in the course of their ordinary business. Allowance must also be made for the fact that the monopoly of spices and the far-eastern trade kept Batavia amply furnished with remunerative cargo for Europe, while for the English merchants in India the problem of filling the homeward ships was often difficult; indigo by itself would not suffice to "drive the trade," and it was important to develop a market in Europe for the cotton goods procurable in such quantities in India. These considerations afford sufficient explanation of the fact that the story of the opening of the market must be traced mainly in the English records.

The English Company was alive to the possibility of trade in cotton goods from the time when it decided to establish mercantile relations with India. The nature of the anticipated demand can be studied in the instructions sent out by successive fleets from the year 1607 onwards, but for the present purpose it will be sufficient to refer to William Finch's commercial report sent home from Surat in 1609 as giving the views formed on the spot by a competent English buyer, who knew what he had to look for. Finch refers first to the different qualities of baftas,[1] the fine makes of Broach, and the coarser goods of other centres; then to semianoes, "broader than the calico, and as I suppose more fitter for England than the baftas," a phrase which indicates that he used calico and bafta almost as identical terms; then come dutties, and then

[1] As explained in a former chapter, *bafta* was the commercial name for ordinary Gujarat calico; *semianoes*, the calico made at Samana in Northern India; *dutties*, the loin-cloths in common wear. *Bairamis* would be of rather better quality if they resembled hollands, but would be calico rather than muslin; the name covers a wide range of texture. *Serribaff* was one of the muslins for which the Deccan was famous.

bairamis, the latter "resembling Holland cloths," these four types representing calico in the general sense of the word. Next he mentions a slighter stuff, or muslin, called serribaff, as probably suited to the North African trade, and a calico of extra width made somewhere near Cape Comorin, which would "sell well in England for sheeting"; and he adds that higher qualities than "these country linens" could be got if required. He then suggests some other goods for the African trade, and *pintados* (the Portuguese word commonly used to describe goods with patterns in colours), as being likely to sell profitably for quilts and for fine hangings; also quilts ready-made of white calico, and of calico dyed red or blue. This completes his enumeration of the cotton goods suitable for export to the West—muslins for Africa, calico of various sorts and some coloured goods for household use in England—and he passes on to the clothing trade with Java and Sumatra.

Trade sprang up very much on the lines indicated in this report, and we may take the first recorded English shipment from Surat as an example of the exports in the initial phase. The table on the following page shows the cotton goods taken by the *Royal Anne* to England in the year 1619; the prices are given in mahmudis, the current coin of Gujarat, which was taken at $\frac{2}{5}$ of a rupee, and they include cost of transit to the ship's side.

It will be observed at once that several of the items in this list are sample consignments, and that the main export was of calico of the ordinary type, baftas broad and narrow, dutties, and semianoes, or three out of the four descriptions recommended by Finch ten years previously. It will also be noticed that there might be substantial variations in the average prices of different consignments bearing the same description, and this point is of real importance to an understanding of the trade. There was, as yet, nothing like a fixed standard of quality: individual artisans wove very much as they chose, and buyers had to pick single pieces to suit their needs. Speaking generally, the best pieces were chosen for England, and the inferior goods sent to Java for the Eastern markets; and I take it that this is what is meant by contemporary

Description.	No. of Pieces.	Value.	Average Price per Piece.
CALICOES—			
(*a*) *Baftas*—		Ma.	Ma.
1. "Gingames"	40	276	6·9
2. Broad	8	120	15·0
,, ...	5302	33,195	6·3
,, ...	1000	6,777	6·8
Extra-broad (?) . . .	1	24	24·0
3. Narrow	980	3,680	3·8
,, ...	20	55	2·7
,, ...	1997	9,950	5·0
4. For table napkins . .	80	218	2·7
5. "Watchetts" (*i.e.* blue) .	20	160	8·0
Coloured	?	3,584	?
"Watchetts"	200	635	3·3
(*b*) *Dutties*—			
1. Not described	290	1,066	3·7
,, ...	480	2,190	4·6
2. Dholka	400	1,291	3·2
(*c*) *Semianoes*—	2330	14,075	6·0
FANCY GOODS AND DOUBTFUL DESCRIPTIONS *			
Sundry stuffs	200	(?) 187	(?) 0·9
"Reeses"	275	1,150	4·2
"Sahum"	50	431	8·6
"Necanies"	420	1,320	3·1
"Eramies"	?	177	?

* Some *reeses* had a pattern of the type known in England as dimity. *Necanies* were striped calico. *Eramies* may have been cloth of the type worn by pilgrims to Mecca (*Ihram*). I have found no description of *sahum*.

writers when they speak of buying "fine" goods for England. They do not mean the finer qualities of Indian cloth, the muslins and other thin goods suited for tropical wear, but worthless as household linen; they mean merely the best pieces of calico suited for the purposes for which they were buying.

The demand for calico increased with remarkable rapidity. The shipment of 1619 totalled about 14,000 pieces (each ordinary piece being from 12 to 15 yards in length): the goods ordered in 1625 exceeded 200,000 pieces; in 1628 the actual consignment consisted of nearly 1000 bales, which would represent 150,000 pieces or more; while in 1630, when the

Gujarat famine was about to bring this phase of the trade to an abrupt conclusion, the Company ordered 100,000 to 120,000 pieces of calicoes, together with small quantities of fancy goods. The large imports attracted the attention of King James I., who in 1623 asked the Deputy Governor of the Company how they were disposed of, and was informed that "much of it is very useful and vends in England, whereby the prices of lawns, cambrics, and other linen cloth are brought down; for the rest, England is now made the staple for that commodity, which having first served His Majesty's dominions, the overplus is transported into foreign parts in the nature of a home-bred commodity. The king approved exceedingly thereof, and said that this was the ready way to bring treasure into the kingdom." Less than two years later, the Governor informed the Company that the sale of Surat goods had much improved, and that the foreign demand for calicoes was so great that from 100,000 to 200,000 pieces could be disposed of in a short time if they were available. The sudden large demand could not be met immediately by Gujarat alone, and buyers were sent to those places in Northern India where the staple goods appeared to be fitted for the London market. The places where we hear of factors being specially sent are Patna and Samana, but purchases were also made in Agra of calico woven in other localities, chiefly in Oudh. Patna was soon abandoned, while we hear of buyers at Samana on various occasions up to the year 1627, but the Company's final verdict on its products was unfavourable, and the indent sent out early in 1630, which has already been quoted, specified only Gujarat calico, and explicitly forbad "Agra goods," including semianoes.

The famine, however, made it impossible to comply with these orders, and it became necessary to extend the sources of supply. In 1635 instructions were sent to Agra to buy "derriabauds, kerriabauds, and echbaryes,"[1] and the two

[1] Dariyabad lies midway between Lucknow and Fyzabad; Khairabad is a short distance north of Lucknow. I have found no description of "Echbaryes," but it has been conjectured that the word denotes some cloth favoured by, or named after, the Emperor Akbar; it was made chiefly in Oudh, sometimes at least in the neighbourhood of Jalalpur, near Fyzabad.

former, the produce of the Oudh towns of Dariyabad and Khairabad, quickly came into prominence, along with a cloth known as mercooli, which was manufactured largely in western Oudh. In the year 1640 a factory was opened in Lucknow, primarily for the supply of Dariyabad goods, those of Khairabad having been condemned, but this prohibition was not continued, and we find both makes on sale in London during the 'fifties. In 1641 the Company expressed a preference for these northern goods; mercoolis were preferred to the broad baftas of Baroda or Broach, Dariyabads were "well accepted of," and Gujarat baftas were to be sent only if the northern supply fell short. The London market was thus definitely opened to the weavers of Northern India.

The entrance of the English Company into the trade of Sind has been described in a previous chapter. The first buyers sent there in 1635 were instructed to inquire chiefly for calico suitable for England, though chequered stuffs for Guinea and cloth for the Java markets were also to be sought; the local calicoes were well reported on by the buyers, and were found acceptable in England, where their sale continued at intervals up to the close of our period, but the quantity available was limited by the conditions prevailing in the locality.

The first attempt to supply London with calico from the East Coast appears to have been made in the year 1621, but sales were unsatisfactory, and the effort was not continued. The subject was revived by the Surat factors in 1630, and the idea was taken up by the Company when the failure of the Gujarat supply became known in England. There was, however, great delay in complying with the indents sent out from London, and in 1636 the factors were severely reprimanded for having provided only £1269 worth of calico against orders for £32,500 given in the previous five years. The result of this reproof is seen in a large consignment sent home by way of Surat in January 1639; nothing seems to have been sent in the following winter, but in 1640 a substantial supply reached Surat, too late for room to be found for it in the ships, and the invoice of that year's cargo shows only a single bale of longcloth sent as a sample, "because it is the first fruits of your new fort at Madraspatam."

The result of these extensions to new areas of supply can be seen in the invoices of the English cargoes despatched from Surat in 1639 and 1640, when the immediate effects of the famine had passed away. The number of pieces of cotton cloth exported stands as follows :—

NUMBER OF PIECES OF COTTON CLOTH SHIPPED FROM SURAT TO LONDON

Source.	Season 1638–39.	Season 1639–40.[1]	Season 1640–41.
East Coast	18,225	...	25
Bengal	6,700	...	...
Gujarat	38,883	13,660	18,918
Agra	2,823	12,122	23,550
Sind	...	28,507	11,360
	66,641	54,289	53,853

All the Agra and Sind goods shown in these figures were calico, as were most of the Gujarat pieces, but these latter included also consignments of "Guinea stuffs," that is to say, fancy goods in stripes or checks suitable for sale in West Africa. The supplies from the East Coast and Bengal forwarded in January 1639 were more diversified, though calico predominated, and a scrutiny of the detailed invoice suggests that the buyers in these regions were still uncertain what to offer the London market, so that this may be regarded as a trial consignment. Nothing further need be said regarding the goods from Bengal, which did not become really important as a source of supply for European markets during our period, but a brief description is required of the principal Coast calicoes, which came rapidly into favour. The names of these take varying forms, but they may be written as percalles, moorees, salempores, and longcloth. Percalles (8 yards by 1) were on the whole the highest grade, though the best moorees

[1] One invoice for this year is missing, and the total export was probably larger than the figures here given.

(9 by $1\frac{1}{4}$) were of about equal value. In the same way, fine salempores (16 by 1) ranked with ordinary moorees, but ordinary salempores were of the same quality as longcloth (30-40 yards long, and a yard or slightly more in width), stout calico well suited for household use. Longcloth was the chief calico made on the Coast. It is apparently identical with what was called Guinea cloth by the Portuguese and the Dutch, but it was sold in the East as well as in the West, either plain, dyed, or figured (*pintado*). By the close of our period it had become the most important calico in the London market.[1]

The figures given for 1638–39 and 1640–41 represent the whole English trade of those seasons, and there is an obvious decline from the standard of over 100,000 pieces yearly attained ten years earlier. The setback was due to the famine in Gujarat. Some time was taken in opening up the alternative sources of supply, and while Gujarat alone could not meet the demand in point of quantity, the quality of its produce showed a marked deterioration, which threatened to ruin the European market. Thus in 1638 the Company wrote that since Indian calicoes had so declined in quality and increased in price, demand for them was at a standstill, and they were being superseded by cloth made in other countries; while three years later it was stated that the loss of reputation caused by the inferior quality of previous consignments was not yet recovered, "for calico here stands upon these terms, that if it may not be afforded to undersell the Germany, Scotch, and French linens, then they will not sell to any considerable quantity; and then one of the main pillars of the Surat trade is overthrown." Calico in fact came into direct competition with goods manufactured in Western Europe, and the market

[1] The descriptions in the text are based on contemporary commercial documents, which must be accepted for our period in preference to the later authorities and conjectures given in *Hobson-Jobson*. Moorees, described there (p. 707) as blue, were occasionally dyed, but were usually shipped brown or bleached. Percalles were not spangled robes (p. 708) but pieces of plain calico. Salempores were not usually chintz (p. 784), though, like all calico, they might be printed. The derivation of such names offers a wide field for conjecture, but indents and invoices are safer guides to the nature of the commodities.

consequently depended entirely on considerations of price and quality.

The next phase of the trade is marked by the growing importance of the East Coast, which was soon to supersede Gujarat as the principal source of supply for Western Europe. After the consignment of 1638–39, which has been mentioned above, there appears to have been an interruption in the exports from this region, for in 1644 the Company wrote that they had received nothing but one bale of longcloth in five years. In 1646, however, goods from Madras had reached England, and sold to advantage; while in 1650, at a time when European markets were depressed, it was recorded that sales consisted chiefly of goods from Coromandel, which "are now preferred before any of the Surat clothing, because they are best fit for French and other foreign sales." It may be said, then, that the trade entered on the new phase about the year 1646, when the supplies from Gujarat, Agra, and Sind began to be supplemented regularly from the East Coast.

I have not succeeded in finding figures to show the volume of exports during the next ten years, but the instructions for purchases at various centres suggest that trade was not expanding beyond the standard of 1640. It is clear, however, that exports rose largely during the years when trade was practically open, for when the Company's monopoly was restored the English market was found to be greatly overstocked. The quantities ordered for supply during the year 1658 were as follows:

From Surat—		
Mercoolis	10,000	pieces.
Narrow baftas	10,000	"
Broad baftas	5,000	"
Sind calico	10,000	"
Dariyabads	10,000	"
Dungaree [1]	10,000	"
Other calico	8,500	"
	63,500	"

also 1000 pieces of chintz, and 300 chintz quilts.

[1] Dungaree was cloth of a very low grade (*Hobson-Jobson*, *s.v.*). It appears in the Dutch invoices as used for packing the bales of other goods.

From Madras—

Longcloth, 20,000 pieces, equal to	50,000	standard pieces.
Salempores	20,000	,,
Others (including some muslin)	14,000	,,
	84,000	,,

Allowing for the extra size of the longcloth, it will be seen that the total demand was for about 150,000 standard pieces, but that considerably more than half was to be provided on the East Coast. The needs of the market proved to have been overestimated, and a year later the indent on Surat was reduced to one-fourth of the quantity previously ordered, or say 16,000 pieces, and this reduction was repeated for the year 1660, on the ground that the market was glutted, and calicoes would scarcely fetch their prime cost. Our period therefore closes with a demand for calico on this side of India only about one-tenth of that which had been reached thirty years previously. The business of the East Coast, however, was satisfactorily maintained, for the indent for 1659 specified over 90,000 standard pieces, viz. longcloth equivalent to 50,000, together with 30,000 salempores and 11,000 of other descriptions; and at the same time a standing order was given to provide roughly 100,000 standard pieces of the same descriptions for future years. Madras had thus definitely replaced Surat as the chief source for supplying the London market.

The story of the Dutch exports to Europe can be told more shortly. Before the year 1620 they were already carrying cotton goods round the Cape, but the exports were almost wholly of the type required for Brazil and West Africa. The Portuguese monopoly of trade in these regions had passed away; the Dutch were rapidly acquiring a predominant position in them; and their exports at this time represent a continuation of the business established by the Portuguese in the course of the previous century. In the next decade this trade began to be supplemented by small consignments of goods suitable to the European market, and the first large order I have noticed was one for 16,000 pieces of calico, which was placed in the year 1634. The European trade increased in the next few years, and its extent can be seen in the indent despatched from Holland in 1639, which may be summarised as follows:[1]

1. *Guinea cloth*	500	bales.
2. *Other calico*—		
Semianoes (Punjab)	1,000	pieces.
Ambertees (Bihar)	1,000	,,
Broad baftas (Gujarat)	5,000	,,
Narrow baftas (Gujarat)	4,000–5,000	,,
Dariyabads (Oudh)	2,000	,,
Salempores (East Coast)	3,000–4,000	,,
Moorees and Percalles (East Coast)	9,000–11,000	,,
	25,000–29,000	,,
3. *Various muslin and fancy goods*— (East Coast and Bengal)	8,000–11,000	,,

As I have said above, Guinea cloth appears to be identical with longcloth, and 500 bales of it would represent the equivalent of nearly 20,000 pieces of calico of the standard length. The total demand was thus for about 60,000 pieces, a small proportion of which consisted of muslins and fancy goods. I have found no later details of the Dutch trade up to the close of our period, but there is nothing to suggest a large extension before 1670; after that year the development was rapid.

The value to Indian weavers of the new export trade can be measured by the prices paid for calico on the spot, excluding the relatively high charges for preparing, packing, and transit to the ship. I have not found any evidence to show that the prices paid changed permanently during our period, though they fluctuated from time to time. Calico bought in Agra and Sind cost from one to two rupees per piece of the ordinary length, while the price in Gujarat was about half a rupee more. The invoice rates for longcloth work out to somewhere about two rupees for the standard length; salempores had a wider range of value, but the qualities most largely bought cost approximately two rupees for the piece; so that the

[1] This indent is in *Hague Transcripts*, II. 114*a*. Ambertees were calico produced near Patna; they are described in *English Factories*, i. 162. The other descriptions have already been explained.

English annual demand of something over 100,000 pieces represents payments to weavers of somewhere about two lakhs of rupees. To this must be added the value of the Dutch exports, and the total value of the trade may perhaps be taken roughly at three lakhs or somewhat more, apart from the disbursements for bleaching and dyeing when required, and also for packing and carriage to the seaboard. As in the case of other exports, the price paid was distributed among a particular class of artisans in a few localities, and the benefit derived by them from the new trade must have been substantial.

Various obstacles were encountered from time to time in the establishment of the export of calico to Europe, some of them due directly to the administration, and others arising out of the conditions prevailing in the industry. Official interference was a frequent cause of complaint: sometimes new taxes, or new extortions, might disorganise operations for the time, and sometimes the looms might be monopolised to provide cargo for an official speculation; but such incidents are illustrative of the general working of the administration rather than of interference with a particular branch of trade. Of greater significance for our present purpose are the difficulties of the second class. The weaving industry within reach of the seaboard was organised, or it may be more correct to say had developed, to serve the specific purpose of providing cloth for particular Asiatic markets, and buyers for Europe had to adapt themselves to the arrangements which they found at work. Thus they had to follow the existing practice of giving advances against future delivery, but they had not the same facilities as Indian merchants for gauging the credit of individual debtors, and the question of security was attended by various difficulties. One remarkable expedient is disclosed in the grant of terms for the settlement at Madras, in which the nayak undertook that "if the English first acquaint us before they deliver out any money to the merchants, painters,[1] weavers, etc., . . .

[1] Painters were the artisans who made *pintados*, or "painted" cotton cloth.

and take our word for their sufficiency and honest dealing, then do we promise, in case those people fail in their performances, to make good to the English all such sums of money as shall remain upon their accounts, or else deliver them their persons, if they shall be found in any part of my [*sic*] territories." Such a State guarantee of credit was, however, an exceptional arrangement, while its practical value might be open to question; and three years after this grant the factors at Madras admitted that the Company had suffered grievous losses by trusting "poor painters and weavers." "But experience," they added, "tells us it cannot be altogether avoided, unless we had one prime merchant (as have the Dutch) who secures all. Such a one we had some time with us," but they explain that he found the business unprofitable and gave it up. Shortly after this, we have a complaint that the English were unable to get weavers to work, because the Dutch, who had ample resources, had bound all the artisans by advances, and thus obtained temporary control of production. It must not, however, be supposed that the distribution of advances enabled buyers to get precisely the quality of cloth they wanted. European consumers were not entirely satisfied with goods manufactured to meet Asiatic tastes, and throughout most of our period we read of efforts to secure some alteration in length, or breadth, or number of threads, but these efforts frequently met with little success. Where purchasers were not competing, weavers might be willing to carry out instructions, as at Nasarpur in Sind, where no difficulty was experienced in increasing the number of threads in the warp, there "being no buyers but us"; but so long as the weavers had a choice of possible customers, they preferred to make the familiar goods in the familiar way. Similarly there were great difficulties in securing the degree of uniformity which was demanded by distributors in Europe. Not only individual pieces, but entire consignments, might be found to fall short of expectations in regard to length, or breadth, or number of threads: in 1638 the Company complained that a consignment was "like a pedlar's pack, not fit for a merchant's foreign export, but for a town retail trade"; and five years later they commented on deficiencies in length, urging the need for so much uniformity that "we may know what we sell, and the buyer what he is to receive." The conditions of production were, however, obviously incompatible with any real standardisation, and so long as India retained a practical monopoly of the industry the defect had to be borne, but there can be little doubt that it became a serious handicap as soon as competition had to be faced.

6. Other Commodities, and General Remarks

The commodities which have now been discussed—indigo, saltpetre, and calico—formed the basis of the new commercial relations between India and Western Europe in the sense that a remunerative trade could not have been maintained without them; but when ships were once placed on the route, an opportunity was afforded of exporting other goods, and the European factors made an exhaustive study of India's possibilities, as the result of which various secondary commodities were brought to the distributing markets of London and Amsterdam. Some of them were quickly discarded, others came gradually into favour, and a few words may be said regarding four items, raw cotton, yarn, sugar, and silk.

The early history of the cotton industry in Western Europe is somewhat obscure, but it is clear that at the opening of the seventeenth century raw cotton was in some demand in England and neighbouring countries, partly for use in preparing candlewicks and other articles in ordinary consumption, partly for the manufacture of the cloths known as fustians, which usually consisted of flaxen warps with cotton wefts. Supplies of raw cotton came regularly from the Levant, where mechanical appliances existed for pressing the fibre into compact bales suitable for sea transport. The factors at Surat were anxious to take a share in this trade, and on more than one occasion asked that presses of the kind used in Turkey should be supplied, but their requests were not complied with, and the bulk of unpressed bales was obviously too great in proportion to value for them to occupy space which could be filled with goods like indigo or calico. Accordingly no regular trade developed during our period, but cotton was occasionally shot loose into the hold to fill the spaces between the bales, while small quantities were sold regularly in London after having served to pack more valuable goods.

Yarn was a commodity much better suited for sea transport, and a regular trade in it developed. The earliest consignments were not indeed welcomed in England, but in 1622 factors were buying yarn suitable for wefts for fustian; in 1628 the English consignment from Gujarat amounted to 525 bales, and two years later the Company wrote that 600 or 700 bales might be sent annually, provided that more valuable goods were not available. Meanwhile the Dutch had established a small but regular export from the Coromandel coast, as can be seen from the invoices summarised in Appendix B, while they were also buying in Surat, though not at first on the same scale as the English, their annual requirements about 1630 amounting to 150 bales. Their demand rose during the next decade to about 400 bales, while the English shipment in 1638–39 amounted to about 300 bales. For the remainder of our period the Dutch trade was maintained at somewhere about 500 bales yearly, taking both coasts together, but the English trade declined. In 1641 the Company reduced their demand to 100 bales; they disliked the commodity, but authorised the purchase of this amount in order not to disappoint English workmen, who, they wrote, had of late found many uses for Indian yarn.[1] Ten years later, only 75 bales were shipped, while in 1653 the indent was for 150 bales, but the general expansion of trade in 1658 extended to yarn, and the demand rose again to about 500 bales. The quality shipped varied within very wide limits,

[1] I have not been able to ascertain what developments in the English industry occurred about this time, but it was certainly progressive, and it is possible that Indian yarn was being found suitable for warps, so that the manufacture of pure cotton goods may date from this period, though evidence of the fact has not yet been discovered. Professor Daniels has shown the untenability of the old view that pure cotton goods were not made in England till late in the eighteenth century, but the date when their manufacture began is still uncertain. (*Daniels*, 21 ff.).

and I have not found definite information as to the grades chiefly handled by the Dutch, but 50 rupees is perhaps a fair average price for a bale (of about 160 lb.), and on this basis the total export may be valued at a maximum of half a lakh.

The trade in yarn was marked by a curious incident in the year 1630, when the English purchases in Gujarat were at their maximum: the weavers feared that their industry would suffer through the export of their raw material, and a regular boycott was organised in Broach, the English being called upon to choose between buying cloth and yarn. There is no sign of similar opposition in subsequent years, and I take the incident to indicate merely that the English buyers had gone ahead too rapidly for the stocks available at the moment; India could produce all the yarn that was wanted, but a sudden large increase in demand might involve hardship to local consumers until production could be extended to meet it.

Conditions in the world's sugar trade have changed greatly since the seventeenth century. The commodity was not, as it now is, an article of general consumption in Western Europe, but must rather be classed as a somewhat expensive luxury. The European beet-sugar industry had not come into existence, and the principal sources of the supply of cane-sugar were China and India in the East, and Brazil and the Antilles in the West. During our period the Dutch controlled the great bulk of the trade from China and America, besides handling most of the exports from India; and since much of the Indian product was inferior in quality and relatively costly to export, it did not at first secure any large share of the European market. Indian sugar was of three main types: the coarse product known as jaggery,[1] which was not handled by exporters, a white sugar of fine grain known as "powder sugar," and large crystals, more thoroughly refined and much more costly, which the merchants knew as "candy." An irregular trade with England in the two latter classes was

[1] *Jaggery*, or *gur*, still the commonest form of sugar in India, is a compost of crystals and molasses produced by the indigenous processes of manufacture. The white sugars were extracted from this compost by elaborate and tedious processes of refining.

maintained by the factors at Surat : sometimes the Company asked for a supply, at other times they prohibited it, and on at least one occasion it was loaded merely to fill the ship ; the quantity sent varied greatly, but it was rarely important, and the factors more than once advised that indents should be made on Bengal, where the commodity was both better and cheaper. The Dutch do not appear to have taken an active part in the Surat trade, but when circumstances became favourable, they developed a substantial business on the other side of India. By the year 1636 they were exporting Bengal sugar from Masulipatam, and in the 'forties their business showed a great expansion, the quantity to be sent annually to Batavia at this period being somewhere about 500,000 lb. Later records are imperfect, but I judge that this export was not fully maintained, either because it was too much for the market, or because the European demand was being met from other sources. The English Company was slow to develop a trade in sugar from Bengal. It was talked about for years, and an investment was ordered in 1651–52, but the first sign of extensive business is an order sent out in 1659 to buy 700 tons, a large amount whether the ton be taken as a weight or a measure. This order was reduced a year later, but the history of the English trade lies outside our period, during which the volume of the total exports was too irregular to justify any estimate of its value to producers.

The trade in silk from Bengal to Europe also lies outside our period. Western needs were met first from China, and afterwards from Persia ; when the Dutch at last secured a regular footing in Bengal, their exports were, as we have seen, directed mainly to Japan ; and I have not found records to show if any progress had been made in developing the European market before 1660. The story of the English trade begins in 1657, when the Company was at last adequately provided with capital, and a sum of £3000 was ordered to be invested in Bengal raw silk, while in the following year authority was given for regular purchases of 100 bales, worth about 20,000 rupees in all.

It will be apparent from the facts which have been brought together in this chapter that in regard to the export trade to Western Europe the first half of the seventeenth century was a period of prolonged experiment. Late in its first decade, we have the Dutch on the East Coast and the English on the West, just beginning to learn by experience what goods could be bought and sold. Ten years later the Dutch had discovered indigo and saltpetre, but the indigo they were buying was nearly the worst, and the saltpetre nearly the dearest, which India could supply. The English, on the other hand, had established the trade in good indigo, and were laying the foundations of the still more important export of the calicoes of Gujarat. By the middle of the half century, Surat appeared to be firmly established as the principal port for Europe; the East Coast was contributing little, and Bengal was still unknown ground to European buyers. The famine of 1630 brought about a startling change, and large parts of India were prospected afresh in order to supplement the inadequate supplies from Gujarat. The superior efficiency of the Dutch merchants gave them a long lead in Bengal, but it was utilised in the first instance mainly for Asiatic developments, and it was only after 1650 that the eastern side of India took a prominent place in European trade. That place was earned partly by the suitability of the Madras calicoes, partly by the cheapness of Bihar saltpetre, partly by the supplies of silk and sugar in Bengal. Gujarat retained its former eminence only in regard to indigo, but this trade was already declining under the stress of American competition, and the political conditions resulting from the rise of the Maratha power were about to prove an additional handicap to the port of Surat, which had at first outdistanced all competitors.

As has already been pointed out, the direct benefit accruing to India from the new export trade was confined to relatively small areas, but in them it was substantial, in that it increased the demand for goods which producers were ready to supply. Indirectly the position of the whole country was changed by the opening up of new commercial relations with the progressive markets of the West. In the previous century the Portuguese had made a poor use of their opportunities for commercial development; but the Dutch and English companies approached India from a different standpoint, employed very different methods, and secured much greater results. Through their agency, Indian goods became familiar in Amsterdam, London, Paris, and other markets; the tastes of consumers were made known in the areas of production; and the East was searched systematically for commodities which might command a profit in the West. A new business organisation was thus brought into existence, and while its initial achievements were by no means negligible, its possibilities in the future were almost unlimited.

One feature of this organisation calls for a word of comment, because it could not easily be paralleled among civilised countries at the present day. In modern business it is the seller who does most of the work. When a country sets out to secure a new market, the enterprise is shared by manufacturers, financiers, and official agents; the market is invaded, often at heavy initial expense; and goods are brought to the doors of those who are expected to buy. India made no such efforts to secure the markets of Western Europe. Indian producers and merchants were eager to sell, and welcomed the foreign buyers who came among them, but their part in the development was passive. We hear nothing at this period of Indians going to Europe to push their goods, or pressing sample consignments on the foreign buyers; in this case the buyers did the work, and it followed necessarily that the large profits accruing from transportation were not shared by India. Had only one European company been engaged in the business, it would thus have been in a position to operate on strictly monopolistic lines, and I think it may fairly be said that in this respect India was fortunate. During our period some of the countries farther to the East learned by experience what a monopoly meant to the merchants of Holland; but in India the competition of the weaker English company usually sufficed to secure to Indians a fair price for what they sold.

AUTHORITIES FOR CHAPTER IV

SECTION 1.—The general position of European markets at this period can be studied in *Cunningham*, vol. II. Reference to the lists of Portuguese cargoes is given in the footnotes; for the secrecy on the subject of their trade, see (*e.g.*) *Renneville*, i. 25; for the inferiority of Indian ginger, *Linschoten*, c. 64. The annals of the Malabar pepper trade must be traced in *English Factories* and the *Dagh Register*; the facts stated in the text are taken from *English Factories*, iii. 62, 90, 92, 157, 327; iv. 9; v. 148, 314; vi. 24; vii. 138; and x. 220. The Dutch attempt to export pepper from the East Coast is mentioned in *idem*, i. 303: some details of it will be found in Appendix B.

SECTION 2.—The Dutch cargo taken as an example is given in *Dagh Register* (Coromandel), November 3, 1642. For Dutch sailings to Europe direct, see Appendix B, *Hague Transcripts*, II. 50, 72, 95; III. F5; and numerous entries in *Dagh Register*. The early Dutch interest in indigo is mentioned in *Terpstra's Surat*, 84, 85. The English exports up to 1630 are taken from *English Factories*, i. 206; iii. 90, 92, 208, 217, 295, 333. The cargo of the *London* (1639–40) is referred to in *idem*, vi. 232, 233 *n.*; exports from 1642 onwards in *idem*, vii. p. xix; viii. 197 *n.*, 256, 295; ix. pp. ix, 41, 149; x. 158, 215, 335. For the period of open trade, see *idem*, x. 44, 57, and *passim*; the activities of Courteen's Association are described in the introductions to successive volumes from v. onwards; for exports from the East Coast, see *idem*, viii. 271; ix. 20, 102, 154; x. 141, 255, 275; and *Letter Books*, ii. 13-17, 196. The admissions of Dutch superiority are quoted from *English Factories*, ii. 121; iv. p. xxxvii; vi. p. xlv; vii. 191, 217; viii. 304; and x. 56, 258, 409. The figures quoted for the Dutch investment in India have been abstracted from the entries in the *Dagh Register* for the years named.

SECTION 3.—The English trade in indigo during our period is summarised by Mr. Foster in *Journal Royal Society of Arts*, LXVI. 362. For the Portuguese monopoly, see *Couto*, X. ii. 572. The references to the Aleppo indigo market are taken from *First Letter Book*, 285; *Letters Received*, ii. 214; and *Purchas*, I. v. 734. A remark in *Hague Transcripts*, II. 52, shows that indigo was still reaching England and Holland from the Levant in 1621. The prices quoted are taken from Mr. Foster's paper, *supra*. For the primary importance of indigo, see *Terpstra's Surat*, 18; *de Jonge*, II. 495; *Letters Received*, i. 28; *First Letter Book*, 285, 308, 328; *Roe*, 447. The production and manufacture of indigo in the north is described at great length by *Pelsart*, but the French translation is inadequate, and the original should be referred to. The best account of the Sarkhej industry is in the *Gujarat Report*. For the export qualities, see (*e.g.*) *English Factories*, iii. 63; vi. 58; *Pelsart*, 4, 5; for their use in England, Mr. Foster's paper, *supra*, and *Court Minutes*, July 2, 1634; and for earliest purchases in India, *Purchas*, I. iv. 429, 483, and *Terpstra's Surat*, 75. Sind purchases are mentioned in (*e.g.*) *English Factories*, vii. 202 and viii. 29; Vengurla, in *Dagh Register*, September 17, 1645, and *passim*; Chittagong, in *idem*, February 13, 1637. For indigo on the East Coast, see the invoices in Appendix B; also *Hague Transcripts*, I. 69, and *Dagh Register*, October 8, 1626, and frequently after that date.

The quantity of indigo exported to England in 1619 is taken from

English Factories, i. 61; for the standard of the next decade, see *idem*, iii. 92, 208. The Dutch exports are compiled from entries in the *Dagh Register*; their indent for 1639 is in *Hague Transcripts*, II. 114*a*. For the effect of price-changes on purchases, see *English Factories*, vi. 111, 273; and for the decline after 1650, *idem*, viii. 253; ix. 29, 82, 196; and x. 322; also *Letter Books*, ii. 1-3.

The first reference I have seen to American exports of indigo is *Purchas*, III. v. 958; see also *Cambridge Modern History*, iv. 706. Later references are *Court Minutes*, January 18, 1633, October 24, 1645; and *English Factories*, x. 322. As regards interference with trade owing to accidents of season, see (*e.g.*) *English Factories*, vi. 278; viii. 62; and *Pelsart*, 5; and for official action, *Terpstra's Surat*, Appendix VII.; *English Factories*, iv. 324 and *passim* (the monopoly); vii. 203 (Sind); and viii. 143 (Ahmadabad). For adulteration, see *idem*, vi. 273; vii. 5; and viii. 12, 31, 33, 303.

The estimates of production in Gujarat are taken from *English Factories*, iii. 232; v. 73; vii. 136; and *Dagh Register*, May 20, 1641; in Agra, *Pelsart*, 5; *English Factories*, iv. 325; and *Dagh Register* (Surat), June 13, 1644; on the East Coast, *English Factories*, vi. 262; and in Sind, *idem*, v. 129. The persistence of the overland trade is referred to in *Dagh Register*, May 20, 1641; *Court Minutes*, December 29, 1643; and *English Factories*, vii. 136, and viii. 253. Purchases by Asiatic merchants are referred to in *idem*, vii. 136, and viii. 243; the quotation from *Pelsart* is taken from f. 6 of the Dutch MS. The assessments made by Akbar on the crop are in *Ain* (translation), ii. 99 ff.

SECTION 4.—Portuguese exports of saltpetre are referred to in *Lisbon Transcripts*, I. 10, 15, and IV. 931; the instances of other non-commercial exports are taken from *idem*, II. 371, and III. 465. The earliest mention I have found of the Dutch trade on the East Coast is in *Hague Transcripts*, II. 30; see also *idem*, I. 162, and the *Dagh Register* from November 20, 1624, onwards. For the saltpetre supply in England, see *Court Minutes*, October 31, 1617; February 20 and December 29, 1624; May 20, 1625, and *passim*; for the beginnings of the English trade, see *idem*, January 5, 1627, and *English Factories*, i. 251; iii. 83, 90. The quantities exported are taken from *idem*, vii. 94, 175, and viii. 203; the figures for 1639 are in *Original Correspondence*, 1656 (enclosure). The use of saltpetre as ballast is mentioned in *English Factories*, iii. 208; vi. 94; and vii. 94, 175. For the English trade in Bengal, see *idem*, ix. 196, and x. 7, 276: the figures for the Dutch trade have been compiled from the *Dagh Register*.

The instances of interference with the trade are taken from *English Factories*, iii. 270; iv. 143; and viii. 34, 53, 79, 108, 203. The parallel of the horse trade is recounted in *Couto*, VIII. 235. The supply of refining plant is referred to in *Dagh Register*, February 19, 1641, and November 29, 1645 (Coromandel); also *English Factories*, ix. 95.

SECTION 5.—The consumption of cotton goods in England is dealt with incidentally in *Baines* and *Daniels*. For the nature of the initial demand on India, see *First Letter Book*, 131, 148, 255, 308, 328, etc.; Finch's report is in *Letters Received*, i. 28 ff. The table of exports in 1619 is compiled from *English Factories*, i. 61, 62; the figures for 1625 and 1628 are *idem*, iii. 92, 208; and the indent of 1630 is *idem*, iv. 8. For the English market at this period, see *Court Minutes*, August 6, 1623, and March 30, 1625; and for purchases in Northern India, see *English Factories*, i. pp. xxi ff.,

212; iii. 141 and *passim*. For the change in trade after the famine, see *English Factories*, iv. 97, 158; v. 146, 278, 341; for Sind, *idem*, v. 118, 129, 164; and for the East Coast, *idem*, i. 343; ii. 336; iv. 64, 228; v. 218; and vi. 295. The exports of 1638–41 are abstracted from the invoices attached to *Original Correspondence*, 1656, 1725, and 1761. The description of Coast goods is based mainly on *Letter Books*, vol. II. 13-17, 196-197; and on details in the Dutch invoices abstracted in Appendix B. The decline in quality of Gujarat calicoes is referred to in *English Factories*, vi. 56, 311. The growth of the East Coast trade can be traced in the latter volumes of *English Factories*; see especially vii. 173; viii. 164, 297; and x. 61, 200, 307, 322. The detailed figures given for this period have been extracted from *Letter Books*, vol. II. 1-3, 13-17, 21-24, 196-197.

The Dutch trade with Brazil and West Africa is discussed in *Elias*, ii. ch. vii. For their export of cotton goods to Europe, see Appendix B, and also *Letters Received*, iv. 34; *English Factories*, i. 41, 44; ii. 336; *Terpstra's Surat*, 76; *Hague Transcripts*, I. 163, 318; II. 52, 114*a*; III. F5.

Interference with trade is recorded frequently; the instances given are from *Dagh Register*, May 20, 1641; *English Factories*, v. 296, and viii. 118, 234. The remarks on advances and security are taken from *idem*, vi. 156, and vii. 46, 164, 191. For defects and improvements, see *idem*, iv. 3; vi. 57; vii. 126; viii. 117; *Court Minutes*, September 6, 1658; and *Dagh Register*, May 20, and September 3, 1641.

SECTION 6.—The English demand for cotton is dealt with by *Daniels*, 2 ff. For requests for baling-machinery, see *English Factories*, iii. 212; v. 206; and for export of raw cotton, *idem*, iii. 62; iv. 9. Sales are recorded in *Court Minutes*, *passim*. The facts stated regarding the English yarn trade are taken from *English Factories*, i. 58; ii. 157, 185; iii. 209; iv. 22; vi. 312; viii. 254; ix. 42, 196; *Letter Books*, ii. 1-3, 13-17. The extent of the Dutch trade has been as usual reached by compiling the figures of cargoes given in the *Dagh Register*; see also *Hague Transcripts*, I. 318, and II. 114*a*.

For the sugar trade at this period, see *Elias*, i. 71. Exports from Surat are mentioned frequently in *English Factories*, *e.g.* i. 51; iv. 4, 9, 323; vi. 58; viii. 255. The Dutch trade on the East Coast has been compiled from the *Dagh Register*, beginning with October 31, 1636. For the English trade in Bengal, see *English Factories*, vols. viii., ix. *passim*. There are occasional references to the silk trade in the earlier vols. of *English Factories*, but as a commercial proposition the history begins with x. 188.

CHAPTER V

THE COURSE OF INDIAN MARKETS

1. General Features of the Markets

From the transactions of the Dutch and English merchants in India we pass to an examination of the conditions prevailing in the markets into which they had secured an entry. A slight experience of the commercial records of the period will suffice to disillusion any one who may have been tempted to regard the India of the seventeenth century as a country of Arcadian simplicity; buyers and sellers resembled in all essentials the buyers and sellers of the present day, and the commercial aptitudes of Indian merchants were certainly not inferior to those of the foreigners who dealt with them. William Finch, the first English merchant at Surat, insisted that a regular factory was required there, on the ground that, when once the foreign ships had arrived, the local merchants would not sell their goods for less than double the value; he emphasised his opinion by a familiar quotation, saying, " They are ' as subtle as the devil,' whose limbs I certainly persuade myself they are " ; and compliments of the same kind could be quoted from various other parts of the country. The ideas, and occasionally even the language, appearing in the records are in this matter altogether modern, and, subject to two important reservations, we need not hesitate to apply the results of recent economic analysis to the transactions which they describe. Throughout the country we find recognised market prices, constantly fluctuating with variations in supply and demand; the conception of a normal price governed by cost of production was perfectly familiar ; and if we find few traces of the more remote process of alterations in the normal cost of production, the reason probably is that the conditions of agriculture and industry afforded very little scope for its operation within the short period to which the attention of the merchants was confined. We meet, too, the keenest competition among buyers and sellers, eager search for exclusive information, the organisation of rings and commercial monopolies, the specialised activities of a large class of brokers, a remarkable development of financial machinery for credit, exchange, and insurance ; a crisis was at least as familiar an event in Surat in the seventeenth century as in modern Bombay ; and, though a bankruptcy law did not exist, the institution itself was generally recognised.[1]

The two reservations which have to be made arise from the risk of official interference, and from the time and cost of transport. As regards the former, merchants dealing in any Indian market had to be prepared for the appearance of the local governor, or his nominee, as buyer or seller of practically any commodity ; and when this occurred, it meant that competition was for the time being displaced by force. In some cases this intervention could be justified by the necessities of the State, though the justification might be merely an excuse, but foreign merchants did not complain very seriously of the Governor's monopoly of lead at Surat, of the restrictions throughout the country on the sale of saltpetre, or of the prohibition of the re-export of copper at a time when the supply for currency was deficient ; their complaints were directed rather against the practice of engrossing or monopolising such staple commodities as indigo, cotton goods, spices, and even food-grains, solely for the profit of the State or its officers, or against other monopolistic developments of a more general nature.

The instances of engrossing or monopoly given in contemporary records are sufficiently numerous to establish the proposition that a local governor was in practice free to enter the market on his own initiative, while at the same time he

[1] *Manucci* (ii. 84) gives a vivid description of a bankruptcy at Patna.

was bound to carry out the orders of his official superiors. We may take as a type of local action the indigo-monopoly set up in 1647 by the Governor of Ahmadabad, regarding which the English merchants wrote as follows :

> Our Governor having most unjustly and unconscionably forced some *banjāras* [itinerant merchants] to sell him a parcel of sugar, and thereby made an unlawful gain of 1000 rupees, is so well encouraged thereby that he is now intended to become the sole merchant of this place, being in hand to engross all the indigo that the city and country will afford. . . . We do not find it probable that he should make any gain hereby this year, the indigo-men being likewise resolved to oppose his proceedings herein to the utmost ; but should he thrive in his project, we may then expect shortly to fetch our butter and rice from him.

As a matter of fact, the profit does not appear to have been great, for shortly afterwards we read that the "indigo-men" bought liberty to sell their stock by the payment of a sum of 250 rupees, "which they must give our Governor as the profit issued from what he bought from them, or (more truly) what he pretended to buy" ; but the very smallness of the payment accepted indicates that a staple industry might be subject to interference on trivial grounds. In the same way spices were monopolised at one time on the East Coast, and a little later, unbleached cloth ; in 1641 the piece-goods of Gujarat were monopolised temporarily for a State consignment to Mocha, and weavers working for any private purchaser were threatened with death ; and in 1632, when Surat was still famine-stricken, the local prices of food were doubled because the governor and one or two merchants had combined to engross the available supplies. Such operations were facilitated by the fact that in some commercial centres local governors were frequently appointed from the mercantile community, and there was nothing corresponding to the modern prohibition of official trading ; being free to enter the markets, it was practically inevitable that they should employ their official powers in their commercial transactions, and the risk of their doing so was always a factor to be taken into account by private dealers.

Of monopolies on a larger scale, the most prominent instance is that which was established in the indigo-market in 1633. By this arrangement, which was apparently modelled on the Persian royal monopoly of raw silk, a merchant undertook to make large payments to the treasury for the privilege of buying all the indigo manufactured in the Mogul Empire, including the produce of Gujarat as well as Biana ; he proceeded to buy in Sarkhej at Rs. 18 and sell at Rs. 27 the local maund (33 lb.), but the arrangement broke down because the principal buyers held aloof, and freedom of trade was restored at the close of the year 1635. The failure of this general monopoly must be attributed to the agreement to defeat it, entered into between the Dutch and English merchants, whose joint demand was the most important single factor in the market ; where individual customers were numerous and carried less weight, similar arrangements might last longer, as in the case of the monopoly of freight on the East Coast, which has been mentioned in a former chapter, but, whether the duration might be long or short, the possibility of such interference had to be taken into account in almost every mercantile transaction.

So far we have spoken of monopolies affecting particular commodities or services, but that there was nothing to prevent a governor from monopolising the entire trade of a seaport is shown by the case of Hooghly, where in the year 1635–36 the Dutch found that an exclusive concession had been given to three individuals, who fixed prices of all goods as they chose. Again, a monopoly might be granted of the business of a group of foreign merchants ; in 1625 the Dutch at Masulipatam were farmed out like any other source of revenue, and thus found themselves debarred from dealing with any merchants except those who had paid for the privilege ; while the existence of a similar arrangement was one of the reasons which led to the English determination to abandon that port in 1628. The system of monopoly was probably most highly developed under Mīr Jumla, the famous Minister of Golconda, who subsequently transferred his allegiance to the Moguls. Manucci tells us that Mīr Jumla was a self-made merchant before he attained to office, and his official proceedings lend credit to the story. We are told that, when he was at the height of his career as Minister, he maintained a large force of land transport for his goods, while he owned ten ships, and was building more, for his trade to various foreign countries. Being offended with the Dutch, he proposed a sort of partnership with the English Company to monopolise the East Coast trade as a whole, and meanwhile he was active on his own account, reserving for himself the services of all the weavers of a large tract of country; and we read that "this course he is resolved to continue, until he can bring a monopoly of all imported goods." The factors at Madras doubted the wisdom of the proposed partnership, fearing that the example might result in the establishment of similar monopolies elsewhere to the detriment of the Company's business, and no student of the records of the period can deny that their apprehensions were reasonable, though the danger of this particular project disappeared when Mīr Jumla abandoned Golconda for the service of the Mogul Empire.

The second consideration we have mentioned, the time and cost of transport, was of not less practical importance than the danger of the disturbance of markets by official interference: the result was to confine markets within limits which nowadays seem extraordinarily narrow, and to make prices depend on the stock of a commodity actually on the spot, rather than on the supply available throughout the world. In the case of imported goods, the dominant factor was time. At the present day an apprehended shortage of a commodity in any part of India would at once set the cables to work, and additional supplies might usually be expected in the course of a few weeks; during our period, the provision of a supply of such a commodity as lead, or coral, or woollen cloth of some particular fashion, required nearly two years, the indent being sent home from Surat in January, and the goods arriving, if all went well, in the next September but one, by which time the conditions of the market might have entirely changed. There was thus a large measure of uncertainty in making up cargoes for remote destinations; goods which had been asked for might prove to be unprocurable, or, if they were available, they might prove to be unsaleable on arrival, and merchants had to be guided partly by local prices and partly by the most recent information, which was already more or less out of date. Some saving of time between India and Europe could be effected by despatching letters overland by way of Basra and Aleppo, a route which came into more or less regular use as experience proved its advantages;[1] transit by it was, however, by no means certain, and while a letter sent overland might effect a saving for practical purposes of about a year, it might in other circumstances take almost as long as one sent by sea. No similar saving of time could be effected in communicating with the Far East, and, speaking generally, the connection between distant markets was so uncertain as to introduce into business a factor which is nowadays practically unknown.

In purely Indian transactions, the factor of time, though it was not negligible, was subordinate to the factor of cost, at least so far as goods had to be collected or distributed by land. It is possible to form a rough idea of the cost of land transport from some details mentioned in contemporary records. Thus in 1619 the rate for conveyance from Agra to Surat by way of Burhanpur was Rs. $14\frac{3}{4}$ for a camel-load of approximately 500 lb.; in 1638 a cartage contract on this route was settled at Rs. $2\frac{3}{4}$ per 74 lb.; in 1651, Rs. $15\frac{3}{16}$ was the charge per camel from Agra to Ahmadabad by the Rajputana route; while in 1639 goods could be carried from Agra to Lahore for Rs. 2 per maund of 74 lb. Reducing these and other rates to a common standard, we find that the cost of carrying 100 lb. a distance of 100 miles in Northern and Western India ranged between half and three-quarters of a rupee, exclusive of anything required for payment of armed guards

[1] The Portuguese occasionally sent information overland by way of Aleppo, and also Suez (see, *e.g.*, *Couto*, X. i. 72), but in the instances I have noticed the news sent was political rather than commercial. In 1616 the Dutch were considering the possibility of overland communication between Amsterdam and Masulipatam, but the route was at this time obstructed by wars (*Hague Transcripts*, I. 83). English use of the overland route becomes noticeable in the 'thirties (*English Factories*, vi. 245, vii. 27, etc.).

and inland customs duties. These latter charges varied greatly according to local conditions; that they might add materially to the cost is shown by Peter Mundy's reference to a contract by which the carriers from Agra to Ahmadabad undertook to discharge all customs demands in return for payments of Rs. 45 per cart and Rs. 9½ per camel-load, but it must be remembered that the number of independent chiefs on this route was exceptional, and these figures cannot be taken as representative of the country as a whole. Confining our attention to the actual cost of carriage, we may say that, while it could be borne by goods of high value per unit of weight, it was absolutely prohibitive in the case of ordinary agricultural produce. At the end of the sixteenth century, the normal price of wheat in Northern India was about 185 lb. per rupee: transport of 100 miles would have sufficed to double this price, and transport to the consuming markets of Gujarat would have multiplied the price from five-fold to eight-fold according to the rate charged. Again we shall find that the normal price of wheat at Surat during our period was somewhere about 85 lb. per rupee; wheat carried to Surat from a distance of 250 miles or less would have required to be sold at that price to cover cost of transport alone, so that the normal radius of import must have been well under 200 miles, and a very large rise in price would have been required to attract food from any considerable distance. Thus we may say that for commodities like indigo, Agra and Ahmadabad were comprised in one market, because inter-transport was a commercial possibility, and the chief buyers could make their purchases in one city or the other; for food grains, on the other hand, India must be regarded as split up into a large number of nearly independent markets, because the cost of carriage by land was so great as to eliminate effective competition. In cases where a route by water was available, the segregation of markets was much less noticeable, and the sea in particular exercised a powerful unifying effect. So far as imports and exports were concerned, Surat and Lahari Bandar were one market, provided that the quantity of goods to be dealt in was sufficient to load a single coasting-boat;

Gujarat and Malabar again were one market, except when the sea-route was closed by pirates or blockade; and the same may almost be said of Surat and Masulipatam. In this last case, the existence of the Dutch headquarters at Batavia was an important factor in equalising the price of imports, because the council could, with very little difference in cost, direct goods such as spices, porcelain, or the precious metals, to whatever point on the coast of India might offer the best market; and the same influence affected the price of many exports, though the specialisation of such commodities as cotton goods in some cases made prompt substitution impossible.[1] So much, however, may be said that, subject to interruption through war or piracy, the coastal markets were closely interdependent when not altogether unified, but even a short stage of transit by land might suffice to sever all connection in the case of goods of low value.

2. Personnel and Organisation

It is easy for a student of the contemporary records to form an exaggerated idea of the importance of the Dutch and English merchants in the Indian markets where they possessed a footing. It is true that, taken together, they had a practical monopoly of the supply of goods from Western Europe, and that they controlled purchases for the same region, but Indian markets were not dominated by the European trade, and the competition between the Dutch and English companies made each of them much less influential than if they had been able to work in harmony. From time to time we find attempts made to eliminate this competition, which was certainly injurious to European interests, though it was beneficial to Indian producers and consumers; but these attempts were short-lived, and even the operation of

[1] In 1627 *Pelsart* (p. 8) pointed out that the Dutch were injuring their trade in Northern India by excessive imports of spices on the East Coast, and recommended a reduction there coupled with increased supplies to Surat. A few years later general orders were issued from Amsterdam to regulate supplies to Persia, Surat, and Masulipatam in such a way as to keep prices level throughout the whole region (*Hague Transcripts*, II. 95).

the agreement to break the official monopoly of indigo in 1634 was seriously hampered by the independent transactions of the buyers at Agra. From time to time the European merchants dominated the markets for particular commodities, but it cannot be asserted that they ever dominated the commercial outlook; that position was held rather by individual Indians—Moslems, banians, or chettis, as the case might be—men who through their wealth and abilities might almost be said to control the entire wholesale trade within the area covered by their operations.

The most prominent of these Indians during our period was Vīrji Vora, the merchant-prince of Surat, who, rightly or wrongly, was reputed to be the richest merchant in the world.[1] The first reference to him which I have noticed relates to the year 1619, when one of his employees in charge of a Surat vessel obtained a recommendation to courteous usage on the part of English ships. From this time onwards he is mentioned frequently in the commercial records, usually as buying or selling various commodities, gold and silver, lead, coral, and ivory, spices, opium, cotton, and practically everything which changed hands in the Surat wholesale market. His dealings were on a large scale, and syndicates dominated by him were ready to buy entire cargoes valued at from five to ten lakhs of rupees. Such purchases naturally secured a temporary monopoly of particular commodities, such as the spices imported by the Dutch, and we find his syndicate selling for Rs. 62 and 65 the cloves which had been bought for Rs. 45 the maund. Apart from foreign goods, he controlled the pepper market in Surat, and the coasting trade to those Malabar ports which were not dominated by the Portuguese. His business had wide ramifications: he had branch offices or agencies at such places as Ahmadabad, Agra, Burhanpur, and

[1] I follow the transliteration of the name adopted in *English Factories*; Professor Sarkar writes Baharji Borah (*Shivaji*, 110), and also Pirji Borah (*Aurangzeb*, i. 325), in passages which clearly refer to the same individual. His reputation as the richest merchant in the world is affirmed in a letter written at Surat in 1664 by the Rev. John l'Escaliot. This letter was printed in Wilkin's edition of the works of Sir Thomas Browne (i. 424): the portion here referred to appeared in the *Indian Antiquary* for 1921, pp. 312 ff.

Golconda, as well as in Malabar and on the East Coast; and he maintained relations with Java, Basra, and Gombroon, occasionally sending his goods to these destinations on English vessels. As time went on, his power in the market increased to a point where it became irksome to the English factors. From being the "usual merchant," he became "the sole monopolist of all European commodities," and in 1634 he was "observed to bear such sway amongst the inferior merchants of this town [Surat], that when they would oftentimes buy, and give greater prices, they are still restrained, not daring to betray their intents to his knowledge and their own sufferance, insomuch that the time and price is still in his will and at his own disposure." The Council which recorded these observations declared itself "weary of his unprofitable correspondence, which they intend to shake off by degrees, and incline to others that promise more fairly"; but the intention was not realised, for in 1642 Vīrji Vora was "awing all other banian merchants to his observance," and four years later the factors were still practically in his hands. In the last decade of our period, we read of a dispute over a particular transaction, which was referred to London for decision; the Company decided against Vīrji Vora, but sent him a valuable present as a mark of esteem, which, however, did not suffice to mollify him, and for a time he was so angered "that he will not hear of lending any moneys upon account of any interest."

Powerful as he was, Vīrji Vora was not always able to disregard the local authorities. In 1630 we find him apprehensive of the Governor's intention to join him in a partnership, which might "ensnare him to his abuse," and a later Governor, Masīh-uz-Zamān, appears to have judged that he was ripe for extortion, for at the end of the year 1638 he was experiencing "most barbarous tyranny" in the Surat prison. The particular charge made against him is not stated, and we do not know whether it was true or false; but the proceedings appear to have been irregular, for the Diwān (the provincial representative of the Imperial revenue authorities) reported the matter to the Emperor, Vīrji Vora was summoned to Court to answer in person, and eventually Masīh-uz-Zamān was removed from his post. From that time to the close of our period Vīrji Vora's career was not seriously checked. He lost heavily by Sivaji's raid on Surat in the year 1664, but a little later we are told that he and another merchant "hold up their heads still and are for great bargains." In 1665 anonymous petitions reached Batavia accusing him of corrupt dealings with the Dutch factory at Surat, and about the same time the traveller Thévenot wrote of him as a friend supposed to be worth at least eight millions. The unit in terms of which Thévenot was writing is not specified, but another contemporary account gives 80 lakhs of rupees,[1] and we may take it that Vīrji Vora was popularly credited with a capital of this amount, an estimate which may of course have been very wide of the truth. I have not come across a notice of his death, but it probably took place before the year 1677.[2]

The question naturally arises whether a man in Vīrji Vora's position welcomed the presence of European merchants in the market. The facts appear to justify an answer in the affirmative, so far at least as the English are concerned, for he willingly financed their transactions during a long period, in the course of which he could probably have driven them out of the country. We have seen in a former chapter that the English were frequently compelled to borrow capital in Surat; it was Vīrji Vora who met most of their needs, and his position in the market was so strong that it is reasonable to conclude that he could have prevented others from making loans if he had wished to do so. On the contrary, he once volunteered a loan of two lakhs at a time when the difficulties of the English were unusually great, and on another occasion he saved their credit by an unexpected offer of half that sum. It would be absurd to suggest that he acted out of philanthropy or charity in these transactions; he took the regular interest, and raised the rate when market conditions justified this

[1] This figure is taken from l'Escaliot's letter quoted in a previous note.

[2] Some curious letters from Surat are printed in the *Dagh Register* of June 1, 1678; their tenor is such that Vīrji Vora's name would almost certainly have appeared if he had been still in business, but no allusion is made to him.

course; he stood out stubbornly for his full terms; and the most reasonable inference is that he valued the presence of the merchants whose business he did so much to facilitate, and judged that more money could be made in Surat when the English were there than if they were away. Another inference which may be drawn from his conduct relates to the importance of personal credit at this period. The records do not show that he asked for security for his loans, and it is tolerably clear that such a request would have been futile, because the English had nothing tangible to offer, their local assets consisting at most of a stock of goods which were temporarily unsaleable. We must conclude therefore that, in the conditions which prevailed in Gujarat, money might be lent by the lakh as a business transaction, if the borrower's personal credit appeared to justify the venture.

Vīrji Vora had a counterpart on the East Coast in the family or firm known by the name Malaya, with headquarters at Pulicat, and connections as far south as Negapatam. Malaya himself died in the year 1634, but the business was carried on by his relatives, and the English records continue to speak of "Malaya" for ten or fifteen years after the date of his death. The business of this firm is more difficult to follow than that of Vīrji Vora, because it was closely intertwined with the complex politics of the south: Chinana Chetti, who was Malaya's younger brother, and succeeded him as head of the firm, appears also as holding various public offices in farm, and on occasion as commanding troops in the field; his career was necessarily marked by vicissitudes, and at one time his debts were regarded as doubtful, but I have not found any record of an actual collapse. In business proper, the firm was largely interested in shipping, and the various manœuvres referred to in Dutch and English records suggest to me that its guiding policy was to play one Company off against the other.

Of ordinary merchants we naturally hear less than of such firms as these, and all that need be said is that their business was on a smaller scale, and that as a rule they worked on the lines set by the men who dominated their market. One instance is on record where a merchant at Surat seems to have thought of defying Vīrji Vora, and bought a consignment of coral, but for two years he did not dare to avow the transaction, and the goods remained in the English storehouse "unrequested and unregarded"; but the correspondence of the period shows that even so much individuality was not to be expected in the ordinary course. Brokers are more prominent in the records than ordinary merchants, and their employment was a universal custom. They were numerous and ubiquitous, and at times they were a nuisance; in 1635 the English factors at Surat

> enacted that no brokers should be permitted to come into the English house, except such as are of the Company's brokers . . . and certain known servants of theirs, unless that they have business that doth concern the Company, and shall first require leave to be admitted; the contrary whereof hath occasioned many inconveniences, not only by furthering all men's private trade of all conditions and qualities, but also by discovering our business, which by that means hath been made as public as the bazar before the affair might be so permitted.

From time to time we read of brokers proving fraudulent or unfaithful, but I take it that, within limits imposed by current mercantile conventions, good service was the rule, and there are some grounds for thinking that the English merchants were for a long time in the hands of a not too respectable clique.[1] Whatever their commercial morality may have been, there can be no doubt that their activities were of the kind which ensures close prices, and, as we shall see in the sections which follow, prices did in fact move rapidly in accordance with the conditions of the market.

[1] The irregularities of the first English broker, Jādu Dās, are familiar topics in the early correspondence, *e.g. Letters Received*, i. 284, 304; v. 115; vi. 232; *English Factories*, i. 21, 42. *Roe* (216), says, "he did more to hinder us than all other lets together"; but also (277), that he was "sufficient in all but his honesty, wherein there is little choice." I take him to have been an aggravating but indispensable subordinate, such as may still be found occasionally in India; and he was certainly successful in placing his relatives in the Company's employment, for in 1632 *Mundy* noted (ii. 79) that his assistant at Patna was "cousin to Gur Das (the broker in Surat), to Dhanji, our broker in Agra, and Panju in Broach, these being the sons of two brothers, whereof Jadu, broker in Burhanpur, is the third."

The line dividing merchants from brokers was, I take it, the possession of capital, and, apart from this particular case, there are few traces of specialisation in the markets of our period. Vīrji Vora was eminently a merchant, that is to say, a buyer and seller of commodities, and his business extended to any class of goods in which there might be hopes of profit; but at the same time he freighted ships, he acted as a banker, he received deposits, and he arranged remittances by means of bills or letters of credit on his branch houses. The activities of the firm of Malaya were equally multifarious, and I have not noticed any record of a banker as distinct from a merchant, or of a prominent merchant confining his transactions to a particular line of goods. The nearest approach to specialisation is perhaps to be found among the dealers in currency, or money-changers; the variety of coins in circulation made this business one for experts, and the "shroffs," as they were called, impressed such visitors as Tavernier with their highly specialised abilities. They did not, however, confine themselves absolutely to dealing in currency, for we read on one occasion that a shroff employed by the English hired one of their small vessels for a trading venture to the Persian Gulf; and in the same way we hear of the English brokers engaging from time to time in business on their own account. It is possible that the business of marine insurance was specialised, but I have found no definite information on this subject. The practice of insurance was quite common, and we read of war risks being dealt in, and also of an "overdue market," but the names or positions of the insurers are not stated, and it is perhaps more probable that the risks were underwritten by ordinary merchants.

We may thus regard an Indian commercial centre of our period as comprising an indefinite number of men of business, not subdivided into numerous branches, but graded in accordance with their ability and command over capital, and all of them eager to take part in any hopeful venture, provided only that it was not of a nature to bring them into conflict with leaders whom they were not prepared to oppose. The inevitable result was that hopeful ventures were often overdone. Thus on the Arab reoccupation of Aden, ships hurried there from various Indian seaports, and the market was so glutted that sales were possible only at a great loss. Conditions were even worse at Mocha owing to official oppression, while no ships had returned from Achin; and the consequence was the bankruptcy of many Hindu and Moslem merchants in Surat, and a fall in the price of cotton goods throughout the country. In 1644 again the Dutch records note that several dealers in currency and some Mocha merchants had become bankrupt in Surat, so that the bullion market was disorganised; and I take it that this trouble is referred to in a letter from the English factors in which it is said that in Gombroon "a commodity can no sooner be in any request but such vast quantities are suddenly sent that it becomes of no esteem. The like it is with Mocha. So that Basra is yet the place that produceth you most profit." This last opinion was, however, soon falsified, for in 1647 the glut at Basra was as bad as at Mocha owing to "the infinite quantity of goods transported there, and the small vend." There was similar trouble in connection with the market at Achin: the tyrant-king of that place died in 1641, and the reputation of his successor for just dealing attracted numerous Indian ventures, so that there was a glut of cotton goods, and not long after the stocks were estimated to be sufficient for two years to come. The general result of these and other incidents of the period is to suggest that the eagerness and lack of restraint which now characterise the markets of Western India are qualities which go far back into history; certainly during our period there was no lack of energy or initiative, and in the conditions which prevailed we cannot wonder that it should have been devoted so largely to business of a highly speculative nature.

3. The Indigo Market in Gujarat

The working of the markets during our period can be illustrated most effectively by tracing the changes in price recorded for a few important commodities. It is scarcely necessary to say that no systematic price-records are available among Indian sources, but the information given in the English correspondence is extensive, and many additional figures have been preserved in the Batavia Journals, so that in favourable circumstances an almost continuous account of fluctuations can be constructed. Unfortunately some of the figures are difficult to interpret; the quality of woollen cloth, for instance, varied so greatly that it would be rash to discuss the prices quoted for it without specialised knowledge of the subject; a somewhat similar danger exists in regard to some other imports such as coral and ivory; while on the export side changes in the sources of supply affect the value of the figures which are available for saltpetre and cotton goods. The illustrations which follow have been chosen so as to avoid these difficulties as far as possible; in some cases, such as lead, or quicksilver, or cloves, there is no question of marked differences in quality, while in others, such as indigo, the figures give the average price paid, or quoted, for large export consignments, and in this way eliminate fluctuations due to variations in the quality of particular parcels. The units in terms of which prices are quoted are discussed in Appendix D. The question of trade allowances, of one or two sers in the maund, presents some difficulty, as it is often uncertain whether their occasional mention indicates a regular custom or a special concession, but the error they introduce cannot be greater than five per cent, and the significant fluctuations are usually much larger, so that we can draw inferences from them which are substantially, though perhaps not arithmetically, correct.

The first illustration relates to the price of the export grade of Sarkhej indigo in the Ahmadabad market, the figures for which are given in the table on following page.

In order to interpret these figures it is desirable in the first place to arrive at the standard of price which was recognised in the market at the opening of the period. There is no doubt that the early English buyers took Rs. 18 as the standard. Writing from Ahmadabad in November 1613, Thomas Aldworth reported that the price had fallen greatly owing to the absence of Portuguese buyers, "insomuch that their

Prices of Sarkhej Indigo at Ahmadabad, 1609-63

Note.—The price is given in rupees (and decimals) for a Gujarat maund of 33 lb. In 1635–36 this maund was raised, and from 1636 the quotations given in the authorities have been reduced by 10 per cent (the new maund standing to the old as 20 to 18), so as to facilitate comparison for the period.

In the references, L.R. stands for *Letters Received*, E.F. for *English Factories*, D.R. for *Dagh Register*, F.R. for *Factory Records*, O.C. for *Original Correspondence*.

Year.	Price, Rs. and Decimals.	Description.	Reference.
Standard . .	18·00	Quoted	L.R. i. 306, and *passim*.
1609 . . .	10·00–12·00	,,	L.R. i. 28.
1612 . . .	14·00	,,	Jourdain, 217.
1613 . . .	14·00	,,	L.R. i. 306.
1614 . . .	10·00–12·00	,,	L.R. ii. 214, 238.
,, . . .	12·00–13·00	Paid	,, ,, 248.
1617 . . .	12·00–15·00	Quoted	Terpstra's Surat, App. IV.
1618 . . .	15·00–18·00	,,	,, ,, App. VII.
1619 . . .	15·00	Paid	E.F. i. 62.
1621 . . .	10·00	Estimate	F.R. Surat, i. 16.
,, . . .	9·25–9.50	Paid by Dutch	E.F. i. 348.
,, . . .	9·25	Paid by English	,, ,, 353.
1622 (Jan.) .	7·00	Estimate	E.F. ii. 19.
,, (Aug.-Dec.)	8·00–9·00	Asked	,, ,, 109, 158, 162.
1623 (Apr.) .	7·50–8·00	Quoted	,, ,, 219.
,, (Nov.) .	8·50–8·75	,,	,, ,, 328.
,, ,, .	12·00	Asked	,, ,, 328.
,, (Dec.) .	10·25	Paid	,, ,, 331.
1625 . . .	12·00	Quoted	E.F. iii. 63.
,, . . .	11·00	Estimate	F.R. Surat, i. 100.
1628 (Jan.) .	14·00–15·00	Asked	E.F. iii. 230.
,, (Mar.) .	12·75–14·25	Asked	,, ,, 275.
1630 . . .	16·00	Quoted	F.R. Surat, 84 (ii.), 52.
1632 . . .	19·00–22·00	,,	E.F. iv. 215.
1633 (Jan.) .	23·00–25·00	,,	,, ,, 255.
,, (Nov.) .	16·00–18·00	Agreed with Dutch	,, ,, 328.
1634 . . .	27·00	Monopoly price	E.F. v. 70.
1635 . . .	27·00 (?)	Paid	,, ,, 142.
1636 . . .	25·20	Estimate	,, ,, 292.
1638 . . .	Under 18·00 (?)	Quoted	E.F. vi. 92.
1639 (Jan.) .	26·90	Paid, average	O.C. 1656.
,, (Dec.) .	17·30	,, ,,	O.C. 1725.
1640 (Jan.) .	20·00	Quoted	E.F. vi. 232.
,, (Dec.) .	16·70	Paid, average	O.C. 1764.
,, ,, .	12·60–14·40	Anticipated	E.F. vi. 273.
1641 . . .	13·50–14·40	Asked	D.R. 3. 11. 42.
1642 (late) .	14·62–14·85	Paid	D.R. 27. 4. 43.
1644 . . .	17·00	Paid	E.F. vii. 104.
1645 . . .	20·70–22·50 (?)	Asked	,, ,, 254.
1646 . . .	20·25–21·60	Asked	E.F. viii. 31.
1647 . . .	17·10–20·25	Paid	,, ,, 77.
1648 (Jan.) .	17·10–17·55	Estimate } Experiment	{ ,, ,, 189.
,, (Apr.) .	19·35–19·80	Actual }	{ ,, ,, 203.
1650 . . .	12·60–13·50	Quoted	,, ,, 305.
1653 . . .	14·22	Paid	O.C. 2309.
1655 . . .	11·81 (?)	,,	E.F. x. 18.
1656 . . .	15·75–16·20	Quoted	,, ,, 76.
1663 . . .	13·25–13·50	Paid	D.R. 21. 6. 63.

Notes.—1635. Perhaps the figure 27·00 should be reduced to 24·30; it is not clear whether the size of the maund had been increased before or after this transaction took place.

1638. Suspicious; quoted by a factor on his defence.

1645. Price is quoted per bale, but this is impossible, and I assume maund to be meant.

1655. Greatly adulterated; described as "half dirt."

best flat indigo, that was wont to be sold for 18 rupees, is now offered for 14 rupees, and like to fall every day" ; and the same rate is used for reference by two or three other merchants in the course of the next year or so. The chief business of these merchants in India was to buy indigo, and it is reasonable to suppose that they had taken all possible pains to ascertain the facts of the market ; but even if we make the rather violent conjecture that they had been deceived by a conspiracy among their brokers, we can safely say that the standard at the time when English purchasers began was certainly above Rs. 15. It is true that the first actual quotation, which was given by Finch in 1609, falls much below this standard, being equivalent to Rs. 10 to 12 per maund, but we are justified in regarding his figures as abnormally low. In the first place, Finch was not buying but only inquiring, and when, as was obviously the case in Gujarat, the market was anxious to attract new customers, *pro forma* quotations were likely to fall below the facts. In the second place, Gujarat was during this season suffering from a severe financial crisis, and it is reasonable to infer that holders of stocks were unusually anxious to sell. In a letter written a few weeks before the date of his report, Finch tells of the sudden bankruptcy of one of the leading merchants, and the flight of another who was involved in the collapse, and in these circumstances the quotation given cannot be regarded as typical of normal conditions, even though it represented the panic price of the moment.

The next figure in the table is for the spring of 1612 ; it is given by Jourdain as having been agreed on as the basis for adjusting certain transactions in the Red Sea, and may safely be taken as representative of the season in Gujarat. In the next two years prices were depressed by the absence of Portuguese buyers owing to the war with the Moguls, but this disturbing cause was quickly eliminated, and, when the Dutch came to Gujarat and appeared as possible buyers, the price was "talked up" to Rs. 18, the figure which I have taken as the standard. The bulk of the cargo despatched by the English in 1619 works out at 40 mahmudis, or say Rs. 16, free on board; charges from Ahmadabad to the ship's side were about one rupee a maund, so that Rs. 15 is a fair figure for this year.[1] From 1621 to 1625 prices were very low, Rs. 7 being talked of at one time. I have found no record of a reason for this drop, a fact which is not in itself surprising, since buyers are usually more ready to defend high prices than to explain prices when they are low; the Portuguese were now buying very little, but the demand of the Dutch and English taken together should have supported the market, and I conjecture that the fall was due to temporary over-production, growers having no means of judging the real requirements of the new customers, and being misled by the vigour of their methods. However that may be, the price had returned to Rs. 14-15 by the year 1628, while early in 1630 there is a quotation of Rs. 16; the fall was therefore a temporary phenomenon. The famine followed, and for a time the market was dead; at the end of 1630 the price was Rs. 18 for what was left of the old stock, "a poor remains of refuse stuff," and there was no new crop in prospect. When cultivation was resumed, food-stuffs at first took precedence; quotations for indigo ranged up to Rs. 25, and late in 1633 the situation was further complicated by the monopoly which has been described in a previous section. The Dutch and English came to an agreement to limit offers to Rs. 16-18, but the monopolists stood out for Rs. 27, and they were supported by the curtailment of production resulting from their operations; in the north the peasants, "being in general a resolute, hare-brained folk," rooted up their standing crops, and, though we are not told of similar action in Gujarat, we may safely infer that sowings were reduced. The price remained about Rs. 25 or over for two years after the monopoly closed, but agriculture was now recovering, and in 1639 and 1640 the English purchases were made at about Rs. 17. The fall continued for some time, because adulteration had become very prevalent, and European buyers were insisting on a high

[1] In the detailed invoice attached to *Original Correspondence*, No. 1725, the charges on 2007 maunds from Ahmadabad to the ships at Swally, the roadstead of Surat, are given as Rs. 2038.

standard of quality, but by 1644 there was a recovery, attributed to improved manufacture and a short crop. In the two following years the price was over Rs. 20, the rise being attributed to the official measures taken to check adulteration: in 1648 adulteration was again troublesome, and the English factors experimented in manufacture, but were unable to reduce the cost appreciably. A reaction came in 1650, as the result of a very good crop both in the north and in Gujarat, while three years later the average price paid was little over Rs. 14. The very low price of 1655 is explained by gross adulteration, and the last available quotations up to 1660 range round Rs. 16; while a Dutch report of 1663 records that purchases below Rs. 14 represented a rise in the price at that time.

It may be added that Tavernier, whose experience covered the last twenty years of our period, puts the ruling price at from Rs. 15 to Rs. 20, a quotation which agrees substantially with the standard suggested for its beginning. Taking then the whole period into review, I cannot point to any evidence of a rise in the normal price; fluctuations can be accounted for usually by recorded alterations in the demand or supply, and the adjustments are at least as rapid as could fairly be expected. Even if we take the view that the first English buyers were deceived, it is not possible to argue that prices in the last decade of our period were materially higher than in 1613, when they began to buy.

4. The Markets for Imported Goods

The next commodity to be considered is quicksilver. There was a limited but insistent demand for the metal, chiefly, I presume, for conversion into vermilion, and, as it was not produced in India,[1] it is a simple case to illustrate the market for imported goods. The offtake of the Gujarat market was estimated at from 15,000 to 20,000 lb. annually,

[1] A quicksilver mine near Agra is referred to in *Letters Received*, iii. 63, but we hear nothing more about it, and I take it to have been an invention put about by buyers in order to lower the price.

and appears to have been fairly constant; any shortage of supply sent up prices rapidly, while even a small excess sufficed to break the market. Supplies came from China as well as from Europe; they might arrive by way of the Red Sea as well as the Cape; and the small bulk of the commodity rendered it suitable for surreptitious private trade. All these factors combined to make the market highly speculative, and the price fluctuated within wide limits. The unit of sale was the Gujarat maund, and in order to facilitate comparison, I have again reduced the quotations by ten per cent from the year 1636 onwards, so that the figures given apply throughout to a maund of 33 lb.; both rupees and mahmudis are quoted in the various Gujarat markets, and I take these in one series, neglecting the cost of transit (somewhere about a rupee per maund) between Surat and Ahmadabad.

In 1609, Finch found the price to vary from Rs. 64 to 80, but this was as we have seen a time of crisis, when buyers were likely to hold off. In 1612–13 sales were made at Rs. 120, and up to Rs. 160, but the arrival of fresh supplies in 1614 brought the price down to Rs. 100, while in 1615–16 it was Rs. 80, "no buyers," on an unfounded report of the discovery of a mine near Agra. From 1619 onwards the level of prices fell, and Rs. 60-90 represents the general trend of the market for the next few years; the fall was probably due to the establishment of the Dutch at Surat, as their supplies competed with those brought by the English. In 1625–26 there was a sharp rise; the Dutch had brought nothing, the Portuguese little, and supplies by the Red Sea route were also scanty, with the result that the price rose to Rs. 100, with small lots at Rs. 120. The next noticeable change was in 1630, when excessive supplies brought by the Dutch and by English private traders, coming just at the beginning of the famine, broke the market, and prices fell below Rs. 50. Private trade continued to keep prices down: in 1633 the rate was Rs. 36, in 1634 it was Rs. 42, and in 1636 the Dutch sold some at Rs. 35¼. I have found no quotations for the next nine years, but the commodity reappears in 1645 at about Rs. 65-70, and in 1649 it was over Rs. 110. The rise appears to have been due in part to the failure of Chinese supplies, for in 1652 the English factors wrote that if that trade revived, the price might go down again to Rs. 60; Dutch, English, and Portuguese were at this time all importing, and there was evidently a sharp fall, for a transaction at Rs. 75½ in 1654 was described as a good advance on the previous price. A recovery had occurred by 1659, when the price was Rs. 100, and in 1661 the Dutch obtained Rs. 84. Generalisation is obviously dangerous in regard to such a market, but I think it may fairly be said that there is no trace of any rise in the normal price, which I should place at Rs. 80-100 over the whole period, while occasional outbursts of excessive competition were of at least temporary benefit to the Indian consumer.

The Surat market for lead offers a great contrast to that for quicksilver. Imports were again the main source of supply, and they came, I think, entirely from Europe,[1] with competition between Dutch and English consignments; but the market was not free, for the local Governor usually asserted a claim to buy all that was offered in the town, and, if it had not been for the existence of alternative outlets, the price would have depended chiefly on his views. In point of fact alternatives existed: there was usually a free market in Ahmadabad, while the masters of coasting vessels were glad to carry the metal as ballast, and we read of sales from Surat to Goa, Lahari Bandar, and Rajapur, as well as to the Red Sea and the Persian Gulf. The position then was that imported lead would ordinarily be sold to the local Governor, but he could not, except by violence, obtain it for much below the market price ruling along the coast, though probably a small concession might be made in order to avoid friction.

At the opening of our period the price of the Gujarat maund ranged between 7 and 8 mahmudis,[2] and up to the year

[1] The Batavia Journals occasionally mention an export of lead from Siam, and some of this may have reached Surat, though I have found no record of the fact.

[2] I give the figures as recorded in mahmudis, because they are so small that to reduce them to rupees would involve the use of minute fractions. The mahmudi was worth about $\frac{2}{5}$ of a rupee, rising to $\frac{4}{9}$ as time went on.

1630 there are no indications of a change though the quotations are fairly numerous. In 1634 we hear that the English Company's lead had been detained in the custom house for nearly two years, because the Governor wanted it at 5½ ma.; but in 1638 the price was up to 7½ ma., and in 1642 to 8 ma. These two quotations, as well as those which follow, should be reduced by ten per cent to allow for the increase in the maund, but fractional deductions from such small figures would give a misleading idea of minute accuracy, and in this case I leave the deductions to be allowed for. In 1646 the merchants hoped to realise 10 ma., and this rate was reached in 1650, but in 1652 the Governor was offering 8 ma., and in 1659 the price paid was 9¼ ma. If we exclude the occasional forced sales, and remember that from the year 1636 onwards the figures are subject to a ten per cent deduction, we see that the range of price in the course of 50 years was from 7 to 9 ma., with no definite tendency in either direction. In this case then we can conclude that the normal price along the Indian coast had not risen materially, for if it had risen, the Governor of Surat would have been forced eventually to increase his offers, or the lead would have gone elsewhere.

A third illustration of the course of the import market may be found in the sales of cloves, a commodity of which the English records have comparatively little to say, but which is mentioned frequently by the Dutch. The trade passed through various phases. In the sixteenth century the commodity was in theory a monopoly of the king of Portugal, but private trade was active, and I suspect that there was in fact a certain amount of competition among sellers even when Portuguese authority in the Moluccas was firmly established. Towards the end of the century, when the political situation in the Spice Islands was increasingly involved, the market at Macassar came into prominence, and the history of the next fifty years covers the Dutch acquisition of the sources of supply, and their prolonged efforts to stop the leakage by way of Macassar; it is only in the 'fifties that we find their monopoly in thorough working order.

The usual price of cloves at the Mogul Court about the year

1595 is given by Abul Fazl at a figure which, allowing for the cost of inland carriage, works out to about Rs. 35 for a Gujarat maund of 33 lbs. landed at Surat.[1] The first quarter of the seventeenth century shows a marked rise, for which I have found no explanation, but which may be attributed partly to the disturbed state of the Spice Islands and partly to increased shipments to Europe; the price at Surat was Rs. 64 in 1617, Rs. 72 in 1621, and Rs. 84 in 1622. The record is broken at this point for eleven years, but prices were still high when information again becomes available, being Rs.77 in 1633, Rs. 55 in 1634, and Rs. 67 early in 1636; the last figure, and all which follow, have been reduced by 10 per cent to allow for the increase in the maund. Later in 1636 there was a sudden fall to about Rs. 40, and between 1641 and 1645 the rate varied between Rs. 27 and 35. In 1648 the price to consumers was raised, for the syndicate which had bought the entire supply at Rs. 41½ resold it at Rs. 55 to 60, and the rate of Rs. 50 ruled in 1649. Another gap in the record occurs at this point, but apparently the authorities in Amsterdam found themselves at last in a position to regulate the spice trade of the world on a uniform basis, for we find that in 1657 India was assigned fixed quantities, to be sold at or above specified prices, and the minimum rate for cloves works out at Rs. 77 for a maund of 33 lb.; the correlation of supply and price was clearly not exact, for sales in 1661 were made at the high price of nearly Rs. 95.[2] It appears then that on this side of India consumers had to pay prices higher than the competitive level from about 1615 to 1636, and again from 1648 onwards. It should be added that in the Surat market allowances were occasionally made to buyers of as much as 4 sers in the maund; I have taken these into account in the figures given in the Dutch records, where they

[1] Abul Fazl's figure is 60 dams per ser, or Rs. 60 for an Akbari maund. Writing in 1626 *Pelsart* (f. 8) mentioned that old merchants had told him that the rate in Agra used to be Rs. 60 or 80, so that Abul Fazl was probably correct.

[2] An entry in *Realia*, vol. iii. under "Spices," suggests that prices had been fixed at any rate by the year 1653, but I have not found a record of the actual date.

are clearly indicated, but it is possible that some of the quotations from English sources should be reduced by about 10 per cent. The error, if it exists, is small in size compared with the actual fluctuations.

The clove market on the East Coast has features of greater interest, because here the Dutch had for a time to meet the active competition of the Danes, who obtained supplies at Macassar. The prices at Masulipatam are given in pagodas per local maund (about 26 lb.), and I have not attempted to convert them into rupees, because the gradual rise in the silver-value of the pagoda cannot be traced with sufficient accuracy to determine the precise ratio in a particular year. It may be said, however, that the rate at Akbar's Court, which I have taken as a starting-point, would represent at the beginning of the seventeenth century very nearly 7 pagodas for the local maund delivered at Masulipatam. We find that here, as in Surat, a marked rise occurred early in the century. A year or two before 1616, the usual price was stated [1] to be 8½ to 10 p., but in 1618 the rate was 14½ p., "an unheard of price"; in 1622 it was 13 p., and by 1631 it had risen further to 20 p. At this point the competition of the Danes became acute, and there was a sudden fall to 8 p. in 1632; in 1638 the price dropped further to 6 p. and in 1639 to 4 or 4½ p., a figure which the English factors conjectured was intended "to break the Danes altogether." Prices remained about 5 p. for the next five years, after which the record breaks off; but when we next hear of the trade, the monopoly is complete, and the minimum prices prescribed from Amsterdam work out between 13 and 14 p. In this case, therefore, consumers benefited for a time owing to the war of prices, but in the end they had to pay, and pay heavily, for the monopoly which the Dutch had established by efforts prolonged over nearly half a century.

The market for mace and nutmegs followed a somewhat similar course, and here also consumers had in the end to pay

[1] This quotation is taken from *Schorer*, f. 7. His report is not dated, but it reached Holland in 1616, and must therefore refer to the market of 1614 or 1615.

higher prices; but apart from these monopoly-goods, I can find no trace of any increase in the normal cost of imports, and the figures available for tin, ivory, and coral suggest that the tendency was if anything towards a small reduction.

5. Food-grains and Silver

It may be urged that the prices of such commodities as lead, or quicksilver, or spices, were of little interest to the population of India taken as a whole. The contention is true, and it applies to all imported goods, because none of them entered largely into the consumption of the masses. The indigo market is of more general significance, for while the crop was grown for export by comparatively few peasants, it came into competition with food-grains, and consequently its price affords an indication of the conditions affecting agriculture; but, at the same time, it cannot be denied that we want most of all to know the course of prices in raw produce—food-grains, oilseeds, and cotton—because, taken together, these commodities represent the bulk of the country's income at this period. Unfortunately the data available under these heads are scanty. I have found no quotations for oilseeds, while those available for cotton are too few to form anything like a connected series, and even in the case of food-grains the materials are very disappointing in point of quantity. The English factors were not ordinarily concerned in the grain trade: the Dutch were, but the available records do not show the prices paid, or the values of the consignments; and regular accounts of housekeeping expenses or of the cost of victualling ships have not, so far as I can learn, been preserved.[1] The information available is therefore fragmentary, but the facts which are on record fit together in a way which makes it possible to draw tentative inferences.

The normal prices of grain in Northern India at the end of the sixteenth century have been preserved for us by Abul Fazl, and we are on fairly safe ground in concluding, first, that the

[1] The *Agra Accounts*, which are quoted elsewhere, extend over only two years, one at least of which was altogether abnormal.

relative values of the various food-grains were much the same as in 1910–12, and, second, that actual prices rose sevenfold between the two periods indicated. I have not found data for the north between 1600 and 1660, but the following facts are on record for the markets of Gujarat. In the year 1609, Finch says that rice " of the best " could be got in Surat at a rial-of-eight per quintal, which is equivalent to about 65 lb. per rupee, and we can safely infer that ordinary qualities were substantially cheaper. In 1611 rice for an English ship was bought at 65¾ lb., wheat at 53¾, and a pulse (*mung*) at 72¾ lb. : probably these figures were substantially above the current market-rates, for the buyers were in a hurry to get the ship provisioned, and they had little experience of the country. The purchase was made in October, when wheat would be near the maximum of the year. In 1619, a consignment of wheat sent to Bantam was invoiced at a price which works out to 78¼ lb. free on board, representing something over 80 lb. in the market. In 1623 we have a record of wheat-meal bought for baking bread for the ships, and, taking the usual contemporary ratio of meal to wheat, we get a rate of 85 lb. of wheat per rupee. The Dutch factor van Twist says that before the famine of 1630, the usual price of wheat was 33¾ Dutch pounds for 10⅔ stivers, which makes nearly 82½ lb. avoirdupois per rupee.[1] In none of the specific cases quoted is there any complaint that the price was exceptional, nor have I found any indications that scarcity prevailed in the years to which they relate; they appear to me to support the definite statement of van Twist, who, as his record and his writings prove, possessed a minute knowledge of Gujarat, and I think the inference is justified that, in the first quarter of the century, the usual, or normal, rate of wheat was somewhere about 80 or 85 lb. the rupee. I have found no indication of the usual price of rice, beyond a statement that in Broach it was about 65 lb. for a rupee.

[1] The *Gujarat Report*, written in 1629, gives the usual price in Broach at a figure which works out to 75½ lb. It is practically certain that van Twist had this report before him when he wrote; perhaps he chose a rather higher figure out of regard for the position of Gujarat as a whole, but the difference is not very material.

In the transaction of 1611 referred to above, it was somewhat cheaper than wheat, and this relation might be inferred from a consideration of the sources of supply; but the difference in value of the varieties of rice was, and is, so great that it would in any case be dangerous to base any conclusions on such figures.

The rise of prices during the famine was enormous. In November 1630, the English factors bought wheat at the rate of 13¾ lb., and a month later they found that grain was unprocurable "though at sevenfold the price of former times accustomed"; if the normal was, as suggested, 80 or 85 lbs., this means that the rate had now risen to 12 lb. or less. The year 1631 was marked by further calamities, and in September we hear of 2½ ser for a mahmudi, giving a rate of very little over 6 lb. per rupee; supplies arrived during the winter, and in January 1632 the rate was about 12½ lb., until the supplies were engrossed, when prices rose again. The next quotation I have found relates to the year 1635, when a consignment of wheat was bought for Goa at 33 lb., and this seems to mark the end of the period of pressure; prices were falling, seasonable rain had produced abundance of all sorts of grain, and in 1636 prices were lower than before the famine. We have seen in a previous section that the price of indigo remained high until 1638, but was down to the normal in 1639 and 1640; this fact appears to confirm the statement that the old normal was restored in the case of food-grains also, and the two years' delay in the case of indigo is what might be expected in view of the precedence naturally given to the former.

There are thus definite grounds for the inferences that the normal price of wheat in Gujarat was about 80 to 85 lb. per rupee in the first quarter of the seventeenth century, that it was not permanently altered by the effects of the famine of 1630, and that the old rate persisted at least to the year 1640. At this point the supply of direct data fails, and, except in seasons of scarcity, I have not found a single positive indication of the price of any food-grain in Gujarat during the next twenty years. This absence of data is not without significance. For the English factors the time was one of drastic retrenchment, and I think we should have heard of it if their bills for wages and household expenses had been materially increased by a rise in prices ; the absence of complaints on this score suggests that causes of complaint were wanting, and that prices kept within the limits regarded by the factors as customary.[1]

In the absence of direct data, some light may be thrown on the question by the rate of wages paid in Surat. A letter written in 1636 says that the wages paid to peons had formerly been from five to seven mahmudis monthly ; the rates were raised in 1634 by three mahmudis, and an attempt to revert to the old rates was successfully resisted by the peons on the ground that, although food-prices had dropped, clothing still remained expensive. In 1636, therefore, when food-prices had returned to the normal, the peons received from 8 to 10 mahmudis. I have found no subsequent reference to their wages for the rest of our period, a fact which by itself suggests that there was no important change, but Ovington, who reached Surat in the year 1690, found that the rate was then 4 rupees, or 9 mahmudis at the exchange current late in our period : thus the rate showed no change after half a century, and the fact supports the inference that prices of food had not risen to such an extent as to necessitate a rise in wages. We are justified then in saying that, while normal prices of food did not change between 1610 and 1640, there is no evidence to show that they changed during the next twenty years, and such indications as are available suggest that they remained fairly constant.

No surprise need be felt that wheat should stand at about 85 lb. in Gujarat a very few years after the rate of 185 lb. had been recorded as prevalent in Northern India : the figures which have been given for the cost of land-transport show that it would have required nearly three rupees to bring 85 lb. of wheat from Agra to Gujarat, and obviously no one would have thought of doing this so long as the total return would be only a rupee. The markets were in fact quite distinct,

[1] In 1650, and again in 1659, we find statements that prices had risen in consequence of failure of the rains, but there is no suggestion of a change in normal rates.

and it required the enormous rise in prices which has been indicated to attract distant supplies to the scene of a famine. The great advantage of water-carriage in such conditions is shown by the fact that during the famine the English at Surat were buying wheat from Persia, while fifteen years later they were able to forward supplies to famine-stricken Madras; the coasts could help each other, but in the interior nothing could be done without such a rise in prices as occurred in Gujarat.

In the India of our period, even more than at the present day, to talk of the price of food-grains was also to talk of the purchasing-power of the money in circulation. Measured in terms of food, the value of the rupee fell as from 7 to 1 in Northern India between 1595 and the period 1910–12, which I have taken as the basis of the calculations I have published on this subject. The wholesale price of wheat in Gujarat during those years was about 20 lb. per rupee, so that in this case the value of the rupee fell as from 4 or $4\frac{1}{4}$ to 1 in the course of three centuries. Whether any portion of this fall took place during our period is a question of real importance, because, until it has been answered, we cannot reach definite conclusions regarding the incidence of the land-revenue, which in the seventeenth century may justly be described as, next to the rainfall, the weightiest factor in the economic life of the country. It is clear that practically all wholesale transactions in Gujarat were settled in silver coin, while there are no grounds for inferring any large change in the velocity of the circulation. Now, with the exception of the clove-market on the East Coast, all the prices hitherto discussed are silver-prices: we have seen that spices eventually became dear owing to the perfection of the Dutch monopoly, but, apart from spices, we have found no trace of a rise in the normal price of imports, of a typical export, or of the staple food-grains; and to say so much is merely to say that we have found no trace of a fall in the value of silver money. It is true that our examination has not extended to all commodities, but, with the exception of cotton goods, raw cotton, and oilseeds, it has covered most of the ground: data for raw cotton and oilseeds are wanting, as I have said above, while, as regards cotton goods, the interpretation of the figures which are available is so dependent on obscure questions of quality that I have thought it best to ignore them. It can be shown, for example, that broad and narrow baftas, the staple calicoes of Gujarat, were bought for England rather more cheaply about 1640 than about 1620,[1] but complaints of the deterioration of weaving after the famine make it dangerous to base any argument on the decline in price; while for tracts which escaped the famine, prices are not on record over a sufficiently long period to justify any inference. The evidence then is incomplete, but it appears to me to permit of the provisional conclusion that the probabilities are entirely against the occurrence of a fall in the value of silver during the half century which we are considering. To establish such an occurrence, it would be necessary to demonstrate two propositions: first, that a rise in price, not otherwise accounted for, took place in a number of commodities, equal in importance to the aggregate of those which have been discussed; and second, that the prices of imports, indigo, and food-grains were depressed by causes of which I have found no trace, so that they failed to respond to the assumed fall in silver. Until some evidence to support these propositions comes to light, it would be unprofitable to discuss the question further, and I shall proceed on the provisional conclusion that in the Gujarat markets silver was a fairly stable standard of value between 1610 and 1660.

If this conclusion be accepted for Gujarat, it can safely be extended to Northern India, taken as a whole. The north may be regarded as one market for silver: there was practically no local production or large influx over the land frontier, and the supply was maintained by the imports on the coast, that

[1] The average prices, free on board, shown for the large consignments of 1619 in the table given in the last chapter were, broad baftas, 6·3 and 6·8 mahmudis per piece, and narrow baftas, 3·8 and 5·0 ma. In the invoice for December 1640 (*Original Correspondence*, 1764), the corresponding prices (including charges to the ship's side) are, broad baftas 5·2 and 5·5; narrow, 3·8 and 4·1 ma.

is to say in Bengal, Sind, and Gujarat. The account which has been given of the maritime trade of Bengal shows that the influx of silver cannot have been great until the last decade of our period, when the Dutch restored and extended the traditional export business; Sind was even less important from this point of view, and I think that students of the contemporary records will agree that the trade of the various ports of Gujarat constituted the principal source of supply. We may then regard the silver-using north as a reservoir replenished chiefly from Gujarat, though subsidiary streams entered it from Bengal and Sind; but we must not regard the silver as absolutely mobile, because the cost and risk of transport were by no means negligible. In these circumstances, if the total supply had exceeded the absorptive capacity of the country, so that the quantity of silver in circulation tended to rise, the resulting fall in its value would have been most apparent in Gujarat, where the principal supplies were received and minted: and since we have found that no noticeable fall in value occurred in Gujarat, we may infer that the stability of silver as a standard extended throughout the country, or in other words that the stream of silver poured in by the Dutch and other merchants was not in excess of the absorptive capacity of Northern and Western India taken as a whole.

In this connection it may be well to notice the history of the Mogul mint at Surat, because at first sight the facts relating to it might suggest a large increase in the currency. Practically all the silver imported, whether foreign coin or bullion, was taken directly to a mint and reissued in the form of rupees or mahmudis.[1] At the opening of our period, the chief mint of Gujarat was located at Ahmadabad, where it had been established by Akbar after his conquest of the country. Akbar had also set up a mint in Surat; it was closed for a time, but was reopened in 1620, presumably in

[1] As explained in Appendix D, mahmudis were coined up to about 1637 in the mint at Mulher in Baglan. I gather that this coinage at Surat was not undertaken when that mint was reopened in 1620, but in any case it was concerned mainly with rupees.

consequence of the growing importance of the seaport. By the year 1634 the amount of silver imported at Surat had outrun the capacity of the local mint, and two years later the difficulty of obtaining currency was one of the reasons urged in favour of a proposal to move the English headquarters to Ahmadabad; but the difficulty was met by increasing the capacity of the Surat mint, which thenceforward appears to have been equal to all ordinary demands. It is certain then that imports of silver into Surat increased largely, but it does not follow that there was an increase in Gujarat taken as a whole, and in point of fact the change must be regarded as an indication of the transfer of business to Surat from Cambay. The chief trade of the Portuguese was conducted at the latter port, and the silver imported by them was naturally taken to the mint at Ahmadabad; when trade passed from the Portuguese to the Dutch and English, Surat prospered but Cambay declined; and the large increase in coinage at Surat was counterbalanced by a decrease at the northern mint.

This change can be traced in the collections of Mogul coins in Indian museums, which in the aggregate are sufficiently extensive to afford a rough indication of the relative importance of the different mints. The following figures have been extracted from the catalogues of the three principal collections.[1]

NUMBERS OF SPECIMENS OF SILVER COINS IN INDIAN MUSEUMS

Reign.	Ahmadabad Mint.				Surat Mint.			
	Lucknow.	Lahore.	Calcutta.	Total.	Lucknow.	Lahore.	Calcutta.	Total.
Akbar . .	153	51	53	257	0	1	0	1
Jahangir .	79	27	32	138	14	4	5	23
Shahjahan .	34	9	12	55	88	22	31	141
Aurangzeb .	21	5	11	37	131	55	91	277
Total .	287	92	108	487	233	82	127	442

Taking the whole period from Akbar to Aurangzeb, it will

[1] The figures of Aurangzeb's coinage include the few specimens minted by Murad Bakhsh in 1658.

be seen that the two mints are about equally represented in the collections, but that Ahmadabad declined as Surat rose. The extension at Surat was carried out early in Shahjahan's reign, and thenceforward it became the chief mint of Gujarat, supplying nine-tenths of the specimens available for the reign of Aurangzeb. These figures then support the inference that during our period there was not a large proportionate increase in the influx of silver into Gujarat; the direct trade to Europe was undoubtedly a new feature, but its volume was small relatively to the existing commerce, which we have seen no reason to think was largely extended; and, taking the business of this part of the country as a whole, we are justified in the view that the course of trade was not such as to produce a general rise in prices of produce.[1]

Turning now to the other side of India, it may be said at once that I have found practically no data for the course of prices of food-grains on the Coromandel coast. We know that famines were frequent in this region, and that in bad seasons prices rose enormously, but we do not know their tendency in ordinary years, and can say only that the absence of complaints regarding increase in the cost of living is a fact consistent with the theory that normal prices did not greatly change. The stability of wage-rates stated in silver points in the same direction. Methwold, who left Masulipatam in 1622, put the rate for the factory servants at a rial-of-eight monthly, or approximately two rupees. In 1658, William Smyth gave the wages of factory servants in the same neighbourhood as from 4s. to 5s. a month; the rupee was at this time taken as equivalent to 2s. 3d., so that the rate is identical with that known to Methwold thirty-six years before, and it becomes highly improbable that any large change in the cost of living can have occurred in the interval.

In Bengal, on the other hand, there is definite evidence of a large and sudden rise in food prices between the years 1650

[1] It is probable that remittances of silver from Persia to Gujarat fell off during our period to an extent which would counteract part of the increased import from Europe, though I have not found sufficiently precise data to justify a definite assertion; the balance of trade must have been affected by the new export of silk from the Gulf.

and 1660, which is of interest as throwing light on the economic position of that part of the country. It will be remembered that the active development of the trade of Bengal began when the Dutch and English settled at Hooghly about the former year. In December of 1658 the English factors applied for an increase in the allowance for housekeeping charges on account of the great rise in the cost of living; their letter is not extant, but from the reply sent by the Company it appears that the allegation was made that provisions had trebled in value, and that the Company did not entirely accept this statement, but called for a detailed account. We may conjecture that the factors exaggerated the extent of the rise, or at least made their case look as strong as possible, and it would be unsafe to conclude that prices had actually trebled, but we are justified in holding that a rise had taken place so great as to render inadequate an allowance which had been fixed less than ten years before.

This rise does not represent the beginning of a divergence between Bengal and the rest of the Indian sea-board, but rather the removal of an anomaly which appears to have been of some standing. By December of 1658, local prices had risen very sharply, but, just eight years before, such commodities as rice, butter, oil, and wheat could be procured "all at half the price or little more that they are in other parts"; in other words, up to the end of 1650, prices in Bengal were abnormally low compared with those which were familiar to the English merchants, that is to say, those which prevailed elsewhere on the coast of India; but a few years of rapidly expanding trade, financed almost entirely by silver, had brought prices up to, or possibly somewhat above, the familiar standard. The natural inference is that the supply of silver in Bengal had previously been inadequate in comparison with what was available on other portions of the sea-board, so that silver prices would be normally depressed, and that the sudden increase in imported supplies occurring from 1650 onwards sufficed to remove this special cause, and bring Bengal into line with the rest of the coast. This inference is in accordance with the fact that for a long time previously Bengal had exported rice to countries which would more naturally have obtained their supplies from Coromandel. To take one instance, Fitch records that Sunargaon (near the present Dacca) served all "India" and Ceylon; by India we may assume that he meant the Western Coast, to which the trade in provisions is mentioned by many other authorities, and we have to ask why rice should be carried thither from Bengal when it could be obtained from Coromandel by a shorter, and much less dangerous, voyage. The only reasonable answer seems to be that the prime cost of provisions in Bengal must have been so much lower as to cover the increased charge for transit, and that prices were, in fact, low is shown by the narratives of various observers from Caesar Frederick to William Methwold. Writing of the years about 1620, the latter spoke of the traffic in provisions and other goods from Bengal to Masulipatam, "which, considering the plenty of the place whereunto they bring them, should come hither as we say of coals carried to Newcastle, yet here they sell them to contented profit"—a striking testimony to the difference in the purchasing power of silver in two coastal regions linked only by imperfect means of communication.

It appears, then, to be a fact that Bengal was inadequately provided with silver until about the year 1650. A probable explanation of this shortage may be found in the working of the revenue system. The land revenue was paid mainly in silver; much of it was usually remitted to the Mogul Court in the same form; and the amount of imported silver retained in the province was apparently insufficient to satisfy the local demand, so that silver would normally be expensive, or, what is the same thing, commodities would normally be cheap. The entire revenue of Bengal is given in the *Ain-i-Akbari* as close on 150 lakhs of rupees, but there is some reason to think that this record is exaggerated, if not fictitious; taking various statements which relate to the reign of Shahjahan, we find that the demand stood at about 130 lakhs of rupees.[1] Some part of this was doubtless spent locally,

[1] The statistics of Bengal given in the *Ain* cover tracts which were outside the Mogul Empire at the time of compilation, and the figures for these, at

but if we allow for the fact that grantees, like the State, commonly remitted part of their receipts to the capital in the form of cash, we must recognise that the regular drain up-country must have amounted to a very large figure, probably something like 50 lakhs a year. We have seen in a former chapter that the sea-borne trade of Bengal had been at a low ebb for many years before 1650, and, while we cannot calculate its actual value, we need not wonder if it were insufficient at once to meet this drain and provide the province with the silver it required. Now the Dutch records show that their trade with Bengal was of the order of a lakh of rupees in magnitude in the years before 1650, but in 1661 it was close on 20 lakhs, the increase representing, as we have seen, new business, and being financed mainly by imports of silver; simultaneously the English were developing new business on a smaller but substantial scale; and it appears to me to be reasonable to infer that this sudden increase in the influx of silver, approaching, if not exceeding, 20 lakhs annually in the closing years of our period, was sufficiently large to effect a material alteration in the monetary position in Bengal. I have not found any figures to suggest that the revenue demand was raised during these years,[1] and, if the drain to the north remained approximately constant, the increased supply of silver would go a long way to satisfy the local demand, and the main cause of depressed prices would be removed.

The final result of this disquisition is that, while the evidence available is incomplete, what evidence there is can be summarised in the tentative conclusion that, during our period, silver was stable in value throughout the north and

---

least, cannot be accepted as representing facts. *Ascoli* (p. 25) gives the revenue of the year 1658 as 131 lakhs of rupees. In the British Museum I find the revenue given as 52,46, lakhs of dams in three MSS. (*Or.* 1842, and *Addl.* 6588, and 6598); taking 40 dams to the rupee, this gives the figure quoted by Mr. Ascoli.

[1] *Ascoli* (*l.c.*), following the Fifth Report of the Select Committee appointed in 1808, says: "It is probable that Shah Shuja's revenue roll [131 lakhs of rupees] was not a new settlement or assessment, but merely a clerical revision." The next assessment on record was not made until 1722.

west of India; but that in Bengal it depreciated rapidly during the closing decade, thereby removing a long-standing anomaly, and bringing prices on the Hooghly into line with those which prevailed elsewhere on the Indian sea-board.

6. Gold and Copper

Having reached the tentative conclusion that, except in Bengal, silver was a stable standard of value throughout our period, it remains to consider the markets for gold and copper, both of which circulated as currency on the basis of their value as commodities. In Appendix D, I have indicated that the silver price of the gold coins known as new pagodas rose during our period on the East Coast, and we should expect to find that the gold market in Gujarat showed a corresponding rise, but the data on record are too few to establish, or to controvert, this proposition. As regards the middle of our period, all that can be said is that this market, like every other, was disorganised for a time by the famine, because the income of the rich had failed so that they could not buy, while poorer people were forced to sell their jewellery in order to purchase food. After the famine, in the year 1635, the English 20-shilling piece sold for 20 mahmudis, while in 1646 its price was 21½ mahmudis, and this rise may be significant, but more data are required for a conclusion, especially as the gold market was subject to professional manipulation; the English factors complained on one occasion that they lay at the mercy of the shroffs or exchangers of money, "who at their pleasures raise and fall the price of either specie as themselves please," and the difference noted may be merely a fluctuation of the market. In 1652 the Surat factors reported that gold was more likely to rise than to fall, but I have not found any actual quotations for the closing years of our period. The circulation of gold in the Mogul Empire was in any case so limited that the question of its value did not affect currency-users in general: in the south we should expect to find indications of a fall in gold prices, but here again data are wanting, and the only commodities for which I have been able to construct a regular series of quotations are the spices, which, as has been shown, were dealt in at rates determined by the Dutch monopolists.

Our information regarding copper is more extensive, and also of more general interest. The position at the opening of our period was that Northern India depended entirely, or almost entirely, on the produce of the local mines, while the south was furnished mainly by the supplies imported by the Portuguese from Japan. The metal was very expensive in the north, as is shown by the fact that the mint price works out at about 84 lb. of wheat for a pound of copper, the corresponding figure in 1910–12 being 16 lb. of wheat; and it cannot have been materially cheaper in the south, for in that case imported supplies would have been diverted from Malabar and Goa to the ports of Gujarat. At this price the metal was a luxury, and utensils made of it were much rarer than is now the case; the industrial demand was small, and, apart from occasional requisitions for founding cannon, the various mints were probably in the aggregate among the principal consumers. Up to about 1620 I have found no signs of a material change in the value of copper in Northern India. The official rate of exchange in Akbar's time was 40 dam, that is 80 Gujarat pice, for a rupee, equivalent to 32 pice for a mahmudi; in 1609 Finch put the current rate for the mahmudi at 31 or 32 pice, "varying as copper riseth and falleth"; and early in 1615 Elkington quoted 34 pice, mentioning the tendency of the rate to fluctuate, so that up to this year, at any rate, there is no sign of a rise in value. Nor had the import into Gujarat begun, for in 1619, when the English factors at Surat wanted a consignment of copper for Persia, they first inquired for it at Burhanpur, that is to say, in the direction of some of the mines, and eventually they sent it in the form of coin, though the amount was only 330 lb., a quantity which would assuredly have been procurable locally if a regular import trade had been in existence. At some time in the next decade a marked rise in price occurred. The earliest reference I have found to an alteration in the rate is Pelsart's statement, made in 1626, that at Agra 58 pice went to the rupee, a remarkable divergence from the former rate of 80. In 1636 the English factors at Surat wrote that for two or three years before the famine the mahmudi was not worth above 20, 21, or 22 pice; on these terms the rupee would be equivalent to from 50 to 55 pice. The rate in 1636 was 25 to a mahmudi, in 1640 it was 24, and twenty years later it was still between 24 and 25, so that, neglecting minor fluctuations, the rupee, which, at any rate up to 1616, was worth 80 pice (or 40 dam), from 1627 onwards was worth 60 pice (30 dam) or a little more or less.[1]

The rise in price was followed by the development of a steady import of Japanese copper into Gujarat. On their establishment in Japan, the Dutch had lost little time in undertaking the supply of the East Coast from that source, but the first recorded appearance of their copper in Surat is in the year 1635,[2] and for the next few years their sales were satisfactory, so that it is clear that a real demand was being met. In 1640 the export of copper from Japan was prohibited, and during the seven or eight years covered by this restriction, we find the Dutch selling copper from Sweden and other European sources both at Surat and at Masulipatam; export from Japan was resumed in 1648, and the trade appears to have continued without further interruption, while supplies were also carried to Bengal, when the Dutch had secured a footing in that province.

Some light is thrown on the conditions of the market at the end of our period by entries in the Batavia Journal for the year 1661. A letter from Surat explained a sudden rise in the price of the metal by two causes: first, that imported supplies were inadequate; and second, that owing to the civil war the northern mines were short of workmen. The authorities in Gujarat met this emergency by prohibiting

[1] The market rate of exchange between silver and copper fluctuated considerably. In the *Agra Accounts* for 1637–39 the rupee was taken as only 50 pice in January 1637, 52 pice in April, 54 pice in September, 55 pice in January 1638, and 58 pice in the following October.

[2] The apparent delay in meeting the needs of Western India is explained by the fact that from 1629 to 1634 the trade of the Dutch in Japan was practically suspended owing to political difficulties; imports of copper began as soon as these had been finally adjusted.

exports of copper (coined or uncoined), and the rate for a rupee rose in consequence from 30 to 33 dams. At the close of our period, then, we find that the silver price of copper had permanently risen by something like 20 per cent, so that the approximate number of pice to a rupee had fallen from the old standard of 80 to nearly the now accepted standard of 64; and further, that the supplies of Northern India were no longer exclusively local, but depended in part on what could be brought from the mines of Japan.

So much for the facts on record. I have found nothing to account for the sudden rise in price, but the results of our examination of silver prices justify the inference that the cause was connected with copper, and not with silver, so that we must look for either a permanent increase in demand, or a permanent decrease in supply. The former is in itself improbable, I can find nothing in the history of the period to suggest it, and I have been unable to conjecture anything which would account for the facts; it appears to me much more likely that the supply from some of the Indian mines failed in the years before 1630, and the permanence of the rise in price indicates that the failure was not a temporary matter. We know that the mines of Rajputana and Central India have failed since Akbar's reign, when they were the only source of supply for the bulk of the Mogul Empire, and I suggest that the failure of some of them occurred at this particular time, and that the resulting rise in the price of copper made it profitable for the Dutch to establish an import trade into Gujarat.

AUTHORITIES FOR CHAPTER V

Taken as a whole this chapter is based on the English commercial correspondence calendared in *Letters Received* and *English Factories*, together with the reports from India contained in the *Dagh Register*. The detailed references given below are illustrative rather than exhaustive; a full appreciation of the course of markets requires the study of these authorities in detail.

SECTION 1.—Finch's view of Indian merchants is in *Letters Received*, i. 30. For monopoly of lead, see *English Factories*, i. 134; of saltpetre, *idem*, viii. 53, and *Dagh Register*, March 31, 1641; for prohibition of export of copper, *idem*, October 18, 1661. For the Ahmadabad indigo monopoly, see *English Factories*, viii. 130, 143; for spices, *Dagh Register*, December 26, 1641; for cloth, *English Factories*, ix. 22, and *Dagh Register*, May 20, 1641; for food in famine time, *English Factories*, iv. 209; for merchants as governors, *idem*, i. 147. The Imperial monopoly of indigo is described in *idem*, iv. 324-28, and v. 1, 70-73. The account of the general monopoly at Hooghly is taken from *Dagh Register*, June 10, 1636; for monopoly of Dutch trade, see *idem*, March 12, 1625; and *English Factories*, iii. 282. *Manucci's* sketch of Mir Jumla is i. 231: his commercial activities are referred to frequently in *English Factories*, ix. and x. The data quoted for cost of land transport are in *English Factories*, i. 74, vi. 135, ix. 52; *Agra Accounts*, MS. 120; and *Mundy*, ii. 278, 291. Prices in Northern India were discussed by the writer in *Journal R.A.S.*, October 1917 and July 1918.

SECTION 2.—Competition between Dutch and English is a regular feature of the commercial records; *e.g. English Factories*, iii. 208, v. 205, 206; for the difficulty experienced in working together, see *idem*, v. 1, 69, 142. Virji Vora's name appears so frequently in the English and Dutch reports from Surat that a full list of references would be tedious; the following will perhaps suffice to guide readers to the principal topics. His syndicates are referred to in *Dagh Register*, October 3, 1641, and June 9, 1645 (Surat); also *English Factories*, viii. 206, 257. His foreign relations, *idem*, iii. 212, vii. 253, viii. 105. His domination of the market, *idem*, v. 24, 218; vii. 18, 108; viii. 5; x. 16, 160. His difficulties with the authorities, *idem*, iv. 31; vi. 94, 108-110. His loans to the English, *idem*, iii. 271, 300; iv. 193, 216; v. 97, 216; vii. 5, 152; ix. 119, 141; x. 360. His wealth, *Thévenot*, 46.

"Malaya" is mentioned occasionally in *English Factories*, but more frequently in the *Dagh Register*; see August 14, 1634, for his death; November 27, 1640, February 19, 1641, February 15, 1643, for his successor's political activities; June 1, 1644, for his financial position; March 14, 1637, November 27, 1640, May 6 and August 19, 1645, for commercial policy.

For the activities of brokers, see in particular *English Factories*, v. 102; for their misconduct, *idem*, iii. 239; iv. 101; v. 171; vi. 225; viii. 209. For shroffs, *idem*, iii. 296; vii. 21; and *Tavernier*, i. 29. For marine insurance, *English Factories*, ii. 101; vii. 92, 161; viii. 259. For gluts and consequent failures, see—at Aden, *Dagh Register*, March 22, 1636; at Mocha and Basra, *idem*, July 18, 1644 (Surat); and *English Factories*, vii. 208; viii. 184; at Achin, *Dagh Register*, May 20 and December 15, 1641; March 10, 1642.

SECTION 3.—The references to quotations for indigo are given in the opening table. For the initial standard and Finch's estimates, see *Letters Received*, i. 23, 28, 306; ii. 152, 214, 248. For the famine price in 1630, *English Factories*, iv. 125; for curtailment of cultivation, *idem*, iv. 325; for adulteration, *idem*, vi. 273; vii. 163; viii. 31, 203. *Tavernier's* statement of price is ii. 9.

SECTION 4.—*Quicksilver*. For demand, see *English Factories*, iii. 325, 334; ix. 121; for private trade, *idem*, iv. 32, and *Court Minutes*, February 13, 1629, and October 22, 1630. Prices up to 1626 are taken from *Letters Received*, i. 32, 235, 305; ii. 191; iii. 9; iv. 296; *English Factories*, i. 55,

327; ii. 158; *Factory Records* (Surat), vol. 102, No. 478; and *Original Correspondence*, 1241. For the glut of 1630 and subsequent low prices, see *English Factories*, iv. 32, 89, 102, 180, 275; v. 82, 205; and for the revival, *idem*, viii. 188, 282; ix. 121, 252; x. 199; and *Dagh Register*, May 1, 1661.

Lead. For the official monopoly, see *English Factories*, i. 323; iii. 157, 196; vii. 210; for alternative markets, *idem*, v. 69, 218; vi. 204, 275; ix. 71, 104. Quotations are from *Letters Received*, i. 33, 235, 238, 300; ii. 193; iii. 8, 9; iv. 296, 336; v. 107; vi. 159; *English Factories*, i. 323; iii. 334; iv. 32, 129; v. 7; vi. 98, 204; viii. 7, 216, 282; ix. 140; and x. 199; also *Original Correspondence*, 1794, 1808.

Cloves. The price at the Mogul Court is given in *Ain* (translation), i. 64. The early quotations at Surat are from *Original Correspondence*, 609; *Terpstra's Surat*, Appendix VII; and *English Factories*, ii. 25. Prices from 1633 to 1649 are from *idem*, viii. 206, 257; *Original Correspondence*, 1543A, 1558; and *Dagh Register*, May 14, 1633, December 26, 1641, July 3, 1643, and June 9, 1645. The final monopoly prices are in *idem*, August 17, 1657; May 1, 1661; and *English Factories*, x. 157. For East Coast prices, see *idem*, i. 41; ii. 136; vi. 47, 186; and *Dagh Register*, March 27, 1631; November 25, 1632; November 29, 1640; December 23, 1641; December 29, 1644; May 14, 1645; June 3, 1661.

Section 5.—The prices of food grains in Northern India are discussed in *Journal R.A.S.*, October 1917 and July 1918. The Surat prices are taken from *Letters Received*, i. 31, 141; *English Factories*, i. 63; ii. 254; and *van Twist*, III. For famine prices and the recovery, see *English Factories*, iv. 95, 122, 165, 196, 209; v. 146, 149, 151, 177. Retrenchment is dealt with in *idem*, vii. 121, 171; viii. 245; ix. 14, 198, 216; peons' wages in *idem*, v. 151, and *Ovington*, 392; for the scarcity of 1658–59, see *English Factories*, x. 196, 306; and for movement of grain by sea, *idem*, iv. 196; viii. 74, 106.

The Surat mint is referred to in *idem*, i. 36, 218; v. 68, 216; vi. 84; also *Ain* (translation), i. 31. For wages on the East Coast, see *Methwold*, 1001, and *English Factories*, x. 261. For the rise in prices in Bengal, see *idem*, x. 407; and for the antecedent cheapness, *idem*, viii. 338; *Original Correspondence*, 2188; *Purchas*, II. x. 1720, 1737; and *Methwold*, 1005. The value of Dutch trade in Bengal has been abstracted from successive entries in the *Dagh Register* for the years in question.

Section 6.—The remarks on the price of gold at Surat are based on *English Factories*, iii. 296; iv. 123; v. 121; viii. 7; ix. 141. The position in regard to copper is discussed at greater length in *India at the Death of Akbar*, 148 ff. The early exchange quotations are from *Pelsart*, 11; *Letters Received*, i. 34; iii. 11; and *English Factories*, i. 100, 114, 142-44; those from 1636 onwards, in *idem*, v. 206; vi. 249; and *Dagh Register*, June 26, 1661. For the import of copper, see *idem*, March 22, 1636, March 14, 1637, February 20 and October 30, 1648, April 12, 1661, and many other incidental entries; also *English Factories*, ii. 260; v. 81 *n.*, 101, 120. The crisis of 1661 is mentioned in *idem*, x. 306, and at greater length in several passages in the *Dagh Register* for that year.

CHAPTER VI

PRODUCTION AND CONSUMPTION

1. Changes in Production

The system of production which prevailed at the beginning of our period has been described in the third and fourth chapters of *India at the Death of Akbar*, and it would be a waste of time for me to go over the same ground a second time. The authorities for the first half of the seventeenth century do not furnish a formal or detailed description of the system, but incidentally they throw much light on its practical working; I do not think it is going too far to say that every glimpse of the activities of producers given in the commercial records is strictly in accordance with the views I stated in the former book, while the records as a whole could not be interpreted on any different hypothesis. The land, by far the most important source of the national income, was cultivated in small holdings by peasants, for the most part short of capital, and contributing a large share of the produce to the revenue of the State. Other forms of production, whether mining or manufacture, were likewise organised in numerous small units, and they were dominated by scarcity of capital and the demands of the Government or its nominees. Producers were, as a rule, anxious to meet the market, but were not in a position to seek new markets for themselves; we look in vain for any traces of productive energy of the type familiar in Western countries at the present day; and the administrative conditions of the period were, as we shall see, more likely to sterilise than to foster any tendency towards enterprise which may have existed among the people. If we compare the close of our period with its commencement, we find no important changes either in products or in methods, and the records tell us only of efforts to meet the demand expressed by buyers, of the degree of success achieved, and of the hindrances arising from various forms of official activity.

As regards agriculture, the list of products of commercial interest shows only a single change, the appearance of tobacco.[1] We have seen in a previous chapter that the dried leaf had become an article of export from the Coromandel coast as well as from Gujarat, and the more important Indian consumption appears to have developed with remarkable rapidity. Jahangir prohibited smoking in the year 1617, and, whatever the effect may have been, his decree may be taken as showing that the practice was already becoming popular. Manucci, writing of the early years of Aurangzeb's reign, says that the farmer of taxes paid Rs. 5000 a day for the tobacco duty at Delhi alone, and, while we may question the precise figure, which appears to be impossibly high, we may accept his statement as evidence of the wide extension of the habit. He adds that the tax was abolished as the result of an outrage committed by the collector, and comments on the benefit accruing from the abolition to the poor, a remark which indicates that consumption had become general. A new and profitable commercial crop had thus become established, but, as I have said, it stands alone.

The agricultural products for which the commercial demand increased were indigo and cotton, to which may be added silk, as the bulk of the silk handled was produced by domesticated worms, fed on the cultivated mulberry. I have shown

[1] Two notes in *English Factories* (i. 296, ii. 70), which suggest that maize was handled commercially, are corrected in *idem*, vii. 66. Potatoes are occasionally mentioned (*e.g. Methwold*, 995, and *English Factories*, ii. 191), but I have found nothing to show that a wholesale trade in them existed, and it is impossible to say with certainty what particular tubers are indicated by the word, which changed its meaning in the course of the seventeenth century: probably the sweet-potato (*Batatas*) is referred to in the passages quoted.

in a previous chapter that at least a large proportion of the European offtake of indigo, yarn, and calico was definitely new, as was the Japanese market for Bengal silk, and the fact that the new demands were met indicates that production responded effectively. Peasants were not governed solely by custom in their arrangements for cropping, but attempted to follow the markets. The scarcity of cotton goods in Gujarat after the famine was attributed by the English merchants in part to lack of raw material, "which we conceive doth chiefly arise from the great price which all sorts of grain hath yielded for some forepast years, which hath undoubtedly disposed the country people to those courses which have been most profitable for them, and so discontinued the planting of cotton"; while early in 1644 we are told that the production of indigo in Sind was falling off year by year in consequence of reduced demand and a heavy fall in price. The adjustment of supply to demand might, however, be imperfect, or at least retarded; I have suggested in the last chapter that the low price of indigo in Gujarat about the year 1622 was probably due to over-estimation of the new demand for Western Europe, and in other cases the want of capital prevented peasants from seizing an opportunity of making a profit, as in Sind later in 1644, and on more than one occasion on the Coromandel coast.

Further light is thrown on this subject by some incidents arising out of a sudden expansion of the demand for a particular commodity. The opposition to the entry of the English into the Red Sea trade, which has been referred to in an earlier chapter, was inspired partly by the fear that there would not be enough cotton goods for all merchants, as actually happened in the year 1618; while ten years later the boycott of the English yarn-buyers was organised by the weavers, who were alarmed for the supply of their raw material. The alarm was, I think, natural in both cases, in view of the small stocks of cloth, or of yarn, ordinarily carried by the market; but the important point is that such incidents did not recur. A few years after these difficulties, the English were buying much larger quantities of cotton goods, and the

Dutch at least equally large quantities of yarn, without arousing any similar manifestations of hostility, and the reasonable inference is that the supply of raw cotton and of yarn had been adjusted to the increased demand. We read of no similar incidents in connection with the earliest purchases of indigo by the English merchants, but in this case, it will be remembered, the Portuguese demand was suspended owing to war just when the English began to buy in earnest, so that the existing supply was probably at least sufficient for all buyers. As regards silk, the Batavia Journals are missing for the critical years, and I do not know whether there was any initial opposition to the Dutch purchases; but when the new trade was definitely established, there are no signs of local hostility to their large exports, such as we should expect to hear of if their effect had been to deprive Indian workers of their raw material, and it is more probable that in this case also the supply was increased to meet the new demand.

These inferences are in accordance with the direct evidence already quoted that the peasants did their best to follow the market, and justify the conclusion that the effect of Dutch and English purchases was to extend the production of indigo, cotton, and, probably, silk. In other respects I can detect no signs of any noteworthy change in agricultural production during our period. The outstanding features of the time relate to distribution rather than production, and can be studied most conveniently in connection with the revenue administration, which was the principal agent at work; for the present it must suffice to say that the surplus income left to the peasant was tending to decrease, where it had not already vanished, and that the impetus to productive effort on his part was being correspondingly weakened. The essence of his business was to adjust his cropping from year to year to the changing conditions of the market demand, complicated, as we have seen, by the possibility of intervention by the State, which might, as the indigo-monopoly shows, intercept his share of the anticipated profit; any attempt to look further ahead would probably have been unwise, and nothing of the sort is suggested in the records which have survived.

What has just been said of agriculture applies in great measure to the remaining forms of production. Under the head of minerals, the most striking feature of the period is the rise to importance of saltpetre, at first on the East Coast, and subsequently in Bihar; the large exports represent the employment of a considerable volume of labour, but the benefit extended to the population of only a limited area. It is possible that the iron-producers in the Golconda country profited to some extent by the demand for Batavia, since the Dutch exports of iron and steel from Masulipatam were at times large, but it is not clear to me how far this was a new development, and its influence was necessarily localised.[1] On the other hand there is the probable failure of some of the copper mines, which has been deduced in the last chapter from the course of the market; and these three changes exhaust our information on the subject.

In regard to manufactures again, there are no signs of important changes other than the increased production of calico to meet the new demand for Western Europe. The position occupied by the weavers stands out clearly in the mercantile correspondence of the period: in one sense each man worked for himself, in another he was in the power of the capitalist who advanced the funds required to buy materials and support him while at work. The system of advances by merchants is too well known to require further illustration; the Dutch and English buyers found it firmly established, and had to adopt it in order to obtain the goods they needed; its working was, as we have seen, by no means easy, but it was indispensable so long as no alternative method existed of providing capital. For the weavers, it is probable that the advent of Dutch and English buyers was beneficial. Once an advance had been taken, the position was substantially unchanged, but the individual weaver had

[1] About the year 1660 the Dutch were active in developing the iron industry in the Godavari delta, and artisans imported by them appear to have introduced real improvements in technique, but the story of these belongs to a later period.

a wider choice of masters, and increased competition for his services made it possible to hope for some improvement in the terms of the contract. The position may be illustrated by the varying reports regarding the possibility of obtaining goods of a particular quality. Where buyers were competing, weavers would make no change, while a practical monopoly enabled the Dutch or the English to obtain goods of approximately the quality required for the European market; and it appears to be probable that the control which could be exercised over the resident artisans was one of the chief commercial advantages derived by the Dutch from their position at Pulicat, and later by the English at Madras.

The weavers were not always free agents. We have seen in the last chapter that their services might occasionally be monopolised on the East Coast and in Gujarat. In Bengal, again, the makers of the finer goods appear to have been under some restrictions imposed by the Imperial Court, for we meet a "*Darogha* (overseer) of the King's weavers"; I have not found a contemporary account of his position, but the Dutch merchants complained of his interference with their trade, and I conjecture that his business was to maintain the supply of muslin for the Emperor's palace, a necessity to which the demand of private merchants would have to give place.

Our information regarding artisans of other classes is scanty, but the system which prevailed in the weaving industry appears to have been general. The supply of saltpetre, for instance, depended on advances in the neighbourhood of Patna, and money had to be provided beforehand to procure indigo in parts of the Biana tract, in Sind, and on the East Coast, though in Gujarat the business of manufacture was in the hands of local capitalists, who presumably financed the growers. The conditions were obviously unfavourable for any spontaneous improvement in processes, and the few changes recorded appear to have been due to Dutch or English initiative. The use of copper vessels for refining saltpetre, the attempt to manufacture indigo in Gujarat of the quality obtainable in the north, some improvements in the practice of dyeing, rope-making, and perhaps shipbuilding,—these items about complete the list, and serve to indicate the stagnant condition of productive industry.[1]

As regards the remuneration of urban workers, there were differences from place to place, but in a given region there was a remarkable uniformity in the wages paid, which were practically independent of the worker's craft. Writing of Agra, Pelsart quoted one set of rates for all classes of artisans; a few years earlier, Methwold had noted the same fact on the East Coast; and the existence of this uniformity would justify us in drawing inferences regarding workers in general from the data available for particular classes, provided that they related to the area under consideration. As a matter of fact, the data regarding artisans are too few for any general conclusions,[2] and we have to rely for comparative purposes on the monthly wages paid to the peons employed in European factories, that is to say, to servants with no exceptional qualifications. There is, however, a pitfall in the interpretation of monthly rates. Pelsart tells us that at Agra forty days were often counted to the month, for which time servants employed in many posts received 3 or 4 rupees; and even then, pay for some months was given in the form of clothes or other articles. A "monthly" rate of 4 rupees might thus represent real earnings substantially less than 3 rupees; and since Agra set the standard in such matters for a large part of India, we may suspect that in some other places also monthly rates may contain a similar overstatement. Similarly, the evils of the

[1] The improvements effected or attempted in the preparation of indigo and saltpetre have been mentioned in Chapters IV. and V. A dye-house was built at Ahmadabad in 1647 (*English Factories*, viii. 59, 127), to put an end to the loss incurred through the inefficiency of the local dyers. *Bowrey* (102, 105) tells of Dutch rope-makers at work regularly on the East Coast, and maintains that the local shipbuilders learned most of their art from the English, but I suspect that any improvements within our period were due rather to Dutch initiative. Attempts were being made to improve the reeling of silk (*English Factories*, x. 296), but the results lie outside our period.

[2] The *Agra Accounts* (*passim*) suggest that nominal wage rates had scarcely changed from those of Akbar's time recorded in the *Aīn* (i. 225). Akbar allowed ordinary labourers 2 and 3 dam per diem; the Dutch in 1637 paid usually 4 pice (2 dam) to ordinary labourers, and 7 pice to superior men. Carpenters were paid 12 and 13 pice by the Dutch; Akbar had allowed 6 and 7 dam for skilled men.

truck system were familiar also in Golconda, for a Dutch account tells us that the governors paid their staff in rice and salt valued at one-third above cost, and it is not improbable that this example was followed by some private employers.

The rates current on the East Coast about the year 1620 were recorded by Methwold as follows. Threepence a day, "finding themselves," represented "great wages to a master-workman; their servants are paid with one penny, and some less"; and household servants received a rial-of-eight, or two rupees, for a month. Taking the rupee at 2*s.* 3*d.*, and assuming that employment was continuous, the monthly rates were then, for the best master-workmen, Rs. $3\frac{1}{3}$; for household servants, Rs. 2; for ordinary artisans ("servants" of master-workmen), Rs. $1\frac{1}{9}$, or less. As was shown in the last chapter, the rate for servants in this region was unchanged nearly forty years later, and I think it is reasonable to assume that artisans' wages were equally stable, though I have found no later quotations to establish the proposition. For Northern India also, I have failed to find comparative figures; and for Gujarat, we have only the comparison of peons' wages drawn in the previous chapter. There is then no evidence of a rise in urban wages during our period, and the analogy drawn from the monthly pay of servants suggests that no rise took place.[1]

In the Mogul Empire the greater portion of our period was marked by heavy expenditure on public works, though not on works of general utility. The only large undertakings I have read of to which the latter description can be applied are Jahangir's waterworks at Burhanpur, and the Punjab canals constructed or repaired in the reign of Shahjahan.

[1] One other item of information may be noticed. In the year 1636, when food-prices had returned to the normal, a messenger detained at Surat was paid an allowance of three pice daily, which may be taken as about the minimum required for the subsistence of a "lean, lazy knave," as the man was contemptuously described (*English Factories*, v. 294). This works out at about Rs. $1\frac{1}{2}$ monthly, and may be compared with the allowance of a dam daily, or three-quarters of a rupee monthly, fixed for the lowest grade of slaves at Akbar's Court; the two figures represent practically identical quantities of grain on the basis of normal rates.

The former work was purely local, and should perhaps be classed rather as military, since Burhanpur was for several years the base of the armies operating against the Deccan, and water was probably provided for the troops rather than the public. The Punjab canals were the result of foreign inspiration, being undertaken by Ali Mardān Khān, who transferred his allegiance from Persia in the year 1637, and shortly afterwards was appointed Viceroy of the Punjab.[1] In 1639 he proposed a canal taking off from the river Ravi, which was sanctioned at an estimated cost of a lakh of rupees, and some years later the existing canal from the Jumna to Delhi was reconstructed under his supervision. I have found no record of the cost of the latter work, but it was probably comparable in amount with the former, and much less than what was being spent on buildings of an ornamental nature. The list of these is longer; Jahangir expended large sums in Agra and Lahore, but it was under Shahjahan that the most remarkable developments occurred. Contemporary writers give figures for the cost of some of his buildings—10 lakhs for the mosque at Daulatabad, 60 lakhs for the palace at Delhi, 917 lakhs for the Taj Mahal at Agra; and, while these may be inaccurate, they are comparable with the estimate of the Lahore canal, which comes from a similar source. The immediate effect of such undertakings was inevitably to hinder ordinary commercial activities. Thus all the carts at Agra were impressed for the works in progress at Delhi, and on one occasion goods in transit for the coast had to lie on the way for some months, after they had been "by the King's officers cast down in the fields, and the carts taken for his use"; but impressment was an ordinary occurrence of the period, and there appears to be no evidence on what is a matter of much greater interest, the treatment and remunera-

[1] Ali Mardān Khān is often spoken of as an engineer, but perhaps projector is a more appropriate term. Abdul Hamid says in the *Badshahnama* (*Elliot*, vi. 67) that "Ali Mardan Khan represented to His Majesty that *one of his followers* was an adept in the forming of canals"; and that, when the canal was sanctioned, "the Khan entrusted its formation to *one of his trusted servants*." I conjecture that the actual engineer was a Persian who had followed Ali Mardān Khān to India.

tion of the large number of labourers employed on these buildings.

Activity in the building industry was not confined to the construction of public works, for, as the face of the country shows, building was a fashionable way of spending money. Francisco Pelsart has some interesting observations on this subject, relating to the latter years of Jahangir's reign. He mentions that the tomb of Itimad-ud-daula at Agra had cost 3½ lakhs of rupees up to the year 1626, and that 10 lakhs more were required for its completion. He speaks also of the numerous *sarais* and palaces built by the Empress Nur Jahan, which he represents as an expression of her desire for lasting fame; and when commenting on the insecurity of wealth among the nobles, he observes that

> nothing is permanent, not even the noble buildings—gardens, tombs, or palaces—the ruins of which give cause for wonder and lamentation in and near every city. The buildings are maintained only so long as the owners live and possess the necessary means; once the builder is dead, no one will care for his buildings, but every one tries to erect buildings of his own. If all these edifices were attended to and kept in repair, in the course of a century the land round every city, indeed every village, would be covered with monuments; but as a matter of fact the roads leading to the cities are strewn with fallen columns.

There can be no question of the artistic value of some of the buildings constructed at this period, but their economic significance is a matter of consumption rather than production, and they lead the way naturally to the subjects treated in the following section.

2. Consumption

In the book to which I have already referred I arrived at the conclusion that, at the opening of the seventeenth century, the population of India consisted of a small but extremely wealthy and extravagant upper class, a small and frugal middle class, and a very numerous lower class, living generally on the same plane of poverty as now, but on the whole substantially worse off. That conclusion is confirmed by the additional evidence which I have since been able to examine; it would be unprofitable to reproduce what has already been published, and in this section I propose to set out only so much of the available material as may suffice for purposes of illustration. This procedure is justified by the absence of any conflict in the evidence: I have not found in the literature relating to our period a single suggestion tending to invalidate the inferences already drawn; I have found much to confirm them; and I believe that they will be accepted as definitely established by any one who studies the authorities as a whole.

The most detailed account of the standard of life in Northern India during our period is that which was drawn up in 1626 by Francisco Pelsart, the chief of the Dutch factory at Agra, on the basis of his seven years' experience of the country. The translation of his account which follows contains, it will be seen, strong expressions, which, when divorced from their context, may suggest the efforts of a sensational writer; but if his lengthy report is read as a whole, it will be found that he was a cool-headed and competent merchant, with a straightforward if occasionally colloquial style, and with a lively interest in his surroundings. He was very deeply impressed by the poverty and oppression he saw around him, and the occasional vehemence of his language must be accepted as indicating the strength of his sympathies with his poorer neighbours. After describing the system of administration in the Mogul Empire, he goes on to write of

> the manner of life of the rich in their great superfluity and absolute power, of the common people in their utter subjection and poverty—poverty so extreme and so miserable that the life of the people cannot be adequately depicted or described, for here is the home of stark want, and the dwelling-place of bitter woe. Yet the people endure patiently, seeing that there is no prospect of anything better, and scarcely any one will make an effort, for a ladder by which to climb higher is hard to find; a workman's children can follow no occupation other than their father's, nor can they marry into any other caste.
>
> There are three classes of the people who are indeed nominally

free, but whose status differs very little from voluntary slavery,—workmen, peons or servants, and shopkeepers. For the workmen there are two scourges, low wages and oppression. Workmen in all crafts, which are very numerous (for a job which one man would do in Holland here passes through four men's hands before it is finished), can earn by working from morning till night only 5 or 6 tackas, that is, 4 or 5 stivers.[1] The second scourge is the oppression of Governor, nobles, Diwan, Kotwal, Bakhshi, and other Imperial officers. If one of these wants a workman, the man is not asked if he is willing to come, but is seized in his house or in the street, well beaten if he should dare to raise any objection, and in the evening paid half his wages, or perhaps nothing at all. From these facts their diet can be readily inferred. They know little of the taste of meat. For their monotonous daily food, they have nothing but a little *khichri*, made of *moth* mixed with rice,[2] cooked with water over a little fire until the moisture has evaporated, and eaten hot, with a little butter, in the evening; in the day-time they munch a little parched pulse, or other grain, which they say satisfies their lean stomachs.

Their houses are built of mud, with thatched roofs. Furniture there is little or none—some earthenware pots to hold water and for cooking, and two beds, for here man and wife do not sleep together. Their bedclothes are scanty, merely a sheet, or perhaps two, serving both as under- and over-sheet; this suffices in the hot weather, but the bitter cold nights are miserable indeed, and they try to keep warm over a little cowdung fire, which is lit outside the door, because the houses have no fireplaces or chimneys; the smoke from these fires all over the city is so great that the eyes run, and the throat seems to be choked.

In this country peons or servants are exceedingly numerous.[3] . . . For their slack and lazy service, the wages are paid by the

[1] *Tacka* is a word which is sometimes difficult to interpret. The Dutch took the rupee as 24 of their stivers, so *tacka* here denotes Akbar's dam, about 30 of which at this time went to the rupee.

[2] The word *khichri* appears in the original. *Moth* is my rendering of *groene ertjens* (literally, green pulse); a similar phrase appears in the *Agra Accounts* as an explanation of the name *moth*, the pulse known to botanists as *Phaseolus aconitifolius*.

[3] The passage omitted is a long description of the duties of different servants, and the punctilious separation of their functions. Pelsart compares the position to life on a Portuguese ship, "where, if the foremast fell overboard, the boatswain would not demean himself by going forward, though he could save the mast by doing so." Portuguese etiquette of this kind was a common subject for jibes.

Moguls only after large deductions. Most of the great lords reckon 40 days to the month, and pay from 3 to 4 rupees for that period ; but wages are often left several months in arrears, and then paid in worn-out clothes or other things. Very few serve their masters honestly ; they steal whatever they can ; and if they buy only a pice-worth of food, they will take their share, or *dasturi* [commission]. . . . Otherwise it would be impossible to feed themselves and their families on such low wages ; and accordingly their position and manner of life differ very little from that of the workman in the wealth of their poverty.[1]

Whatever he may deal in—spices, drugs, fruit, cloth, or anything else—the shopkeeper is distinctly better off than the workman, and some of them are even well-to-do ; but they must not let the fact be seen, or they will be victims of a trumped-up charge, and their property will be legally confiscated, for informers swarm like flies round the officials, and make no difference between friends and enemies, perjuring themselves when necessary in order to remain in favour. Further, they are so oppressed that if the Emperor's nobles or governors should require any of their goods, they must sell them for very little—less than half price. . . .

This is a short sketch of the life of these poor wretches, who in their submissive bondage may be compared to poor, contemptible earthworms, or little fishes, which, however closely they may conceal themselves, are swallowed up by the great monsters of a wild sea. Now we shall write a little of the manner of life of the great and the rich, but, in order to do so, we must entirely change our tune ; for the pen which has described bitter poverty clothed with the woeful garment of sighs, the foe of love, friendship, and happiness, but the friend of loneliness wet with the daily dew of tears—that pen must entirely change its style, and tell that in the palaces of these lords dwells all the wealth there is, wealth which glitters indeed, but is borrowed, wrung from the sweat of the poor. Consequently their position is as unstable as the wind, resting on no firm foundation, but rather on pillars of glass, resplendent in the eyes of the world, but collapsing under the stress of even a slight storm.

Pelsart then enters into many details of the luxurious life of the nobles, and of the insecurity of their position, and

[1] Literally, "in their rich poverty," apparently a fanciful phrase, of a kind popular at the time.

concludes by recognising that exceptions were to be found, nobles who were thrifty as well as rich, but he insists that what he has described is the standard of the great majority. His account of life in the country is much less detailed. In one passage he says that "so much is wrung from the peasants that even dry bread is scarcely left to them for their food": in another place we read that "the land would give a plentiful, or even an extraordinary yield, if the peasants were not so cruelly and pitilessly oppressed"; but he was essentially a townsman, and his references to the country are merely incidental.[1]

The other commercial reports drawn up by Dutch factors at this period follow somewhat different lines, and do not attempt a formal description of the standard of life, but occasional remarks indicate conditions similar to those which Pelsart depicted. The merchant who described Golconda recorded his astonishment at the amount of the revenue extracted from the people, who were very poor and lived miserably, and he described the country as desolated by exactions. The Gujarat report depicts the weavers as too poor to deal on credit, but living from hand to mouth, and requiring advances to enable them to buy yarn; while, owing to the high revenue, the peasants earned barely the cost of their labour, and differed very little from slaves, compelled to work for the luxury of the great. The Dutch merchant van Twist tells the same story of Gujarat a few years later—the peasants forced to surrender the entire profit of the land, and the authorities unable in consequence to find peasants in sufficient numbers. Methwold and his Council at Surat, describing the gradual recovery after the famine, wrote as

[1] A detailed verbal comparison makes it clear that the passages of Pelsart's report quoted above were comprised in the material on which J. de Laet based his description of the standard of life in the Mogul Empire (*De Imperio Magni Mogolis*, pp. 116 ff.). De Laet also had before him the *Gujarat Report*, from which he occasionally quotes; and most of what he indicates as taken from Dutch sources will be found in these two authorities. It is unnecessary therefore to reproduce de Laet's account here; it is an accurate summary of his sources, but is secondary evidence. It may be added that the French translator was not very successful with these paragraphs of Pelsart's report; the rendering I have given is, I hope, as nearly literal as is possible.

follows: "The villages fill but slowly, yet it betters with them also; and if the excessive tyranny and covetousness of the governors of all sorts would give the poor people leave but to lift up their heads in one year's vacancy from oppression, they would be enabled to keep cattle about them, and so to advance the plenty which the earth produces." Ten years later, the English Council reported regarding Sind that "the people are so exceedingly oppressed and kept so miserably poor that, notwithstanding the soil is fertile and proper, and would produce large quantities of good indigo, they have neither will nor means to manure [cultivate] and sow the ground."

The observations recorded at first hand by Bernier and Tavernier show that the conditions which have been described persisted up to the closing years of our period. The former, who spent the years from 1656 to 1658 in the Mogul Empire, gives, in his *Letter to Colbert*, a melancholy description of the state of the peasantry:

> Even a considerable proportion of the good land remains untilled from want of labourers; many of whom perish in consequence of the bad treatment they experience from the governors. These poor people, when incapable of discharging the demands of their rapacious lords, are not only deprived of the means of subsistence, but are bereft of their children, who are carried away as slaves. Thus it happens that many of the peasantry, driven to despair by so execrable a tyranny, abandon the country, and seek a more tolerable mode of existence either in the towns or in the camps. Sometimes they fly to the territories of a Raja, because they find less oppression and are allowed a greater degree of comfort.

Further on, the same writer declares that

> the ground is seldom tilled except under compulsion, and no person is willing or able to repair the ditches and canals; the whole country is badly cultivated, and a great part is rendered unproductive for want of irrigation. . . . No adequate idea can be conveyed of the sufferings of the people. The cudgel and the whip compel them to incessant labour for the benefit of others.

Tavernier, who travelled in India at intervals between 1640 and 1660, writes of the Mogul Empire in a similar strain.

"The peasants," he tells us, "are reduced to great poverty, because if the governors become aware that they possess any property, they seize it straightway by right or by force. You may see in India whole provinces like deserts, from whence the peasants have fled on account of the oppression of the governors."

These quotations are perhaps sufficient to indicate the state of the agricultural population. Of the artisans in the cities, Bernier wrote that

> it should not be inferred that the workman is held in esteem or arrives at a state of independence. Nothing but sheer necessity or blows of a cudgel keeps him employed; he never can become rich, and he feels it no trifling matter if he have the means of satisfying the cravings of hunger and covering his body with the coarsest garment. If money be gained, it does not in any measure go into his pocket, but only serves to increase the wealth of the merchant.

In the same spirit van Twist insisted on the contrast between the comfort enjoyed by the merchants and the poverty of the craftsmen; while as regards the weavers, the largest section of the industrial population, the cumulative effect of numerous incidental references in the Dutch and English correspondence is to exhibit them living on a dead level of poverty throughout the country. In a former chapter I have examined in some detail the course of the export trade in Indian slaves. The facts of that trade fall into line with such observations as have been quoted above. We see the mass of the population living on the margin not of comfort but of bare subsistence, with no incentive to energy, and no possibility of escape except by emigration in one of the two forms which were then within reach—either flight to some region where for the moment conditions seemed to be more favourable, or surrender of personal freedom in return for a promise of subsistence in some foreign country. Such was the position in years of normal production: in the next chapter we have to examine the results which ensued when the ordinary course of production was interrupted.

AUTHORITIES FOR CHAPTER VI

SECTION 1.—The references for the use of tobacco are *Elliot*, vi. 351, and *Manucci*, ii. 175. The adaptation of cropping to market-conditions is deduced from various passages, especially *English Factories*, v. 64, vii. 136, and *Dagh Register* (Surat), June 13, 1644, April 12 and June 9, 1645. Instances of want of capital will be found in *English Factories*, vii. 203, and *Dagh Register*, August 14, October 6, 1634, and October 6, 1636. For apprehensions of scarcity of material, see *English Factories*, i. pp. xv, 92, and iv. 22; and for ease or difficulty in obtaining goods of special quality, *idem*, iii. 209, vii. 187, viii. 117, and *Dagh Register*, January 31, 1633, August 14, 1634, October 31, 1636, and May 20, 1641. The restrictions on weavers in Bengal are in *idem*, November 29, 1661; the subject is referred to in *Taylor's Dacca*, 173, 189. For advances for saltpetre, see *Dagh Register*, April 12, 1661; and for indigo, *English Factories*, iii. 246, vii. 208.

The facts given regarding wages are taken from *Pelsart*, 16 ff.; *Methwold*, 1001; *Begin ende Voortgangh* (van den Broecke's journal), ii. 77 ff.; and *English Factories*, v. 151, x. 261. As regards public works, the Burhanpur waterworks are described in *Imperial Gazetteer*, ix. 105; the canals, in *Elliot*, vii. 67, 86; the estimated cost of buildings, in *idem*, vii. 86, 142, and *Sarkar's Studies*, 30. For impressment, see *English Factories*, ii. 230, viii. 253, 299. For private buildings, see *Pelsart*, MS. ff. 2, 21.

SECTION 2.—The long translation from *Pelsart* has been made from ff. 23 ff. of the MS.; his observations on the peasants are on ff. 18 and 20. The Golconda reference is *Begin ende Voortgangh*, p. 77 of van den Broecke's journal; for Gujarat, see the *Gujarat Report*, ff. 7, 20, 21, *van Twist*, xxxiv, xli, and *English Factories*, v. 65. For Sind, see *idem*, vii. 209. For the close of the period, see *Tavernier*, i. 391, and *Bernier*, 205, 226, 228, 230.

CHAPTER VII

THE ECONOMIC RESULTS OF FAMINE

1. The Nature and Frequency of Famines

From what has been said in the previous chapter, it will be apparent that during our period production followed a generally uneventful course, responding to, but not creating, developments in demand, and impeded from time to time by administrative interference, or by the occurrence of famine. The results of administrative interference will be considered later; in this chapter we have to examine the frequency and the effects of famine, and the subject requires careful study because a change in the implication of the familiar word has given rise to ideas which rest on an erroneous foundation. At the present day the "famines" which are spoken of in India are emergencies in which the State has recognised the existence of unemployment on a scale which, in the absence of a general poor-law, requires special measures of relief. The famines which we read of in the chronicles of the seventeenth century were not work-famines but food-famines in the strictest sense, times when it was not a question of obtaining the means to pay for food, but of getting food at all; and the attempt sometimes made by popular writers to use these materials for a comparison of the frequency of famines at different periods is vitiated from the outset by this change of meaning. On the one hand, there have been no extensive food-famines in India for many years; on the other, we have no systematic record of work-famines before the middle of the last century, and no valid conclusion could be drawn from the fact (if it were a fact) that work-famines are now more common than food-famines were in former times. Further, it can easily be shown that the record of food-famines in the published chronicles is incomplete, because we find several mentioned in the Dutch and English commercial correspondence of which no other account is known. To take one instance, I can trace no Indian record of famine between the years 1632 and 1650, but the Dutch tell us of heavy mortality in Golconda in 1635, the weavers on the East Coast were dying of hunger in 1646, and a year later a part of Rajputana was "wholly depopulate" owing to the same cause. Abandoning, then, any attempt at direct comparison, I have constructed a list of the years lying within our period in which production is known to have been seriously impeded through deficiency of agricultural produce, whether food or raw materials.

It cannot be asserted that this list is complete. The Batavia Journals, which are exceptionally valuable as sources of such information, are wanting or imperfect for several years, particularly between 1647 and 1660, and the missing records may have contained details of dearth or famine which would not be found elsewhere. Even, however, if the commercial records were available throughout the period, they would not cover the whole of India, but only those portions with which the merchants maintained relations: Bundelkhand, for instance, which is a tract peculiarly liable to vicissitudes of season, is altogether outside their scope; and the same is true of the Punjab, which, before the construction of the modern canal-system, must have resembled Bundelkhand in many important features. We may say, then, that production was certainly interfered with in the years shown in the following list, but we should not be justified in saying that the years not entered in it were prosperous throughout the whole of India. It will be noticed that recorded dearths are more numerous in the second half of our period than in the first; the difference may possibly be significant, but it is more probable that it results from the extension of the foreign merchants' connections, and, in the case of the Dutch, from improvements in the system of recording events, the Journals which have survived for the 'forties being much fuller than those relating to the years before 1630. The list is as follows :

1614–15 (?).—The Emperor Jahangir records a pestilence in the year ending in March 1616, which was attributed by some authorities to the effects of drought, the country having suffered from want of rain for two years in succession. The area affected by the pestilence was the Punjab as far east as Delhi, and presumably the drought was localised in the Punjab. The description does not indicate the precise years in which the rains were deficient.

1618–19.—Writing from Masulipatam in 1622, a Dutch factor accounted for his small purchases of slaves by the comparative prosperity of the times, saying that, according to his information, the large supplies obtained four years previously were due to the extreme dearth and famine in Pulicat and the vicinity, when many hundreds of deaths occurred ; but conditions had changed, supplies of rice were ample, and at the moment no large number of slaves could be procured. This information points to a severe famine on the Coromandel coast in 1618 or 1619. The historian M. de Faria y Sousa records of the latter year that dearth and famine destroyed many people ; the exact locality is not indicated, but the reference is clearly to Southern India. Methwold, who left the East Coast in 1622, writes of such extreme want and famine in some parts of the territory of Vijayanagar "that parents have brought thousands of their young children to the seaside, selling there a child for 5 fanams of rice." I take these three accounts to refer to one calamity, a disastrous famine about the year 1618–19.[1]

1630.—The terrible calamity following on the failure of the rains in this year is described by various Indian, Dutch, and

[1] Mr. Loveday shows 1623 and 1628–29 as years of famine (Appendix A of *The History and Economics of Indian Famines*), but these entries are not correct. His authority for the former year is *Etheridge*, p. 40 ; Etheridge wrongly took 1623 as the equivalent of the Hijra year 1040 (which really began in July 1630), and the events which he attributes to 1623 in fact occurred in the great famine of 1630. *Etheridge* (p. 63) is also the authority for 1628–29, but the facts which he records under it are clearly the same as those which he gives under the Hijra year 1040, and should be assigned to 1630. The seasons of 1628 and 1629 were not favourable, and the yield of indigo had been reduced (*English Factories*, iv. 20) ; in the latter year the rains began late and were unduly heavy at the close (*Hague Transcripts*, I. 298) ; but the commercial correspondence gives no hint of anything like a famine, and in April 1630 both Dutch and English merchants were busy and hopeful.

English authorities. Its effects on the economic condition of the country are examined in detail in the next section.

1635.—The Dutch factors at Surat reported that provisions were unprocurable throughout the whole kingdom of Golconda, and that the mortality from famine was heavy. The report reached Batavia in March 1636, and may therefore be taken to indicate a failure of the rains in the previous year. The extent appears to be somewhat exaggerated, since no reports of intense famine were received from the East Coast, though rice was difficult to obtain in Masulipatam, and the supply of raw cotton on the coast was still deficient in the following autumn. Probably there was severe famine in the western districts of Golconda, whence news would naturally reach Surat, and some scarcity on the side of Masulipatam.

1640.—Early in 1641 the Dutch reported deficiency of rain near Pulicat and Madras, so that provisions had to be imported by sea. From the subsequent reports from the coast, it does not appear that the famine became acute.

1641.—The season appears to have been unfavourable to the cotton crop in Northern India, for the Dutch reported that piece-goods had risen seriously in price owing to the scarcity of cotton. Cotton was scarce in Ahmadabad also during the summer of 1642, so that the previous season was probably unfavourable in Gujarat as well as in the north.

1642–43.—In January 1643 rice was reported to be very scarce and almost unprocurable owing to extraordinary drought in the neighbourhood of Pipli (Orissa). The winter rains of 1642–43 failed in Bengal.

1645–46.—This was a time of intense famine on the southern section of the Coromandel coast. The few letters of 1645–46 extant from the English factors do not mention a failure of the rains of 1645, but that this had occurred is shown by a letter written at Achin in October 1646, which reported the arrival from Negapatam of a cargo of starving slaves, and news through them of "a very strong famine for 13 months past . . . insomuch as the people give themselves for slaves to any man that will but feed them." The rains of 1646 also failed, and by January of 1647 the position on the coast was desperate. Heavy mortality was reported from Pulicat, S. Thomé, and Madras, "so that all the painters [1] and weavers are dead"; rice sent from Surat was sold at "great rates"; and the famine continued until the rains

[1] "Painters" is the term ordinarily used to denote the producers of *pintados*, or painted cottons.

of 1647. In October of this year the factors at Madras reported that the famine had then lasted two years, so that the earlier failure was not confined to the Negapatam country; they added that half the people in the kingdom were dead, and referred to "the stench of the dead carcases that lieth most fearfully to behold in all places that we go, as well as the noise of the dying people, which can be no less terrors to the hearers thereof."

1647.—This year the rains failed in parts of Rajputana, and "occasioned a famine, insomuch that those parts are, either by mortality or people's flight, become wholly depopulate and impassable."

1648.—A recurrence of the famine on the Coromandel coast was so imminent that arrangements were made to forward rice from Surat, but a plentiful fall of rain came in time to remove the danger.

1650.—The Surat factors reported that "this year there hath very little rain fallen in all parts of India, and since the middle of July little or none, so that corn is risen in many places already [October] to double the price, and a dearth is extremely and generally feared." This drought was widespread, being experienced in Oudh as well as Gujarat, and crops were short "almost all India over," but apparently its intensity was not great, for we have not the familiar records of mortality or voluntary enslavement.

1658.—Want of rain in this season had doubled the price of all sorts of provisions in Surat by February 1659, but the calamity was heavier in Sind, for in September of that year it was reported that famine and disease "hath swept away most part of the people," and the Surat factors sent grain to Lahari Bandar to be distributed to the weavers so as to keep them alive.

1659–60.—Scarcity was experienced on the East Coast in the summer of 1659, as the result of deficient rainfall, aggravated by the demand for supplies for armies in the field. A letter written in October 1659 from Masulipatam says that people were dying daily from want of food, and famine continued on the coast into the year 1661. The want of rain had also been experienced in Gujarat, where in April of 1660 prices were very high, while in Sind famine still raged, "the living being hardly able to bury the dead." The historian Khafi Khan writes of the Hijra year 1070 (which began in September 1659), that want of rain, combined with war and movements of armies, made grain very scarce and dear; that many districts lay entirely waste, and that crowds of people made their way to the capital. Scarcity was reported also from Negapatam in the far south, so that our period closes with a calamity of unusual extent.

The list which has now been given makes depressing reading, and if the defects in its sources are borne in mind, the conclusion appears to be justified that the Indian climate in the seventeenth century was very much what it is to-day. I do not think that the record of the years from 1640 to 1650, imperfect as it may be, has been exceeded in the course of any decade in modern times; and without attempting a detailed comparison, we may say that local dearths were frequent, while acute or widespread famines occurred sufficiently often to influence the calculations of merchants and producers. The difference lies rather in the results which followed. The cost of transporting grain long distances by land was, as we have seen, prohibitive, and consequently a local shortage of food could not be met by importation; people might die in thousands, as on the East Coast in 1647, though there were ample supplies in other parts of the country, and the economic life of the area affected might be broken up through mortality and migration in a way which the modern railway-system has rendered impossible. At the present day the effect of a local shortage is spread over a large area, and its intensity is thereby reduced, because food can be imported in sufficient quantities, so that the very idea of a food-famine has been banished from all but the few tracts still inaccessible to the merchant: during our period, food-famines on varying scales might be expected in any season, and their present unfamiliarity makes it desirable to explain in some detail the economic consequences which followed in their train. The records of the famine of 1630 are sufficiently copious to make this possible, and the next section will be devoted to their examination.

2. The Famine of 1630–31

The immediate cause of the great famine was the failure of the rains in the year 1630. The failure occurred in the central parts of India. The Gangetic plain was not affected, and Peter Mundy's account of his journey northward from Surat shows that most of Malwa had escaped. The chronicler of the reign of Shahjahan says that no rain whatever fell in the

Mogul provinces of the Deccan and Gujarat, while there was a deficiency in bordering countries. English letters from the East Coast show that the calamity extended right across India, and a merchant who visited Masulipatam in July 1631 wrote that "the major part of both weavers and washers are dead, the country being almost ruinated." Towards the south, we know that the drought was experienced in Armagon, but no information is on record as to the country beyond. Sind also was affected, but the letters written thence in 1635 suggest that the distress cannot have been very intense, because no traces of it are mentioned such as were still visible in Gujarat. The detailed information which has survived relates chiefly to this latter province, and for the present our attention may be confined to it.

The rains had been somewhat unsatisfactory for the three previous seasons, but not to such an extent as to affect commerce very materially, and in April of 1630 prospects were considered to be favourable. The monsoon, however, failed, and the immediate results can best be stated in the words of the Dutch senior merchant van Twist, who included an account of the famine in a short description of Gujarat, first printed at Batavia in 1638, and subsequently reissued in Amsterdam.[1] His description is written in a dry and matter-of-fact style; it is a business document, drawn up by a man who knew the country well, and whose ability is indicated by his selection not long after for duties of great responsibility; the horrors described in it derive additional emphasis from this setting, while their occurrence is amply confirmed by the more fragmentary English narratives, as well as by the rhetoric of the Moslem chronicler.

[1] The title-page of van Twist's pamphlet shows that he had been senior merchant in Ahmadabad, Cambay, Broach, and Baroda. He is mentioned incidentally in the *Dagh Register* from 1631 onwards: in 1636 he was sent on a special mission to the Court at Bijapur; and not long afterwards he was appointed Governor of Malacca, where he died. I have not seen a copy of the Batavia issue of his pamphlet, but the title-page of the reprint in *Begin ende Voortgangh* states that it was reproduced from the edition printed at Batavia in 1638. The English narratives of this famine have been brought together in *Mundy*, ii. Appendix A; they appear also in *English Factories*, iv. Abdul Hamid's account is translated in *Elliot*, vii. 24.

So little rain fell, says van Twist, that the seed sown was lost, and no grass grew. Cattle died. In towns and villages, in fields and on roads, men lay dead in great numbers, causing such a stench that it was terrible to use the ways. For want of grass cattle fed on the corpses; men took the carcases of beasts to eat; some in desperation went about searching for bones which had been gnawed by dogs. . . .

As the famine increased, men abandoned towns and villages, and wandered helplessly. It was easy to recognise their condition: eyes sunk deep in the head, lips pale and covered with slime, the skin hard, with the bones showing through, the belly nothing but a pouch hanging down empty, knuckles and knee-caps showing prominently. One would cry and howl for hunger, while another lay stretched on the ground dying in misery; wherever you went you saw nothing but corpses.

Men deserted their wives and children. Women sold themselves as slaves. Mothers sold their children. Children deserted by their parents sold themselves. Some families took poison, and so died together; others threw themselves into the rivers. Mothers and their children went to the river-bank, and drowned themselves hand in hand, so that the rivers flowed full of corpses. Some ate carrion flesh. Others cut up the corpses of men, and drew out the entrails to fill their own bellies; yes, men lying in the street, not yet dead, were cut up by others, and men fed on living men, so that even in the streets, and still more on road-journeys, men ran great danger of being murdered and eaten. . . .

Terrible tragedies were seen every day. Even a heathen might wonder and pity when he learned that a mother had killed and cooked her only son: much more might a Christian conscience, when it was known that husbands had eaten their wives, wives their husbands, children their parents—but it would be tedious to describe everything in detail. Many hundred thousands of men died of hunger,[1] so that the whole country was covered with corpses lying unburied, which caused such a stench that the whole air was filled and infected with it. Some of our Dutchmen, coming from Ahmadabad, found some people sitting at a little fire where hands and feet were cooking, a terrible thing to see. Even worse was it in the village of Susuntra, where human flesh was sold in open market. This terrible divine punishment fell chiefly on the poor, who had nothing in store.

[1] This number is not to be taken literally, but rather as an idiomatic expression signifying that the mortality was incalculable.

The narrative then gives the details of prices, which have been examined in a previous chapter, and passes to the season of 1631, when the rains were at first promising, and prices began to fall. But, continues van Twist, the improvement did not last, and it was seen that the punishment was not yet over. The Almighty sent locusts, rats, mice, and other vermin, which wrought great damage to the young crops: then continuous heavy rain when the crops were ripening caused much grain to perish in the fields; flooded rivers caused even greater loss in towns, villages, and country; and prices rose higher than ever. Thus famine lasted throughout the year, and pestilence and fever followed, so that scarcely a healthy man could be found. The dead lay scattered in the streets. Corpses lay for days in the houses, because men could not be paid to carry them out. Wood could not be had for the pyres, and unburnt corpses were buried or thrown into the river. May the Almighty protect all Christian lands from such terrible calamities!

The main features of this narrative will not come as a surprise to students of Indian famines of the type now obsolete. The break-up of family life, loss of agricultural capital, aimless wandering, voluntary enslavement, deaths from suicide or sheer starvation, cannibalism—all these could be illustrated from both Indian and foreign accounts of similar calamities. It will be noticed that van Twist has nothing to say of State measures of relief, but from Indian narratives we can form some idea of their nature and extent. Public kitchens were opened, taxes were remitted, and money was allocated for gratuitous relief, but the facts on record show that the effect of these measures was trifling, and from the nature of the case they could not counteract the actual deficiency of food which was the dominant factor in the situation; they might operate to improve the distribution of such stocks as were available, but they could not bring grain into the country, and though their inadequacy may be obvious, it is not easy to suggest what more could have been done. Casual references in letters of 1631 and 1632 show that the English merchants had ordered large quantities of grain from Persia, but the course of shipping imposed narrow limits on supplies from that source; Sind was itself affected; the Malabar coast ordinarily imported a large proportion of its food; the East Coast was starving;

and it appears to be at the least doubtful whether the best and most humane administration in the world could have organised imports by sea sufficient to meet the situation. There was surplus grain in the north, but the cost of carriage by land was, as we have seen, exceedingly heavy, and it is hard to see how pack-animals could have moved through country without fodder or water in numbers adequate to the emergency.

It would be unjust, therefore, to blame the Mogul administration for failure to avert a calamity which, in the circumstances of the time, must be regarded as inevitable; but it may be pointed out that the measures actually taken were not only inadequate but tardy, and that the leaders of the people acted in a manner likely to aggravate rather than mitigate the distress. The authority for these statements is Peter Mundy, who, after describing his observations on the route from Surat to Burhanpur, lays stress on the fact that no course was taken to remedy the evil, "the rich and strong engrossing and taking perforce all to themselves." The same observer points out that relief from the north was hopeless, because the Mogul armies at Burhanpur lay across the route by which grain must come; and though the country near Sironj was well stocked with food, "poor Gujarat was never the near[er], where there was most need, it being all sent to Burhanpur to supply the King's *lashker*" [army]. This last obstacle was, however, temporary: by the end of 1631 the *banjāras*, or grain-carriers, were coming through, the sea-trade was helping, and from this time forward it appears that the needs of the reduced population were not too great to be provided by the ordinary course of trade, though at prices still far above the normal.

The immediate effect of this calamity on industry and commerce may be illustrated by a few facts gathered from the English correspondence of the period. By October 1630, the impending scarcity of indigo was realised at Surat, and arrangements were on foot to buy in Agra instead of Ahmadabad. In the same month special precautions were found necessary to protect provisions on the way to the ships from "assault by the poor starved people of the country." In November, Masulipatam reported scarcity of cotton goods, and a fall in the price of gold and other imports; while the factors at Surat had for the moment the rare experience of having more funds than could be invested owing to the shortage of cotton goods and indigo, were suggesting importation of rice from Macassar, and were reducing the rations allowed on the English ships. Spirits had by this time become unprocurable because the distillers had "departed into the parts of more hoped plenty, as are many thousands besides, as well weavers, washers, dyers, etc., that puts us almost into despair of a competent lading for the succeeding year's home returns." In December, Armagon reported that the inferiority of cloth was due in part to a fourfold rise in the price of cotton, and on the last day of the year Surat wrote that the artisans were abandoning their habitations in multitudes and perishing in the fields. Gold was falling in price because the poor were selling, while the rich could not buy; the yield of indigo in Gujarat was about one-twentieth of the normal, and nothing but old refuse was available in the market; cotton and yarn were doubled in price; the roads were unsafe owing to bands of desperate robbers, and even messengers ran the risk of being murdered. The famine, together with the war in the Deccan, had "disjointed all trade out of frame."

Early in the new year we hear of the increased cost of land transport; there is a warning not to pass saltpetre through the inland customs as sugar, lest it should be detained as provisions and the fraud be discovered; and the ships coming from England were advised to lay in rice on the voyage; but by this time the factors were perhaps resigned to the situation, and the correspondence is scanty. In June the rains promised well, and activity was renewed; cloth was coming in at Broach and Baroda "with the help of a ser of corn delivered out to the weavers on every piece brought," and there were hopes of making up some sort of a cargo for England. In September, however, the cost of indigo and cotton goods was found to be prohibitive, while food prices were at the highest point (about 6 lb. of grain for a rupee), and agues, fevers, and pestilential diseases prevailed in every house. The English merchants did not escape, for in October every one except the President was either dead or sick, and the President died in the following month. Gujarat, "the garden of the world," was turned into a wilderness, with few or no cultivators or artisans; indigo was rotting on the ground for want of men to gather it; and the places which had yielded fifteen bales of cloth in a day could now produce barely three bales in a month. A Dutch factor writing at this time saw no hope of trade for three years to come, and the year 1631 closed in desolation.

Early in 1632 the tide of distress began to recede. It will have been apparent from van Twist's description that the calamities of 1631 were more local than those of the previous year; supplies were therefore available from less remote areas, and prices began to fall as grain arrived from outside. The worst of the misery was over, but the restoration of industry and commerce was a matter of years. Its slow progress may be traced in the reports of the English merchants. By February 1632 wheat was procurable at Broach, but the supplies at Surat were engrossed by the Governor and one or two traders. Ample rain fell this year on the East Coast, and there are no complaints regarding the season from Surat, but at the end of the year indigo, cotton goods, and other commodities were still very dear, while imports were almost unsaleable. Prices in November 1633 were so high as to offer no hope of profit in England, while in October 1634 India offered little or nothing on which to found a profitable trade. Prices on the East Coast were also too high for business, but a return to normal conditions was expected as the result of the good crops of that year. In December the factors at Surat wrote to the Company that the losses were incalculable, and that they could not see how to restore the trade; and they estimated that at least five years were still necessary for recovery. The rains of 1634 had, however, been exceptionally good, artisans were returning, and the cities were becoming repopulated. What follows has been quoted in part in the last chapter, but it will bear repetition.

The villages fill but slowly, yet it betters with them also; and if the excessive tyranny and covetousness of the governors of all sorts would give the poor people leave but to lift up their heads in one year's vacancy from oppression, they would be enabled to keep cattle about them, and so to advance the plenty which the earth produceth that all things would be much more abundant, and there would be no want but of time to make the children capable to exercise the functions of their fathers.

This last phrase is noteworthy: one of the most lasting effects of such famines was the lowered level of skill resulting from the death of expert peasants and workmen, and the cotton goods of Gujarat suffered in reputation owing to this cause for many years. The gradual recovery proceeded unequally in different places; by September 1635 steps were taken to re-establish factories at Ahmadabad and Baroda, but Broach was still "not well peopled with weavers," and a separate establishment there was considered useless.

The recovery of commerce is marked by a letter of December 1635, when the Surat factors reported that prices were steadily falling owing to the cheapness of grain and the return of inhabitants, and that they had decided to borrow enough capital to make a fresh start; Gujarat could not, however, supply all they wanted, and they were extending their field of operations to Sind and Northern India in order to obtain sufficient goods. In January 1636, freight-goods for Persia were being offered by Indian merchants, and the correspondence about this time begins to record activity of the kind which had prevailed before the famine. By March the price of grain was below the old normal, and in April food-grains and raw cotton were sent from Surat to Masulipatam, where the effects of the Golconda drought of 1635 were being experienced. Baroda was now making good cloth in some plenty, but Broach was "broken," for, as a letter written in September says, "the people are fled and dead, and now want of employment makes men afraid to return." The correspondence of the year 1637 throws little light on the progress of events, but in December of 1638 a factor wrote that the country had recovered from famine, goods were to be had in abundance, and the prospects of commerce were very encouraging. We may say, then, that Gujarat was again prosperous by 1639, but with a reduced population, and a loss of skill, which was still affecting the quality of cotton goods and other manufactures. In the last respect, however, steady improvement was noticeable, and even Broach was beginning to make some progress : there remained the loss of reputation abroad, and the advantage which Gujarat had gained by priority in European markets had definitely passed away.

No detailed account can be given of this famine in the Deccan, since European factories did not exist there, but there are indications that the calamity was comparable in intensity to that which fell on Gujarat. The *Badshahnama*, which was written about the year 1650, classes the four Deccan provinces along with Gujarat as constituting exceptions to the general conditions prevailing in the Mogul Empire. The author gives figures to show that in the first twenty years of Shahjahan's reign the Imperial revenue had increased largely, but that these five provinces were stationary or even showed a decline in yield ; and he expressly attributes this fact to the famine of 1630–32. When Prince Aurangzeb became Viceroy of the Deccan in 1653, he found that, though the revenue demand had been reduced, it was still excessive, and the country, so far from contributing to the Imperial treasury, could not even pay for the local administration in his charge. The Deccan, therefore, remained impoverished for at any rate a generation.

This lengthy review of the progress and results of the famine of 1630 is justified by the frequency of similar events in the history of India. The extent and the intensity of famines varied within wide limits, but all that we know leads to the conclusion that their effects were similar in nature though they differed in degree. When once an actual insufficiency of food is known, or even suspected, to exist, and where adequate imports are impossible, it is certain that the people will endeavour to migrate, and in the circumstances of the time the attempt to migrate could result only in that "aimless wandering in search of food," which had become so traditional that, even in the present century, its first symptoms were regarded as the surest index to the need for immediate relief.[1] The economic life of a village, a town, or a district, when once broken up by migration, disease, and death, could not quickly be renewed, and there are no signs in the literature of the period of such constructive measures of relief as would have been required to accelerate the process. Those wanderers who had survived would naturally return on the advent of a favourable season, and the old life would gradually be restored, but the recovery was a tedious business at the best, and, as we have seen in Gujarat, it might be delayed further by "the tyranny and covetousness of the governors." The loss of capital, particularly the peasant's working animals, the decline in the level of skill and knowledge, and the disrepute accruing in foreign markets are the features which concern the economist most directly: the attention of the social historian will be drawn rather to the waste of life and the intensity of human misery recurring so frequently on varying scales.

[1] See the *Report of the Indian Famine Commission*, 1901, p. 14.

AUTHORITIES FOR CHAPTER VII

SECTION 1.—The references for the list of famines are as follows:—For 1614–15, *Elliot*, vi. 346; *Tuzuk*, i. 330. For 1618–19, *Hague Transcripts*, I. 162; *Faria y Sousa*, iii. 298; and *Methwold*, 993. For 1635, *Dagh Register*, March 22, June 10, and October 31, 1636. For 1640, *idem*, March 31, 1641. For 1641, *idem*, December 26, 1641; June 20, November 3, 1642. For 1642, *idem* (Coromandel), February 15 and October 16, 1643. For 1645–46, *English Factories*, viii. 46, 54 *n*., 68-74, 163, 198. For 1647, *idem*, viii. 157, 192. For 1648, *idem*, viii. 246, 259. For 1650, *idem*, viii. 322, ix. 10, 29, 82. For 1658, *idem*, x. 196, 210. For 1659–60, *idem*, x. 257, 263, 306, 401, 407; *Dagh Register*, January 13, February 17, and May 16, 1661; *Elliot*, vii. 263.

SECTION 2.—For the extent of the famine of 1630, see *English Factories*, iv. *passim*; *Mundy*, ii. 55 ff.; *Elliot*, vii. 24. Its story is scattered all through *English Factories*, iv.; *van Twist's* narrative is c. III. For relief measures, see *Elliot*, vii. 24; *Etheridge*, 39, 63; *Mundy*, ii. 49, 50, 56. The account of effects on industry and commerce is compiled from *English Factories*, iv.; and of the gradual recovery, from *idem*, iv., v. The facts regarding the Deccan are taken from *Badshahnama*, ii. 710, and *Sarkar's Aurangzeb*, i. 170 ff.

CHAPTER VIII

THE ECONOMIC INFLUENCE OF THE ADMINISTRATION

1. The Position of Foreign Merchants in Indian States

We must now turn to the last branch of our study, and examine the economic significance of the administrative and financial institutions which existed in India during our period. Our knowledge of the practical working of the various administrations is derived so largely from the observations of Dutch and English merchants that it is important for us to realise at the outset the position occupied by the observers, the more so that nothing like it can be found in India at the present day. If a company of foreign merchants, Americans let us say, or Japanese, were to decide on establishing an agency in modern Calcutta or Bombay, their resulting rights and liabilities would be clearly known beforehand. They would not require official permission to occupy offices and warehouses, nor would they have to enter into preliminary negotiations regarding the customs tariff, the harbour-dues, or the transit charges applicable to their particular business. The ports and cities would be open to them, but the fact of their settlement would involve automatically their submission to large sections of the law of India; they would not be exempt from the ordinary jurisdiction of the civil or criminal courts, and they would be under legal obligation to comply with the regulations in force regarding customs tariffs and many other matters. This arrangement, which nowadays seems as natural as it is convenient, is, in Asia at least, quite modern. At the time of which I am writing, ports and cities were not open to settlements of foreign merchants as a matter of course; such settlements were based on special conventions or agreements, and the position of the merchants with regard to the authorities was determined by these conventions rather than the ordinary law. It has sometimes been asserted that the privileges of foreign merchants were forcibly acquired by the first arrivals from Europe, but the truth appears to be that similar privileges were enjoyed by Asiatic merchants before European vessels had entered Indian waters, and that the new arrivals accommodated themselves to arrangements which they found already in existence.

The nature of these purely Asiatic arrangements may be illustrated by two instances in which the facts are clearly on record—Malacca, the greatest seaport in the Farther East, and Calicut, which, before the changes resulting from the advent of the Portuguese, was probably the greatest port in India. When Alboquerque reached Malacca in the year 1511, the city already contained several foreign mercantile settlements; the men of each nation lived under their own laws and customs; and each nation had a chief or head-man of its own, who exercised the functions of a governor in regard to his nationals. Alboquerque's arrival resulted in a divergence of interest among these foreign communities: the Chinese and the Javans welcomed him, but the Moslems from the west coast of India, supported by their Malay co-religionists, were bitterly opposed to the establishment of a Portuguese settlement, and it was their predominant influence over the King which led to the outbreak of hostilities. The motives actuating the two parties are not formally on record, but it is obvious that the question at issue was essentially commercial; Malacca being the port of transhipment between East and West, the Chinese and Javans, who brought Eastern goods there for sale, would naturally welcome competing Western buyers, while the Indian Moslems, apart from their existing quarrel with the Portuguese, would naturally make every effort to maintain their monopoly of the westward trade. The Portuguese could not establish a trading settlement at

Malacca as a matter of course, but required permission from the King; their settlement was opposed by the other foreign merchants with whom they would compete; and their attempts to negotiate a convention were unsuccessful. In the result Alboquerque effected a settlement by force of arms, and the city passed into the possession of the Portuguese, under whom the old privileges of foreign merchants gradually disappeared.

The position at Calicut some years earlier was essentially similar. When the Portuguese attempted to secure a settlement there, they were supported by the subjects of the Zamorin or King, who were engaged in the import trade from the East, while they were opposed by the Arab and Egyptian merchants, who controlled the export trade to the Red Sea; here, as in Malacca, importers were eager to welcome new customers, while exporters exerted all their influence to keep out new competitors. In this case also the exporters prevailed with the authorities, and the Portuguese found that no convention could be arranged. Now these Arabs and Egyptians were not subject to the jurisdiction of the Zamorin of Calicut, but had a resident governor of their own; there was thus a foreign commercial settlement in Calicut, governing itself and outside the control of the local law, just as there were several foreign and self-governing commercial settlements in Malacca.

Nor was Calicut the only Indian seaport where the institution of mercantile extra-territoriality was recognised in the early years of the sixteenth century, for the description left to us by Barbosa shows that it prevailed on extensive sections of the coast. In Malabar, we read that the Chettis from the East Coast "manage their own affairs, the King may not enquire into their crimes; they do justice to one another, with which the King is satisfied." In the same region the foreign Moslems "have in the town itself a Moorish [Moslem] Governor of their own, who rules and punishes them without interference from the King, save that the Governor gives an account of certain matters to the King." In Kayal again the Moslem farmer of the pearl-fishery "executes judgment and justice on the Moors [Moslems] without interference from the King"; and speaking generally, Barbosa's account shows that mercantile extra-territoriality existed on the coasts of India before Portuguese influence had an opportunity of altering the institutions of the country. The arrangement was of course familiar to the first arrivals from Europe, and we find the Dutch and English merchants accepting it without comment both in India and in the islands farther east; but the suggestion that they imported it must be set aside as unhistorical.

The first settlements made in India by the Portuguese must not be regarded as conforming to this Asiatic custom, because they were much more than commercial: the commanders of their early expeditions usually insisted on territorial concessions, or in the alternative seized territory by force, but in doing this they were acting as representatives of the king of Portugal, and not as merchants. Some of their later commercial settlements, such as Hooghly, conformed more nearly to the Asiatic type, but even in these they were assisted by, and presumed on, the prestige of their existing dominion. The chronicler Khāfi Khān wrote that the Portuguese started at Hooghly with a grant of land for stores and residences, but in course of time they overstepped the sufferance they had obtained, and I take it that in a general way this statement is correct, and that Portuguese merchants assumed rights of sovereignty in their settlements, relying on the naval power which had been established in Asia by their nation.

The earliest Dutch settlements, on the other hand, were purely commercial, and were made in accordance with existing Asiatic practice. In regard to them it is important to bear in mind the distinction drawn in an earlier chapter between the Voyage and the Factory. The original idea of a trading voyage, where a ship merely stayed at a port long enough to sell and buy, did not involve any necessity for a durable convention, but at the most a temporary agreement regarding customs and port dues; and accordingly the narrative of the first Dutch expedition under Houtman, which is the type of a trading voyage, does not throw direct light on the position of foreign settlements in Java, though there is a hint in it that the Chinese merchants may have had privileges such as foreigners enjoyed in other Asiatic seaports.[1] The question of similar privileges for the Dutch can have arisen only when the mere trading voyage had been found unsuitable, and the step was taken from Voyage to Factory: when once it was decided to settle Dutch merchants at any seaport, their position towards the authorities would have to be laid down with precision, because, in the absence of the ships, the few Dutchmen on land would be dependent on them for protection. The published narratives of the expeditions which succeeded Houtman's are incomplete, and I have been unable to find an account of the first actual settlement of a Dutch factory, but factors were certainly resident in Achin before September 1602, and others were appointed at Bantam in December of that year. There is good reason to suppose that extra-territorial privileges were enjoyed from the outset, because the earliest extant regulations for the factories, which were issued in 1603, provide for the exercise of independent jurisdiction, not as a novelty but as an existing institution, by the authorities in charge of the factory, and definitely authorise the infliction of punishments. In 1603, therefore, and probably for some time before, the Dutch enjoyed privileges similar to those of the Arabs in India a century earlier; their settlement, or factory, was already a foreign self-governing community. In the case of the earliest English settlement there is no room for doubt, for the Commander of the first fleet commenced his operations at Achin by negotiating a convention, which provided definitely for internal self-government, and this Achin convention was quoted as a suitable precedent in the instructions issued in England to subsequent fleets.

The same procedure was followed on both sides of India. In the year 1606 the Dutch attempted to obtain a settlement

[1] In the description of Bantam given in the Journal of Houtman's voyage, mention is made of the separate settlement occupied by Chinese merchants, but no details are given of their status (*Houtman*, i. 108). The fact that the Dutch recognised a "captain" of the Chinese in Batavia suggests that the earlier Chinese settlements in Java had been self-governing.

at Pulicat, but on this occasion opposition was offered by the Portuguese, and no convention could be negotiated. The vessel sailed therefore for Masulipatam, where negotiations were carried on, first with the local authorities, and then with the king of Golconda, until an agreement was reached, and factories were established under it. A few years later we have similar negotiations with the Hindu authorities farther south, leading to settlements in Tegnapatam and Pulicat, as well as a convention with Calicut, which, however, was not followed up; while the experience gained on the East Coast was utilised in drafting a set of terms for a Dutch settlement at Surat, which again include reservation of criminal jurisdiction, the distinctive mark of self-government. In the Mogul Empire, however, the lead was taken by the English, and the position proved to be unlike that which existed in the maritime Asiatic states. The authorities at Calicut, Masulipatam, and Pulicat, like the kings of Bantam and Achin, were familiar with the institution of mercantile extra-territoriality, but the Great Mogul had the outlook of Central Asia, where such ideas are not likely to have been known, and in his Empire the grant of a concession was not a matter of course. Hawkins, the commander of the first English ship to reach Surat, was informed that the local authorities could allow him to trade, but that the settlement of a factory required the Emperor's orders, and he travelled to Agra to endeavour to secure "capitulations" for that purpose. His diplomacy was unsuccessful, as we have seen, and the effective settlement dates from 1612, when Best and Aldworth negotiated a convention with the local authorities, and received what they understood to be the Emperor's formal ratification. The discovery of their mistake was followed by further negotiations, which are recounted at length in the journal of Sir Thomas Roe; for a long time he pressed for a definite treaty, but eventually he was satisfied by a concession, which was in essence a convention, but in point of form fell short of his original aim. For our present purpose, the most important article was that which provided that the Englishmen in the settlement should live according to their own religion and laws without interference, thus securing to them an extra-territorial position.

In the same way it could be shown that other settlements established in India by both Companies were based on conventions securing to the merchants certain terms in matters of commerce and also exclusive jurisdiction over men of their own nation, but enough has been said to justify the statement that the position of both Dutch and English in India was essentially similar to that of Asiatic foreigners in places like Malacca or Calicut; the merchants had not submitted to Indian jurisdiction, as modern merchants would necessarily do, but lived and traded in the country on terms which had been settled with the authorities, and which both sides were bound to observe. The point is of practical importance, because it explains the nature of certain transactions which bulk largely in the records of our period, and which are almost unintelligible without a knowledge of the actual conditions. Conventions were infringed on several occasions by the authorities in various Indian States, and when a State breaks a convention the normal result is the risk of an outbreak of hostilities. The few Dutchmen or Englishmen in one or other of the factories could not, of course, enter on a war on land with the Mogul Emperor or the king of Golconda, but they could on occasion make war successfully on the sea, because, as we have seen, the Indian States maintained no naval forces; and thus we find the usual course of trade broken from time to time by events which are described as Reprisals, and which consisted of coercive measures taken against Indian-owned ships. These measures must be regarded as acts of war; the State had infringed a convention, and the sufferers considered themselves justified by the principles of international morality as then understood in exacting redress by force. Like other acts of war, they must be judged mainly by their efficacy, and in this respect the superiority lay definitely with the Dutch.

As an example of reprisals conducted by the English, we may take the events of 1623–24, a clear account of which will be found in the Introductions to the volumes of *The English Factories in India* for 1622–23 and 1624–29. Omitting unnecessary details, the position was that the English factors at Surat held that they had been oppressed in contravention of the terms of their settlement. They decided, therefore, to seize some Gujarat ships which were returning richly laden from the Red Sea, and to hold them as security until redress should be granted; they carried out this project successfully, and there can be no doubt that their action constituted an act of open hostility against the Mogul Empire. The immediate result was that the Mogul authorities capitulated; a new convention was framed and ratified, granting compensation for past injuries, and favourable terms for the future; the Indian vessels were restored to their owners; and the English force, consisting of four ships in all, dispersed to England, Persia, and Sumatra. This was, however, only the first act of the drama. Almost as soon as the English were left without means of offence through the departure of their ships, the Moguls reopened hostilities, and early in 1624 seized the various factories; negotiations were then renewed, and eventually a fresh convention was ratified, under which the English lost much of what had been gained, but retained permission to trade as well as the right of self-government. The idea of further action was considered by the English and rejected; the convention of 1624 therefore remained in force, and no similar trouble occurred for some years. The English at Surat have been blamed for committing an outrage in seizing the Indian ships, but, regarded as an act of war, their conduct was undoubtedly legitimate; their fault lay in their misjudgment of the position, for it should have been obvious to them that their strength lay only in their ships, and, since the needs of commerce prevented them from keeping the ships in harbour, it was injudicious to enter on hostilities with an enemy who, in the absence of the ships, was infinitely superior in force. This was the view taken at the time by the Italian traveller, della Valle, who was then living at Goa. His information came from Portuguese sources, and consequently presented the details of the English activities in an unfavourable light, but his verdict on the general question was as follows:

For my part, I think the English have not managed their business discreetly in this case; for it is not possible for a few strangers and immigrants to contest with and get the better of a great king in his own country. And upon the rising of the like differences I should account it the best course to settle them with good words, and amicably with the said king, . . . otherwise if redress cannot be obtained, then before a manifest feud, 'twere best to get out of his power and war upon him securely, not in his own country, where there are so many people, and the king undoubtedly hath more power than any other.

The contemporary neutral view was, then, that such reprisals were permissible, but that the English acted foolishly in attempting them in unfavourable circumstances. With the English action on this occasion we may contrast the conduct of the Dutch a few years later, when they were driven by oppression to break with the king of Golconda: they first withdrew their factory from Masulipatam, and then, acting from their base at Pulicat, opened hostilities by a blockade of the enemy's port. This measure proved successful. The authorities entered into negotiations with the commander of the blockading squadron, the governor of Masulipatam was dismissed, and a royal decree invited the Dutch to return and re-establish their trade. The success achieved in this case was clearly due to the existence of a convenient base of action outside Golconda territory. The State had no naval forces, and consequently Masulipatam lay at the mercy of Pulicat, where a few gunboats sufficed to dominate the coast; the Dutch factors possessed, what the English at Surat lacked, sufficient power to threaten their enemy at a vulnerable point without exposing themselves to greater danger, and thus they were in a position to insist on adherence to the terms of their convention.

The fortress at Pulicat, which proved so serviceable on this occasion, marks the second stage in the gradual progress towards European territorial dominion in India: as the Voyage had led to the Factory, so the Factory led to the Fort, because an unprotected factory offered no guarantee for the safety of its inmates or the maintenance of the terms under which it had been established. The foundation of Pulicat thus possesses peculiar interest for students of commercial history, because it was the first fort in India to be held by the merchants of a European Company, and it led directly to Armagon and to Madras. I know of no connected account of its establishment, but contemporary documents show that it must be described as an accident rather than as the outcome of deliberate policy. As we have seen in Chapter II., the Dutch soon learned that their first Indian factories, which were located in the Kistna delta, would not serve all the markets in which they were interested, and they were thus led to look farther south. In the first instance they applied to a nayak, or chief, for a settlement near Tegnapatam, and the nayak offered to grant them a fort, but they refused the offer, and preferred to settle under his protection; in other words, they were then contented with a factory.[1] A year or two later they desired to extend their business to Pulicat, and obtained from the king of Chandragiri terms for a settlement there, which were modelled on those in force at Tegnapatam: at the outset, therefore, Pulicat was merely a factory. Its transformation was due primarily to the hostility of the Portuguese at S. Thomé, itself a settlement of a somewhat anomalous nature.[2] In 1612 the Portuguese attacked Pulicat and expelled the Dutch. The King was anxious to fulfil his obligation to protect the sufferers, but he was not in a position to take decisive action against the aggressors, and the outcome was a further convention concluded by him with the Dutch agent. Under this convention a fort was to be built at the cost of the local authorities, and was to be occupied partly by them and partly by the Dutch, but the local authorities neglected to perform their part of the agree-

[1] The documents I have seen do not explain why the nayak should have offered a fort, but presumably he supposed that the Dutch would follow the precedents set by the Portuguese in the vicinity; the point is that the offer was made, and was refused.

[2] I make out S. Thomé to be one of the places where the Portuguese assumed greater power than they had been granted. *Couto* (X. i. 49) distinguishes it from the Portuguese territories on the West Coast as not being the King's "patrimony," but says it was "peopled by his vassals" and "governed by the laws of his kingdom." *Methwold* (994) says it was governed by Portuguese, "who notwithstanding must acknowledge some dependency from the nayak." The Portuguese in the town certainly governed themselves, but they were not in sovereign possession of its area.

ment, and left the fort half-built; the Dutch agent completed it at the cost of the Company; friction inevitably arose over the joint occupation; the Indian troops were withdrawn; and by a convention made in the year 1616 the Dutch were left in sole possession of Fort Geldria, as they named it. For some time it was a fort and nothing more, for Methwold, who had lived in it, tells us that the Dutch claimed no sovereignty over the native inhabitants, exacted no duties, and prescribed no laws, contenting themselves with confronting the Portuguese and transacting their mercantile affairs. It is true that, as time went on, they assumed more extensive dominion, but the possession of the fort, which enabled them to do so, was the result of circumstances, not of policy: at the outset they sought from the king of Chandragiri protection against the Portuguese, and they came by stages into possession of a fortress which was to set a new fashion throughout India.

We have seen already the advantages conferred by the possession of Pulicat in the dispute at Masulipatam. In 1626 the Dutch Company desired to secure a similar fortified harbour to command Surat; and about the same time the English were considering a plan for taking Bombay from the Portuguese.[1] These designs were abandoned, but the first English fort, built at Armagon on the East Coast, was an imitation of Pulicat, and was intended to overawe the rulers of Golconda as well as to facilitate trade, while Madras, the successor of Armagon, was designed to serve the same purposes. Andrew Cogan, one of its founders, wrote thus:

> The Company must give order for the making good a place for the security of their estate[2] in India; which how much prejudice the want hath been is very visible, for are we not continually subject, and have not your estates made good all demands from time to time, be it right or wrong? And lastly, are we certain of continual peace with the Portugals and Dutch? No; for the peace we enjoy by them is but for their own ends.

[1] Some years earlier Roe had been attracted by the idea of a fortress on the coast of Gujarat, but he gave it up on the ground of expense (*Roe*, 344).

[2] The word estate had not yet been restricted to its modern signification of landed property, but was used in the wider sense of property in general. The older sense survives in such legal phrases as personal estate.

All which being duly considered, 'twere very requisite that the making good a place were first put in practice; from which will arise these benefits: you shall be ever secured of the most part of your estate, and if any affront [be] offered be enabled to do yourselves right.

In this way the Dutch and the English Companies obtained possession of the fortresses on the East Coast.[1] Ten or fifteen years after the founding of Madras, the English at Surat were anxious to imitate the precedent, and here also two motives were prominent: on the one hand, they desired to be independent of Indian officials, on the other they were anxious for protection against the Dutch, just as the Dutch at Pulicat had been anxious for protection against the Portuguese. In the year 1653 we hear of a project for obtaining possession of Bombay: in 1658 the Company authorised the President at Surat to negotiate for Bombay, Bassein, or some other suitable place; and though no definite result followed within our period, a few years after its close the English were established in Bombay, while the Dutch had secured the fortress of Cochin. From this time forward, the Fort may be regarded as an essential part of the equipment of a European trading venture on the coast of India: the later steps in the acquisition of territorial dominion lie beyond the scope of this book.

In the foregoing paragraphs I have attempted to describe the gradual development of commercial policy, from the Voyage to the Factory, and from the Factory to the Fort. The ideas of European merchants in the sixteenth century did not extend beyond the familiar trading voyage, but the conditions prevailing in Eastern markets required the establishment of factories, and, when the factories were in existence, the political and administrative environment led almost inevitably to fortresses upon the coasts. But whether Dutch and English merchants were living in factories or in forts, they had not submitted, nor had they been required to submit, to Indian jurisdiction: under conventions with the

[1] The Danes also had obtained a fort at Tranquebar, but I do not know of any account showing in detail the circumstances of its acquisition.

authorities they formed self-governing communities, and they could view the conduct of those authorities from the outside. They were not bound to the subjects of Indian States by ties of common political interests, and their observations of the relations between States and subjects are entitled to the respect us uallyaccorded to the views of independent witnesses. They thus fill an important gap in our knowledge, for the Indian literature of our period is written almost wholly from the official standpoint, and presents only one side of the case, frequently in terms coloured by conventional flattery of the rulers: we are dependent on this literature for accounts of existing institutions as seen through the atmosphere of the Court or the Capital, but we must turn to Dutch and English records to know how those institutions actually worked, and how they were regarded in the towns and villages of the country.

One other preliminary observation seems to be required. In the discussions which follow I estimate the various Indian administrations strictly from the economist's standpoint, and the conclusions I have reached are sufficiently unfavourable to suggest that the India of the seventeenth century must have been an Inferno for the ordinary man. It is perhaps arguable that that view is applicable to Asia as a whole, but among Asiatic States a relatively high position must be assigned to the administration of Jahangir and Shahjahan. It was indeed inferior to that of China, but, on the evidence left by travellers and merchants of many nations, the Mogul Empire may fairly be placed on about the same level as Persia or Japan, and far above the rule of the Turks to the West, Achin to the South, and Arakan, Pegu or Siam to the East. Had my object been to discuss the comparative value of the institutions of different countries, I should have gone into this subject at length; but in a book which deals solely with India this general statement must suffice, and readers who may think that the description of Indian administrations is too unfavourable to represent the truth may be advised to examine for themselves the position in some of the other States which I have named.

2. Indian Administrative Systems

A study of the materials whose nature has been briefly indicated in the preceding section leads us to the conclusion that in the India of our period the working of the administration was, next to the rainfall, the most important factor in the economic life of the country. It acted directly on the distribution of the national income to an extent which is now difficult to realise, for in practice the various governments disposed of somewhere about one half of the entire gross produce of the land, and they disposed of it in such a way that the producers were left with a bare subsistence or very little more, while the energies of the unproductive classes were spent in the struggle to secure the largest possible share. The reaction on production was inevitably unfavourable: producers were deprived of the natural incentive to energy, because they could not hope to retain any material proportion of an increase in their income; men of ability or talent were discouraged from producing, and attracted by the very great prizes to be won in the struggle for distribution; it was better to be a peon than a peasant; and critics who express surprise at the tendency of Indian brains and energy to seek employment in the service of the State will find ample explanation in the history of the centuries during which no other career was possible. We must, therefore, examine the nature and working of the administration in greater detail than would be necessary if we were concerned with the present day, and I shall first attempt to sketch the outline of the systems which prevailed, and then pass to a fuller consideration of their actual working.

The Indian governments with which we are concerned were in all cases despotic, and there are no traces of any popular institutions exercising political authority or even influence. The seat of power was at the capital of the State, and everything that was done was in theory done by order of the Ruler, though it might in fact be the work of a subordinate acting in his master's name. There was no code of written law as the term is now understood, and no public machinery existed for promulgating or harmonising the orders or regulations of the State : apart from religious obligations, the Ruler was untrammelled, and an order given one day might be reversed the next.[1] But while there were no legislative or deliberative institutions, there was in every State an organised administrative machine designed to carry the Ruler's orders into effect. The Ministers at Court directed and controlled the activities of a regular hierarchy of localised officials, whose primary duty was to collect the revenue, but who had to carry out whatever orders might be given, and who owed obedience to the Ruler and not to his subjects. The actual government of the country can best be described, therefore, as a union of despotism with bureaucracy, and the emphasis on either element depended at any given time mainly on the personal character of the Ruler. Under Jahangir, for instance, the local officials had in practice very wide powers, because the Emperor was disinclined to enter into details : in Golconda, there were times when the King scarcely counted, and the group of Persian Ministers at his Court were practically uncontrolled ; while conditions in the Hindu territories appear to have varied with the individuality of the nāyaks or local chiefs, some of whom might be obedient to their king, at a time when others were practically independent. Wherever orders might originate, the duty of the subjects was obedience to the officials with whom they came directly in contact ; a particular order might come from king, or minister, or subordinate, but its source was a matter of little moment to merchants, peasants or artisans, who had to reckon with the men on the spot. There are cases on record in which individuals or communities appealed successfully against oppression by local officers, but there are, perhaps, an equal number where an official whose acts had been questioned returned to his duties exonerated through bribery or influence, and the facts appear to justify the inference that oppression was always possible, and that the prospects of an appeal were dubious.[2] Thus the welfare

[1] In the greater part of India the canon law of Islam was recognised in theory, but not in such a way as to hinder the practical freedom of the executive (*Pelsart*, MS., f. 21).

[2] The experience of Vīrji Vora, recounted in Chapter V., may be taken

of the people depended partly on the character of the local officials, partly on the efficiency of the system of control, and partly on the ideals of the Ruler.

In the matter of control two distinct systems prevailed. In some cases public office was farmed, that is to say, an official agreed to pay a fixed sum for his post, and retained whatever surplus revenue he could collect; this system, which in Indian official terminology is described as holding office *pakka*, or *pukhta*, appears to have been practically universal throughout our period in the south of India,[1] and it was making headway, I think rapidly, in the Mogul Empire, in which Akbar had aimed at establishing the alternative system of "direct" administration. In direct administration, which Indians describe as holding office *kachcha*, or *khām*, the official receives a fixed salary, and accounts to his superior for all the revenue which he collects. In the India of our period it took two different forms, according to the method in which the salary was paid. Akbar's ideal was the modern practice of paying salaries in cash from the treasury, but the older Indian method of paying by *jāgīr* was generally adopted by his successors. A *jāgīr* was the assignment, by way of salary and allowances, of the revenue yielded by a tract of land, which the assignee took under management almost as if it had been his own estate, and from which he attempted to collect at least the amount stipulated, and in some cases was able to realise a substantial additional sum. Assignments of revenue were also granted for other purposes, which may be described rather loosely as charitable; a tract of land might be held in

as an example of a successful appeal against local oppression. Against it may be set the fact, recorded in the next section, that a Governor, who had been called to the Court for punishment, had been liberated by bribes and influence, and returned to his duties, threatening vengeance on his accusers. Manucci tells us in his account of Shahjahan's captivity that the old King justified his past administration by the fact that months would pass without any one presenting a petition to him; the inference that nobody had any grievance against his officers will, however, scarcely commend itself to students of the period (*Manucci*, ii. 19).

[1] In *India at the Death of Akbar* I stated the prevalence of farming in the south as an inference drawn from indirect evidence. I had not then come across the materials utilised in the next section, which show that the system was in fact prevalent early in the seventeenth century.

this way by the custodians of a mosque or temple, or by a family or individual to whom it had been granted for maintenance or as a reward for past services, and in some of the Mogul provinces the aggregate of these charitable assignments was relatively large. Lastly, the administration of large areas was left in the hands of chiefs or persons of local influence known as *zamindārs*, who in practice exercised very considerable power so long as they paid the stipulated revenue. The actual status of a *zamindār* approximated to that of a farmer, but the normal duration of the tenure was greater, and the position was, I think usually, hereditary, though it could, of course, be terminated in a moment by the decision of the Ruler. An Indian peasant might thus find himself under a master of one of five different classes, a farmer of the revenue, a salaried official, a *jāgīrdār* in temporary possession, a private person or corporation with a longer and possibly a permanent tenure, or, finally, a *zamindār*; and the powers of his master were so great, and the chances of superior interference so small, that his welfare depended principally on the master under whom he happened to come.

Administrative progress has rendered the farming system so nearly obsolete that it may be well to say a little regarding its nature. The system was not, of course, peculiar to India, but at one time might almost have been described as general, and it may be recalled that the English Company had regular transactions with the farmers of the customs in London, while its factors were dealing with the farmers of the customs at Surat or Masulipatam. Its existence may be taken as connoting two things, obstacles in the way of detailed control, and emphasis on the financial as opposed to the ameliorative side of administration. The obstacles to control were mainly the result of imperfect means of communication, and no small part of the history of the art of administration is made up of the gradual development of methods of supervision which depend on the modern posts, telegraphs, and means of locomotion. So long as a subordinate remained isolated at a distance, little detailed supervision was possible, and in practice there was something to be said for a system which did not attempt impossibilities, but concentrated on what was regarded as the essential point, the punctual payment of a fixed revenue. At the same time allowance must be made for the fact that the ameliorative side of administration is itself largely modern; a foreign observer may be pardoned for questioning the appropriateness of the designation of an Indian Collector at the present day, but during our period there was no question that a collector's first duty was to keep the treasury supplied with funds, and it is easy to realise that in some circumstances the most effective way of securing this was to bind him to pay a fixed sum whatever happened, and leave him a large measure of freedom so long as the essential stipulation was fulfilled.

The farming system could not in any ordinary case commend itself to a modern administrator, but its actual effects might vary within wide limits. The first English officials in India gained much practical experience of it while bringing into order the financial system inherited by them, and their conclusions may be summarised in a sentence which now reads like a commonplace. The evils of farming will, it may be said, be minimised if the farmer is carefully chosen, if his payments are fixed at a moderate figure, and if his tenure is sufficiently long to enable him to pursue a constructive policy; on the other hand, the oppression of the people will be greatest when the farm is given for a short period on purely financial considerations, for then the farmer will have no interest other than the immediate exaction of the largest possible sum. The practice of annual auctions of the farms of the revenue, which prevailed, as we shall see, in the kingdom of Golconda, may be described as on the whole the most oppressive method of administration which has hitherto been devised; we are not entitled to infer that peasants in other parts of the country were exposed to the same degree of oppression, but we are bound to recognise that oppression was a real danger wherever the farming system prevailed.

The peasant holding land in an assigned tract might be either fortunate or unfortunate according to the nature of the assignment. When the grant was intended to be durable, and the grantee could pursue a constructive policy, the peasants might be comparatively well off, as appears to have been the case in Farid Khan's *jāgīr* near Benares in the sixteenth century, or under Shaista Khan in Bengal at the close of our period; but when assignments were changed frequently, as in the reign of Jahangir, the temporary possessor thought only of extracting as much as the peasants could pay, or in the words of Hawkins, "he racketh the poor to get from them what he can, who still thinketh every hour to be put out of his place."[1] The peasant whose land was included neither in a farm nor in an assignment was in theory fortunate, since his master had less direct incentive to oppress him, but in practice the lack of effective supervision made oppression possible; and though our information on the subject is necessarily defective, it appears to be probable that those peasants were best off who held land from a *zamindār* of an old-established family. It must not be inferred that the life of such peasants was idyllic, but such evidence as that of Bernier, which will be quoted in a later section, indicates that the average of oppression was lower under *zamindārs* than under either officials or assignees.

While the peasant was concerned primarily with the collector of the land revenue, the interests of merchants and artisans centred in the arrangements for realising an indefinite number of taxes on production and transport. The farming system appears to have been adopted generally for the customs revenue, for we find it in existence in Sind and Gujarat as well as on the East Coast, and, as we shall see, the position of the farmers was such as to render oppression almost inevitable. The situation in regard to duties on production and inland transit cannot be summed up in a phrase; the subject will be examined in the next chapter, and for the present it must

[1] Hawkins' pointed description of the system of assignments will be found in *Purchas*, I. iii. 221, and *Early Travels*, 114. The prosperity of the peasants under Farid Khan is described in *Elliot*, iv. 313, and Shaista Khan's beneficence in Bengal is recounted in a chronicle translated in *Sarkar's Studies* (155 ff.), but both these documents are eulogies, and their language is subject to a rather high rate of discount. In both it is easy to see the extent of the general oppression with which these favoured areas are contrasted.

suffice to say that while such duties were nearly universal, their assessment was left in the hands of local officers, who thus exercised an important influence on the prosperity of merchants and artisans.

The foregoing summary will show that production was dominated by the administration to an extent which has no parallel in British India at the present day. The sections which follow will be devoted to a more detailed examination of the subject, and we may begin with the practical working of the farming system, which prevailed throughout the southern regions.

3. The Farming System in the South

The fullest account of the system of administration which prevailed during our period in Golconda is contained in "A Description of the Domains of the King Kotebipa lying on the Coromandel Coast," which appears as an insertion in the later editions of the narrative of Pieter van den Broecke's Voyages.[1] The arrangement of the text suggests that the description is by a different author, and this is made certain by internal evidence, for the writer had spent six years on the coast, while van den Broecke was there for a few weeks only; presumably the editor thought a fuller account of Coromandel was desirable to complete van den Broecke's story, and inserted the description with this object. The author's name is not given, but the date of composition is fixed by a reference to the war "during the last two years" between Ahmadnagar and the Portuguese at Chaul; the only war to which this can refer is the fighting which took place in that region between 1612 and 1614, and we are justified in accepting the description as the work of a Dutch factor who was stationed at Petapoli (Nizampatam) from about 1608 to 1614, and whose duties,

[1] The description did not appear in the edition of the Voyages published in 1634, soon after the author's return to Holland. Its first appearance seems to be on p. 77 of the reprint in vol. ii. of *Begin ende Voortgangh*, and it is also given in the independent reissue of 1648; no MS. appears to have survived. "Kotebipa" is an obvious mistake for Kutbshah, more correctly Kutb-ul-Mulk, the title of the Golconda dynasty.

as his narrative shows, required him to travel through the villages; we have, therefore, the experience of one who was in a position to appreciate the every-day working of the administration.

According to this description, the chief authority at the Court of Golconda was at this time in the hands of Persians, "the proudest nation in India," who would not usually take a local appointment, but were employed as farmers-in-chief or as inspectors over the subordinate officers. The kingdom was divided into districts under "Governors,"[1] whose chief duty was to collect the revenue, and these posts were farmed by the year to the highest bidders. Most of the local governors were brahmans or banians, "the craftiest and most knavish people in all India," who gave lavish presents to their superiors at Court, so that the complaints of the poor could never reach the king. The amount of revenue collected from the peasants was so great as to surprise the narrator; often, he says, "when I was travelling in the kingdom I wondered whence such large sums could be obtained, for the people are very poor and live miserably"; and in other places he writes of the severity of the governors, the difficulty they experienced in fulfilling their contracts, and the resulting impoverishment of the country. We may take the district of Petapoli as an example of the financial arrangements in force. The farm was for 55,000 pagodas, but it had been sublet to the actual governor for 1000 p. more; out of this, 8000 p. were allowed to the governor for salaries of subordinates, while a cess levied by him brought 5000 p. for the same purpose. Most of the salaries, though calculated in cash, were paid in grain and salt of inferior quality, valued at least one-third above their cost, and in this way a profit was made. The narrative does not say how the

[1] I retain the word "Governor" because of its regular use in the contemporary authorities, but its meaning is more nearly that of District Officer. The head of a Mogul province is usually described as Viceroy, or by an Indian title such as *Sahibsuba*: the Portuguese appear to have applied their word *governador* to the chief local authority with whom they came in contact, and it was doubtless through Portuguese interpreters that this use passed to the Dutch and the English. In the Mogul Empire it usually signifies the *Amil*, who was subordinate to the provincial Viceroy.

revenue was assessed, and other accounts are also silent on this point, so we are left to infer the probable standard of payments from the necessities of the governors, who were kept under strict discipline. The stipulated annual sum had to be paid in three instalments within the year, and default was visited with severe floggings; the narrator says he had personal knowledge of some cases in which defaulting governors had been permanently injured by the punishments inflicted on them. Flogging could, however, be avoided by borrowing from the Persian officials at Court, who made a business of usury, and "were not ashamed" to charge a governor five per cent monthly if he was known to be in difficulties, thus "draining him to the dregs."

This description is confirmed in substance by the concise report which another Dutch merchant, Antony Schorer, sent home from Masulipatam in 1615, and it agrees in all important points with the slightly later account written by William Methwold on his return to England after several years' service on the East Coast. In Methwold's view, the king of Golconda's subjects were

> all his tenants, and at a rack rent. . . . The government is farmed immediately from the King by some eminent man, who to other inferiors farmeth out the lesser ones, and they again to the country-people, at such excessive rates that it is most lamentable to consider what toil and misery the wretched souls endure. For if they fall short of any part of their rent, what their estates cannot satisfy, their bodies must, so it sometimes happens they are beaten to death, or, absenting themselves, their wives, children, fathers, brothers, and all their kindred are engaged in the debt, and must satisfy or suffer. And sometimes it so happens that the Principal, failing with the King, receives from him the like punishment, as it befell to one Basbell Raw (Governor at Masulipatam since the English traded thither), who, for defect of full payment, was beaten with canes upon the back, feet, and belly, until he died. Yet hold they not these their governments by lease, for yearly in July all are exposed in sale unto him that bids most; from whence it happeneth that every Governor, during his time, exacts by tolls taken in the way and other oppressions whatsoever they can possibly extort from the poorer inhabitants, using what violence within their governments they

shall think fit; for in them, during their time, they reign as petty kings.

This system of administration appears, as I have said in the last section, to be perhaps the most oppressive which has yet been devised. The annual term, the auction of posts, and the severity shown to defaulters combined with the extortion and usury at headquarters to make up a method of stripping producers practically bare, and we need not wonder at the statement of the Dutch narrator that no rich man dare let the fact of his wealth be known, or openly raise his standard of living, since the governor would at once find some pretext for his ruin. The general accuracy of the narratives is confirmed by various incidental remarks of other observers. As regards the position at Court, we read in one place that the "chancellor" of the kingdom and other great men were working against an English petition in order to secure bribes, "which in these parts will open any passage. . . . Such is the miserable condition of this country, whence justice and truth are fled long since, the poor exceedingly suffering the riches' tyranny without redress." Somewhat later we are told that the King was kept in the dark by the officers at Court, and believed that claims had been satisfied which were in fact being actively pressed; while a Dutch record describes how, when complaints regarding a local official actually reached the King, the offender secured an acquittal by gifts and influence, and returned to his post threatening vengeance on the complainants. We find also confirmation of the statement that the local officials exercised great severity in their administration. In 1632 the governor of Petapoli with his own hand cut a village headman in two pieces for not sowing his land, and by this and other outrages drove the country into rebellion; and a little later the scanty supply of merchandise in Masulipatam was attributed to the governor's intolerable exactions. The truth appears to be that in Golconda a governor could not afford to think of anything except extracting the entire surplus income of the country, and ordinarily he would farm any possible source of revenue to the highest bidder. Thus the English factors at Masulipatam explained the sudden institution of a monopoly of dealings in gold and silver by saying that " this government is farmed at a rack rent, and he best welcome to the principal undertaker [farmer, or contractor] that can devise a new course of raising new revenues." This is the obvious explanation of the incident noted in a former section, when the Dutch were made the subject of a farm, and admission to their place of business was prohibited to any one except the licensees of the syndicate which had paid for the privilege; the Dutch were making a profit, and in Golconda profits were made primarily for the benefit of the authorities. It is noteworthy that individual towns and villages were frequently taken in farm by Dutchmen and Englishmen, sometimes for their Company and sometimes for their private benefit, a fact which confirms Methwold's statement that the farming system permeated the whole country: the governor had undertaken to pay a rack rent, and the obligation was passed on to the multitude of subordinate farmers throughout his jurisdiction. A final instance of the severity of the system may be drawn from some correspondence regarding the farm of Masulipatam itself. In the year 1626 the authorities in Holland were so exasperated by the continual difficulties at this seaport that they were tempted to take the contract for its government, but the proposal was set aside by the Governor General at Batavia on the definite ground that the Dutch merchants could not hope to extort by tyranny the amount required by the Golconda administration; and the decision is significant to students familiar with the administrative efficiency of the Dutch in Eastern countries.

The incidents which I have quoted are spread over the greater part of our period, and indicate that the administrative system in force at its opening remained substantially unchanged so far as the kingdom of Golconda was concerned. The commercial records give very little information regarding the system in the neighbouring kingdom of Bijapur, but where we get a glimpse of it we see similar processes at work. The local governors would not pay any attention to an order from the King until their immediate masters had instructed them to comply with it; and a Dutch report tells how a "high governor" came to Vengurla under a contract to pay a lakh of pagodas in three years, and how, after a short period of active extortion, he was suddenly ejected in favour of a competitor who had offered an increase of 25 per cent. Such incidents do not, at the least, enable us to infer that the people were substantially better off in the west of the Deccan than in the east; and we have the authority of Professor Jadu Nath Sarkar for the statement that the Hindu subjects of Bijapur were depressed as a deliberate policy in the time of Muhammad Adil Shah.

As to the Hindu territories in the south, we know from a large number of references in the Dutch records that farming was the regular practice from Pulicat at least as far as Negapatam. The farms were, sometimes at least, of short duration, for we read that the nayak of Tanjore put in new governors almost every month (doubtless an exaggeration); and the post commonly went to the highest bidder in Tanjore, and also in Pulicat. From time to time we hear of severity and extortion. The trade of Kayal had been ruined by official oppression; the districts round Pulicat were described as held by mean and cunning extortioners, so that people found little security; in the same locality the governor's demands for money had driven many artisans to abscond; and in Tanjore exceptional taxation and extortion sent some hundreds of weavers fleeing to other places in the hope of securing better treatment. On such data as these, it is not easy to distinguish the Hindu system from the Moslem, but the weakness of the central authority resulted in additional risks for the people. Thus we read of towns having two or more governors at once, each appointed by one of the contending parties, and from time to time villages held in farm by the Dutch were attacked and pillaged by the forces of a nayak, who presumably had some sort of claim to their possession. No redress could be expected in such cases. On one occasion when a village had been burnt, the crops carried off, and the inhabitants driven away, the Dutch complained to the king of Chandragiri, but the result was merely a polite letter in which the King said in effect that he could not allow his merchants to suffer such injuries, and that he had told the nayak not to do it again. I have no doubt that individuals differed: some nayaks, and some governors, were probably worse than others; but throughout the whole region the system in force appears to have been such as to render extortion and oppression practically inevitable. The Courts insisted that money should be provided; the local authorities had somehow to find it; and the merchants and producers had to pay. Such a system, once introduced, tends to intensify itself, for no remunerative measure will be dropped, and new expedients will be invented from time to time; its logical result is the reduction of the people to the bare minimum of subsistence, with the possible alternative of a revolutionary change, and, short of the appearance of a strong and beneficent despot, there is no prospect of peaceful amelioration.

As has been said above, our authorities do not indicate the proportion of the gross produce which was claimed by the State, and their silence is probably significant. The governor, who had to pay a rack rent for his district, was bound to claim a rack rent from the farmers of individual villages, while governor and farmer alike hoped to make a profit out of the transaction, and risked their persons in the event of failure to fulfil their undertaking. In these circumstances it does not seem possible that any traditional standards of revenue should have remained effective in practice; the need and the greed of the farmer were the dominant factors, and the only limit to collections was the risk of checking cultivation or driving the peasants to rebellion or flight. The short term of the farms rendered a constructive policy impossible, and I think it is justifiable to conclude that for the south of India, taken as a whole, the first half of the seventeenth century was a period when the masses of the people were forced by the administrative system to live on the border-line of starvation or rebellion.

4. Administrative Changes in the Mogul Empire

When we turn to the north of India, we are met at the outset by a measure of uncertainty as to the practical working of the Mogul administration at the opening of the seventeenth century. Akbar had instituted in a large part of his Empire a revenue system which, though undoubtedly severe by modern standards, was in theory substantially just; it required, however, close supervision, and there are indications that, even in the lifetime of its founder, practice lagged some way behind theory. At the same time we must not underrate Akbar's efficiency as an administrator: the traditional estimate of his great capacity is borne out substantially by independent evidence, and it appears to me to be impossible to accept the view that his regulations existed only on paper. The more reasonable inference is that they were put into practice largely, but not completely; that while many old abuses were checked, some may have survived; and that unscrupulous subordinates may have been finding new methods of oppression to replace the old. On this view the official record of his institutions, known as the *Ain-i-Akbari*, is to be regarded neither as an infallible guide to practice nor as a work of merely theoretical interest, but rather as an authoritative indication of the standard of administration which Akbar endeavoured to secure; we cannot infer that the revenue was everywhere assessed and collected in precise accordance with his regulations, but we can safely compare them with those which were issued by subsequent rulers. Such a comparison will disclose changes in the standard, while incidental observations may assist us to estimate within wide limits the extent of the gulf between standard and practice at different stages in history. It is beyond dispute that Akbar was far superior as an administrator to Jahangir or Shahjahan in their later years, or to Aurangzeb in the greater part of his reign; [1] we should be

[1] Jahangir's rank as administrator can be judged from his own statements in the *Tuzuk*, as well as from the accounts given by *Roe* and other contemporary writers; *Pelsart* (p. 2) traces the commercial decline of Agra to the time when this Emperor abandoned the drudgery of administration for his pleasures, and justice was replaced by violence. I think there are

justified therefore in inferring that the same standard would have been worked more oppressively in 1660 than in 1600, and when we find that a new standard had come into existence in the interval, itself much more oppressive than the old, the conclusion becomes irresistible that for the masses of the people our period was one of growing impoverishment.

Akbar's administrative system was not entirely uniform throughout his dominions.[1] The framework was given by the division of the Empire into provinces (*suba*), of the provinces into districts (*sarkār*), and of the districts into subdivisions (*mahal*), which last usually, but not invariably, coincided with the traditional local areas known as *pargana*. The methods of assessment were adapted to local conditions and might vary within the province, or even within the district. The outlying provinces, Bengal,[2] Berar, Khandesh, and Sind, were left under the systems prevailing at the time of their conquest; in Sind the crops were actually divided by the traditional method, while in the other three provinces some easier and more summary alternatives were in vogue, the precise nature of which is not on record. In the northern

good grounds for the view that Shahjahan's capacity deteriorated with age, though it would carry us too far to set out the evidence at length: in 1636 we are told that "every man honours the king, but no man obeys him"; in 1645 we read of daily appointments and removals of high officials; and a year later of "the king's wavering mind, which like a weathercock turns with the wind" (*English Factories*, v. 204, vii. 302, viii. 51). *Manucci's* favourable account of this Emperor (i. 188) is obviously coloured by time; his caustic descriptions of Aurangzeb's methods (*e.g.* ii. 382) are perhaps better evidence of fact.

[1] The text omits reference to the systems in force in Kashmir and the country which is now Afghanistan; they were very intricate, and the population affected by them was too small to justify their discussion in this connection.

[2] The position in regard to Bengal is somewhat obscure. The long discussions of the eighteenth and early nineteenth centuries (summarised in *Ascoli*) started with the revenue settlement made by Todar (Tooril) Mal in 1582, but the nature of the action taken by him has not yet been made clear; the passage describing it in the *Ain* (translation, ii. 122) is obscure, the MSS. are discordant, and I have not found one of them which makes tolerable sense. The inference that Akbar continued existing arrangements seems, however, to be permissible, and the form of the statistics shows that, whatever Todar Mal may have done in Bengal, he did not introduce the system usually associated with his name. It is possible that some of the extant MSS. were deliberately falsified in the eighteenth century, when the secrets of the revenue system were jealously guarded by Indian officials.

plains from Multan to Bihar, as well as in large parts of Rajputana, Malwa, and Gujarat, the revenue was assessed on the special system identified with the names of Akbar and Todar Mal, and known technically as *Zabt*, but in nearly every province we find areas where a different system is known, or may be suspected, to have prevailed. In most of these areas the determining factor was the presence of tribal chiefs or other men of local influence, who were described collectively as landholders (*zamindār*), and were allowed to engage for the revenue in a lump sum, in some instances at lower rates than would have resulted from assessment on the regulation system. The essence of this system was the determination of fixed cash rates, payable, in place of a fluctuating share of the produce, on each unit of area sown with each crop; the peasant thus knew beforehand the precise amount of his liability to the State, and could adapt his course of cropping to all the circumstances, including the differential revenue rates. These rates once fixed, the procedure required for assessment was limited to the measurement and record of the areas cultivated in each season; given the rates and the areas, a simple calculation sufficed to show the revenue to be demanded from each peasant. The rates were the average value of one-third of the average gross yield as determined once for all by local investigation; the pitch of the revenue demand was thus much higher than is considered wise at the present day, but in other respects the theory of the *zabt* may be regarded as sound. The practical difficulties in its working arose mainly from the quality of the staff available. The seasonal record of crops field by field was a laborious and expensive affair; most of the cost appears to have fallen on the peasants, in addition to the revenue due from them, but the real objection was the scope for extortion by the measuring staff, while in addition to this there was no security in practice against the levy of additional payments by officials of intermediate rank.

A study of Akbar's orders on the subject indicates that he attached great importance to two general principles: whatever the system of assessment might be, he desired that the officials should be paid cash salaries instead of receiving assignments of land, and he insisted that, wherever possible, they should deal directly with the individual peasant cultivators. Our knowledge of the activities of his successors is incomplete on many points, but it is possible to show that these two principles disappeared in the course of the next half century; assignments multiplied, the farming system spread, and the growth of what may be called summary settlements of the revenue gave increased scope for tyranny within the village. These three changes all point to deterioration in the position of the ordinary peasant; in addition we have evidence of increasing pressure to extend the area under crops beyond the economic possibilities of the time; and lastly, we have the standard of assessment raised from one-third of the gross produce to one-half. The cumulative effect of these measures cannot be stated in precise figures, but the facts appear to justify the conclusion that the small margin left by Akbar was swept into the Imperial treasury or the pockets of officials, and that a very large proportion of the peasants were brought dangerously near to the bare level of subsistence. The evidence of these changes must now be set out.

In regard to assignments, it must be remembered that this method of remunerating officials was of old standing: Akbar endeavoured to abolish it, but there are indications that he was not entirely successful, and, when his personal influence was removed, the system quickly regained its previous vogue. The frequent references to assignments in Jahangir's *Memoirs* show that they were normal incidents of his administration, and the same inference can be drawn from the experience of William Hawkins at his Court. If the practice of payments in cash had been at all common, it would almost certainly have been followed in the case of a foreign visitor, but as a matter of fact Hawkins found that, as soon as he had been appointed to an official position under the Emperor, he had to join in the scramble for assignments which he describes so vividly. His narrative shows further that at this time changes of assignment were frequent; a man could not "continue half a year in his living, but it is taken from him, and given unto another"; and consequently it was the assignee's interest to extract the utmost possible sum from each successive grant. Terry also noted the frequency of transfers, saying that officials were usually removed annually, and, while Hawkins' language is probably exaggerated, there is no reason to doubt the substantial truth of his account.

The practice of granting assignments was continued by Shahjahan, as can be seen from Peter Mundy's account of his journey through the Gangetic plain, in the course of which he notes the numerous assignments through which he travelled. According to him, transfers were at this time less frequent, being made at intervals of three or four years, but about the same period van Twist noted their frequency in Gujarat, and some incidental remarks in the commercial correspondence suggest that, with the weakening of the Emperor's will, this source of danger to the peasants increased. It is clear that under Shahjahan a very large proportion of the revenue was assigned. In the careful account of the Empire about 1650 given in Abdul Hamid's *Badshahnama*, the total revenue is shown as 880 karors of dams, while the *khālisa,* or portion available for the Imperial treasury, was 120 karors ; on this basis, nearly seven-eighths of the revenue at this period was received by assignees or other intermediaries, and a still larger proportion appears in statistics of the reign of Aurangzeb. The ordinary peasant was therefore subject to an assignee rather than an official collector.

I have not traced any instance of a farm of the land revenue being granted during Akbar's later years, and, while the absence of evidence is not by itself conclusive, it is rendered significant by the fact that the system is utterly opposed to the Emperor's ideal of direct relations with individual peasants. The earliest indication I have found that farms were given in the Mogul Empire is in van Ravesteyn's account of Gujarat in the year 1615, in which the farms of various "governments" (or districts) are formally set out. Writing about the same time, Roe referred to "the new Farmer, rather than Governor, of Surat" ; and his record of an interview with the Viceroy of Patna seems to show that by 1616 the provinces were ordinarily administered on this system. In this interview he was told that "the government of every province did yearly pay a rent, as for his government of Patan only he gave the King 11 lakhs of rupees: all other profits were his, wherein he had regal authority to take what he list." Whether the practice continued to be general is a point on which I have found no direct evidence, but in Gujarat, the only part of the Empire regarding which we have detailed knowledge, it certainly persisted under Shahjahan. The Batavia Journals show that both Cambay and Surat were held in farm in the year 1636, and the farmer of the latter place was reported to be five lakhs to the bad, which he was expected to recover "in one way or another"; the peasants were complaining of his intolerable extortions and the area under tillage was falling off. Two years later the English at Surat reported that the local governor "is just now outed of his government by Mezer Mulcke [Muizz-ul-mulk, *alias* Mīr Mūsa], whom he also wrought out and succeeded by farming Surat at a greater rent"; and a subsequent letter makes it clear that the farm applied to "this adjacent country, mint, and custom house," in the affairs of which none of the King's ministers intermeddled. Mir Musa, however, was unable to fulfil his contract, and vacated it in debt for 31 lakhs, "which he yet owes the King, and is therefore called to Court to clear accounts, which it is known he cannot do. And therefore this his failing induced the King to think on some more provident course," and so he appointed certain officers to the government, "and a certain exhibition [stipend] allowed all of them yearly from the King, unto whose account whatever this country, mint, and custom house produceth is brought." The factors added that, though the change to direct management involved some delay and increase in work, they and all other merchants rejoiced exceedingly. The Dutch factors made a similar report to Batavia, and the fact that both Dutch and English explained the system of direct administration in detail shows that in their experience it was a novelty. There is no reason to think that during this period the farming system was peculiar to Gujarat: the government of Lahari Bandar in Sind was certainly farmed in the year 1640; and, if similar evidence is not on record regarding other provinces, the imperfection of the sources makes it impossible to draw any inference. We hear of farming from the provinces where we happen to possess a certain amount of information, but we have practically no detailed knowledge of the conditions prevailing in the remainder of the Empire. It is noteworthy also that, at the end of Jahangir's reign, assignees frequently farmed their land, handing it over "to farmers or *karoris*, who have to take the risk of good or bad harvests."

So far we have seen that the changes in the terms of appointment of officers were such as to curtail the power of the central authority, and place a very large proportion of the peasants at the mercy of men whose main object was to realise as much money as possible. Coincidently with these changes, there was an administrative revolution in the method of assessing the revenue, which made it easier for assignees and farmers to raise the level of their demands. I have not found a record of this revolution in the chronicles of the period, but its occurrence is established by a comparison of Akbar's regulations with orders issued in the early years of Aurangzeb. Akbar, as we have seen, required the revenue to be assessed on individual holdings at rates previously sanctioned by himself, and he explicitly forbade the practice of making summary settlements, under which the village headmen contracted to pay a lump sum for the village as a whole, a practice which he condemned as conferring undue authority on high-handed oppressors.[1] Orders which were issued by Aurangzeb to take effect from the eighth year of his reign (A.D. 1665–66) show that by this time the normal procedure was that which Akbar had prohibited: the assessors proposed each year a lump sum based on general considerations, and applied Akbar's methods in detail only when a village or a larger area refused to accept their proposals. It has been explained above that the main objection to Akbar's methods was the risk of extortion, and

[1] The published translation of this regulation (*Ain*, ii. 45) does not give the exact sense. There is nothing in the original about "entrusting the appraisement" to the headmen; the text says simply, "He shall not make a summary settlement (*nasaq*) with the headmen."

knowledge of ordinary human nature is sufficient to show that, when those methods were used as a threat, the risk became a practical certainty, so that we are justified in concluding that annual summary assessments had become the working rule, and that the less influential peasants were thus exposed to the risk, apprehended by Akbar, of having to pay more than their fair share of the demand on the village. The village as a whole had become more directly subject to the assessors, and the individual peasants to the stronger men among them.

Meanwhile it appears that the pressure on the assessors had also increased. Their immediate masters, whether farmers or assignees, were in a position to demand more for themselves, while at the same time the needs of the State were increasing, and it was the assessors' business to see that both claims were satisfied. There is no doubt that Shahjahan's tastes and methods resulted in a large rise in public expenditure, and it is sufficient to quote on this point the eulogy passed on him by the chronicler, that "the expenditure of former reigns, in comparison with the one in question, was not even in the proportion of one in four ; [1] and yet this King, in a short space of time, amassed a treasure which it would have taken several years for his predecessors to accumulate." If then expenditure rose largely, while surplus receipts were accumulated, we should expect to find either that fresh taxation was imposed or that the yield of existing sources was increased. We do not hear of new taxes, and, as will be explained farther on, the miscellaneous duties were devoted to provincial or local expenditure, so that it was mainly the land revenue which had to meet these increased demands.

The first obvious method of increasing the land revenue was to extend the area under cultivation. That this development was actively pressed forward is indicated by the eulogy just quoted, which refers to the favourable consideration given to those officials who were successful in extending cultivation ; but the nature of the pressure exercised by them

[1] The proportion is probably exaggerated, but the large increase in expenditure is indisputable.

is more fully explained by the orders issued by Aurangzeb in the year 1668, which described the existing practice of revenue officers in the following terms:

> At the beginning of the year inform yourself as far as possible about the condition of every peasant, and whether they are engaged in cultivation or are abstaining from it. If they have the means to cultivate, ply them with inducements and assurances of kindness, and show them any favour they may desire. But if it be found that, in spite of having means to cultivate, and of a favourable season, they are abstaining from cultivation, then you should urge and threaten them, and make use of force and the whip.

In other words, the standard of cultivation was to be determined not by the peasant, but by the assessor, whose momentary interest was that it should be as large as possible, and who was authorised to enforce his views if necessary by flogging. If this regulation be compared with the directions on the same subject given by Akbar, the change in emphasis will be apparent; Akbar laid stress on friendly arrangements, Aurangzeb laid stress on the whip.

Apart from this insistence on the largest possible area of cultivation, the required increase in revenue was obtained by raising the standard of the State's demand from one-third of the gross produce to one-half, an enhancement of 50 per cent. Apparently the rise was not immediately universal, for Aurangzeb's orders of 1668, in which the new standard is recognised as already well established, indicate that the lower rate might still be accepted in some localities, or from peasants of particular classes, but their general tenor justifies the statement that a collector or assignee would demand one-half of the produce in all ordinary cases. I have not found a notice of the introduction of this standard in any of the chronicles, but I suspect that the change was made early in the reign of Shahjahan,[1] since van Twist, writing before 1638, records that half the produce, or more, was claimed by the

[1] Some figures given in the next section indicate a possibility that Jahangir in his last years had introduced the higher rate in two provinces, but they are open to more than one interpretation.

authorities in Gujarat; and probably the measure is covered by the phrase "generous attention towards the improvement of agriculture and the collection of the revenue," on which the chronicler already quoted lays such stress. The general standard of 50 per cent was perfectly familiar to Manucci and other writers in the reign of Aurangzeb, and it reappears in regulations of the next century, so that it cannot be regarded as a temporary measure; and since it was defined in terms of produce, it must be thought of as independent of alterations in the level of prices.

We may then state the change in the ordinary peasant's position in the following terms:

(1) His liability to the State had risen from one-third to one-half of his gross produce.

(2) He might be required to pay at this rate for more land than he could cultivate effectively, so that he would actually pay more than half his produce.

(3) He might have to contribute to the revenue of the more influential men, who distributed the burden on the village among the individual peasants.

(4) The probability of additional levies was substantially increased by the administrative changes which have been indicated.

In order to realise the deterioration in the position of the ordinary peasant, it is necessary to bear in mind that the revenue, though it was assessed on the gross produce, had in fact to be paid out of the net income, that is to say, out of the produce which remained after defraying the expenses of cultivation and the cost of maintaining the peasant and his family. In a previous work [1] I suggested that something like half the gross produce must have been required to maintain the "representative" peasant as an efficient cultivating unit with a small margin to meet losses in unfavourable seasons; on this view the effect of enhancing the revenue to one-half the produce was to bring the peasant dangerously near to the level of subsistence in ordinary times, and to leave him practically nothing to make his life worth living, while even

[1] *India at the Death of Akbar*, c. iv.

moderate losses might be ruinous. Under Akbar's regulations, the distribution of the gross produce of the soil was nearly one-half for necessary expenses, one-third for the State, and a margin of one-sixth or a little more for the peasants' comforts and luxuries, or for unfavourable seasons: under Shahjahan, nearly one-half was for necessaries, one-half, or more, for the State and intermediate claimants, and practically nothing was left at the disposal of the peasant. Judging by modern experience, Akbar allowed the peasant just about the minimum required to keep agriculture going, but Shahjahan did not; and, arguing merely from the official regulations, we should expect to find that the industry was becoming unpopular, and that men who found the life not to be worth living were deserting it for other forms of employment.

There is direct evidence that this change had in fact set in before the end of our period. Many of the detailed provisions contained in Aurangzeb's orders indicate that peasants were absconding to an extent which seriously embarrassed the administration, but the fact is brought out most clearly in Bernier's *Letter to Colbert*, which was based on his experiences about the year 1656. In this letter, after commenting on the severity of the Mogul officials, he goes on:

> Thus it happens that many of the peasantry, driven to despair by so execrable a tyranny, abandon the country, and seek a more tolerable mode of existence, either in the towns, or camps; as bearers of burdens, carriers of water, or servants to horsemen. Sometimes they fly to the territories of a Raja, because there they find less oppression, and are allowed a greater degree of comfort.

Farther on he writes of the tyranny

> that drives the cultivator of the soil from his wretched home to some neighbouring State, in hopes of finding milder treatment, or to the army, where he becomes the servant of some trooper. As the ground is seldom tilled otherwise than by compulsion, and as no person is found willing and able to repair the ditches and canals for the conveyance of water, it happens that the whole country is badly cultivated, and a great part rendered unproductive from the want of irrigation. The houses, too, are left in

a dilapidated condition, there being few people who will either build new ones, or repair those that are tumbling down. The peasant cannot avoid asking himself the question, "Why should I toil for the tyrant who may come to-morrow and lay his rapacious hands upon all I possess and value, without leaving me, if such should be his humour, the means to drag on my miserable existence?" The Timariots,[1] governors, and revenue contractors on their part reason in this manner: "Why should the neglected state of this land create uneasiness in our minds? And why should we expend our money and time to render it fruitful? We may be deprived of it in a single moment, and our exertions would benefit neither ourselves nor our children. Let us draw from the soil all the money we can, though the peasant should starve or abscond, and we should leave it, when commanded to quit, a dreary wilderness."

These somewhat lengthy quotations are justified by their importance, for they state as observed facts the inferences which have been drawn from official regulations and other indirect evidence. The concentration of the authorities on immediate gain, their severity to the peasants, the compulsory cultivation, the neglect of agriculture, the desertion of the land for other employments, the gradual impoverishment of the country, all these features were sufficiently obvious to attract the attention of a foreign observer. It has occasionally been suggested that Bernier was inclined to exaggerate, but each fact alleged by him, though not the magnitude of each fact, follows almost necessarily from the changes known to have been introduced in the administration; and the concurrence of the two lines of evidence justifies the conclusion that by the end of Shahjahan's reign the economic system of the Mogul Empire had been strained almost to breaking-point, because the burdens on the principal industry were becoming unbearable, and that production was ceasing to be worth while, because the life of the producer was ceasing to be worth living.

The foregoing observations relate to the area of the Mogul

[1] "Timariot" denotes the holder of a military tenure in the Turkish Empire (*Dictionnaire de l'Académie*, s.v.). The brief descriptions of it which I have seen indicate that the tenure was practically the same as that of an assignee in the Mogul Empire, and the expression in the text may be read as "assignees, governors, and farmers."

Empire as it stood at the beginning of our period, and they require to be supplemented by a brief account of the changes in the southern territory acquired by Shahjahan. In the course of the struggle to maintain the independence of the kingdom of Ahmadnagar, Malik Ambar introduced a revenue system obviously modelled on that of Akbar, but it did not survive the downfall of the kingdom. This region suffered terribly from the famine of 1630, and for twenty years or so it remained in a deplorable condition, with a falling revenue demand, which was still far in excess of the collections. When Prince Aurangzeb became Viceroy of the Deccan in 1653, he found that the area which had formerly belonged to Ahmadnagar could not pay even for the local administration. The Emperor sent repeated orders to extend cultivation so as to increase the revenue, and the administration was reorganised under Aurangzeb's revenue officer, Murshid Kuli Khan, who re-introduced the methods of assessment approved by Akbar. The results lie outside our period, but the fact is significant that the two outstanding administrators in this region should have taken Akbar's regulations as their model. The same inspiration is apparent in the system applied by Sivaji to the dominion which he secured, and it is noteworthy that at first he followed Akbar in claiming only one-third of the gross produce, though the proportion was subsequently raised to two-fifths.

It is important, however, to distinguish Sivaji's dominions (or *swarāj*) from the area which he drained of its resources but did not administer. He treated his own subjects comparatively well, but he was able to do so only because he was in a position to draw a large income from the subjects of neighbouring rulers. The exactions of *chauth* and *sardeshmukhi* in Mogul territory lie outside our period,[1] and it must suffice to say that

[1] *Chauth* was an old-standing tenure in the Deccan; some sixteenth century references to it will be found in *Dalgado* (*s.v.* Chouto), which suggest that it originally denoted liability to pay one-fourth of the gross produce, but the proportion varied in practice, and under the Marathas the word seems usually to have meant one-fourth of the revenue. *Sardeshmukhi* was a cess, or extra demand, of ten per cent on the revenue. *Manucci* (ii. 25) asserts that Sivaji had obtained a grant of *chauth* in the Mogul Deccan as early as 1658, but the statement seems to be inconsistent with the careful account of the transaction in question given in *Sarkar's Shivaji* (p. 65).

they came as the proverbial last straw on peasants who were already assessed to the uttermost. There can be no doubt that the system inaugurated by Sivaji contributed materially to hasten the economic collapse of the Mogul Empire, but the evidence which has been adduced shows that the evil was already at work when the Marathas first appeared upon the scene, and to my mind there is no doubt that the national bankruptcy which ensued must be attributed primarily to the enhancement of the land revenue, coupled with the administrative methods by which it was assessed and collected.

Before we leave the subject of land administration under the Moguls, a few words may be said on the rise of the modern rental system. Akbar's regulations disclose no trace of rent in the sense of a sum payable merely for the right to occupy land; his revenue was charged not on occupation, but on cultivation, no payment was claimed on land which lay fallow, and his system was in essence the traditional one of taking a share of the produce of whatever land was cultivated. This system was still predominant in the time of Aurangzeb, but by its side an alternative had come into existence, under which a peasant could compound for his revenue by annual cash payments agreed on with the authorities for the land in his occupation, altogether independent of the income which he might actually draw from it. This system was known as *kharāj-i-muwazzaf*, and the detailed provisions regarding it which are contained in Aurangzeb's orders show that it had already become practically important. I have traced no account of its origin, but I conjecture that its extension at least was due largely to the oppressive methods of assessment which have been indicated above; pressure to get the land cultivated would be unnecessary when payments were independent of cultivation, and contracts covering a term of years would seem convenient both to assessors and to peasants at the moment, however disappointing their eventual results might prove. Whatever were the causes, the system was in existence at the outset of Aurangzeb's reign, and it furnishes a link between Akbar's methods and those which were found to prevail on the establishment of British rule; when the Mogul assignee or official was transformed into a landholder, the contract payments of revenue made to him would naturally become rents in the modern sense of the term.

5. The Statistics of Mogul Land Revenue

In the last section we followed two distinct but converging lines of evidence to the conclusion that during our period administrative pressure on the peasants increased so seriously as to affect the productive resources of the Mogul Empire. The increase is apparent also in some statistics of the revenue demand which happen to have survived, and an examination of these is required in order to present a complete view of the subject; but the interpretation of the figures presents numerous difficulties of detail, the discussion of which is necessarily technical, and is of interest only to those readers who may wish to carry the subject further. I have therefore thought it best to relegate the detailed figures and their explanation to Appendix C, and to offer here only the broad results which appear to me to be established, subject to the warning that the manuscripts I have used have not yet been critically edited, and consequently the conclusions based on them cannot be regarded as absolutely final.

Before, however, we compare statistical data extending over more than half a century, we must inquire whether the monetary unit in which they are expressed can be regarded as reasonably stable, since a general rise or fall in prices would make an important difference in the financial position of the peasantry. In a previous chapter the tentative conclusion has been drawn that the relation of value between silver and agricultural produce did not vary materially within our period, and the restatement of this conclusion would have sufficed, if the land revenue had been assessed and collected only in silver. In fact, however, the assessments which we have to use were almost certainly made in terms of copper, and since we have seen that the silver price of copper rose during our period by something like

30 per cent, it might at first sight be inferred that, apart from any formal enhancement, the real burden of the revenue had increased in a corresponding proportion. An examination of the official regulations seems to show that this inference would be erroneous, because peasants could pay the revenue in either metal, and the official ratio between them was not apparently altered to follow the market. Akbar's directions to the official treasurers make it clear that peasants could pay in gold, silver, or copper, whichever they might choose, and Aurangzeb's orders of 1665 show that silver could still be paid, since they permit the receipt of Shahjahan's rupees in cases where coins of the current reign were not available. The official ratio in Akbar's time was 40 dam to a rupee: I have found no record of its alteration, while it is used repeatedly in chronicles of Shahjahan's reign, and Manucci, writing many years after the close of our period, states definitely that the old rate was still in force in his time for the conversion of salaries. So long as the official rate remained unaltered it is obvious that when a rupee cost less than 40 dam in the market, the cultivator would never pay 40 dam in copper to the treasury, but would buy a rupee at the market rate; and consequently, though he might have given more produce than before for his copper, he would give less copper for his rupee, and his real burden would depend on the relation between silver and commodities, which as we have seen was probably unchanged. We may assume that while the rise in the price of copper was in progress, the peasant's burden was increased, because he would naturally, as is still the case, get the worst of the market, but this loss would not be cumulative, and when the metal settled down at the higher level, his payment, measured in produce, would be about the same as before. We can therefore compare the statistics of different years without the necessity of allowing for a large change in the value of the unit in which they are expressed; but if evidence should come to light showing that the peasants bore the burden of the enhancement in the value of copper, it would strengthen the considerations I have put forward to show that their position deteriorated greatly during the period we are examining.

One other preliminary remark seems to be required. The value of these statistics has been occasionally questioned on the ground of the discrepancies between the various tables which have survived, but this objection overlooks the fact that the revenue was assessed annually and not, as now, for a term of years. If, then, two tables of revenue were in exact agreement, we should have to conclude that they referred to the same year, and even large proportionate differences in the entry for a district or subdivision need excite no surprise if we remember that war, famine, or rebellion might suddenly transform the economic position of an extensive region. In my opinion the true way of using these tables is to ascertain the date to which each refers—unfortunately a matter of some occasional difficulty—and then, having arranged them in chronological order, to see whether they tell an intelligible story. For the present purpose, I make use of six tables. The first shows the revenue demand under Akbar about the year 1594 ; the second gives the demand at the accession of Shahjahan ; the third relates to 1647, or perhaps a year or two earlier ; the fourth and fifth are not precisely dated, but refer to years very near the end of Shahjahan's reign ; while the sixth is taken from a chronicle which closes with the year 1668, and may be presumed to relate to one of the early years of Aurangzeb. In the table on the following page I have excluded the southern provinces, the boundaries of which are known to have varied ; the province of Bengal, because the initial record of its revenue is obviously not in accord with the administrative facts ; and the small province of Sind, the figures for which are doubtful and incomplete.

Looking first at the changes between the year 1594 and the accession of Shahjahan, we see that the revenue of nine provinces rose by 29 per cent, but that the increase was by no means uniform. In four, the increase was less than 20 per cent, a rise which cannot be taken as evidence of unduly increased pressure, since it may be accounted for by a reasonable extension of cultivation. Of the provinces where the increase was greater, we know that Allahabad and Bihar were very much under-cultivated about the year 1594, and the increase in them may well represent mainly a recovery from the low state of cultivation which then prevailed. In Ajmer also the increase of 48 per cent probably represents a process of levelling up: the administration of this province was not very effective in Akbar's time, when the standard of revenue was only one-seventh or one-eighth of the produce, and the extension of Mogul authority which was effected by Jahangir must have meant a larger revenue, which was the primary

PROPORTIONATE INCREASE IN THE MOGUL REVENUE DEMAND
(Stated in terms of Akbar's revenue of about 1594, which is shown as 100.)

Province.	Akbar about 1594.	Shahjahan				Aurangzeb before 1668.	Aurangzeb before 1668; figures in column 3 equated to 100.
		Accession.	About 1647.	Late.	Late.		
1.	2.	3.	4.	5.	6.	7.	8.
Bihar	100	138	176	173	175	?	?
Allahabad	100	146	194	202	214	208	142
Oudh	100	114	147	136	155	157	138
Agra	100	151	165	158	196	193	128
Malwa	100	119	170	174	166	181	152
Gujarat	100	117	122	117	105	102	87
Ajmer	100	148	212	213	229	224	151
Delhi	100	110	168	205	200	196	178
Lahore	100	147	161	160	153	162	110
Multan	100	?	187	147	144	164	?
Total	100	129	166	170	175	175	136 (eight provinces)

NOTE.—As indicated in the appendix, there are uncertainties regarding the figures for Multan in column 3 and Bihar in column 7, and these provinces have been ignored in calculating the ratios of the totals of these two columns.

object of all such developments. There remains the anomaly that Agra and Lahore show large increases, while Delhi, intermediate in situation and probably in economic condition, shows the lowest increase of all. Various conjectural explanations of these figures could be suggested, but I have found no positive basis for any of them, and the anomaly must stand until further facts come to light; but, taking all the provinces together, the figures justify the statement that during Jahangir's reign there was no large general increase in the revenue, though the demand on some provinces was levelled up, and Lahore and Agra show large unexplained enhancements.

Turning to the reign of Shahjahan, it will be seen that the index for nine provinces rose from 129 at his accession to 175 in the early years of his successor, while the figures given for his reign prove that the increase occurred within it, since the index in his time had already risen to that level. In order then to measure the increase in this reign, we may take the figures for Shahjahan's accession as the base, and re-calculate those of Aurangzeb as percentages, as is done in the last column of the table for eight provinces, the figures for Multan being doubtful in one year and those for Bihar in the other. The first obvious anomaly in this column is the actual fall in the revenue of Gujarat, but it is adequately accounted for by the persistent effects of the famine of 1630, which has been described at length in an earlier chapter: the lapse of a generation had sufficed to restore the economic life of the country, but even at this time its revenue had not increased materially above the amount claimed by Akbar. Shahjahan's enhancement over the eight provinces works out at 36 per cent, but if Gujarat be excluded, the figure for the remainder rises to nearly 44. The other anomalies are the relatively low increases in Lahore and Agra, with a relatively large increase in Delhi, and it will be noticed at once that their effect is largely to obliterate the unexplained anomalies observed in the reign of Jahangir. In general terms, then, it may be said that under Shahjahan the revenue rose by 40 to 50 per cent —more in Delhi, where the revenue at his accession was low, and less in Agra and Lahore, where it was exceptionally high.

There are no statistics later than 1594 of the area brought under assessment; apparently these figures were recorded only under Akbar's regulation system, and they disappeared with its abandonment, so that it is impossible to compare the incidence of revenue on cultivation, but, notwithstanding this drawback, I think the claim may fairly be made that the figures I have given tell an intelligible and probable story. Under Jahangir the pressure of the revenue did not greatly increase except in two provinces: under Shahjahan, it increased by nearly one-half, apart from those two provinces, and from Gujarat, which was desolated by famine during his reign. No part of the large increase can be accounted for by a rise in the value of produce, and it must be attributed partly to extended cultivation, and partly to the rise in the standard of assessment. But at this time extension of cultivation was not, as it would be now, a measure of the increase of population or resources; it was forced by the administration, and, according to Bernier, cultivation was in fact tending to decline in Shahjahan's later years, so that most if not all of the increase must be attributed to administrative action. We have seen that the standard of assessment was raised by one-half, and we have seen that the revenue demand rose by nearly the same proportion. The coincidence is of course not exact, for a new standard can rarely yield a precise arithmetical result in practice, but speaking in general terms it may be said that the increased pressure on the peasants, which is indicated in official orders and in contemporary observations, is clearly reflected in the revenue statistics which have survived.

Before passing from this branch of our study, a few words may be said regarding the suggestion which is occasionally made, that these statistics give an exaggerated idea of the administrative pressure, because the sum actually collected as revenue might fall far short of the demand. The suggestion that the revenue could not be realised in full will be recognised as, at the least, probable by any one familiar with the conditions of the period; but the point is that the demand was made. I do not myself suppose that Shahjahan's revenue could possibly have been collected in full over a series of years, but that fact serves only to show how great the pressure on the peasants must have been. An energetic subordinate might not hope to realise everything, but he could sweep the country clear in the attempt to minimise the total of arrears; while the severity of the methods of recovery in force, including the sale of a defaulter's family into slavery, makes it practically certain that not much could be saved by bribery, for the amount of the bribe would approximate to that of the demand.

It would probably be a mistake to take the figures I have given as representing money actually brought to credit as received: they may be accepted with safety as a measure of the threat which, from season to season, impended over the agricultural population.

AUTHORITIES FOR CHAPTER VIII

SECTION 1.—The description of the position of foreign merchants in Malacca is based on *Alboquerque*, III. 96, *Barros*, II. ii. 33 ff., *Correa*, ii. 253 ff., *Castanheda*, iii. 179 ff.; see also *Journal R.A.S.*, 1920, p. 517 ff. For Calicut, see *Correa*, i. 189, *Castanheda*, i. 111, and *Barbosa*, ii. 76; for the rest of the coast, *idem*, ii. 73-122; and for Hooghly, *Elliot*, vii. 211, *Smith's Akbar*, 137, and *Campos*, 50 ff. The earliest references I have found to Dutch factories are in *Begin ende Voortgangh*; the factory at Achin is p. 44 of Spilberg's voyage; Bantam is p. 23 of Harmansz.' voyage; the first regulations for a factory are printed in the voyage of Warwyck and de Weert. The English convention at Achin is in *Purchas*, I. iii. 156, and *First Letter Book*, 69. The early history of the Dutch on the East Coast is in *Terpstra's Koromandel*, 35-123: the draft Dutch-Mogul convention is in *Terpstra's Surat*, Appendix VI.

The references to the English negotiations with the Mogul are *Purchas*, I. iii. 206, 210, and I. iv. 458, 461; *Letters Received* (Introduction to ii. and iv.); *Roe*, *passim*; and *English Factories*, i. 39, 40. For English reprisals, see *idem*, i. ii (the facts are summarised in the Introductions); iii. 24, 27; *della Valle*, 418. The facts of the Dutch reprisals are taken from *Hague Transcripts*, I. 284, 291, 298, and *Dagh Register*, June 16, 1628.

The history of Pulicat fort is compiled from *Methwold*, 994; *Terpstra's Koromandel*, 85 ff.; *Hague Transcripts*, I. 69, 86; *van Dijk*, 20-35; *Elias*, ii. 53. Early plans for forts on the West Coast are referred to in *Hague Transcripts*, II. 73, 95; *English Factories*, iii. 198. The founding of Armagon is in the same volume (*passim*, especially 128, 134): Madras, in v. 90, 161, and vi. Introduction, and 156: later projects for the West Coast, ix. 170, and x. 151, 208, etc.

SECTION 2.—This section is mainly a summary of the conclusions reached in *India at the Death of Akbar*, and a forecast of the results to be reached in the sections which follow. Detailed references will be given in these, and it is unnecessary to repeat them here.

SECTION 3.—The war at Chaul is referred to in *Faria y Sousa*, iii. 168, 185, etc., and *Letters Received*, ii. 150, 239. *Schorer's* description of the administration is ff. 3, 4. *Methwold's* account of Golconda is p. 996. The instances of oppression, etc., in Golconda are taken from *English Factories*, ii. 46, iv. 228, 232, vii. 41, and *Dagh Register*, March 12, 1625, March 31 and October 23, 1633, November 23, 1636, and March 14, 1637. For European farmers, see *idem*, October 31, 1636, and *English Factories*, v. 45, vi. 188, ix. 6: the Masulipatam farm is discussed in *Hague Transcripts*, I. 261, II. 73, and III. J4. The references to conditions in Bijapur are *Dagh Register*, April 30, July 11, 1661, and *Sarkar's Shivaji*, 34. I have found no systematic account of administration in the Hindu territories; the occurrences mentioned are taken from *English Factories*, vii. 49; and *Dagh Register*, February 19, 1641; April 23 and 24, and July 16, 1642; November 20, 1643; June 21 and July 29, 1644; January 18, August 19, and September 17, 1645.

SECTION 4.—Much of this section is based on two papers in *Journal R.A.S.*: (1) Akbar's Land Revenue System, January 1918; (2) The Development of the Land Revenue System, January 1922. The original authority for Akbar's system is *Ain*; the changes during the period are deduced from two of Aurangzeb's farmāns, of which the text was printed with translations in *Journal A.S.B.*, June 1906. Translations are also available in *Sarkar's Studies*, 168 ff. For Akbar's capacities, see Dr. Vincent Smith's *Akbar, the Great Mogul, passim.*

References to assignments are *idem*, p. 121, *Akbar-nama* (translation) ii. 95, *Tuzuk*, *passim*. Hawkins' account is in *Purchas*, I. iii. 221, and *Early Travels*, 114; Terry's statement is in *Purchas*, II. ix. 1480. For the prevalence of the system under Shahjahan, see *Mundy*, ii. *passim*; for frequency of changes, *idem*, ii. 85, and *van Twist*, XVIII.; and for statistics, *Badshahnama*, ii. 710 ff.

Ravesteyn's account of farms in Gujarat is in *Terpstra's Surat*, Appendix VI. Roe's observations on the subject are pp. 124, 239: see also *Dagh Register*, October 31, 1636, January 28, 1642 (Surat); *English Factories*, vi. 100, 276, and vii. 23, 24; and *Pelsart*, MS. f. 20. The account of Shahjahan's expenditure is in *Elliot*, vii. 171, 172. The demand of one-half the produce is mentioned in *van Twist*, XLI., *Manucci*, ii. 451, *Ovington*, 197, and other writers. The peasant's position in regard to revenue is discussed at greater length in *India at the Death of Akbar*, 295 ff. Flight of peasants can be inferred from Aurangzeb's orders in *Sarkar's Studies*, 172, 189, 191; *Bernier's* discussion of the subject is p. 205 ff.

For the Deccan administration, see *Sarkar's Aurangzeb*, especially i. 179 ff., and *Shivaji*, 470; also an article by S. Sen in Calcutta University Journal (Department of Letters), 1921, p. 237. The paragraph regarding the rental system is based on Aurangzeb's farmāns, quoted above.

SECTION 5.—The sources of the statistics discussed in this section are given in Appendix C. The option of paying revenue in either metal is stated in *Ain* (translation), ii. 49, and *Sarkar's Studies*, 193: the persistence of the official ratio is indicated in *Badshahnama*, ii. 712, 715; *Majalis-us-Salatin*, f. 115-118; and *Manucci*, ii. 363 ff. The deficiency of cultivation in Bihar and Allahabad is discussed in *Journal*, United Provinces Historical Society, 1919: the condition of Ajmer is indicated in *Ain* (translation), ii. 267.

CHAPTER IX

THE SYSTEM OF TAXATION

1. A General View of the Fiscal System

In this chapter we have to examine the economic aspects of the financial institutions, other than the land revenue, which existed in India during our period, and we can most conveniently begin with a description of the fiscal system which we find in the Mogul Empire. The key to this system is the distinction between what we should now call Imperial or Central, and Provincial or Local, income and expenditure. The Emperor relied on a small number of recognised heads of income, which he disposed of at his pleasure, while the provincial and local authorities enjoyed a large measure of freedom in levying revenue for their own needs within the area under their jurisdiction. It follows from the nature of the sources of information which are available, that we know much more of central than of local finance ; the magnitude of the Imperial resources was a stock topic for the chroniclers of the seventeenth century, as well as for European visitors to the country, but the details of the local administration can have possessed little attractions for writers of either class, and our knowledge of them is drawn mainly from incidental remarks in the commercial correspondence.

The central heads of income were land revenue, customs, mint, inheritance, and presents, which may be classed as ordinary, together with occasional special receipts, such as monopolies, or what may be described roughly as indemnities. The land revenue has been discussed in the preceding chapter, and the other ordinary heads will be examined in the next section: as to the extraordinary items, no general statements can be made, and it must suffice to refer as examples to the indigo monopoly of 1633, which was designed to bring in several lakhs of rupees,[1] or the tribute imposed on Golconda after the military operations of 1636. We have no trustworthy figures to show the central income as a whole, but it is, I think, safe to say that land revenue was much the most important single item, and we have seen in the last chapter that its incidence on the old provinces rose by 75 per cent during our period. Its gross total was increased further by annexations of new territory, and in order to get a rough idea of the development which occurred, we may contrast the figure of 880 karors of dams given in the *Badshahnama* with the 363 karors accounted for in the *Ain*.

The bulk of the land revenue was, as we have seen, assigned to meet the ordinary expenses of the army and the general administration. These two heads of expenditure cannot be separated, because the maintenance of troops was a condition of practically all assignments, while the administration in all its branches was conducted by officers holding military rank.[2] Apart from these two heads, the normal central expenditure consisted chiefly of the outlay of the Court, a term which covered the maintenance of the artillery and other special troops, together with a considerable volume of charitable and miscellaneous items. The extraordinary charges met from central revenues consisted primarily of the cost of military operations, and secondly of buildings or other works of utility or ornament. The large rise in the standard of expenditure under Shahjahan is established by general testimony, and in particular by the eulogy quoted in the last chapter, which suggests a four-fold increase; the precise figure is perhaps exaggerated, but the record of wars and buildings speaks for

[1] The amount to be paid by the monopolist is variously stated as four and six lakhs, in addition to repayment of a loan from the treasury (*English Factories*, iv. 324).

[2] The features of the Mogul administrative organisation here summarised are explained at greater length in *India at the Death of Akbar*, chaps. ii., iii.

itself regarding this Emperor's extraordinary budget, while a large part of the increase in recurring expenditure must be attributed to inflation of the salary list. Akbar remunerated his officers on a scale which may fairly be described as extravagant, but in Shahjahan's time the numbers in the higher grades, and the incomes of the leaders, both show a remarkable rise. About the year 1594, not more than 58 individuals held the "rank" of 1000 horse or upwards;[1] about 1647 the corresponding number was 218, and a detailed comparison of the two lists indicates that, after allowing for certain curtailments in the scale of remuneration, the total cost of salaries must have been multiplied three-fold in the course of this half-century. It cannot, I think, be maintained that the expansion of the Empire justified anything like so great an increase at the top of the list, and a large proportion of it must be attributed to the lavishness of the Emperors and to lack of effective control on the financial side.

We may conclude, then, that, while the central gross revenue was very large, the bulk of it was pledged to recurring expenditure on an exceedingly costly bureaucracy and on an army whose actual numbers fell far below the nominal strength: the balance was at the disposal of the Emperor, and so much as could be provided was devoted mainly to wars of aggression.[2] To ensure the supply of funds for these and other undertakings, branches of the Imperial treasury were maintained throughout the country, and a representative of Imperial finance, known as the Diwān, was stationed in each province. The revenue paid into a

[1] Mogul officers ranked according to a scale drawn up in terms of mounted men; the position of a "commander of 1000," for instance, was nearly as definite as that of a Commissioner of a Division at the present day. All that need be said here is that the number of men denoted by the rank was far greater than the number required to be maintained.

[2] The Indian tradition was to accumulate a large surplus, which was hoarded in the treasury, in the form of either cash or jewellery. The chronicler quoted in the last chapter asserts that Shahjahan followed this tradition successfully. On the other hand, *Bernier* (p. 223) says that his accumulations were less than six karors of rupees, a small amount considering the duration of the reign, but this writer excludes precious stones and other articles of value, which the chronicler presumably took into account, so the discrepancy is not very material.

branch treasury was not held at the disposal of the Viceroy or the local Governor: any sums sanctioned by the Emperor for expenditure within the province were disbursed on the authority of the Diwān, and the balance was remitted periodically to the Court, or to one of the reserve treasuries which were maintained in various fortresses. From some remarks scattered through the chronicles, I gather that each province was expected to produce a surplus for remittance, and that the special attention which Shahjahan paid to the Deccan finances was the result of the abnormal deficit which existed there after the famine of 1630; but, however this may be, the fact is clear that the surplus, if there was a surplus, was wholly at the disposal of the central government, and was not available for provincial or local needs except under the Emperor's express authority.

The question then arises how these needs were met. The administrative staff in the provinces was certainly remunerated by assignments of land revenue,[1] and it may be assumed that the troops employed on police and revenue duties were drawn from the contingents which the officers were bound to maintain at their own cost. It may also be assumed, though I have found no authority for the statement, that expenditure on clerks and routine work generally was meant to be covered by the assignments given; but we have still to take into consideration the facts, firstly, that frequent and costly presents to superiors were in practice compulsory, and, secondly, that administrative employment was regarded as a legitimate source of private profit. Towards the close of our period, the Mogul officials, taken as a whole, were poor, for extravagance had at least kept pace with the rise in remuneration, and, as Bernier wrote of the upper ranks, "most of them are in embarrassed circumstances, and deeply in debt; not that they are ruined, like the nobility of other countries, by the

[1] These assignments were usually of the type already described, in which the assignee was expected to collect the income, but cash assignments were also recognised, which would be paid out of the treasury under the order of the Diwān. Thus when Aurangzeb was Viceroy of the Deccan, he held large assignments of land, but received also a fixed sum in cash (*Sarkar's Aurangzeb*, i. 179).

extravagance of their table, but by the costly presents made to the king at certain annual festivals, and by their large establishments of wives, servants, camels, and horses." In such an environment it is obvious that the profit to be drawn from military or administrative rank must have been a primary consideration, and that there were the strongest motives for developing local sources of revenue. I have not found any Imperial orders granting specific powers of local taxation to viceroys or governors, but there is abundant evidence that these officers in fact levied taxes distinct from those which were accounted for in the Imperial treasury, and the conclusion appears to be justified that they had in practice a free hand to raise revenue for local needs, or for their personal profit, so long as they did not drive their charges into rebellion, or cause a scandal so great as to require Imperial interference. On this view it becomes easy to understand the wide diversity of conditions disclosed by the commercial correspondence: quite apart from the Imperial sources of revenue, there were numerous duties closely adapted to local possibilities, but most of them exceedingly burdensome in their nature; and the instances on record of the scale of taxes changing with a change of governor make the conclusion, to my mind, certain.

In the following sections then, we have to examine, firstly, the Imperial sources, other than the land revenue, and secondly, the expedients employed to raise funds for local or provincial objects; but before entering into the details of these topics we may glance at the financial systems in the countries lying to the south of the Mogul Empire. Here the universality of the practice of farming the revenue at least made for simplicity. The net payments made by the farmers-in-chief constituted the central revenue at the disposal of the King and his ministers, while within the "government," or district, the farmer-in-chief could farm out any possible source of revenue, the balance of receipts after making good his contract remaining at his own disposal. To recur to the instance given in the last chapter, the governor of Petapoli had to pay 48,000 pagodas *net* for his year of office, and that sum represented the total accruing to the central government from his charge, though individual ministers might obtain something additional by way of bribes or presents. Those liabilities discharged, the governor could retain all that he collected in excess of necessary expenditure, and his sole object was to make the collections as large as possible, and, as the account which I have quoted shows, to cut down administrative expenditure to a minimum during his short term of office. The financial system in southern India was thus perhaps the simplest, as it was the most oppressive, which it would be possible to devise.

2. The Mogul Imperial Resources

Apart from the land revenue, the Imperial budget, if such a document was drawn up, contained on the receipt side four ordinary heads, Customs, Mint, Inheritance, and Presents. The Customs appear to have been usually administered along with the land revenue, in so far that the governor of the district held also the farm of the seaport, but this relation was not invariable, and it may be recalled that when Hawkins arrived at Surat, he found the port under the Viceroy of the Deccan, while the land was under the Viceroy of Gujarat. The duties on imports and exports were fixed by the Emperor, and the privilege of collecting them was farmed, or occasionally assigned, to the governor or some other authority. The rates of which we read were distinctly low. At Surat in 1609 they were 2½ per cent on goods, 3 per cent on provisions, and 2 per cent on "money," a term which I take to include gold and silver, whether coined or not; they were increased somewhat during our period, but at its close they were still less than 5 per cent; and the Surat schedule may be taken as typical. Under these arrangements it was the interest of the farmer to foster foreign commerce as much as possible, since, his principal disbursements being fixed, the duties in excess of the farm were practically clear profit, while a serious fall in trade might result in his ruin; and, as a matter of fact, we find that the authorities were disposed in a general way to welcome foreign merchants. But the lack of continuity in administration made it impossible for an individual farmer to pursue a constructive policy. A port might, for instance, require protection against pirates, but such a measure would have involved immediate expenditure, while the returns would have benefited the farmer's successors rather than himself; and the records of our period disclose nothing in the way of far-seeing measures for the benefit of trade, while on the other hand, the need for realising the amount of the farm, and the natural desire for an immediate profit, resulted in the adoption of various questionable expedients, some of which were undoubtedly injurious in the long run.

Perhaps the least harmful of these expedients was the practice of tempting away traders from a competing port. An instance of this practice is recorded by Sir Thomas Roe, who, at a time of difficulty in Surat, was approached by the authorities of Cambay with the object of diverting the English trade thither, and who successfully played off the competitors against each other. Somewhat later we hear of similar competition between various ports in Gujarat; and, while the affair was largely one of promises, it appears to be probable that the fear of loss of trade may have operated to impose a limit on active extortion, and that the Indian merchants of Ahmadabad were pursuing a recognised line of action when in the year 1647 they transferred capital for investment from Surat to Lahari Bandar on account of the oppression practised at the former place. The expedients which were obviously injurious may be classed as delay, over-valuation, and compulsory sales. Delay in clearing goods is referred to so frequently that it must have been a common experience throughout India, and it must be regarded as practised with the definite object of extorting bribes, or of bringing pressure to bear on traders to fall in with the officials' schemes. The English merchants attributed such delays to the "innate accustomed villany" of the officials, who, they added, "will do nothing without bribes, which, however extorted, is made a continual custom, enforced as a duty"; and we may safely conclude that the sanctioned schedule of duties was supplemented to a substantial extent by such charges.

The practice of over-valuation was more serious. The schedules were *ad valorem*, but, while the rates were fixed by superior authority, the valuation of goods was left to the discretion of the officers on the spot, who could, if they chose, double their demands by doubling the values placed on the consignments passed through the customs. The practice was not universal, for fixed values were recognised at the small port of Lahari Bandar, but it was very common at Surat, from which place an English merchant wrote as follows :

> Here the governor's will is a law ; so that he sets what prices he pleaseth on commodities, that thereby it cometh to pass that, while you think you pay but 3½ per cent, your customs stand you in twice as much, for the goods are often times rated at double the prices they cost, as was that indigo I bought in Agra, which costing 61 rupees per maund was here rated by Mazel Mulk at 110 rupees, because (he said) it was worth so much in Persia. But at Bandar Laree [Lahari] it is not so, for there the prices are known and set down in a rate book, not to be innovated or altered at every covetous or unjust governor's will.

The practice of over-valuing is recorded at Surat as early as 1615, and is mentioned frequently thereafter: that the valuation might be at least doubled is shown by some figures given by a Dutch merchant in 1641 (saltpetre costing 1½ rupees being valued at 4 rupees, and cotton goods costing 9 rupees at 18 rupees); and the obvious result was to make the incidence of the duties much heavier than could be inferred from the official schedule, while the lack of certainty as to the basis of the calculation must have been a serious handicap to trade.

The farmer's ability to hasten or delay clearances, and to raise or lower the valuation, put him in a position not merely to extort bribes, but to make a profit by forced dealing in goods which came into the custom house. In the year 1615, we find the English merchants complaining that their goods were taken away by the governor and customer, and either not paid for at all, or paid for at inadequate rates ; thirty-five years later their successors reported that goods were refused clearance for two years and upwards, if they declined to accept the inadequate price offered by the customers; and various other statements show that these instances were not exceptional. Such claims could on occasion be settled by bribes, as in the year 1620, when a demand for the sale of imported coral at an inadequate price was evaded for "1000 rials-of-eight bribe to the governor, 100 ditto rials to the broker, and the sale of 2000 maunds lead into the Prince's warehouse [1] at a mahmudi per maund less than we ordinarily sold at." In one way or other, however, money had to be paid, and if we take account of bribes, forced sales, and over-valuation, we shall find that the schedule of duties sinks into insignificance in comparison with the demands which might have to be met in practice. I cannot find that the burden of these demands altered materially in the course of our period; it varied from time to time with the rapacity of individual farmers; it could scarcely be worse than is depicted in the representation of 1615 already quoted; and I have found nothing to suggest that any permanent improvement took place.[2]

Regarded as sources of revenue, the Mints were of much less importance than the Customs. It is clear that they yielded something, for they were farmed, but, so long as the standard of coinage was maintained, the legitimate profit cannot have been large. The administration was minutely controlled by the Imperial authorities, and must be regarded as of political rather than fiscal importance; the issue of coin was the prerogative, and also the most direct evidence, of

[1] Prince Shahjahan was at this time assignee of the revenues of the port.

[2] The prevalence of such practices as I have described may be inferred from the fact that even passengers' personal luggage was not exempt. It is dangerous to rely on the available editions of *Mandelslo's* journal, because his editors added so much to the original, but the following passage (p. 12) appears to record his personal experience at Surat: "The Sultan or Governor, nay, the Customers themselves, oblige merchants and passengers to part with, at the price they shall think fit to put upon them, those goods and commodities which they had brought for their own private use. Accordingly the Sultan, having found among my things a bracelet of yellow amber and a diamond, would needs buy them both of me."

sovereignty, so that it is easy to understand that no local official, "or any man whatever" would dare to make alterations "without the King's especial order and warrant." Judging by the commercial correspondence, the administration of the mints in Gujarat compared favourably with that of the customs, for, apart from the complaints of delays at Surat, when, as has been explained in a previous chapter, the local mint was temporarily overworked, there is scarcely a grievance on record, and the claim may fairly be made that the mercantile community enjoyed during our period the advantage of honest money. I have found no contemporary account of the working of the mints in the interior of the country, but just after the end of our period the Dutch were complaining bitterly of delays and malpractices at Rajmahal in Bengal, so that it would be unsafe to conclude that the high standard of Gujarat was generally maintained.

I have not found any official statement of the precise claim made by the Mogul Emperors to inherit the estates of their subjects. The accounts of European visitors disclose certain variations, some asserting that the claim was universal, others limiting it to the estates of the official nobility, and others extending it to the wealthier merchants; but legal exactitude is not to be expected from such sources, and if we consider these statements in the light of incidents recorded in other authorities, the most probable conclusion is that the rule was not absolutely rigid. The Emperor certainly claimed the estates of his nobles, and occasionally we hear of the claim being extended to estates of merchants; probably the practical questions which arose in any case were the value of the particular estate and the amount of bribes offered to avert confiscation. This view is in accordance with a letter written by Aurangzeb to Shahjahan, a portion of which was preserved by Bernier. "We have been accustomed," wrote Aurangzeb, "as soon as an Omrah [noble] or a rich merchant has ceased to breathe, nay sometimes before the vital spark has fled, to place seals on his coffers, to imprison and beat the servants or officers of his household, until they made a full disclosure of the whole property, even of the most inconsiderable jewel. This practice is advantageous, no doubt; but can we deny its injustice and cruelty?" In this passage I take the expression "rich merchant" to be significant, and to denote that, while no general claim was made on merchants as a body, the risk must always have been present in the minds of successful men. The severity described by Aurangzeb was not a novelty, for it is prominent in the following extract from the account given by Pelsart of the procedure under Jahangir.

Immediately on the death of one of the lords, be he great or small, without any exception—sometimes even before the breath has left his body—the King's officers are on the spot, and make an inventory of the entire estate (provided it has not been concealed), recording everything down to the value of a single pice, even to the clothes and jewels of the ladies. The king takes the whole estate absolutely for himself, but if the deceased had done good service in his lifetime, the women and children are given enough to live on, but not more. It might be thought that wife, or children, or friends, could conceal enough to support the family while the lord was alive, but this would be very difficult, because all the acts of the lords, and their possessions, are perfectly well known. In every palace there is a *diwān* [steward], through whose hands everything passes, and he has many subordinates, each of whom has some definite charge, for which he must account. [When the lord dies], all these subordinates are arrested, and compelled to show from their books and papers where all the cash or property is deposited, and how their master's income has been disposed of; and if there is any suspicion about their disclosures, they are tortured until they reveal the truth.

The income derived by the Imperial treasury from this source cannot be stated precisely, but it must have been substantial. A Dutch report asserts that Shahjahan realised 19 karors of rupees on the death of the famous Asaf Khan in the year 1641: the figure is probably a gross popular exaggeration, for the items of the estate enumerated in the *Badshahnama* amount to only 2½ karors; but in any case the windfall was important, and, as Father Sebastian Manrique tells us, the land routes leading out of India were closed to prevent the removal of any portion of the property. Estates of such magnitude were doubtless exceedingly rare, but the revenue derived from lesser accumulations was, as Aurangzeb said, "advantageous," and it is noteworthy that, while he condemned the system, he did not abandon it in practice; for Manucci tells us that in his time, though the claim had been formally renounced, the estates left by officials were still regularly appropriated on the pretext of debts due from them to the State.

Some sidelights on the working of the system are thrown by casual entries in the commercial correspondence. Thus in the year 1646, we read that woollen cloth was unsaleable at Court, partly because the King was "plentifully furnished with that specie by the death of some of his umraws" [nobles]. At one time an attempt was made to apply the rule of inheritance to the estates of foreign merchants dying in the country, and on the death of the English chief at Ahmadabad everything in the factory was sealed up without discrimination of the goods belonging to the Company; but, so far as the English were concerned, this claim was finally abandoned in the settlement of disputes affected in the year 1624. A transaction of the year 1647 suggests an extension of the practice of seizing Indian merchants' estates. The estate of a prominent Sind trader was seized, and incidentally his brother was subjected to ill-usage which was resented in the locality;

> . . . it is said the King have fined him 100,000 rupees, which is a-paying in Tatta; besides which the Prince's and other great men's fees will carry away at least 50,000 rupees more. This all men exclaim against, being the worst (they say) of all ill customs that ever came up yet; for now, if a merchant of fashion, or any other that hath but means dies, his wealth will be all seized on, though he hath children and brothers to leave it unto, and, having so, the King ought not to pretend any right.

The same letter mentions that, on the death of a local governor, all his goods were seized by the King's officers, "as the manner is when any umbraw [noble] deceases," and the phrases I have quoted indicate that, while a claim to an official's estate was regarded as a matter of course, a claim to inherit from a merchant came as a novelty to the people of Sind, the "fine" of a lakh being presumably what would now be called a composition.[1] Apart from this indication that the demands of the State were being extended to new areas, I have found nothing to show that any material change occurred during our period. It would be superfluous to insist at length on the economic evils resulting from the system. So far as officials were concerned, it may fairly be said that the liability was part of the contract under which they served, and that since the condition of the administration impelled them to predatory courses, there was some reason for a rule which ensured the reversion of their gains to the State; but as regards the wealthier merchants, it is obvious that trade must have suffered, and that productive enterprise must have been rendered impossible, by the risk of a sudden demand for the whole visible capital at the moment when the death of its owner had probably involved the business in temporary uncertainty. The instances which have been given show that the risk was real, and its existence must be taken into account in any estimate of the economic condition of the Mogul Empire; so long as the claim persisted, there was no possibility of either the establishment of wealthy families independent of the State, or the development of capitalistic production in any form.[2]

The last main head of the Imperial revenue consisted of the presents which were offered to the Emperor on every possible occasion. The custom appears to have been general

[1] Up to 1635, there were probably no wealthy merchants in Sind, other than the Portuguese, who almost monopolised its trade. It cannot be inferred, therefore, that similar protests would have been heard if the transaction had occurred in Agra or Gujarat.

[2] In his *History of Jahangir*, which reached me while these paragraphs were in the printer's hands, Mr. Beni Prasad writes (p. 85 *n.*) that in *India at the Death of Akbar* I have fallen "into the mistake of supposing that the effects of merchants also escheated to the State." I can find no such assertion in my former book, but on page 51 I wrote that the Emperor certainly claimed the goods left by the wealthier merchants. The extant evidence, some of which is set out in the text, appears to me to justify that statement; the mistake, if there be one, is primarily Aurangzeb's.

throughout Asia, and we read occasionally of places where presents of equivalent value were returned, but the rule of equivalence was not observed in the Mogul Empire or the kingdoms of the Deccan, where the articles given in return were sometimes of comparatively trifling value. Writing of the Emperor Shahjahan, Manrique recorded that the presents received at his ceremonial weighing far exceeded his own gifts and expenses on the occasion, and we find in the Batavia Journals records of expenditure and receipts which show a large balance in the Emperor's favour, as when a present costing some thousands of rupees, and including an elephant, great copper candelabra, broadcloth, and various other items, was requited by a horse and a dress of honour, the whole valued at 520 rupees. On another occasion we hear that the English merchants gave presents worth about Rs. 13,000, and received the equivalent of Rs. 3500 in return. The net receipts were thus large, as can be inferred from a perusal of Jahangir's Memoirs, where the values of many presents are recorded, while the burden of the practice was a standing grievance with foreign merchants. It must not, however, be supposed that the balance received by the Emperor represented a clear financial gain. Officials who presented large offerings could usually hope for early promotion, and since there were no regular cadres or limits to the numbers in any particular rank, many transactions of the kind must have involved a contingent liability greater than the actual receipt. Foreign merchants again usually expected some sort of concession in return for expensive presents; in the case which has just been mentioned, the Dutch obtained a series of concessions of considerable value from the commercial point of view; and speaking generally, the system bears some resemblance to modern financial methods in which a State receives an immediate payment in lieu of an annuity, but with the important difference that the annuity was by no means certain, since concessions might at any time be cancelled, or an officer might be summarily dismissed shortly after his promotion. It is impossible to say whether on balance the Mogul Empire gained or lost by the system in the long run; it produced an immediate visible income, but at the same time it created contingent liabilities, and, having regard to the financial conditions of the period, the former fact was probably sufficient justification for its existence.

In order to complete the survey of the normal sources of Imperial revenue, reference may be made to a small number of entries in the statistics given in the *Ain*, which show that miscellaneous income was occasionally brought to account under the head of land revenue. Nearly all of these occur under Bengal, where there are about twenty entries of comparatively small sums under "markets," "salt," "transit dues," and the like; but on the view I have put forward that the figures recorded for Bengal represent only the claims of the kingdom to which Akbar succeeded, these entries do not justify any inference as to the financial system of the Empire. Outside Bengal I have found only three cases of the kind, one of road-tolls at a village in Berar, one of ferry-tolls at Attock in the Punjab, and the maritime customs in the province of Gujarat. The last of these shows merely that in Gujarat customs were brought on to the land revenue accounts: the two former indicate that inland tolls were credited to the Imperial treasury in two cases, and, if we consider the great detail in which the statistics are presented, we may fairly infer that these two cases stand by themselves, representing exceptions to a general practice. There were thus only two instances in Akbar's Empire, outside Bengal, where duties other than those which have been described were brought separately to account. It is possible that some items of miscellaneous income may have been included in the totals shown as land revenue, but a detailed examination of the figures leads to the conclusion that, if this was done, the amount was insignificant,[1] and consequently we may accept the view already given of the Imperial resources as substantially, if not absolutely, complete. The Emperor was in a

[1] I examined this question in a paper on the agricultural statistics of Akbar's Empire, in the *Journal* of the United Provinces Historical Society, 1919.

position to take from the estates of the rich practically as much as he chose: his direct revenue from commerce consisted of the receipts from customs and the mints: and he claimed first one-third, and eventually one-half, of the gross produce of the soil of his dominions. The income of artisans and ordinary merchants, together with the balance of their produce retained by the peasants, remained available for local and provincial needs.

3. Provincial and Local Resources

Our authorities indicate that revenue required by provincial or local officials might be raised either by supplementary imposts on Imperial taxes, or by duties imposed independently, while their income might be increased largely by presents, fines, and bribes. The practice of adding cesses for local purposes to the regular revenue is still familiar in India, and its prevalence during our period is sufficiently established by Aurangzeb's orders to endeavour to prevent it. An illustration of a similar practice in relation to customs may, however, be given from the kingdom of Golconda, because it is in itself of some historical importance. When the Dutch began to negotiate for trade at Masulipatam in the year 1606, no difficulty arose about the general scale of the King's duties, which were moderate, but the local authorities claimed as much as 16 per cent on exports of cotton goods, a duty which they described as belonging to themselves. The Dutch carried this question to the Court, and obtained a decree fixing export duties in their case at 4 per cent, and expressly relieving them from the impost (known as *chhāpa-dalāla* [1]) of 12 per cent on cotton goods, which was paid by subjects and foreigners alike. In this instance we find that the claim of the central administration was quadrupled by a duty levied simultaneously for local purposes; and the events of the next few years show that the exemption granted to the Dutch by the King was resented by the local authorities, who tried various expedients to recover what they had lost. The incident in fact is by

[1] Obviously, a fee for stamping (*chhāp*, a stamp or seal), and brokerage (*dalāl*, a broker).

itself a sufficient explanation of the constant friction of which we read at this seaport.

An idea of the number and nature of the duties, or taxes, or levies, imposed independently can be formed from the occasional orders by which some of them were formally prohibited. The edicts issued by Jahangir on his accession condemned the levy of cesses and other burdens which the assignees of "every province and district" had imposed for their own profit, an expression which brings out the wide prevalence of such imposts. About seventy years later Aurangzeb issued more detailed orders on the subject.[1] The texts of his orders vary somewhat in detail, but Professor Sarkar enumerates fifty-four imposts under six main heads; there is no certainty that the list is exhaustive, but it seems to cover practically every kind of transaction in which ordinary people were likely to engage, such as sales or purchases, transport of goods or journeys of passengers, and the like, besides such incidents as the birth of a son, or the demarcation of a boundary. A contemporary view of the system is contained in the following extract from the chronicle of Shihabuddin Talish, as translated by Professor Sarkar:

> From the first occupation of India and its ports by the Mohammadans to the end of Shahjahan's reign, it was a rule and practice to exact *hāsil* [revenue] from every trader—from the rose-vendor down to the clay-vendor, from the weaver of fine linen to that of coarse cloth—to collect house-tax from new-comers and hucksters, to take *zakāt* [2] from travellers, merchants, and stable-keepers. As Sadi has said, "At first oppression's basis was small, but every successive generation increased it," till at last in all provinces, especially in Bengal, it reached such a stage that tradesmen and merchants gave up their business and householders took to exile, saying,
>
> We shall flee from the oppression of the Age,
> To such a place that Time cannot track us there.

[1] Aurangzeb's exemptions are set out and discussed in Professor Sarkar's *Lectures on Mughal Administration*, p. 120 ff.

[2] *Zakāt*, which occasionally appears in the commercial correspondence in forms such as *jagat*, properly denotes an income-tax recognised by Moslem law, but at our period its popular meaning had come to be a duty levied, not at fixed intervals of time, but at uncertain intervals of space.

The rulers, out of greed for *hāsil*, gave them no relief. On the roads and ferries matters came to such a pass that no rider was allowed to go on unless he paid a *dinar*, and no pedestrian unless he paid a *dirham*.[1] On the river highways, if the wind brought it to the ears of the toll-collectors that the stream was carrying away a broken boat without *hāsil*, they would chain the river. . . . They considered it an act of unparalleled leniency if no higher *zakāt* was taken from rotten clothes actually worn than from mended rags, and a deed of extreme graciousness if cooked food was charged with a duty lower than uncooked grains. None of the Delhi sovereigns, in spite of their efforts to strengthen the Faith and follow the rules of the Prophet, put down these illegal practices, but connived at them.

Allowing for the writer's picturesque style, this account may be taken as substantially correct: everything was taxed, and the system tended to intensify itself as time went on. Shihabuddin proceeds to say that Aurangzeb abolished the evil, but this statement proved to be premature, and the lists of miscellaneous duties actually levied in Bengal during the eighteenth century bear a strong resemblance to those of the remissions ordered by successive Mogul Emperors.

A comparison of Aurangzeb's prohibitions with those which had previously been made by Akbar discloses similarity amounting to practical identity, and the story is really older, going back at least to the time of the Emperor Firoz Shah. There is thus evidence of a conflict between the central administration, which attempted spasmodically to abolish these burdens, and the local authorities, who maintained and developed them to meet their need for funds. It is scarcely worth while to discuss the question whether this need was public or private in its nature, because the two spheres were not clearly distinguished in practice; but, whatever the object might be, the conclusion must be accepted that the conflict was decided in favour of the local authorities, who in fact continued to levy prohibited duties, subject only to the primary administrative consideration that there should be no scandal to provoke the Emperor's personal interference. Various

[1] *Dinar* and *dirham*: traditional Moslem coins. Their precise value is immaterial for this passage, which is obviously rhetorical.

incidents could be quoted to show that such interference would result from greed or oppression carried beyond the point which the people would stand, but the people were habituated to endurance, and exaction could be carried far without reaching the breaking-strain.

From the nature of the case, we hear little in detail of the duties levied on artisans, retailers, or consumers; they did not directly affect the business of the foreign merchants, from whose reports most of our information is derived, and who noticed them only when they became important to the export trade, as in the case of the various monopolies instituted from time to time. The duties on internal transit stand in a different position, because they were collected from the English and Dutch, whose experience may be accepted as evidence of the ordinary working of the system. These duties are a very common topic in the commercial reports, where they are spoken of as *rāhdāri* or *jagāt*,[1] and the constant friction which arose over their levy indicates that they must have been a very real hindrance to trade, not only for the foreigners who tried to escape them, but for the Indians who presumably submitted to them as inevitable. As early as the year 1615, we find the English complaining that three separate duties were collected on goods brought from Ahmadabad to Surat for export, and a few years later they were contesting the charges demanded at Burhanpur, and on the road thence to Surat. The agreement made at Surat in 1624 provided that no land customs should be demanded at places belonging to the Emperor, and this was confirmed by Jahangir's farmān, but the duties were collected all the same, and in 1627 the merchants sent instructions to Lahore to obtain more effective orders from the Emperor; "otherwise," they said, "we will bribe no more to have the King's farmāns." The duties, however, were still demanded, and in 1644 a mission was sent to Court, not on this occasion to evade the duties, but to obtain orders regarding the valuation of goods for assessment purposes. From time

[1] For *jagāt*, or *zakāt*, see the note above. *Rāhdāri* appears to have meant originally payments for travelling guards, but in our period it means transit dues, whether guards were supplied or not.

to time we read of exemptions in particular localities, but these were favours granted by individual officers, and lapsed when they vacated office; and in 1650 renewed efforts were made to secure a general exemption. Again a farmān was granted, and it was occasionally effectual, though one caravan had to pay as much as formerly, and individual officers refused to take notice of the orders; but at the close of our period payments were still being made at Burhanpur and elsewhere in the Mogul Empire.

The experiences of the Dutch were similar. A farmān was obtained in 1634 exempting them from all tolls and duties on the road to Surat, but seven years later the merchants were discussing whether it was worth while to press for new orders; the old farmān was useless, the duties were still levied, and it was thought better for the moment to conciliate the local officials. In 1643, however, a new farmān was obtained, and it had some effect, for though it was ignored by the officials at Agra, where it was granted, a personal representation to the Emperor secured an order for refund. Meanwhile complaints were frequent on the other side of India: tolls on silk were already heavy, and were greatly raised on the advent of a new Viceroy in Bengal; in Orissa on the other hand some authorities were anxious to foster trade, and the duties were reduced by three-quarters, but they were raised again shortly afterwards; and we are told that Indian merchants were refusing to transport goods owing to the increase in the burdens.

It will be apparent from these experiences that transit dues might be levied even when exemption had been granted by the Emperor, and we may safely conclude that for Indians, who had obtained no similar privileges, the charges were hard facts. The Mogul administration cannot be blamed for the existence of the system, because it was by no means confined to the country under Mogul control, and indeed there are indications that the charges were higher and more frequent in independent territory. That the Imperial exemptions were not intended to apply to the Hindu Chiefs or Rajas whose territory lay within the Empire, is apparent from a comparison of the first and final settlements of the English troubles at

Surat. In the first settlement, when the Moguls were temporarily helpless, exemption was granted, among other places, for the territory of the Raja of Dhaita ; but in the second, when the Moguls were free agents, this territory was not included, and the exemption was limited to " places belonging to this King," a phrase which was obviously intended to exclude the country administered by Chiefs. This distinction had been drawn a few years previously when a request for exemption at Dhaita was met by the reply that the Prince (Shahjahan) could not interfere with the Raja's collections, seeing that they supplied the tribute which he paid ; and various incidents in later years show that as time went on the English recognised that the demands made by Chiefs, especially in Rajputana, stood on a different footing from those of the Mogul officials. But the claim for transit dues was not made by Chiefs only, for on occasion it was asserted even by villagers. In 1637 such a claim was made only a few miles from Agra, and an English merchant was killed in a skirmish which ensued ; while Peter Mundy mentions various cases where the country-folk, having become rebels, levied customs on their own authority. Outside the Mogul Empire the system was perhaps more oppressive than within its borders. Thévenot was struck by the change when he entered the kingdom of Golconda, and passed sixteen taxing-posts in 23 leagues' journey ; Manucci comments on the severity of the toll-collections in Bijapur ; exemptions from junckans,[1] as the duties were called locally, are prominent in the various farmāns obtained by the English at Masulipatam ; and the demand was a frequent source of trouble in the Hindu territories in the south. We are therefore justified in regarding land-transit duties as an Indian, rather than a Mogul institution, leviable in all parts of the country by any one who possessed, or asserted, administrative authority.[2] Perhaps

[1] Junckan is apparently the Tamil word *chungam*, a toll : in the East Coast correspondence it represents duties of the same general kind as were called *rāhdāri* in the north and west.

[2] In the Maurya Empire, " the merchant was mulcted in dues at the frontier, by road-taxes and tolls, and by octroi at the gates of the cities " (*Cambridge History of India*, i. 478).

we get a suggestion of its origin in an explanation offered by an English factor for a change of route; "I purposed," wrote John Parker in 1622, "to have come Handia way; but here I understand that of late the Raja of the country, whereas formerly he only took custom, now robbeth merchants and passengers of what he findeth with them. Within these eight days a merchant was robbed of eight camels laden with goods, himself and three men killed." From robbery to blackmail, and from blackmail to transit duties, is a natural development; and occasional reversions to the initial practice were not unknown even in recent times. Whatever the origin may be, the universality of the system makes it easy to understand its persistence in the face of repeated prohibitions and exemptions: the people were accustomed to pay transit duties, and were unlikely to protest effectively, even though the levy might have been formally forbidden.

In the circumstances it is not possible to define the burden on commerce in quantitative terms, since any one might claim a tax of any amount, even if goods had paid taxes in an adjoining jurisdiction. Some of the charges of which we hear were in themselves moderate, while others were apparently excessive. In one case we read of a charge of two rupees per cart, in another of 65 rupees, and payments clearly varied within wide limits; but the real evil consisted in the uncertainty of the demand and the violence with which it was collected. Merchants could not make a confident forecast of what they would have to pay on any particular journey, and goods would not be transported unless the anticipated profit was sufficiently large to leave a margin for unforeseen demands; in the long run the consumer doubtless paid the duties which were actually levied, but consumers and producers alike must have suffered by the curtailment of trade resulting from the uncertainty in the operation of the system.[1]

[1] The *Gujarat Report* (f. 19) shows that about the year 1628 Ahmadabad enjoyed marked advantages over other cities in that local taxation was both light and certain, and the writer attributed to this fact its extensive and flourishing trade and industry. Probably some other places enjoyed similar advantages from time to time, but they were exceptions to the general rule.

It may perhaps be worth while to point out that, in some cases at least, transit duties benefited the Imperial treasury indirectly, though they were not brought to credit in the Imperial accounts. The case of the Raja of Dhaita, which has already been quoted, shows that Shahjahan would not interfere with the dues charged by a Raja because they supplied the tribute which he paid ; and some remarks of the historian Khafi Khan indicate that similar considerations were applicable to the demands enforced by assignees. This writer tells us that in the famine of 1660 Aurangzeb gave orders for the remission of transit dues, as well as various other cesses, but that officers and assignees continued to collect them, partly because the Emperor was not respected, and partly

"... because the revenue officers, through inattention, or want of consideration, or with an eye to profit, contrary to what was intended, made deductions (for these cesses) from the *tanhkwāh* accounts of the *jāgīrdārs* ; so the *jāgīrdārs*, under the pretext that the amount of the cesses was entered in their *tanhkwāh* papers, continued to collect the *rāhdāri* and many other of the abolished imposts, and even increased them. When reports reached the government of infractions of these orders, the offenders were punished" . . . but after a while they got their rank restored, so that "the regulation for the abolition of most of the imposts had no effect."

The highly technical language of this quotation may be explained as follows. An officer got an assignment of land estimated to yield him a certain income. He did his best to make it yield more, while the officials endeavoured to see that he did not, and kept records (the *tankhwāh* papers) of what he collected, with a view to claiming an adjustment of any excess. If then an assignee collected transit dues, the amount was entered in these records ; and the assignee could thereupon argue that his demand was recognised by the authorities, and that consequently he was entitled to enforce it on the public. There was in fact a continuous struggle between assignees and the Accounts officials, and transit dues were merely one of the items on which the ingenuity of both sides might be exercised.

Khafi Khan adds some comments which are worthy of reproduction as showing the views of a well-informed Indian on these imposts.[1]

"The *rāhdāri* in particular is," he says, "condemned by righteous and just men as a most vexatious impost, and oppressive to travellers, but a large sum is raised by it. In most parts of the Imperial territories the *faujdars* [commandants] and *jagirdars* [assignees], by force and tyranny, now exact more than ever from the traders and poor and necessitous travellers. The *zamindars* also, seeing that no inquiries are made, extort more on roads within their boundaries than is collected on roads under royal officers. By degrees matters have come to such a pass that between the time of leaving the factory or port and reaching their destination, goods and merchandise pay double their cost price in tolls. Through the villainy and oppression of the toll-collectors and the *zamindars*, the property, the honour, and the lives of thousands of travellers and peaceful wayfarers are frittered away."

Khafi Khan, like most chroniclers, writes from the point of view of the consumer and the traveller, but the references which have been given to the Dutch and English correspondence show that his condemnation of the entire system of transit dues was substantially in accordance with commercial opinion, and there is nothing to be said in its favour beyond the fact that it was endured by the people, and consequently profitable to the authorities.

As has been said above, our knowledge of the other duties levied on trade and industry is much less detailed. It is natural to assume that the payments required from artisans and petty traders had settled down on a more or less customary basis, but sufficient evidence exists to justify the statement that any marked development of business was likely to lead to an increase in the demand made either by the State or by its officers. The Imperial monopoly of indigo which, as we

[1] Khafi Khan's personal experience was later than our period, and where he writes in the present tense he is probably referring to the beginning of the eighteenth century, when administrative disorganisation had progressed and the check on local abuses had been weakened; things were doubtless worse when he wrote than under Shahjahan, but the system was identical.

have seen, was established in the year 1633, involved a tax on production of practically 33 per cent, since producers had to sell at Rs. 18 when the market price was about Rs. 27. The earlier provincial levy in Gujarat was at first sight even heavier, for it works out at a charge of Rs. 10 on indigo valued at about Rs. 16, but in this case it is reasonable to suppose that the initial demand was pitched high in order to give a favourable start to negotiations, and the sum actually realised was probably less. Again we read that the Mogul Emperor had made saltpetre an Imperial monopoly in the year 1655, when the export trade had just begun to assume large dimensions; while ten years earlier a Dutch report mentions that a new toll had been imposed on the same commodity. In this connection we may notice a levy made by Mir Jumla in Bengal. A Dutch narrative tells how he called together the grain-merchants at Dacca, and demanded from them Rs. 50,000 on the ground that they had made twice as much by way of what might now be called excess profits owing to the prolonged presence of his large camp. The merchants offered Rs. 10,000; they were mercilessly beaten with whips, but refused to offer more, urging that they were only retailers; the two leaders were then seized and thrown in front of elephants, and, in fear of death, they compromised by paying Rs. 25,000; after which the bankers of the city paid three lakhs, apparently without the need arising for similar coercive processes. It is, I think, fair to conclude from such occurrences that industrial or distributive enterprise must have been seriously discouraged by the risk that novel demands might be imposed in the event of any profitable development of business.[1]

Before leaving the subject of local duties, a few words may be said regarding three heads of revenue, octroi, excise, and

[1] The reputation earned by Mir Jumla in Bengal is indicated in an entry in the *Dagh Register*, under date September 3, 1663. The letter which described his encounter with "death, his last enemy," went on to say: "And this is the end of a man, who, rising out of obscurity, must be classed among the most eminent, inspiring such awe that even his master, the Great Mogul, appeared to fear him; but now he is little mourned, indeed every one seems absolutely delighted at his death."

salt, which are familiar in modern India. Our authorities do not distinguish between octroi and transit duties, and probably the attitude of Indians was similar, but the levy of duty on goods brought into a city for consumption was certainly a recognised institution. In the sixteenth century these duties were familiar in Vijayanagar, where nothing could come through the gates without payment, and even head-loads were charged; while Akbar's regulations for urban administration recognise and define the taxing power of the Kotwal, or city-governor. We may say, then, that octroi formed part of the system of local taxation during our period, and probably its incidence varied in practice with the individuality of the administrator.

There is no trace of any general system of excise, and such an institution would have been inconsistent with a strict adherence to Moslem religious law. Prohibition of the sale of alcohol was not rigorously enforced by Jahangir, but we hear of it under his successor. In his journal for 1632 Peter Mundy refers to the heavy penalties on distillation or sale of spirits; near Allahabad supplies could be obtained by stealth, but farther east none could be got for any money, there being "a strait prohibition, with death to the party, and destruction to that house where it shall be found." The same writer, however, records that the Governor of Surat had farmed the palm trees from which intoxicating liquor was obtained; distillation was a recognised craft in that neighbourhood in the year 1630; and it is clear that while the Emperor's orders were strict, their enforcement depended on the local administration, which might, as in the instance just given, draw revenue from consumption.

There is no doubt that under the Moguls salt was taxed, but the rates of duty do not appear to be on record except for the mines in the Punjab, where in Akbar's time the charge was considerably more than double the prime cost. This duty is said to have been paid "to the *diwān*," an ambiguous phrase, which, however, probably denotes the Imperial authorities. The sources in Rajputana were under the local Chiefs at this period, and nothing is said about them in the

Ain. Most, if not all, of the supply obtained in Gujarat and from the Ran of Cutch was taxed by the local Chiefs. In Bengal the tables of Imperial revenue include certain salt-duties, but, as has been said before, these tables appear to bear little relation to the administrative facts of the period. Speaking generally, then, we may conclude that, while salt was taxed, there was nothing like a uniform system of administration, and the duties were usually provincial or local rather than Imperial. The prominence of salt in the budget of modern India arises from the fact that—with the exception of the octroi levied in some municipalities—the tax is the sole survival of the mass of duties and imposts which during our period left scarcely any branch of industry untouched.

Apart from taxes, local authorities could hope to realise a large income from presents, fines, and bribes. The first of these heads does not call for detailed description; the practice of giving presents was universal and binding, and what has been said regarding it in the previous chapter applies generally to officials of all ranks. As regards fines, the Dutch commercial reports make it plain that fines went into the pocket of the officer by whom they were imposed. Writing primarily of Agra, Pelsart recorded that criminals were rarely executed unless they were poor, but their property was confiscated for the benefit of the Governor and the Kotwal. He added an expression of pity for those who came before "these godless and unrighteous officers; their eyes are bleared with greed, their mouths gape like wolves for their prey, their bellies hunger for the bread of the poor; every one stands with hands open to receive, for no mercy or compassion can be had except on payment." Similarly the Gujarat Report shows that in the Empire generally fines were ordinary punishments, not only for minor offences, but even for murder, theft, and robbery, because all fines went to the Governor, whose pocket would not benefit if such criminals were executed. The line between fines and bribes was thus indistinct, and the report shows also that armed gangs of robbers infested the vicinity of some of the principal cities with the connivance of the

Governors, who benefited both by the bribes they received, and by the savings in police expenditure. In the case of citizens also the authorities were in a position to extort money almost with impunity ; a trumped-up charge would bring either fine or bribe, and there was no lack of informers to set the law in motion, for Pelsart wrote that in Agra they swarmed like flies. Nor could the provisions of the Moslem law be relied on : the Kāzi, whose business it was to interpret the law, might be sitting in the court, but in practice the Governor was absolute, and as the same observer says, " Who can excommunicate the Pope ? and who can challenge the decision of the Governor ? " The possibility of appeal existed, and we have seen in a previous chapter that a man of great wealth, like Virji Vora, might be successful before the Emperor ; we do not know how much Virji Vora spent on that occasion, but it would be rash to infer from his success that men of moderate means were efficiently protected against the rapacity of local officials. To my mind the correct inference is that which has already been suggested, that in levies of all kinds, whether imposed on classes or on individuals, officials had to avoid such a scandal as might provoke interference from above, but that, short of this limit, they had very large opportunities of raising money by methods which would not be tolerated by public opinion at the present day, and which were undoubtedly injurious from the economist's point of view.

AUTHORITIES FOR CHAPTER IX

SECTION 1.—I know of no contemporary description of the Mogul fiscal system as a whole. The account I have given is based on statements scattered through the chronicles, and on *Sarkar's Aurangzeb*. The heads of revenue are stated most clearly in *Manucci* (ii. 415), but his list includes items which were added after the close of our period. For the gross yield of land revenue, see *Ain* (translation), ii. 115, and *Badshahnama*, ii. 710 ff. The nature of the outlay debited to the Court can be learned from Book I. of the *Ain*. Shahjahan's increased expenditure is emphasised in *Elliot*, vii. 171, 2. The comparison of salaries is based on *Ain* (translation), i. 308 ff., and *Badshahnama*, ii. 717 ff. Regarding the remittance of surplus revenue, see *Sarkar's Aurangzeb*, i. 171 ff. The poverty of the officials is stated by *Bernier*, 213. Authorities for the fiscal system in the south have been given under Chapter VIII.

SECTION 2.—For the Surat customs, see Hawkins in *Early Travels*, 171; *Purchas*, I. iv. 423; and *Thévenot*, 7: for competition between seaports, *Roe*, 45, 57, 82, and *English Factories*, iii. 192, viii. 134. Delay recurs frequently: see for instances, *Letters Received*, iv. 78, and *English Factories*, i. 137, ii. 311, iii. 29, viii. 302; also *Schorer*, f. 8. Over-valuation is also a common topic; the instances given are *English Factories*, v. 244; *Letters Received*, iv. 78; *Roe*, 152; *Dagh Register*, July 31, 1641. Instances of forced dealing by customs authorities are *Letters Received*, iv. 78, *English Factories*, i. 187, viii. 302.

The references to the Surat mint are *English Factories*, iv. 103, v. 18, vi. 84, vii. 23, viii. 185, x. 120. Abuses at Rajmahal are stated in *Dagh Register*, September 3, 1663, and numerous entries in the next few years. Statements of the Mogul claim to inheritance will be found in *Purchas*, I. iii. 218, II. ix. 1480; *Roe*, 110 ff.; *Bernier*, 164, 204, and elsewhere: Aurangzeb's letter on the subject is in *Bernier*, 167: the description of Jahangir's practice is translated from *Pelsart*, MS. f. 21. For Asaf Khan's estate, see *Dagh Register*, September 4, 1642; *Elliot*, vii. 68; and *Manrique*, lxxi: for Aurangzeb's attitude, *Elliot*, vii. 161, and *Manucci*, ii. 415 ff.: for notices in the commercial correspondence, *English Factories*, ii. 125, iii. 29, viii. 7, 102, 119.

The system of presents is mentioned by most writers: the specific passages referred to in the text are *Manrique*, lxiv, and *Dagh Register* (Surat), April 27, 1643, January 18 and June 9, 1645. The items of miscellaneous Imperial revenue must be sought in the statistical tables of *Ain* (translation), ii.

SECTION 3.—The levy of cesses on the revenue is referred to in *Sarkar's Studies*, 194; the local cess in Masulipatam in *Terpstra's Koromandel*, II., and *Renneville*, v. 179 ff. Jahangir's prohibition of local duties is in *Tuzuk*, i. 7; Aurangzeb's orders are discussed in *Sarkar's Administration*, 120; the persistence of such levies can be traced in numerous later works, *e.g. Taylor's Dacca*, 197. The passages referred to in connection with transit dues are *Letters Received*, iv. 79; *English Factories*, i. 88, 331; iii. 28, 176, 273; vii. 160; viii. 58, 71, 108, 301, 320; ix. 10, 26, 38, 84; x. 63; and *Dagh Register*, February 24, 1634; March 31, May 20, 1641; April 27, December 12, 1643 (Surat); April 17, 1643, January 5, 1645 (Coromandel). For the levies by authorities other than the Moguls, see *English Factories*, i. 331; ii. 96, 310; v. 17; vi. 13, 150, 258; vii. 306; ix. 235: *Mundy*, ii. 111, 119: *Thévenot*, 279: *Manucci*, ii. 171: *Letters Received*, v. 128. Khafi Khan's account is in *Elliot*, vii. 246-248.

As regards other duties, the monopolies mentioned have been discussed in Chapter IV. Dues on saltpetre are mentioned in *English Factories*, x. 15, and *Dagh Register* (Coromandel), August 19, 1645; for Mir Jumla's levies, see *idem*, November 29, 1661. Town duties are recorded in *Sewell*, 364 ff., and *Ain* (translation), ii. 42: excise regulations in *Mundy*, ii. 32, 97, 134; and salt duties in *Ain* (translation), ii. 242, 249, 315. The quotations regarding fines and bribes are taken from *Pelsart* (MS. ff. 22, 24), and *Gujarat Report*, ff. 20, 21.

CHAPTER X

SUMMARY AND CONCLUSION

In the foregoing chapters I have discussed such information as I have been able to collect regarding the economic conditions which prevailed in India during the reigns of Jahangir and Shahjahan. The task remains of estimating the changes which took place during this period, and of attempting a rough balance-sheet, which may go some way towards answering the questions whether the national income was increasing or diminishing, and whether its distribution was approaching to, or receding from, modern standards of equity. At first sight, the outstanding facts are the appearance in India of agents of the great commercial companies formed in Holland and England, and their gradual penetration into all the most productive regions of the country; but on a closer examination the economist, while recognising the eventual significance of those phenomena, is led to attach greater immediate importance to the administrative changes of the period, which intensified existing defects in the system of distribution, and thereby brought about a marked and cumulative reaction on productive industry. On the one hand, India benefited by an increase in the efficiency of the marketing agencies at her disposal, but on the other she suffered from the intensification of the economic parasitism which was destroying her productive energies: some localities, and some classes of producers, profited by the new external facilities, but the country taken as a whole was being impoverished by the operation of internal forces; and in my judgment there can be no question that the final balance is on the adverse side of the account.

Among the external agencies at work, the Dutch Company was much the most important. On the eastern side of India Dutch enterprise secured the initiative, and maintained its predominance throughout our period : in the west it quickly surpassed the results attained by the English, who had there the advantage of priority. From the Indian point of view, the presence of two competing organisations was undoubtedly beneficial. The English merchants during our period realised very scanty profits after allowance has been made for the heavy losses incurred from time to time, but they succeeded in retaining a position in Indian trade, and it was mainly through their efforts to do so that the country was saved from the grip of a commercial monopoly such as the Dutch established in some other parts of Asia.

The conditions which prevailed in India were such as to prevent any large development of the import-trade. The masses of the people were too poor to be interested in such foreign goods as were then available : the middle classes were few in number, and were debarred from ostentatious expenditure by the fear of official rapacity ; while the market offered by the Courts and their dependant nobles was small in volume, and was governed mainly by fashion or caprice. Indian consumers benefited where there was competition among importers, but suffered where a monopoly was established, and payment for most of the new exports was taken in the precious metals. The additional imports of gold and silver were not, however, in excess of the absorptive capacity of the country taken as a whole, and they produced no marked change in the general level of prices, though the sudden extension of trade in Bengal resulted in that market being brought more nearly on a level with the conditions prevailing elsewhere on the coast.

On the export side, the main result of the Dutch and English activities was to secure new and extensive markets for Indian producers of indigo, calico, saltpetre, raw silk, and a variety of other items of less individual importance. Indian merchants had made no effective attempts to exploit these markets, while Portuguese activities during the preceding century had produced only limited results: the large consumption of Indian silk in Japan, and of Indian calico and saltpetre in Western Europe, are definitely new facts of commerce, while the increase in the use of indigo in the latter region was so great that it may fairly be placed in the same category. Some allowance must indeed be made for a temporary decline in the export of pepper, but this loss cannot be regarded as equivalent to more than a small proportion of the new trade. The direct advantage accruing to India was confined to particular localities, which were enabled to dispose of an increased amount of material, and to find remunerative employment for certain classes of the people; the increase in the income of these localities may be described without exaggeration as substantial, but it could scarcely make a large difference if it were spread over the whole population of the country.

The insistent Indian demand for the precious metals led the European merchants to take a large share in the Asiatic carrying-trade. It is possible, but in my opinion it is unlikely, that their activities in this direction resulted in a large proportionate increase in the existing export-trade to other parts of Asia; it is certain that they resulted in important changes in the shipping industry. The burden of these changes fell mainly on the Portuguese ship-owners, who lost most of the business they had acquired in the course of the preceding century, but Indian owners also were injuriously affected to an extent which differed in different regions, but was probably greatest in Gujarat; on the other hand, Indian exporters benefited by the provision of a more efficient carrying-service, the charges for which were kept down by active competition.

The immediate effects of European activities were thus local and partial. It is unquestionable that they brought substantial economic benefit to growers of indigo and cotton, to weavers, to producers of silk and saltpetre, to the land-transport industry, and to export merchants, classes of much greater importance in the aggregate than the pepper-growers, ship-owners, and ship-builders who may have been adversely affected by their operations; there was thus a substantial balance of advantage for India, but not, in my opinion, of such magnitude as to represent a proportionately great increase in the total of the national income. Further, there was the gain resulting from the establishment of a new business organisation, by which Indian producers were brought into close relations with the markets of Western Europe; in the latter portion of our period there was a practical certainty that whatever India had to sell would be offered in London, Paris, and Amsterdam, while the competition between the Companies usually sufficed to secure reasonable prices to the sellers. The development of external relations had thus brought substantial benefit at the moment, and a promise of greater benefit to come.

On the other hand, the internal forces in operation were wholly injurious. The demands made by the various Governments on producers were so large that there is no exaggeration in the statement that administrative activities were the most important factors in the distribution of the national income. Speaking generally, their effect was to leave to producers very little, if anything, above the minimum required for their subsistence, and to offer the surplus in rewards to energy or ingenuity exerted in unproductive ways. In the south of India the administrative system operated steadily in this direction throughout our period, and here the changes to be recorded are comparatively slight: pressure on producers tended to intensify, because the local authorities had the strongest motives to discover every possible form of income, and to increase their demand to the utmost on those forms which were already familiar; but the system itself was unchanged, and even at the opening of our period its severity was such that a great increase of pressure could have led only to starvation or rebellion. In the north, on the other hand, there was a definite change in system. Akbar's financial institutions, which, judged by modern standards, were severe, but not necessarily inequitable or destructive in their operation, gave way under his successors, and the direct demand on production was largely increased, while the simultaneous deterioration in administrative methods resulted in a steady approximation to the conditions which already prevailed in the south. The effect of these changes is shown by direct contemporary evidence to have been a diversion of energy from productive to unproductive pursuits, a process which was necessarily cumulative in its effects, and which is to my mind the outstanding economic fact of the half-century. Almost throughout India the tendency was to reduce the reward of production to a point where it ceased to offer an adequate incentive, to attract brains and energy to the struggle for a share in what had been produced by others, and thus to lead the way towards the national bankruptcy which eventually occurred.

Such are the conclusions which I have drawn from the evidence which has been examined. The question has still to be asked whether the account is substantially complete, or whether other important developments may have occurred of which the evidence on record gives no hint. So far as the departments of production and transport are concerned, this question can be answered with practical certainty. The records of the Dutch and English commercial activities cover practically the entire field; the possibilities of every commodity and every means of transport were discussed and tested by competent men, not governed by routine, but energetically exploring every course which might yield a profit; and it does not appear to be possible that any development of real economic importance can have been overlooked. The same conclusion is certainly true of the consumption of imported goods, the trade in which fell mainly into the foreign merchants' hands; the need for curtailing the use of the precious metals urged them to foster the import-trade in every possible way, and the small results known to have been secured may safely be taken to cover the whole ground. The possibility remains of unrecorded changes in the Indian consumption of Indian goods. The Dutch and English had not yet entered largely into the internal trade by land, though they were familiar with most branches of the coasting trade, and it is conceivable that internal changes might have occurred without finding a record in their correspondence. It is difficult, however, to conjecture any important changes of this kind ; I have found no suggestions of them in chronicles or journals of the period ; there are no signs of any marked alteration in the standard of living ; and the spending-power of the people was in any case so small that the presumption is altogether against the occurrence of anything of the sort. We may infer that some weavers, saltpetre-makers, or indigo-growers found themselves in a position to eat rather more food, or to spend rather more on clothes and metals ; we may infer in the same way that large numbers of peasants found life harder ; but there do not appear to be grounds for travelling further into the region of conjecture.

The low standard of life, and the small spending-power of the people, are, however, facts established by direct evidence, and perhaps the best way of bringing this study to a conclusion will be to attempt a reduction to its lowest terms of the economic system from which these facts emerge. Let us imagine, then, a self-supporting community, consisting of five producers, each securing about the same income, and one non-producing consumer, whom we may describe either as a policeman or as a parasite. A simple sum in arithmetic shows that, in order to secure equality of income in this community, each producer should surrender one-sixth of his income to the parasite or policeman. If now, in place of a rule of equality, we introduce the revenue system as it worked under Shahjahan, so that each producer surrenders one-half instead of one-sixth, then the income of the policeman or parasite will be five times that of each individual producer, and, provided that the conditions of his existence are in other respects tolerable, there will be an exceedingly strong temptation for each producer to secure his place. If we multiply this community by some figure of the order of 4 millions,[1] we get something very like the economic skeleton of the India of our period. The bulk of the peasants and artisans of all classes lived on practically

[1] That is to say, about 20 to 25 million households, which I take to be about the standard of the population of India at this period.

the same level, and, while there must have been individual differences due to skill or fortune, we are justified in assuming that they diverged from the norm to about the same extent on either side, so that we can think of the mass as homogeneous. The proportion of " parasites " to producers cannot of course be determined accurately, but the figure I have taken seems to me to be probably an over-statement.[1] Neither cities nor armies had greatly increased during our period, for local advances are offset by retrogression elsewhere, and there is no doubt that peasants formed the bulk of the population, while the proportion of artisans was at any rate substantial; and, without attempting to secure numerical exactitude, it is safe to say that a relatively large number of producers contributed half their gross income to the support of a relatively small number of economic parasites. The latter class was not, however, economically homogeneous, for it extended from the greatest noble to the humblest slave; in point of fact, most of the parasites lived on substantially the same plane as the producers, and it was only the small minority which engaged actively in the struggle for the surplus product. There was thus a very large income to be divided between a very small number of competitors, and, since saving resulted only in confiscation at death, the dividend was usually spent as quickly as it accrued. The conditions thus rendered inevitable the extravagant luxury of the nobles which struck foreign observers so strongly, and the dissipation of the surplus income of the country in unproductive channels. The humbler parasites, while living on the same plane as producers, were in some important respects substantially better off. If, for instance, seasons were bad, the peon's wages might buy less food, but the peasant might see his wife and children sold into slavery; and the general result of the administrative changes which occurred during our period was to increase this disparity to a point where the producer's life ceased to be worth living. He bore the brunt of the struggle with natural forces, but he could hope to retain no appreciable portion of the spoils,

[1] The figures of the census of 1911 give a proportion of about one " parasite " to nine producers, as against the assumed ratio of one to five.

which were employed in maintaining a few parasites in luxury, and a much greater number in a life of comparative security.

The unproductive population was to be found mainly in towns or camps, while production was carried on chiefly in the villages, so that, from a somewhat different standpoint, the economic system of our period may be regarded as operating to provide the urban population with subsistence below cost. The harvest-glut is still a familiar fact in India : a disproportionate amount of the season's produce has to be marketed within a few weeks in order to provide for necessary payments in cash ; and forced sellers have to be content with lower prices than would be obtainable in a market to which they were not compelled to come. At the period we are considering, this recurring glut must have been much more acute than now,[1] because the proportion of produce to be sold was much larger, while the penalties attaching to default were much more severe. At each harvest, then, there was an urgent demand for coin, and the merchants who held coin in stock could practically make their own terms. They had, however, to turn over their stock of produce in time to be in funds for the next harvest, and, since the urban population was proportionately small, this condition secured to them supplies of food and other produce at less cost than if the markets had been free. The cheapness of food in Indian towns was one of the first facts to strike foreign visitors, who were usually content to attribute it to the fertility of the country ; but there can be no doubt that the working of the revenue system was a factor of at least equal importance in transferring to the towns a large proportion of the profits earned in the villages.

Such was the economic system which at the close of our period was drawing towards collapse. Weavers, naked themselves, toiled to clothe others. Peasants, themselves hungry,

[1] The statement in the text is correct whether revenue was paid in cash or in grain. The treasury required silver, and, while in some provinces receipts of grain may have been disbursed for local needs, much of it must have been sold in order to provide silver for remittance, and in fixing prices merchants would take that fact into account. The regulations of the period contemplate cash payments as the rule, but there were probably local exceptions.

toiled to feed the towns and cities. India, taken as a unit, parted with useful commodities in exchange for gold and silver, or in other words gave bread for stones. Men and women, living from season to season on the verge of hunger, could be contented so long as the supply of food held out: when it failed, as it so often did, their hope of salvation was the slave-trader, and the alternatives were cannibalism, suicide, or starvation. The only way of escape from that system lay through an increase in production, coupled with a rising standard of life, but this road was barred effectively by the administrative methods in vogue, which penalised production, and regarded every indication of increased consumption as a signal for fresh extortion. The period of which I have written is characterised primarily by the extension and the intensification of those methods: the story of the century which followed is the story, first of the eventual collapse, and then of the gradual change, which was in time to render a new economic system possible.

APPENDIX A

THE DUTCH AND ENGLISH COMPANIES

The constitution and management of European trading companies are topics which lie outside the scope of a book dealing with the economic history of India, but some knowledge of these subjects is required in order to understand the principal authorities for the commerce of our period, which consist of the records of such companies, and assume a familiarity with details which cannot be expected of ordinary readers at the present day. Some explanation, therefore, is called for, and the need for it is increased by the changes in the meaning of various terms which have occurred in the course of three centuries. The very word "Company" calls up a false picture: to speak of shareholders is in some respects misleading; and it is equally dangerous to talk of capital and dividends.

The development of the joint-stock company with limited liability has been a lengthy process, and it had made comparatively little way in England when "certain adventurers" were incorporated "for the discovery of the trade for the East Indies" on the last day of the year 1600. At that date there were no Company Acts in existence, no settled forms of procedure, no recognised rules of accountancy; and, while it was not altogether a novelty, the enterprise may fairly be described as an adventure even in the modern sense of the term. What happened was this. Certain merchants agreed together to risk, or adventure, some money in a trade of which they had no experience. They applied for, and obtained, Letters Patent, or as we should now say a Charter, from the Crown, incorporating them as a Company, and thus giving them a legal status, laying down rules for their procedure, and granting certain privileges, notably a monopoly of the trade for a term of years. The first adventurers became by this charter the original members of the Company, but the identity did not continue. The Company was, as the charter says, a Fellowship, and what we should call its members were known as brothers or freemen. Admission, or the freedom of the Company, could be obtained in the recognised ways, by patrimony, or by service, or on payment of what was called a fine; there was no inherent obligation on the freeman to adventure any capital, and thus the Company consisted of members who were privileged, but not bound, to take part in its enterprises.[1] The adventurers at any moment were those members who had invested capital; the Company had no permanent capital of its own, and the funds with which trade was carried on belonged to a fluctuating body of its members. The word "fluctuating" is justified by the fact that the adventures were at first made for short periods and specific purposes. The original adventure was for a single voyage; the whole capital subscribed was spent on ships and goods, and when the ships returned, they were disposed of, and the adventure was wound up. In this way twelve voyages were undertaken in succession, each with its separate capital subscribed by bodies of adventurers, and returned to them, with any profits that had been earned, on its conclusion.

This system of separate voyages proved to be exceedingly inconvenient, mainly owing to the conditions prevailing in Asiatic markets, which, as has been explained in Chapter II., made it necessary to keep factors on the spot, to dispose of imports as opportunity offered, and to get together goods for export in advance of the arrival of shipping. In 1613, therefore, a joint stock was subscribed, which undertook all the business up to 1616, and two other joint stocks cover the period from 1616 to 1640. By the latter year, the trade had lost its initial attractions for Englishmen. Dutch competition was vigorous and successful; profits had fallen off; King Charles I. had encouraged the rival enterprise known as Courteen's Association; and the political situation in England made it undesirable to lock up funds in prolonged speculative undertakings. The subscription for a new joint stock failed to fill, and in 1642 a reversion was made to the system of Single (now called General) Voyages. Later in this year a fourth joint stock was launched, but with wholly inadequate capital: a Second general voyage was undertaken in

[1] An adventure was not necessarily confined to the existing members or freemen. Thus the Court decided in 1607 that if the Fourth voyage were not fully financed by the "old adventurers," any of the King's subjects might be permitted to subscribe (*Court Minutes*, May 13, 1607); such subscribers would presumably have been admitted as freemen in due course.

1646; and in 1650 the "United Joint Stock" resulted from the inclusion of certain merchants who had hitherto stood outside the Company. This in turn was exhausted in a few years; in 1655 a subscription failed, and for a time the trade was practically open, that is to say it was carried on by individuals; but in 1657, on the grant of a fresh charter, capital was again attracted, and the New General Stock was started with subscriptions of nearly three-quarters of a million sterling, only half of which was eventually employed. Unlike its predecessors, this adventure was made for an indefinite duration, and, since a regular market for the shares developed in London, it became permanent; adventurers sold their shares instead of looking for repayment, and thus the share-capital of the Company came into existence.

The procedure followed by the Company makes it impossible to calculate the exact dividends paid during our period. When one or more ships had arrived in the Thames, a "division" (as it was called) was usually made to the adventurers concerned, sometimes in cash, sometimes in pepper, indigo, calico, or whatever goods might be on hand; other divisions might follow at uncertain intervals; and in some cases we do not know the precise period for which the capital was actually employed. It is certain, however, that while the first ten or twelve years' trading, covered by the single voyages, was comfortably, though not extravagantly, remunerative,[1] the first joint stock was marked by a serious fall in profits, the second and third paid very little, and the fourth resulted in a loss of half the capital. The details as set out in the records of the Company are as follows.

The First and Second voyages were eventually united, and gave an "advance" over the original capital of 95 per cent, which has to be distributed over the period of its employment; the annual rate of dividend depends not only on the total period, but on whether we take the return of capital first, or proportionately from each division, and on various other factors. The Third and Fifth voyages, which were also combined, yielded 234 per cent, but the Fourth was practically a total loss, the ships being cast away, and this fact must be taken into account in any attempt to strike an average of profits. The "advance" given by the next seven voyages (Sixth to Twelfth) varied between 120 and 220 per cent; and that these returns were considered to be satisfactory is shown by the large subscription (£400,000)

[1] Macpherson, in his *History of European Commerce with India* (p. 92), calculated the annual return of the separate voyages as something under 20 per cent, which he regarded as "scarcely an adequate premium for the risk."

secured for the first joint stock. At this point the tide of profit began to ebb as the difficulties with the Dutch increased. This joint stock gave 87½ per cent advance in the course of about four years, but the second gave only 12½ per cent, and the third 35 per cent, so that, taking the latter two together, the dividend calculated on modern lines would have been somewhere about 2 per cent annually. The effect was seen in the difficulties experienced in raising capital for fresh ventures, difficulties increased by the failure of the fourth joint stock, which eventually lost half its capital; and, while the United Joint Stock did somewhat better (gaining 105 per cent in all), it seems to be certain that from about 1615 to 1655 the Company was not really a commercial success.

The Dutch Company was in some respects more in keeping with the modern sense of the word, for it had from the outset what may fairly be termed a permanent capital of about £550,000, and consequently its payments to shareholders are comparable with modern dividends, though the fact that they were paid sometimes in cash, sometimes in bonds, and sometimes in spices, would have to be allowed for in a precise calculation of the rate of profit.[1] Its constitution was, however, peculiar. The shareholders had no control whatever over the managing body, which was complex. The different organisations which had united to form the Company retained their individuality, in so far that there were several distinct "Chambers," one located at each of the principal seaports. Each chamber consisted of a number of directors (*bewinthebber*), who were in the first instance nominated; subsequent vacancies were filled by the provincial government on the nomination of the existing directors. The central management consisted of a "College" of seventeen, representing the chambers in fixed proportions; its members were often spoken of as "the Seventeen." The college framed the policy of the Company, which was executed by the chambers, each acting for its own seaport. Thus the size and equipment of the annual fleet was determined by the college, which allotted ships to each chamber: the chamber sent out the ships allotted to it, and marketed the goods brought back in its ships. In practice, then, the business of the Company was entirely in the hands of an oligarchical body, maintaining its continuity by nominating to vacancies. The charter provided that serious disputes in the

[1] Under the terms of the original charter shareholders were free to withdraw their capital after each triennial settlement of accounts, but the development of a market for the shares, usually at a premium, rendered this provision unimportant in practice.

college should be referred to the Central Government (the States General), but the historian of the Company is justified in the statement that the directors were practically autocrats, in no way responsible to the shareholders, and only nominally responsible to the State. The accounts of the Company were not published, there were no meetings of members or shareholders corresponding to the General Courts of the English Company, and it is said that no minutes were kept of the proceedings of the college. Our knowledge of the policy and motives of the Company is therefore incomplete; in later years its financial methods were dubious, and apparently some of the dividends were paid out of capital; but there seems no reason to doubt that during our period the sums distributed were really earned.

The early profits of the Dutch Company were high. The figures given by different writers are discordant, but the average dividend from 1605 to 1609 was certainly 35 per cent annually, and perhaps much more. From 1610 to 1619 the resources of the Company were devoted largely to the struggle for monopoly in the Spice Islands, and in these years the distribution averaged about 21, or, according to another account, 28 per cent. The dividends for the five decades from 1620 to 1669 averaged 12, 20¾, 29, 18, and 14¾ per cent annually, payments being made in most years, but the amounts varying within wide limits; and if we consider that the rate for loans in the London market ranged during part of this period from seven to nine per cent,[1] we are justified in regarding the Dutch returns as satisfactory, but not very much more. An important point to realise regarding this Company is what may be described as its national aspect.[2] It was formed at the instance of the State by the amalgamation of existing ventures: the interests of each important seaport were represented on the governing body; authority was given to it to enter into agreements with foreign Powers in the name of the Dutch

[1] In 1609 the English Company was inquiring for a loan at nine per cent or under, and in 1614 it was offered money at ten, and borrowed at nine, per cent (*Court Minutes*, February 13, 1609, January 24, 1614). Ten years later, the Company was paying seven and eight per cent (*idem*, August 25, 1624), while in 1635 the rate was 6¼ to 7 per cent (*idem*, February 1, 1635).

[2] The power of the Dutch Company appears very clearly in the records of the negotiations carried on from time to time in London and in Holland. In 1627, for instance, when the English Company was considering the abandonment of its undertaking, a "mixed court" recorded the opinion that there was very little hope of redress for the losses caused by the Dutch, since "the Government of the Low Countries is so intermixed with Bewinthebbers that in a trial they will be both parties and judges" (*Court Minutes*, July 20, 1627).

Government; and when the first Governor General was appointed in 1609, the position assigned to him was very nearly that of an officer of State, with practically a free hand in matters of Asiatic policy. The protracted negotiations between the English and Dutch Governments indicate a great difference in the position held by the two Companies. The impression left on my mind by a perusal of the Calendars of State Papers is that, while James I. regarded the protection of the Eastern trade as important but not vital, the States General and the Dutch Company acted practically as a single body, ready to stake everything for the attainment of the objects of the latter. It is true that the States condemned the action of the Company's officials in the affair of Amboina, but their diplomatic efforts were directed to keeping what had been gained rather than to satisfying the English demands, and their success in doing this is a matter of history. The English Company could usually count on fair promises from the two Stuart kings, but it could count on nothing more: the Dutch acted with the certainty that its Government stood behind it; it had been given wide powers by the State, but at the same time it constituted a power within the State, and one with which the State could hardly have ventured to break.

The national position enjoyed by the Dutch Company was a material factor in its commercial success, but does not by itself explain its marked superiority over its English rival. Apart from national support, that superiority may be attributed to the advantages resulting from priority, financial strength, sound administration, and possibly a higher level of capacity in the staff employed. The fact of priority is obvious: the Dutch had six years' experience of the markets when the first ships of the English Company reached Java, and were known as customers in every promising seaport which the English visited as strangers. Their financial strength arose mainly from their large permanent capital, which was in marked contrast to the sums adventured in England for successive voyages; and thus they started in the struggle for the Spice Islands with a definite handicap in their favour. Moreover, they were quick to realise, what seems obvious now, that a strong centralised administration was essential in the East: during the critical years from 1610 onwards the direction of their whole resources was concentrated under the Governor General in Java, while the English factors and commanders, not infrequently at variance, could look for guidance only to London. Add to these considerations the emergence of a really great man, the masterful and ruthless Jan Pieterszoon Coen, who, first as director of the factories in Java, and then as Governor

General, may fairly be said to have dominated the Eastern seas as Alboquerque had dominated them a century before, and the initial success of the Dutch in securing the monopoly of the Spice Islands and the Farther East is seen to have been the only possible result of the conditions which prevailed.

Their commercial success during the rest of our period depended very largely on that monopoly, but continued sound administration was also an important factor. The Council at Batavia stands out in the records as highly efficient: the chain of subordination was strict, each of the chiefs at such centres as Taiwan, Amboina, Pulicat, or Surat being held directly responsible to the Council for the various factories under his control; and the occasional inspections made by high officials from Batavia were so conducted as to maintain discipline and curtail abuses, as well as to develop and extend trade on profitable lines. During this period, the English factories, spread over a much smaller area, were usually grouped under two co-ordinate authorities, the councils at Surat and Bantam, whose views not infrequently differed, and whose conflicts of opinion had ample time to bring serious losses before they could be removed by orders from the Company in London. The discipline exercised by these councils must, I think, be described as lax, and it is hardly going too far to say that, while the Dutch carried on their business as a trained and disciplined team, the English achievement was largely the work of individuals. It is difficult to compare *personnel* after the lapse of nearly three centuries, but the impression left on my mind by the records of the two Companies is that the Dutch had on the average an advantage, though it is of course impossible to say whether, given equal discipline, the English might not have done equally well.

The lack of discipline in the English organisation is most apparent in the matter of Private Trade, a topic which recurs so frequently in the records that some explanation of it is due to modern readers. The factors were employed by the Company, which was entitled to claim the results of their work and knowledge, and suffered more or less serious injury when, as so commonly happened, they devoted time and brains to making money for themselves. The private trade which they carried on may be classified, from the Company's point of view, as imports, exports, and local trade. Imports to Europe by returning factors and ship's companies were the least open to objection, and individuals were formally allowed to bring home a certain amount of goods subject to certain specified exceptions. They did not, however, confine themselves within these limits, but brought cargo by the tun, filling up space on the ships which belonged to the Company, and sometimes interfering with its markets.[1] The Company treated such infractions of its orders with extraordinary leniency, entering into negotiations with each individual, sometimes taking over the goods at a fair price, sometimes merely charging freight, and sometimes imposing a fine, the amount of which depended on the quality of the individual's past service ; and no one who has glanced through the *Court Minutes* for our period can wonder that the practice was almost universal. Private imports were, in fact, speculative business, the profits on which had usually to be shared with the Company, but a factor whose record was good could hope to keep a large portion for himself.

Private exports, of course, tended to affect the Company's markets abroad, but they were discouraged mainly, I think, because they represented capital which later on could be used in local trade.[2] Outgoing factors were often allowed to invest capital in the "adventure" by which they were employed, and this course was obviously advantageous; but the profits of successful private speculation might be so great that a man who went out with even a small sum in his own possession might come home with what in those days was a comfortable fortune, gained by trading in the East. The mere buying and selling, though it was sometimes on a scale sufficient to affect the local markets, was the least objectionable part of the business. Some factors employed the Company's capital in their private ventures ; with the same object, others borrowed money ostensibly on the Company's account; vessels belonging to the Company were diverted to carry the goods of individual merchants ; transactions were so handled that the profits accrued to the individual, while the Company bore the losses; and secret partnerships were arranged with local merchants, who thus obtained the benefit of knowledge which belonged by right to the Company. The whole thing must have been utterly demoralising, and a sound administration would have endeavoured to stamp it out; yet in 1634, when a merchant chosen as President of Bantam asked for powers to do so, his request was refused, and he was advised to use his authority "not with too much rigour and severity." The truth appears to be that the scales of salaries and expenses allowed

[1] Captain Weddell, for instance, brought home 40 tuns of goods, a quantity which would occupy an appreciable proportion of the whole cargo-space available for the year (*Court Minutes*, December 18, 1626).

[2] As has been indicated in the text, quicksilver was a favourite form of private export. In 1630 the London price of the metal was raised owing to the quantity bought by mariners and others going on the voyage (*Court Minutes*, October 22, 1630).

by the Company were in themselves inadequate to attract competent merchants; the directors recognised that the hope of gain by private trading was in fact part of the contract, and they endeavoured to keep such trade within reasonable limits while tolerating its existence, an attempt which was obviously hopeless.

The stronger Dutch administration attempted no such compromise, and, so far as can be judged from the published records, it suffered much less from the practice, at least until the closing years of our period. Raynal, writing in the eighteenth century, laid stress on the frugality and probity of the Dutch merchants, and asserted that before the year 1650 not even one remarkable fortune had been made; but he alleged that after that date luxury and corruption made rapid strides. Contemporary records suggest a continuous struggle over this question, though an absolute prohibition of private trade had been issued in 1603. As early as 1610, we hear of private goods being detected and confiscated, a stern measure which, I think, was never at this period taken by the English authorities in the East. Twenty years later, orders sent out from Amsterdam suggest that the evil was increasing, and we hear of Dutch factors transacting business through English intermediaries. Tavernier tells of much private trade after the year 1640, but he had a quarrel with the Dutch, and possibly exaggerates the extent of the evil; at the same time he allows that heavy penalties were enforced in some instances. An order issued at Batavia in 1653 suggests that the practice was then extending, for informers were promised a share of confiscated goods; while three years later we hear of two high officers being sent for trial on charges of gross private trading; and from 1664 onwards the Batavia Journals indicate increased attention to the subject at headquarters. These incidents suggest that the Dutch were gradually yielding to temptation, and the same inference may be drawn from an order of the year 1676 in which the directors at Amsterdam reiterated their prohibition of the practice, "which is nothing else than a plague and canker in the Company's body, and yet flourishes everywhere in spite of all the orders decreed and the notices issued." On the strength of this order it may perhaps be said that by this time private trade had definitely been established among the Dutch merchants, but we may accept Raynal's statement and the other evidence quoted above as showing that in the earlier years of its existence the Dutch Company secured, to a greater extent than its English rival, the best services of its employees in the East.

This "private trade" must be distinguished from the business carried on by Europeans not in the service of one of the Companies, who are sometimes described as "private traders." The operations of these individuals were, however, unimportant during our period. There were free Dutchmen living at Batavia and some other places in Asia, but their business was closely controlled by the Company in whose settlements they lived, and they were probably a help rather than a hindrance to the official merchants. The English Company had little trouble with individual Englishmen until the last few years of our period. One result of the years of open trade (about 1655) was the settlement on the East Coast of individuals not under direct obligation to the Company, and from 1658 onwards they begin to take a prominent place in the commercial correspondence.

AUTHORITIES FOR APPENDIX A

The early history of joint-stock companies can be studied in *Scott.* The first Letters Patent of the English Company are given in *Purchas*, I. iii. 139; its subsequent history must be traced mainly in the *Court Minutes*. The evils resulting from separate voyages are indicated in *Jourdain*, 304, among other writers. The eventual establishment of share-capital is recorded in *English Factories*, x. 113; the introductions to the earlier volumes of this series give the salient facts regarding the position of the Company, while the financial results are reviewed in *Court Minutes* for November 1654. For the constitution of the Dutch Company I have relied mainly on *Van der Chijs*, who in chapter XII. gives the charter in full; its working is discussed in *van Loon*, 61 ff. The dividends paid are set out in *Renneville*, i. Introduction, and, with some discrepancies in the early years, in Macpherson's *Annals of Commerce*, iv. 488, while *Edmundson*, p. 124, mentions one very large payment not shown in either table. The orders defining the powers of the Governor General are in *de Jonge*, III. 130; the general course of the prolonged Anglo-Dutch negotiations can be followed in the *Calendar S.P.*

The evils of private trade among the English appear all through the *Court Minutes* and *English Factories*; some remarks of *Roe* (442) show that it was rampant within a few years of the Company's foundation. The case in which the Company explicitly discouraged zeal is in *Court Minutes*, January 3, 1634. *Raynal's* view of private trade among the Dutch is i. 191. The original prohibition is given in *de Jonge*, III. 206: the early instance of confiscation, in *Terpstra's Koromandel*, 144: the orders of 1632, in *Hague Transcripts*, II. 95, 97: the assistance rendered by the English, in *English Factories*, iv. 166, and *passim*: *Tavernier's* account in i. 311, ii. 43-50, 327 ff.: the later orders quoted, in *Dagh Register*, December 31, 1653, November 6, 1656; and *de Jonge*, VI. 163. For private traders not in the English Company's employment, see *English Factories*, x. 149, and later entries.

APPENDIX B

EARLY DUTCH EXPORTS TO EUROPE

There is a gap in the published information regarding Dutch commercial activities on the Coromandel coast from 1610, when Dr. Terpstra's account of their establishment breaks off, to 1624, when the series of the Batavia Journals begins. Some idea of the exports to Europe during this period can be formed from the following abstracts of some invoices preserved in Holland, photographic transcripts of which have been supplied to me by the Public Record Office at The Hague. The values are given in guilders ($\frac{5}{8}$ rupee); I have eliminated fractional entries, and have rounded the quantities in converting to English pounds and yards.

1. Invoice of the *Black Bear* (*Swarte Beer*) from Masulipatam for Holland, most probably in 1615–16. (*Kol. Archief, portef.* O.)

The invoice itself is not dated on the first page, but each of the inner pages is headed "*Anno 1616 : Masulipattan*"; I take these headings to have been added in Amsterdam, and the year to be that of arrival. We know from the English records that another ship, the *White Bear*, was expected to sail for Holland in 1616 (*Letters Received*, iv. 34), and it is probable that the *Black Bear* left late in 1615, a year in which the English records do not give the name of any ship sailing for Holland direct.

Goods.	Bales.	Quantity.	Value in Guilders.
Indigo	450	2800 maunds = about 73,000 lb.	23,992
Cotton yarn . .	155	968¾ „ = „ 25,000 „	12,689
Guinea cloth . .	66	1322 pieces = „ 66,000 yards	7,778
Bengal taffacylles (sample) . . .	1	135 „ (length not given)	716
		Total . . .	45,175
		Add packing, loading, and export duties . .	4,554
		Value of cargo . .	49,729

The bales of indigo and yarn are entered as 6¼ maunds. The weight of the maund is not given; taking the usual Masulipatam maund of about 26 lb., the bales would be 162½ lb., while in the subsequent invoices the bales are given as 150 lb. Dutch, or 163 lb. avoirdupois. It may be inferred that the ordinary local maund was intended, and the figures given in pounds are calculated on this basis.

The pieces of Guinea cloth are given as 100 cobidos or 70 ells. The Amsterdam ell was equivalent to about 0·68 metre, so the "cobido" is here obviously the *asta*, or true cubit, of about 18 inches, not the larger Surat covad.[1] "Taffacylles" were probably what English records call tapseels; the name is applied to both silk and cotton goods, and the precise nature of this sample bale is doubtful.

2. Invoice of the *Black Bear* (*Swarte Beer*) from Masulipatam for Holland, 1619. (*Kol. Archief, portef.* P.)

The English records show that the *Black Bear* arrived at Masulipatam in July 1618, to be laden for Holland (*English Factories*, i. 41): presumably she sailed after the monsoon, and reached Amsterdam in the following spring. The date 1619 is not given on the invoice itself, but on a title-page which I take to have been added in Amsterdam.

Goods.	Quantities.		Value in Guilders.
Indigo	693 bales	= about 113,000 lb. avoird.	46,833
Wax	13,528 lb. Dutch	= „ 14,750 „ „	3,340
Cinnamon	48 bales	= „ 7,800 „ „	900
Borax	8 „	= „ 4,200 „ „	1,329
Yarn	30 „	= „ 4,900 „ „	1,548
Guinea cloth	10,406 pieces	= 246,000 yards	46,583
Bengal cloth	180 „	(not given)	6,474
Gingham	294 „	„	1,750
Other cloth	170 „	„	355
Carpets	50 „	„	784
Misc. goods		..	596
			110,492
	Ballast, packing and loading, and customs		11,192
	Correct value of cargo		121,684

[1] See Appendix D for these measures.

The total given in the invoice is 122,084 *f.*, but errors aggregating 400 *f.* have been noted on it, presumably in Amsterdam.

This cargo was drawn from a wider area than the first, but it consisted essentially of indigo, Guinea cloth, and samples or odd consignments. We may assume that the cinnamon came from Ceylon, the wax and borax from Bengal.

The pieces of Guinea cloth were not on this occasion of a fixed size, but the contents of each bale is given in *astas*, from which I have calculated yards. It was priced not by the piece, but by the 70 *astas*, most of the pieces falling short of this length.

The lengths of the other cloths are not given, but the "Bengals" were evidently of very high quality, being invoiced at 36 *f.* the piece, while the gingham cost 5 *f.* to 7 *f.*

3. Invoice of the *Medenblick* from Masulipatam, May 1621, for Holland. (*Kol. Archief, portef.* T.)

The English records mention that the *Medenblick* was nearly laden in May 1621 (*English Factories*, i. 254): the date of sailing is given on the invoice itself.

Goods.	Quantities.	Value in Guilders.
Indigo . . .	452 bales = about 73,900 lb. avoird.	31,473
Diamonds . .	..	27,094
Guinea cloth .	12,348 pieces = „ 308,750 yards	57,666
Bengal ginghams	80 „ (length not given)	384
		116,617
	Ballast, packing and loading, and customs	11,877
	Value of cargo	128,494

This cargo was purely local, except for the 80 pieces of ginghams. The Guinea cloth was invoiced on the same lines as in No. 2.

4. Invoice of the *Naerden* from Masulipatam, October 1621, for Holland. (*Kol. Archief, portef.* V.)

The date is given on the invoice, and confirmed by entries in *English Factories*, i. 297, 303.

These records show that this cargo was largely experimental, the pepper which formed the chief item being obtained overland from Malabar by way of Tegnapatam.

Goods.	Quantities.	Value in Guilders.
Pepper . . .	About 156,000 lb. avoird.	36,457
Saltpetre . . .	„ 47,500 „ „	2,964
„ refined .	„ 8,700 „ „	1,170
Diamonds . . .	..	1,326
Borax	„ 650 lb. avoird.	175
Yarn	„ 5,400 „ „	2,390
Guinea cloth . .	65,000 yards	11,918
Moorees . . .	900 pieces (length not given)	3,154
Betilles . . .	100 „ =1200 yards	1,200
		60,754
	Miscell. charges, and some small errors	2,000
	Value of cargo . . .	62,754

The pepper was "dear enough," and this branch of trade did not become important. Of the cotton goods, I take the moorees (superior calico) to be a trial consignment, but no particulars are given. The betilles (muslins from the Deccan) were expensive, costing a guilder per yard.

5. Invoice of the *Dordrecht*, from Masulipatam, probably September 1622. (*Kol. Arch.*, *portef.* X.)

This invoice is not dated, but there are indications that it relates to the voyage mentioned in *English Factories*, ii. 147. The bulk of the cargo consisted of Malabar pepper (200,000 lb.), saltpetre (180,000 lb.), indigo (60,000 lb.), and yarn (55,000 lb.), together with a re-export of 35,000 lb. of pepper from Achin. The cotton goods comprised about 325,000 yards of Guinea cloth, 2720 pieces (about 22,000 yards) of percalles, and 600 pieces of other sorts.

6. Invoice of the *Schoonhoven*, from Masulipatam, October 1624. (*Kol. Arch.*, *portef.* DD[i].)

The invoice is dated August 1624, but a supplement was added in October. This vessel carried no pepper, but there were ordinary quantities of indigo, yarn, and saltpetre. The cotton goods consisted of about 100,000 yards of Guinea cloth, nearly 30,000 yards of moorees, about 3000 yards of percalles, and the same quantity of salempores (an ordinary calico).

Invoices are also available of the direct shipments from Surat to Holland in 1624 and 1625, almost, if not quite, the first Dutch efforts in this branch of trade.

1624. Early in this year two vessels, *Heusden* and *Vrede*, sailed for Holland ; duplicate invoices of each have been preserved (*Kol. Arch. portef.* AA. DD[i]. EE), and dates are given in one copy of each.

The cargoes consisted principally of indigo and saltpetre, with small lots of yarn, lac, borax, and other goods. The pieces of cotton goods entered are Guinea cloth (1520), mentasses (9240), baftas of sorts (2928), semianoes (200), and cassas (muslin) (120). The Guinea cloth was as usual in long pieces, each of 50 ells, or say 37 yards. I have found no description of mentasses, but from the detailed entries they must have been short, because 280 pieces went to the bale (against 120 baftas), while the price (about Rs. 8 per 20 pieces) shows that they were of very low quality. I suspect that they were bought for Africa and not for Europe. The baftas were of all colours and dimensions: some bales are marked as samples, others as " for Holland." It appears safe to infer that the bulk of the cotton goods was intended for the African trade, while various trial consignments were included to test other markets.

1625. Invoices exist for two vessels, *Weesp* and *Dordrecht*. They are not dated, but a note in the *Dagh Register* of June 28, 1625, makes it clear that they relate to the voyage made by these vessels in April of that year, after they had taken part in the naval action off Gombroon (*English Factories*, iii. 47, 76). On both vessels the most valuable item of the cargo was Persian silk, the first-fruits of Dutch enterprise in that direction ; indigo and saltpetre took most of the space. As regards cotton goods, the *Weesp* carried only a single bale of samples ; the *Dordrecht* had 6000 pieces of mentasses, 1000 of Guinea cloth, 200 semianoes, and 800 cassas (described as " of Bengal "). If my conjecture regarding mentasses is correct, this shipment, like that of the previous year, may be described as intended mainly for Africa, with some samples for Europe.

APPENDIX C

MOGUL REVENUE STATISTICS

Chroniclers of the seventeenth century occasionally wound up their narratives by giving a list of the provinces included in the Mogul Empire, and the revenue assessed on each at the time they wrote. Similar figures are to be found in some manuscript records which are described as *Dastur-ul-amal*, and several specimens of which are available in the British Museum, where they are catalogued under the heading "Official Manuals." From these sources I have compiled the following table for ten of the Mogul provinces. The figures are in lakhs of dams, a lakh being equivalent to 2500 rupees at the official rate of exchange current during our period.

The table does not cover the entire Empire. It excludes, first, the Deccan provinces, where the Mogul rule was expanding. The names given for these provinces differ, and their limits varied from time to time,[1] so that any useful comparison would depend on a detailed knowledge of the administrative arrangements in force at a given date. It excludes, secondly, Bengal, because there is no satisfactory starting-point for a series of figures; the revenue-roll of this province as given in the *Ain* includes large areas which remained outside the Mogul administration until the reign of Aurangzeb, and it probably represents the demand as it stood before the Mogul conquest. My impression is that Akbar was content to take as much as could be collected from whatever area might be under his authority at the moment. Jahangir ordered a settlement of the country in the year 1605, but no result is recorded, and we know nothing of any formal revision of the revenue-roll until 1658.[2] Thirdly, I have excluded the small province of Sind because there appear to be very large

[1] See, *e.g.*, *Badshahnama*, ii. 710-714.

[2] Jahangir's orders are in *Tuzuk*, i. 22; the revision of 1658 is discussed in *Ascoli*, 23.

errors in some of the figures relating to it, including those given in the *Ain*; and, lastly, I have ignored Kabul, Kandahar, and Kashmir, provinces which had revenue-systems of their own. There remain the ten provinces which formed the heart of Akbar's Empire, and continued under the administration of his successors.

REVENUE DEMAND AT DIFFERENT PERIODS (LAKHS OF DAMS)

Province.	c. 1594.		Shahjahan.				Aurangzeb.
	Original.	Adjusted.	Accession.	c. 1647.	Late.	Late.	Before 1668.
	A.	*B.*	*C.*	*D.*	*E.*	*F.*	*G.*
Bihar . . .	22,19	22,70	31,27	40,00	39,43	39,60	[73,18]
Allahabad . .	20,83	21,00	30,70	40,00	42,43	44,96	43,67
Oudh . . .	20,17	20,34	23,22	30,00	27,95	31,52	32,01
Agra . . .	54,62	54,47	82,25	90,00	86,12	1,07,19	1,05,17
Malwa . . .	24,07	23,51	28,00	40,00	40,83	38,99	42,55
Gujarat . .	43,68	43,27	50,64	53,00	53,65	50,70	44,01
Ajmer . . .	28,84	28,34	42,05	60,00	60,29	65,12	63,69
Delhi . . .	60,16	59,56	65,61	1,00,00	1,22,29	1,19,35	1,16,84
Lahore . . .	55,95	55,91	82,50	90,00	89,30	85,47	90,70
Multan . .	15,14	14,95	[40,00]	28,00	21,98	21,62	24,53
Total . . (by addition)	3,45,65	3,44,05	[4,76,24]	5,71,00	5,84,27	6,04,61	[6,35,35]

NOTE.—The figures in square brackets are doubtful, as explained below; the totals in which they are included are similarly marked, and these have been adjusted before calculating the percentages given in the text.

The first set of figures (column A) is taken direct from the tables in the *Ain* (vol. ii. of the translation). In the *Journal of the United Provinces Historical Society* for 1919 I showed that these figures contained some large errors, which could be eliminated by a process which I described in detail. The results of adjusting the figures by this process are given in column B; it will be seen that, while the errors are important for individual districts or subdivisions, they do not make a serious difference in the provincial totals. I have used column B as the base of the percentages given in the text.

The figures in column C are taken from Elliot's *History*, vii. 138. The *Majālis-us-Salātīn* in which they are contained was (according to its chronogram) completed in the year 1628; it is a history of India up to and including the reign of Jahangir, and the historical portion closes with the accession of Shahjahan. The precise date of the revenue figures is not stated, but they must in any case be earlier than 1628, and the context suggests that they relate to the end of Jahangir's reign and show the revenue to which Shahjahan succeeded. The province of Multan does not appear separately in this record,[1] which speaks of "the province of Sind, including Multan, Thatha, and Bhakkar." Figures for Sind in some of the other records are doubtful, and I cannot suggest how much of the 40 lakhs entered should be assigned to Multan, so I have omitted this province from the text, and excluded its revenue in calculating the percentage of increase of the total.

As I have explained in the text, the only surprising figures in this column are those for Agra and Lahore: I suspect that possibly the initial 8 may in each case, or one of them, be a mistake for 6, an accident which might very easily happen if the original were in the *raqam* notation. I have been unable to test this suspicion, because the only MS. of *Majālis-us-Salāṭīn* which I have traced in this country is the copy prepared for Sir Henry Elliot, and now in the British Museum (Or. 1903); and, as was to be expected, the figures in Elliot's translation agree with the source he used. They are given in words, not in *raqam*, but it is possible that the copyist had *raqam* before him, and expressed the figures in words for his employer's convenience. This part of the copy—it is near the end—contains a large number of obvious mistakes in the writing, so that a mistake in the figures would not be surprising; but the point could be cleared up only by the original MS., which I do not know where to find. There is one curious feature in the copy. The revenue of Lahore is given as "present" (*hāl*), a word which is not used in the other entries, and this may possibly indicate that the Lahore figure is of later date than the others, but it may also be merely a copyist's mistake.

The figures in column D are taken from Abdul Hamid's *Badshahnama* (ii. 710 ff. of the printed text). Unlike most of the data, the figures have been rounded by the chronicler, and aim apparently at giving a general idea of the existing revenue rather than the precise figures for a particular year. The chronicle stops at the year 1647, and I take the statistical account of the Empire, which follows it, to relate to this year, or possibly a year or two earlier. The text inspires confidence, for the totals agree with the items, and the writer has been at pains to explain the increase during his period, while he mentions the famine of 1630–1632 as the reason why the revenue in Gujarat and the Deccan provinces was no larger.

[1] It may be conjectured that Multan and Sind had been farmed as a unit for the year to which these figures relate.

The figures in columns E and F are taken from unedited MSS. in the British Museum, the former from "Additional, 6588," the latter from "Oriental, 1779," and "Oriental, 1842"; the last is, I think, copied from 1779, with some incidental mistakes. These MSS. are catalogued under the name "Official Manuals"; so far as I can make out, most of the MSS. under this heading are copies made in the eighteenth century for the use of British officers in Bengal, and there are some grounds for suspecting that some of them may have been falsified so far as Bengal is concerned, but I have found no reason to doubt the substantial accuracy of the information relating to other parts of India. The MSS. I have used give the revenues at some unspecified period of Aurangzeb's reign, and then, for comparison, those of Shahjahan; dates are not assigned for these (or, if they are, I have missed them), but I think the circumstances justify the presumption that they refer to the latter portion of Shahjahan's reign. I have chosen these two sets of figures from a larger number, partly because they contain no blanks or obvious errors, and partly because they are, comparatively speaking, legible. The figures are in the *raqam* notation.

The figures in column G are taken from Elliot's *History*, vii. 164. The chronicle in which they are found does not go beyond the tenth year of Aurangzeb's reign, and I presume that the figures relate to one of those ten years; but their actual date is not of great importance, because they agree so closely with the two previous columns as to show that no great change in revenue had occurred in the interval, whatever it was. The province of Bihar furnishes an exception to this statement, but, in view of previous and subsequent figures, I think the entry of 72 karors for it must be regarded as doubtful. The amount is clearly given (in words, not figures) as 72 karors in the India Office MS. (Persian 126) of this chronicle, the *Mirāt-i Jahānnumā*; but the rise in revenue is exceedingly large, and the later figures I have seen for Aurangzeb's reign, while showing further general enhancements, do not bring Bihar much over 50 karors. Either the figure is a mistake; or it represents a speculative contract for an amount which could not be maintained; or possibly the revenue of the hill-country to the south, which in some later records appears separately as Gondwana, was temporarily included in Bihar. In view of this uncertainty, I have excluded this figure in calculating the percentages given in the text.

The notation used in the printed text of the *Ain*, and in those MSS. of it which I have consulted, is the ordinary Arabic notation, which presents no difficulty. In some of the MSS. from which the later figures have been taken the notation is *raqam*, which is by no means easy to transcribe. I have found, however, that in the MSS. which I have used the karors and lakhs are usually clearly written, while the thousands and lower digits are frequently cramped and much less legible. For the present purpose it is obviously unnecessary to take less than a lakh of dams into account, and I have neglected the smaller figures altogether; the totals given above may therefore have errors in the right-hand digits, but a lakh is insignificant when we are thinking in terms of the arb and the karor.

Some of the MSS. in question give the revenue under two or three forms—as *jama dāmi, hāsil kāmil,* and *hāsil sanwāt* (or *hāsil 'amali*). These are obviously technical terms, for occasionally we find the heading *Kaifiyat dāmi wa hāsilāt, i.e.* "Statement of the *dāmi* and the *hāsils*." The *hāsils* are given in rupees, and the *dāmi*, as the name implies, in terms of the dam. It has been usual to render *hāsil kāmil* as "standard revenue," and *hāsil sanwāt* (or *'amali*) as "current revenue"; but I have found no contemporary explanation of the terms. It is clear from the *Ain* that the actual assessment of revenue was made in copper, not silver, though the sum assessed was payable in either metal; and the position occupied by *jama dāmi* in the later MSS. suggests strongly that it was the original figure. I have acted on the hypothesis that *jama dāmi*, like the figures in the *Ain*, represents the gross revenue demand as reported by the local assessing authorities, and that the *hāsils* were derived from it by some process of calculation, of the details of which I have found no record. I cannot offer a formal proof that the *jama dāmi* is the original assessment, but it seems much more probable that the revenue continued to be assessed in copper, as it certainly was assessed under Akbar, and that the revenue offices calculated from this basis certain rupee-figures required for administrative purposes, than that the basis of assessment had been changed from copper to silver, and that the copper equivalent in the later MSS. was calculated from the rupee basis. The question what the *hāsils* actually represent is one of some interest, and could possibly be solved by study of the available MSS., but it does not arise on the hypothesis I have stated, according to which the *jama dāmi* furnishes the basis of fact throughout the period under consideration.

Some of the figures used in this Appendix were considered by Thomas in *The Revenue Resources of the Mughal Empire*, and it may be well to indicate the differences in the data. Thomas was concerned mainly with the total revenue and took all provinces into account; his aggregates, therefore, bear no relation to those which I have given for the ten old provinces. The figures he took from the *Ain* are practically identical with those in column A. except for Multan; the MSS. justify either 38,40 or 15,14 for this province, and, while Thomas took the former, I have been led to accept the latter by the tests to which I have already referred. Thomas did not use the figures in columns C., E., F., or G.; he used those in column D., and here there is no discrepancy. On the other hand, I have not used his figures for 1654, or for "Bernier's return"; nor do I refer to his later figures, which lie beyond our period.

The figures attributed by Thomas to 1654 are drawn from two MSS. (British Museum, Addl. 6598, 6599), which are in effect one authority. Each contains two returns of revenue: Thomas took the first in order of these, and referred to the second only as "illustrative" (*vide* his footnote on p. 33), but I can find no authority in the text for this differentiation, and it appears to me to be an open question which of the returns (if either) refers to the date specified in the MS. There is, too, a difficulty regarding this date. The opening of the MS. describes it as "*Dastur-ul-'amal m-h-m-li*[1] *hasb-ul-hukm* Aurangzeb (with titles) in the regnal year 3 and the Hijri year 1065." These two dates do not agree; the latter is, as Thomas noted, 1654–55 A.D., and this would give the official date of Aurangzeb's accession as 1652–53. I know of no authority for fixing it so early, his reign being usually reckoned officially from the deposition of Shahjahan in 1658. Whatever be the date, it is to my mind doubtful whether it can be applied to either of the revenue returns given in the MS.; the heading may mean only that the Dastur was prepared in accordance with a *hasb-ul-hukm* (a technical name for an order less formal than a farmān) issued in that year, and figures in such a Dastur might refer to any subsequent date. The use of these figures for 1654 would strengthen the conclusion reached in the text of a very large enhancement during Shahjahan's reign, but the uncertainty regarding their date has led me to discard them.

As to Bernier's figures, the chances of errors creeping in before they were finally printed in Paris appear to be so great as to make it undesirable to place them on the same footing as the authorities I have used. The total of his rupee-figures for the ten provinces

[1] The vowel-points are not given, and I can find no word of this precise form in dictionaries or glossaries; the hyphens merely indicate that there may be some short vowel. From words such as *mahmil* or *muhammal*, it may perhaps be conjectured that the meaning is "current."

is equivalent to 6,05,77 lakhs of dams, which is very close to F., but there are some large discrepancies in the items, which may represent errors in transcription or calculation. In the case of Thévenot's figures, which are given, but not tabulated, by Thomas, there is the additional uncertainty of the ratio which he used for converting rupees or dams into livres. Taking the livre at about the usual value, the total of his figures is equivalent to 5,91,60 lakhs of dams for the ten provinces, but in this case also the items present some difficulties, which may be due to the same causes as those suggested in Bernier's case. It seems safer to place these travellers' figures apart, as confirming the order of magnitude of the revenue demanded at this period, but too uncertain in detail to be used alongside of the data drawn from chronicles and other Indian records.

APPENDIX D

CURRENCY, WEIGHTS, AND MEASURES

ONE of the minor difficulties attendant on a study of the commercial records of our period is the diversity of units employed by the writers. The most convenient method of coping with it is to select for general use one unit of money, another of weight, and another of length, and in the text I have, as a rule, confined myself to the Mogul rupee, the pound avoirdupois with its multiples, and the English yard. In this Appendix I examine the relations of the common units to these standards.

CURRENCY

The composition of the rupee did not vary during our period: it contained about 175 grains of silver, and was thus nearly equivalent as bullion to the coin now current of 180 grains (out of which 165 are silver). Rupees of several denominations were in circulation, but at any particular time the current issue (known as *chalani*) was accepted as the standard, and older issues (known as *khazāna*) were received subject to discount of varying amount, while worn coins were also subject to discount. There was, of course, no regular exchange market between India and London, but for purposes of account the factors usually converted the rupee first at 2s. 6d., and later at 2s. 3d. The purchasing power of the rupee at this period is discussed in Chapter V.

Jahangir coined a rupee heavier by 20 per cent than the standard, apparently to square with the increase in the maund which is mentioned below. Some coins of this size occur in modern collections, but they are greatly outnumbered by those of the standard weight, and the change produced no permanent result.

Apart from the rupee, the monetary units most commonly

met with are as follows, it being understood that the value given is in each case subject to fluctuations in exchange.

Name.	Metal.	Where used.	Value in Terms of Rupee.
Guilder or florin .	Money of account	Dutch accounts and records	Fixed at $\frac{5}{8}$ rupee.
Rial of eight .	Silver	Spanish: well known throughout the East	2 rupees
Mahmudi . . .	Silver	South Gujarat	At first $\frac{2}{5}$ rupee, rising to $\frac{1}{2}$.
Dam (or pice) .	Copper	Mogul Empire	At first $\frac{1}{40}$ rupee, rising to about $\frac{1}{30}$.
Pice (half dam) .	Copper	,,	$\frac{1}{80}$ rupee, rising to about $\frac{1}{60}$.
Pagoda, new .	Gold	South India and East Coast	Rising from about 3 to $3\frac{1}{2}$ rupees.
Pagoda, old . .	Gold	,,	Rising from less than 4 to 5 rupees or over.
Fanam . . .	Gold	,,	Variable; several fanams are mentioned in the records.

Guilders.—Guilders (or gulden, or florins, represented by the sign *f.*) were not generally current in the East, but the Dutch accounts were usually kept in them, local currencies being converted at conventional rates, and consequently, so far as India is concerned, they are best described as money of account. The guilder contained 20 stivers, and the rupee was valued by the Dutch at the fixed rate of 24 stivers, making the guilder $\frac{5}{6}$ of a rupee: this rate is also obtained from numerous entries in the Batavia Journals, where sums of money are given in both currencies. The only aggregate of guilders mentioned in the Dutch records is the " ton of gold," an expression which must not be interpreted literally; it stands for 100,000 guilders.

Rial of Eight.—The commonest European coin in the East was at this time the Spanish rial of eight; it may be taken as equivalent to two rupees, but, in localities where silver was not minted, temporary variations from this standard might be considerable.

Mahmudi.—The mahmudi was the chief coin of Gujarat at the time when it was an independent kingdom. Akbar introduced the coinage of rupees at Ahmadabad in 1572–73, the year of his conquest, but the coinage of mahmudis was continued at Surat for some time longer. The coin was also struck by Raja Partap Sah at the fort of Mulher, lying in his territory of Baglān, some way south of the Tapti, and, after its coinage at Surat was discontinued, this appears to have been the only source. The mint at Mulher is mentioned by Finch in the year 1610, and in a Surat letter of 1619 ; in 1622 a safe-conduct for transport of coin was obtained from the Raja ; and coinage continued until 1636. At the opening of our period, the north of Gujarat had already adopted the rupee, but the southern towns, Surat and Broach, continued to do their business in terms of mahmudis, and the English factors used it consistently in their accounts. The rate of exchange was, of course, subject to fluctuations, but the normal rate was 5 mahmudis for 2 rupees when the factory at Surat was started, and this rate was maintained in the English accounts until after 1650, though the mahmudi tended to rise in value, and we find occasional statements that the correct rate was 9 for 4, and complaints that the Surat accounts were to that extent inaccurate. The rise was recognised by the English Company in 1651, when the rates for adjustment of accounts were fixed at 2s. 3d. for the rupee, and 1s. for the mahmudi, making the latter $\frac{4}{9}$ths of the former.

Dam and *Pice*.—The word pice was used during our period to denote various coins, and can be interpreted only as the commonest copper coin circulating in that particular part of the Mogul Empire to which the statement under examination relates. The name dam was given by Akbar to the large coin of about 324 grains, which in his time exchanged at the rate of 40 to the rupee ; but we know that this coin was often called pice in Northern India, and we find it commonly referred to in the expression, "a ser of 30 pice," used to describe the Akbari standard of weight, the ser having been fixed by Akbar at 30 dam. In Surat, on the other hand, the coin usually called pice was not the dam but the half dam, or *adhela*, as is shown by the fact that at the opening of our period the mahmudi exchanged for 32 pice, or 80 pice to the rupee. These copper coins were not tokens, but circulated on the basis of metallic content, and the rise in their value relatively to silver has been discussed in Chapter V. : judging from the catalogues of the museum-collections at Lahore and Calcutta, the weight of the common coins remained unchanged throughout our period, but was reduced under Aurangzeb. It may be added that the modern subdivisions of the rupee (anna and pie) do not appear in the accounts which have survived for Northern and Western India, which show only rupees (or mahmudis) and pice ; the anna was, however, familiar as a unit of account, though not of currency, in Bengal and Bihar.

Pagodas.—Gold coins, known to Indians as *hun*, but spoken of by Europeans as pagodas, were the usual currency of the kingdoms of Golconda and Bijapur, as well as of the Hindu territories farther south. Two kinds were in circulation during our period, known respectively as "new" and "old": the former were the current coinage, and circulated on the basis of metallic content, while the latter were no longer coined, and circulated at a fictitious value.

New Pagodas.—These were coined in Golconda and Bijapur, in various Hindu mints, and in the Dutch and English mints established by permission of the authorities. In the year 1621 the new pagoda was worth about 1½ Spanish rials, or very nearly 3 rupees. In 1633 the "Armagon pagoda," which was clearly "new," was taken as 1⅗ rials, or practically the same rate; in this order the rial was taken as 5s., and the new pagoda was thus worth about 6s. 8d. Later, the new pagoda was taken regularly at 8s., and the change appears to justify the inference that gold was rising relatively to silver; seeing that in 1651 the Company fixed the rupee at 2s. 3d. and the new pagoda at 8s., we may take the latter coin as worth about 3½ rupees in the last decade of our period as against 3 rupees in the earlier years. As is well known, the rise in the silver value of gold continued after our period closed.

Old Pagodas.—I have failed to find numismatic data showing the precise metallic contents of the different pagodas, but it seems to be safe to follow the account given by Tavernier, who traded extensively during his travels in Southern India, and is not likely to have been mistaken on a question of the kind. According to him, the old pagodas were the surviving coins of the Empire of Vijayanagar; they were of the same intrinsic value as the new pagodas, but commanded a premium (in his time) of about one rupee, apparently because some classes of transactions, and notably payments of revenue, had to be made in these particular coins. He adds that the melting of old pagodas was condemned by a superstition current at the time, and that the money-changers paid the king of Golconda a large annual sum to prevent their withdrawal for re-coinage. If this account is correct, we should expect to find the old pagodas appreciating relatively to the new, for while the premium would operate to prevent melting or export, casual losses would gradually reduce the quantity in active circulation, and thus the money-changers could count on a steady profit so long as the demand continued. As a matter of fact, we find that the old coins appreciated during our period in terms of the new, which were themselves appreciating in terms of silver. The recognised ratio about 1632 was 125 new for 100 old, but by 1651 the ordinary rate was over 130, and in 1656 it was above 145.[1] The actual

[1] A letter written from Madapollam to the English Company in the

value taken by the English merchants was 8s. 4d. when the new pagoda was 6s. 8d., and 10s. when the new was 8s., but the latter rate was admitted to be misleading. In terms of Mogul currency, the old pagoda rose during our period from under four to well over five rupees.

The fractional currency employed with pagodas varied greatly; the small gold coin, called fanam, was reckoned at different times or places as 12, 15, 16, 18, 24, and 32 to the pagoda, while the copper cash also had a wide range. These units become important only when rates are quoted in terms of them, and such quotations must be interpreted in the light of the context.

Weights

During our period there was nothing like a general unit of weight in India, and for a standard we must adopt the pound avoirdupois, which was used by the English factors, and has not varied in the interval. Care must be taken to distinguish the pounds (or *livres*) of writers of other European nations, which differed from the pound avoirdupois by amounts which were in some cases relatively great: the most important of these is the pound used in the Dutch commercial records.[1]

The Dutch Pound.—Several different pounds prevailed in Holland at this time, and in the original charter of the Dutch Company it was laid down that all spices should be sold by the Amsterdam pound, the weight of which was 0·494 kilograms,[2] or practically 1·09 lb. Examination of various equivalent weights in the Batavia Journals shows that the pound prescribed for spices was, in fact, used for all purposes by the Dutch factors in the East. To convert the Dutch weights into pounds avoirdupois, it is necessary to increase them by 9 per cent, but in ordinary reading the addition of one-tenth gives a fair approximation to the quantities denoted.

The French *livre* of the period was slightly less than the Dutch pound, and can be treated for ordinary purposes as its equivalent.

---

year 1667 shows that the local authorities had then secured a practical monopoly of old pagodas, and had forced the ratio up to 170 by insisting on the payment of revenue in the more valuable coin.

[1] The printed Batavia Journals use two distinct abbreviations for the pound. In case students may be tempted to think, as I was tempted, that the symbols might denote different units, I may mention that inquiry made from the publishers showed that the two signs are interchangeable, and mean the same thing.

[2] This figure is taken from Staring and van Wieringen's *Past and Present Measures, Weights, and Coins.* I am indebted for the reference to Dr. W. R. Bisschop; I have been unable to obtain a copy of the book itself.

It is dangerous to take the *ton* as a unit of weight at this period; usually, though not invariably, it denotes a measure of shipping space, representing about 60 cubic feet.[1] This is equally true of the Dutch *last*, which was equal to about 120 cubic feet or 2 tons (measurement). Thus in one place we are told that 158 last of rice weighed 474,200 lb. Dutch; this makes the last of rice 3270 lb. avoirdupois: in another place, some rice of different quality came out at 3750 lb. to the last, while a last of pepper weighed 2616 lb.

The *quintal*, or *kintal*, a Portuguese unit used widely in the East, was about 130 lb.

The chief Indian unit of weight bore the name *man*, now familiar as maund. All of those with which we are concerned contained 40 ser, but the weight of the ser differed widely.[2] From Akbar's time onward the maunds of the Mogul Empire had what may be called a scientific basis, the ser being fixed at the weight of a certain number of the copper coins called dam. Akbar's own ser contained 30 dam: the Akbari maund, therefore, represented the weight of 1200 dam (each of about 324 grains), or about 55½ lb., and can be thought of as half a hundredweight, but the English factors usually took it at 55 lb., and perhaps this was correct in practice, as the sellers' weights may have been based on slightly worn coins. The Dutch took it at 50 of their pounds, giving 54½ lb. avoirdupois, but from the frequent use of round numbers I suspect that their equivalents were selected partly for practical convenience, and not solely for minute accuracy.

[1] The ton made its way gradually into the avoirdupois table during the seventeenth century: school-books published early in the century used no weight larger than the cwt., but eventually the ton earned recognition. It appears to be uncertain when merchants adopted it as a general unit of weight, but it is probable that the schools followed the markets, and in particular passages the word may denote a weight of iron, or lead, or other heavy goods, but its ordinary use during our period is that of a measure. I have been unable to find any discussion of this subject, and the views I have expressed are based on examination of a number of commercial and educational manuals published during the century.

[2] One occasionally finds references to maunds of 39, 41, or 42 ser, but I take these to indicate commercial allowances made in particular transactions or classes of transactions: a seller might allow one ser extra in the maund, or a buyer take a maund reduced by one ser, where modern merchants would speak of an allowance of 2½ per cent. In a few cases there is mention of a maund containing 60 ser, but these seem to mean that the writer is explaining an unfamiliar maund in terms of the ser which he ordinarily used. To say that the Akbari maund contained 60 ser would be natural in the case of a merchant who transacted business on the basis of the Gujarat ser of 20 pice, for 60 of these ser, in fact, make one Akbari maund.

In 1619 Jahangir was told by a religious mendicant that according to the Hindu scriptures the ser ought to weigh 36 dam, and he promptly made this standard applicable to the Empire. We read of the Jahangiri maund at Patna in 1620, and the ser weighed 36 pice at Burhanpur in 1622, so that the order had widespread effect; the weight of this maund would be about 66 lb. Apparently this maund persisted in Bengal for some years after Shahjahan had introduced another standard, for the Dutch records mention a maund of about 66 lb. at Hooghly in 1636, and at Balasore in 1642, but in 1645 the Shahjahani maund was used at the port of Pipli. Mundy in 1632 found the maund in use at Patna to be based on a ser of 37 pice: this may represent the Jahangiri maund with a trade allowance of one pice in the ser, or it may be a local unit. In 1620 Hughes had found in the same market the Akbari ser of 30 pice, and another of 34½ pice.

Shahjahan in his turn fixed the ser at 40 dam, giving a maund of nearly 74 lb. I have not found a definite statement showing when it was introduced, but it was in use in Agra in 1634, when a Dutch record speaks of the maund of 67 pounds Dutch, which is nearly 74 lb. We meet this maund in various localities from Sind to Bengal during the remainder of our period, but its use was not universal, and it is important to note that indigo, in particular, continued to be bought in Agra by the Akbari maund.[1] It may be added that the "standard" maund of over 82 lb. is quite modern, and was unknown during our period.

So far I have written of the official Mogul maund. Gujarat had a system of its own. At the opening of our period we read of two maunds current there, one of about 27 lb., the other of 32½ lb., but nearly all important transactions were conducted in terms of the latter, which is usually taken at 33 lb., and is described as based on a ser of 18 pice.[2] In Dutch pounds it is taken sometimes at 30 and sometimes at 30½, the latter being, I think, nearer the truth, but the former being preferred as a round number. Shahjahan altered this local, or Gujarat, ser from 18 pice to 20. The change is recorded as follows in Methwold's diary for 1636: "February 12th. By order from the king, who sent his farmān to that purpose, the ser of this place [Surat], which hath in all

[1] Indigo was not the only exception in the Agra market, for a factor writing in 1655 about a transaction in cochineal reported that the ser used "is 40 pice, and not 36 pice as we were formerly made to believe; that custom being three years since altered" (*English Factories*, x. 18). In other words, the Jahangiri ser was retained for cochineal until the year 1652.

[2] The smaller Gujarat maund was obviously the southern maund, mentioned below as prevailing on the coast.

former times been but 18 pice weight, was now made 20 pice; according whereunto all weights were rectified. In Ahmadabad it hath been so for more than a year, and now the maund of this place is just the half of the maund Jahan, which consisteth of 40 sers, and every ser of 40 pice weight."[1] The rectification of the weights shows that the order was really effective, and from this time onwards the Gujarat maund was taken at or near 37 lb. in English records, while the Dutch took it as 34½, which is slightly more. Surat factors occasionally wrote of the Shahjahani as a "double maund," a term which is accurate from their point of view.

Southwards from Surat, and up the East Coast as far as Masulipatam, the maund was apparently not subject to official interference, and was equal to about 26 lb. (1 lb. more or less); we have 27 at Nizampatam, 26 at Masulipatam and Calicut, 25 at Dabhol, Tegnapatam, and Madras; and in this region the *candy*, or *bahar*, was usually 20 maunds.

It may be noted that the weights spoken of as maunds by the factors in Persia were much smaller than those mentioned above. At Tabriz the maund was only 6 lb. 5 oz., while at Ispahan the *man-i-shahi* or *batman* was 12½ lb. On the other side of India the Arakan maund was about 46 lb.

The principal maunds in use in India may thus be tabulated as follows:

Name.	Approximate Weight in lbs.		Weight of Ser in Dams.	Current.	Period.
	Avoirdupois.	Dutch.			
Akbari	55	50	30	North India	Up to 1619.
Jahangiri	66	60	36	"	From 1620 to about 1634, but in Bengal up to 1642 or later.
Shahjahani (or double maund)	74	{67 / 68}	40	"	From about 1634.
Gujarat, old	33	{30 / 30½}	18	Gujarat	Until 1634–35.
Gujarat, new	37	34½	20	"	From 1635–36.
Southern	26(±1)	24(±1)	..	South India and East Coast	Throughout our period.

[1] An entry in the *Dagh Register*, October 22, 1634, shows that the old maund was still in use at Ahmadabad in 1634, so the change in that city must have been made in the winter of 1634–35.

Some knowledge is needed of the Chinese scale of weights, which prevailed throughout the markets from Sumatra eastward, the weights being known among the islands by their Malay names. The large unit is the picul, which contains 133⅓ lb.: below this is the catty of 1⅓ lb., 100 catties going to the picul. Very little variation appears in regard to these units, but in reading of the spice trade it is important to remember that the catty of the Banda Islands was much larger, being almost 6 lb., and that mace and nutmegs were weighed by this unit.

Measures of Capacity

No Indian measures of capacity are prominent in the records of this period, and all that need be said under this head is to repeat that the word ton usually means a quantity of goods sufficient to occupy about 60 cubic feet, and that a last similarly denotes about 120 cubic feet.

Measures of Length

Gaz, Covad, and Hasta.—There is no Indian measure of length which can be adopted as a standard for our period, and we must employ the English yard, which has not changed in the interval. The measures of length prevailing in Northern India were known as *gaz*; they varied greatly, and Akbar attempted to standardise them in his *Ilahi gaz*, which, according to the data given by Abul Fazl, ought to be about 31 inches, but appears in practice to have been rather more than an inch longer. The *Ilahi gaz* was used in the North, but not universally. Jahangir increased the *gaz* by 20 per cent, following the corresponding changes in the maund and the rupee; we meet this *gaz* of 40 inches at Patna in 1620, but I have found too few references to it to show the extent to which it was adopted. About the year 1646 Shahjahan made a trifling reduction in the *gaz* then in use at Agra to assimilate it to the Lahore standard; I have not read of other official changes during our period, but in 1647 the Agra unit was still about 32 inches.

In Gujarat two measures were in use. The larger, almost exactly a yard, was used in Surat for woollen goods, while Ahmadabad seems usually to have employed the *Ilahi gaz* for this purpose; but for cotton cloth there was a shorter measure of just under ¾ yard, which was in general use along the West Coast. Whatever the length, the *gaz* might be divided either into 16 *girih*, or 24 *tassuj*, and both subdivisions are met with in the commercial correspondence.

The Portuguese on the West Coast applied *covado*, their word for a cubit, to whatever *gaz* they found in use in the markets, and the terms used by the English (covad, covett, etc.) are corruptions of this word. In the Gujarat piece goods trade it is safe to take the covad as nearly ¾ yard. In Sind we are told that 17 of the local covads made 20¾ covads of Gujarat; this gives 32½ inches for Sind, so we may infer that the word covad was there applied to the *Ilahi gaz*. I think it always refers to the *Ilahi gaz* in Agra also, but this is not quite clear: in Patna we have the Jahangiri covad of 40 inches as already mentioned.

On the East Coast we find the true Indian cubit, described as *hasta* by the English and *asta* by the Dutch, and usually taken as half a yard or very slightly more. Covads are frequently mentioned in the coast records, but in this case the word is used as a synonym for *hasta*, and not as denoting a different unit. An instance has been given in Appendix B, where 100 cobidos are equated to 70 Dutch ells; the standard length of salempore cloth is given sometimes as 16 yards, and sometimes as 32 covads; and various other incidental references establish the use.

The measures of practical importance are thus:

On the East Coast .	Hasta (or covad), about 18 inches.
In Gujarat . . .	Covad, nearly 27 inches.
In Sind	Covad (Ilahi gaz), about 32 inches.
In Northern India .	Ilahi gaz (or covad), about 32 inches.
" " .	Jahangiri gaz (or covad), about 40 inches; the precise range of the latter is uncertain, but it did not last for long.

Corge and Piece.—Transactions in the piece goods trade were not, as a rule, carried out in terms of yards, or covads, or hastas, but by the corge or by the piece, a corge (or score) being 20 pieces; and in order to appreciate the volume of trade, it is desirable to form some idea of the ordinary length of the piece. In the case of the Gujarat calico trade to Europe, this can be done with reasonable accuracy, because the cloth exported in quantity was of a few well-known kinds, and while individual pieces varied with the idiosyncrasies of the weavers, variations were usually a matter of inches rather than of yards. The standard lengths of some kinds exported were as follows:

Baftas of Gujarat . .	14 to 15 yards.
Dutties of Gujarat . .	About 12 yards.
Semianoes of Samana .	About 10 yards.
Joorees of Sind . .	Between 12 and 15 yards.
Mercoolis of Agra . .	About 15 yards.

I have not found a definite statement of the length of dariyabads as purchased in Oudh, but in 1662, when the English Company ordered this make to be imitated in Gujarat, the dimensions prescribed were 13 to 14 yards long by ¾ yard broad. An ordinary cargo from Surat may thus be taken as running rather less than 15 yards to the piece, the amount of the deficiency depending on the proportion of dutties, short joorees, or semianoes included in it; 100,000 pieces would represent from 1¼ to 1½ million yards. This figure would not apply to a cargo containing a large proportion of guzzees from Agra, as this cloth was made in long pieces varying from 30 yards upwards, but I have not noticed any such cargo during our period, and the export of guzzees to Europe did not attain large dimensions.

On the East Coast matters were more complicated, because the European shipments thence consisted largely of longcloth, which, like the guzzees just mentioned, might be of very considerable length, usually between 35 and 40 yards.[1] In the indent sent out from London in 1657, the Company complained that the length had in many cases been reduced to 36 yards, and a year later they directed that the length should be 37 to 38 yards, so that these figures may be used for approximate calculations. The letter just quoted shows further that salempores may be taken as 16 yards, moorees as about 9 yards, percalles about 8 yards, and white ginghams about 21 yards.

Consignments for the North African trade consisted mainly of turban cloth, the pieces of which were perhaps about 12 yards long on the average. Some of the goods for Guinea were much shorter, "negro-clouts" (Dutch *negroscleeden*) being only 4 yards; but the bulk of what is called Guinea cloth was longcloth, and was usually invoiced by the cubit. As to the export to Sumatra, Java, and beyond, the number of varieties of cloth is far too great for any accurate average to be deduced from the few records available; some of the common cloths were of the length given for calicoes, very few were longer, and a large number were much shorter, ranging from lengths of 8 yards down to what we should call handkerchiefs. Probably the average of an ordinary cargo for the southward was much less than 15 yards, but how much less cannot be calculated with precision.

[1] The number of pieces and also the number of "covads" are specified for three consignments of longcloth in the invoice of the year 1639 attached to *O.C.* 1656. The average per piece works out as 62½, 71, and 72 covads respectively; taking the covad at half a yard, these consignments averaged 31¼, 35½, and 36 yards, the first being much below the standard, and the others approximating to it.

Bales, Packs, Fardles, Etc.

So much information relating to the trade of our period is given in terms of bales, or other packages, that it is desirable to arrive at some idea of their significance. The packages of which I have found average or standard weights recorded are as follows; in some cases the weights are net, in others they probably include packing materials, but this has usually to be guessed:

Commodity.	Source.	Contents of Bale.	Means of Transit.	
Indigo . . .	Agra	220 lb. net	Camel	(English records)
" . . .	"	230-240 lb.	"	(Dutch records)
" . . .	Gujarat	148 lb. net	Not stated	(English records)
" . . .	"	145-155 lb.	"	(Dutch records)
Sugar . . .	"	296 lb.	"	"
Saltpetre . .	"	295 lb.	"	"
Silk . . .	Bengal	143 lb.	"	"
Cotton yarn .	Coromandel	165 lb.	"	"
" . .	Surat	188 lb.	"	"
Piece goods . .	Agra	110 pieces calicoes	Buffalo	"
" . .	Gujarat	100 pieces baftas	Not stated	"
" . .	"	200 pieces bairamis (6 yards)	"	"
" . .	East Coast	25 pieces longcloths (36 yards)	"	"

It will be understood that the size of a bale was a matter of convenience, and when goods were packed at the waterside, the limit of weight was presumably set by the possibility of handling the bales without the aid of modern mechanical appliances. I take the bales of sugar and saltpetre in the foregoing statement to indicate approximately this limit, so that bales were not likely in any case to exceed 300 lb., though they might be of less weight in the case of bulky articles such as yarn. Goods brought down by land were packed to suit the method of transport, the general principle being that two bales made one load, slung across the ox or camel. The load of an ox was somewhere about 300 lb.,[1] and the

[1] *Tavernier* (i. 39) puts the ox-load at 300 to 350 *livres*. *Mundy* (ii. 98) allows $2\frac{1}{2}$ cwt., or 280 lb. net. On p. 95 he takes 4 "great maunds," which may be either Jahangiri (=265 lb.), or Shahjahani (=296 lb.); he also gives the equivalent of the maund as 16 gallons, or two bushels, "London measure," but I am not sure what London measure he was thinking of.

bales of Gujarat indigo and Bengal silk were of a size consistent with this method of transit: indigo from Agra was frequently carried on camels, the load of which was about 500 lb., and the weights given are about half-camel loads. In cases, then, where goods were brought by land it appears reasonably safe to take the bales at about 150 lb. each, unless it is probable that camels were employed, when they may be taken at nearly 250 lb.; but when goods were re-packed at the waterside, the bales were probably larger, up to a maximum of 300 lb. As to cotton goods, where the weight is not given, it will be seen that calicoes were made into bales varying from about 1000 to 1500 yards.

Of packages made up outside India, only two require notice, the sack of pepper and the suckle (suckell, sockel) of mace. The sack of pepper at Bantam was about 62 lb. The suckle [1] of mace varied in weight rather widely, the limits indicated by numerous details in the Batavia Journals being 120 and 140 lb.

AUTHORITIES FOR APPENDIX D

The questions dealt with in this Appendix have usually to be determined by examining a number of incidental statements in commercial documents. I have not attempted to give a complete list of these, but I hope that the following references will suffice to justify the conclusions reached.

CURRENCY.—For the rupee, see *Ain* (translation), i. 16-35; and for discount on various issues, *English Factories*, i. 113, 236, 248. Jahangir's large rupees are mentioned in *Pelsart*, 11, but the French translation is not quite accurate on them. For equivalent values of guilders, see *Dagh Register*, June 21, 1634, July 31, 1641, February 17, 1659; and for rials, *English Factories*, i. 8, 187, 314. The mint at Mulher is mentioned in *Purchas*, I. iv. 424, and *English Factories*, i. 91, ii. 25, v. 225. For the value of the mahmudi, see *Letters Received*, i. 34, *English Factories*, vi. 91, viii. 256, and *Court Minutes*, May 9, 1651.

For Mogul copper coins, see *Ain* (translation), i. 31; for the Gujarat pice, *Letters Received*, i. 33, and *English Factories*, i. 269; for the anna,

---

The ordinary gallon of wheat about this time was 8½ lb. Troy, or say 7 lb. avoirdupois, which would make the maund 112 lb., so either he was using some other English unit, or he made a mistake in his calculations. (The weights and measures used for grain in England are discussed in Sir C. M. Watson's *British Weights and Measures*, London, 1910.) The conventional load of an ox in Northern India is still 4 maunds, or say 330 lb.

[1] The conjecture that suckell may be a misreading for picul (*Hobson-Jobson*, s.v. Catty) is negatived decisively by the Dutch records; and the fact that a suckle was a package is established by an invoice entered in the Batavia Journals under date May 31, 1657, where the cost of suckles and other packing materials is given separately from the price paid for the mace.

idem, i. 194, vi. 316. Pagodas are discussed in *Hobson-Jobson*, s.v. For the change in value of new pagodas, see *English Factories*, i. 262, iv. 300, ix. 15, 21, x. 33, and *Court Minutes*, May 9, 1651. For old pagodas, see *Tavernier*, ii. 90 ff., and *English Factories*, iv. 80; for their appreciation, *idem*, iv. 291, 300, ix. 51, x. 42, 103. For fanams and cash, see *Hobson-Jobson*, s.v.; *Bowrey*, 114; and *Schorer*, *passim*.

Weights.—The adoption by the Dutch Company of the Amsterdam pound was prescribed in Article 40 of the Charter, printed in *van der Chijs*, c. 12. The livre is discussed in *La Grande Cyclopédie*, s.v. The size of the shipping-ton is examined in Appendix D of *India at the Death of Akbar*. The use of the word last is deduced from numerous passages in the *Dagh Register*, *e.g.* February 19, 1641, November 14, 1644, and June 8, 1645.

For Akbar's maund, see *India at the Death of Akbar*, 53, *Purchas*, I. iii. 218, *Dagh Register*, June 21, 1634. Jahangir recorded the change made by him in *Tuzuk*, ii. 108; his maund is mentioned in *English Factories*, i. 199, ii. 230; *Pelsart*, 11; *Dagh Register*, February 8, 1634, June 10, 1636, and January 5, 1645 (Coromandel). The change at Pipli is noted in *English Factories*, vii. 72; the weights at Patna in *idem*, i. 193, and *Mundy*, ii. 156. The first record I have found of the Shahjahani maund is in *Dagh Register*, October 22, 1634; the survival of the Akbari maund for indigo is mentioned in *Tavernier*, i. 38, and *English Factories*, vii. 84, viii. 202.

For the Gujarat maunds, see *Letters Received*, i. 34, v. 106, vi. 167; *English Factories*, i. 60; *Dagh Register*, May 14, 1633, February 24, 1634. Methwold's record of the change is in *English Factories*, v. 156. For southern maunds, see *Schorer*, *passim*; *English Factories*, i. 153, 255, 289, viii. 216, and *Letters Received*, i. 319; and for the Candy, *English Factories* i. 262, 304, iv. 76. Persian maunds are given in *Letters Received*, v. 194, 237, 248, 288: those of Arakan in *Dagh Register*, February 6, 1636, February 13, 1637. For the Chinese scale of weights, see *Hobson-Jobson*, under *Catty*, and *Picul*, also *Dagh Register*, March 15, 1637; for the Banda catty, *idem*, September 27, 1626, and *Purchas*, I. iii. 203.

Measures.—For the *gaz*, see *Ain* (translation), ii. 58-61, *English Factories*, i. 192, 236, viii. 190; for Gujarat measures, *idem*, i. 21, iii. 355, vi. 241, and *Letters Received*, i. 34; for Sind, *English Factories*, v. 129; and for the East Coast, *Purchas*, I. iv. 391, *Letters Received*, vi. 71, *Dagh Register*, February 13, 1637; *Master*, i. 272. References to the length of piece goods are: for baftas, *Letters Received*, i. 29, 74, *English Factories*, iii. 247, iv. 8; for dutties, *idem*, i. 62, iv. 8; for semianoes, *idem*, vi. 134, and *Letters Received*, iv. 239; for Sind goods, *English Factories*, v. 129, vi. 136, viii. 78; for mercoolis, *idem*, vi. 311, vii. 123; and for guzzees, *idem*, vii. 7.

The size of longcloths and other coast pieces is taken from *Letter Book*, II. 13, 196: of North African goods, from *Letters Received*, i. 29, iv. 35; of goods for Guinea from *Dagh Register*, February 13, 1637, and various Dutch invoices. Examples of the sizes required for the Asiatic trade will be found in *English Factories*, iv. 204, v. 297, and *Dagh Register*, March 15, 1637; December 29, 1644; and May 14, 1645.

Bales, etc.—References to sizes of bales are: for Agra indigo, *English Factories*, vii. 84, *Dagh Register*, May 20, 1641, and June 20, 1642; for Gujarat indigo, *O.C.*, 1656 (invoice), and *Dagh Register*, May 20, 1641, and July 3, 1643; for sugar, *idem*, May 20, 1641; for saltpetre, *idem*, June 20,

1642; for silk, *idem*, May 20, 1641; for yarn, *idem*, December 4, 1634; for piece goods, *idem*, March 14, 1637, May 20, 1641; and *O.C.* 1656 (invoice). For pack animals, see *English Factories*, i. 73-76, ii. 123.

For sacks of pepper, see *Purchas*, I. iii. 161, and *Dagh Register*, August 21, 1631; for suckles of mace, *idem*, September 29, 1625, September 29, 1628, May 7, 1637, and many subsequent entries.

APPENDIX E

LIST OF AUTHORITIES

NOTE.—This list is arranged in the alphabetical order of the abbreviations or " key-words " which have been used in the notes to the text.

AGRA ACCOUNTS. The Accounts of the Dutch factory at Agra, 1637–1639, being Nos. 120 and 123 of the W. Geleynssen de Jongh Collection in The Hague Public Record Office.

AIN. The Āīn-i Akbari. By Abul Fazl-i 'Allāmī. Persian text, edited by H. Blochmann, and translation by Blochmann and Jarrett, both printed for the Asiatic Society of Bengal.

AKBAR-NAMA. The Akbar-nāma. By Abul Fazl-i 'Allāmī. Persian text, and translation by H. Beveridge, both printed for the Asiatic Society of Bengal.

ALBOQUERQUE. Commentarios do grande Afonso Dalboquerque. 3rd Portuguese edition. Lisbon, 1774.

ASCOLI. Early Revenue History of Bengal, and the Fifth Report, 1812. By F. D. Ascoli. Oxford, 1917.

BADSHAHNAMA. The Bādshāh-nāma. By 'Abd al-Hamīd Lahawri. Bibliotheca Indica, printed for the Asiatic Society of Bengal.

BAINES. History of the Cotton Manufacture in Great Britain. By Edward Baines. London, 1835.

BARBOSA. The Book of Duarte Barbosa. Translated by M. Longworth Dames for the Hakluyt Society. (The Portuguese text is vol. ii. No. VII. of *Colleção de Noticias para a Historia e Geographia das Nações Ultramarinas*, issued by the Lisbon Royal Academy of Sciences.)

BARROS. Da Asia (Decadas). By J. de Barros. Lisbon, 1777, etc.

BEGIN ENDE VOORTGANGH. Begin ende Voortgangh van de Vereenigde Nederlandtsche Geoctroyeerd Oost Indische Compagnie. Amsterdam, 1646.

BERNIER. Travels in the Mogul Empire, 1656–58. By F. Bernier. Revised edition by A. Constable. London, 1891.

BOWREY. A Geographical Account of the Countries round the Bay of Bengal. By T. Bowrey. Edited by Sir Richard Temple for the Hakluyt Society.

CALENDAR S.P. Calendar of State Papers. Colonial Series, East India, etc., 1516–1634. By E. Sainsbury. London, 1862, etc.

CAMB. MOD. HIST. The Cambridge Modern History, vols. i.-iv. Cambridge, 1902.

CAMPOS. History of the Portuguese in Bengal. By J. J. A. Campos. Calcutta, 1919.

CASTANHEDA. Historia do descobrimento e conquista da India. By F. L. Castanheda. Lisbon, 1833.

CORREA. Lendas da India. By G. Correa. Lisbon, 1858, etc.

COURT MINUTES. (1) Calendar of the Court Minutes of the E.I.Co. By E. B. Sainsbury. Oxford, 1907, etc. (2) The MS. Court Minutes in the India Office Records. (I have given the dates of the entries quoted, which serve as references equally to the Calendar and the original records.)

COUTO. Da Asia (Decadas). By D. de Couto. Lisbon, 1777, etc.

CUNNINGHAM. Growth of English Industry and Commerce. By W. Cunningham. 3rd edition. London, 1903.

DAGH REGISTER. Dagh-Register gehouden int Casteel Batavia, 1624–1681 (the official Journal kept by the Dutch authorities). Batavia and The Hague, 1896–1919. (A name, *e.g.* Surat, after the date of entry quoted, means that the entry will be found in the section dealing with that administrative centre. Only a few of the volumes are arranged in sections, and as a rule the date is a sufficient guide to the passage quoted.)

DALGADO. Glossario Luso-Asiatico. By S. R. Dalgado. Coimbra, 1919–21.

DANIELS. The Early English Cotton Industry. By G. W. Daniels. Manchester, 1920.

DANVERS. The Portuguese in India. By F. C. Danvers. London, 1894.

DE JONGE. De Opkomst van het Nederlandsch Gezag in Oost-Indie. By J. K. J. de Jonge. Amsterdam and The Hague, 1862, etc.

DE LAET. De Imperio Magni Mogolis. By J. de Laet. Leyden, 1631.

DELLA VALLE. The Travels of Pietro della Valle to India. Edited by E. Grey for the Hakluyt Society.

DUTCH IN MALABAR. Selections from the Records of the Madras

Government. Dutch Records, No. 13: The Dutch in Malabar. Madras, 1911.

Early Travels. Early Travels in India. Edited by W. Foster. Oxford, 1921. (Contains the narratives of Fitch, Mildenhall, Hawkins, Finch, Withington, Coryat, and Terry.)

Edmundson. History of Holland. By G. Edmundson. Cambridge, 1922.

Elias. Het Voorspel van den Eersten Engelschen Oorlog. By J. E. Elias. The Hague, 1920.

Elliot. The History of India as told by its own Historians. From the papers of Sir H. M. Elliot. London, 1867–77.

English Factories. The English Factories in India. By W. Foster. Oxford, 1906, etc. (The volumes are distinguished by the years they cover, from 1618 onwards. In order to abbreviate the references, I have distinguished them by numbers, i representing 1618–21, and x 1655–60.)

Etheridge. Report on past Famines in the Bombay Presidency. By A. T. Etheridge. Bombay, 1868.

Factory Records. *See* India Office Records.

Faria y Sousa. The Portuguese Asia. By M. de Faria y Sousa. Translated by J. Stevens. London, 1695.

First Letter Book. The Register of Letters, etc., of the Governor and Company of Merchants trading into the East Indies, 1600–19. London, 1893. (This title is taken from the title-page: the cover bears the title, "The First Letter Book of the East India Company.")

Fryer. A new account of East India and Persia. By J. Fryer. Edited by W. Crooke for the Hakluyt Society.

Gujarat Report. A Dutch MS. report on the various Gujarat markets, relating to the years before 1630; forming No. 28 of the W. Geleynssen de Jongh Collection at The Hague.

Hague Records. This denotes unpublished records of the Colonial Archives in the Dutch Public Record Office at The Hague.

Hague Transcripts. The series of copies of Dutch records in the India Office, entitled "Transcripts from Archives at The Hague." I have distinguished the three series by Roman numerals: I refers to "Letters from the East"; II, "Letters from the Dutch Co. to the East"; and III, "Letters from the Governor General to his subordinates."

Hay. De rebus Iaponicis, Indicis et Pervanis. By John Hay. Antwerp, 1605.

HOBSON-JOBSON. A Glossary of Colloquial Anglo-Indian Words and Phrases. New edition, edited by W. Crooke. London, 1903.

HOUTMAN. De eerste Schipvaart der Nederlanders naar Oost-Indie onder Cornelis de Houtman, 1595–97. (Lodewycksz' journal of the First Dutch voyage round the Cape.) Edited by G. P. Rouffaer and J. W. Izerman for the Linschoten-Vereeniging, 1915.

IMPERIAL GAZETTEER. The Imperial Gazetteer of India. Oxford, 1908.

INDIA OFFICE RECORDS. A description of these records will be found in " A Guide to the India Office Records," by W. Foster. London, 1919. The series from which I have quoted are—" Original Correspondence," " Court Minutes," " Factory Records," and " Letter Books," all of which are described in the Guide in more detail.

JOURDAIN. John Jourdain's Journal of a Voyage to the East Indies. Edited by W. Foster for the Hakluyt Society.

JOURNAL A.S.B. The Journal of the Asiatic Society of Bengal. Calcutta.

JOURNAL R.A.S. The Journal of the Royal Asiatic Society of Great Britain and Ireland. London.

LETTER BOOKS. *See* INDIA OFFICE RECORDS.

LETTERS RECEIVED. Letters Received by the East India Co. from its Servants in the East (1602–17). London, 1896–1901.

LINSCHOTEN. The Voyage of John Huyghen van Linschoten to the East Indies. Translation edited by A. C. Burnell and P. A. Thiele for the Hakluyt Society.

(I have used also the Dutch text, edited by H. Kern for the Linschoten-Vereeniging, 1910. The references I have given to chapters apply equally to both publications.)

LISBON TRANSCRIPTS. The copies and translations of Portuguese Records in the India Office. All the references I have given are to the translations of the series called " Books of the Monsoons."

MAJALIS-US-SALATIN. Extracts from this chronicle are in ELLIOT. The only MS. I have been able to find is Or: 1903, in the British Museum.

MANDELSLO. Voyages and Travels into the East Indies. By J. A. de Mandelslo. Translated by John Davies: second edition, London, 1669. (I have not seen the original work; much in this " translation " is the work of editors. Its value as an authority was discussed by Dr. Vincent Smith in *Journal R.A.S.*, April 1915.)

MANRIQUE. I have not had access to the original *Itinerario* of Fray Sebastian Manrique. The references are to the translation of some chapters published by Sir E. Maclagan in the *Journal of the Panjab Historical Society*, 1911, vol. i. 83, 151.

MANUCCI. Storia do Mogor. By N. Manucci. Translated by W. Irvine. London, 1907.

MASTER. The Diaries of Streynsham Master, 1675–80. Edited by Sir Richard Temple. London, 1911.

METHWOLD. This refers to the *Relations of the Kingdom of Golckonda and other neighbouring nations*, written by W. Methwold, and printed in *Purchas His Pilgrimage*, 4th edition. London, 1626.

MIDDLETON. The Voyage of Sir Henry Middleton to Bantam and the Maluco Islands. Edited by B. Corney for the Hakluyt Society.

MUNDY. The Travels of Peter Mundy in Europe and Asia, 1608–1667. Edited by Sir Richard Temple for the Hakluyt Society.

ORIGINAL CORRESPONDENCE. *See* INDIA OFFICE RECORDS.

OVINGTON. A Voyage to Suratt in the year 1689. By J. Ovington. London, 1696.

PELSAERT. An Account (*Remonstrantie*) of life in Agra, written in 1626 by F. Pelsart for the information of his superiors in the Dutch E.I.Co. A French translation is included in the *Relation de divers voyages curieux* published by M. Thévenot, Paris, 1663, but it is greatly condensed, and in places inaccurate; I have relied on photographs of the contemporary Dutch MS.

PURCHAS. Purchas His Pilgrimes. By S. Purchas. (The references are to the original paging, which is given in the margin of the reprint issued for the Hakluyt Society, Glasgow, 1905.)

For *Purchas His Pilgrimage*, see under METHWOLD.

PYRARD. The Voyage of François Pyrard, of Laval, to the East Indies. Translated and edited by A. Gray for the Hakluyt Society.

RAYNAL. A Philosophical and Political History of the Settlements and Trade of the Europeans in the East and West Indies. Translated from the French [of Raynal] by J. Justamond. Edinburgh, 1776.

REALIA. Register op de Generale Resolutien van het Casteel Batavia. Leyden and The Hague, 1882–85.

RENNEVILLE. Recueil des voyages. . . . Rouen, 1725. (A translation of BEGIN ENDE VOORTGANGH, with some additional matter.)

ROE. The Embassy of Sir Thomas Roe . . . 1615–19. Edited by W. Foster for the Hakluyt Society.

SARKAR'S ADMINISTRATION. Mughal Administration. By Jadunath Sarkar. Calcutta, 1920.

SARKAR'S AURANGZEB. History of Aurangzeb. By Jadunath Sarkar. Calcutta, 1912, etc.

SARKAR'S SHIVAJI. Shivaji and his Times. By Jadunath Sarkar. Calcutta, 1919.

SARKAR'S STUDIES. Studies in Mughal India. By Jadunath Sarkar. Calcutta, 1919.

SCHORER. Cort Verhael van de Cust van Chormandel. A concise MS. account of the Coromandel Coast, which reached Holland in 1616. (Overgekomen Brieven, 1616; eerste boek; Hague Records.)

SCOTT. Constitution and Finance of English, Scottish, and Irish Joint-Stock Companies to 1720. By W. R. Scott. Cambridge, 1910.

SEWELL. A Forgotten Empire. By R. Sewell. London, 1900.

SMITH'S AKBAR. Akbar the Great Mogul. By V. A. Smith. 2nd edition. Oxford, 1919.

TAVERNIER. Travels in India. By J. B. Tavernier. Edited by V. Ball. London, 1889.

TAYLOR'S DACCA. Sketch of the Topography and Statistics of Dacca. By Dr. J. Taylor. Calcutta, 1840.

TERPSTRA'S KOROMANDEL. De Vestiging van de Nederlanders aan de Kust van Koromandel. By H. Terpstra. Groningen, 1911.

TERPSTRA'S SURAT. De Opkomst der Wester-Kwartieren van de Oost-Indische Compagnie (Suratte, Arabië, Perzië). By H. Terpstra. The Hague, 1918.

THÉVENOT. Les Voyages de M. [Jean] de Thévenot aux Indes Orientales. Amsterdam, 1727. (For Melchizedech Thévenot's collection of voyages, see under PELSART.)

THOMAS. The Revenue Resources of the Mughal Empire in India. By E. Thomas. London, 1871.

TUZUK. Memoirs of Jahangir, translated by A. Rogers. Edited by H. Beveridge for the Royal Asiatic Society. London, 1909–14.

VALENTIJN. Oud en Niew Oost Indien. F. Valentijn. Amsterdam, 1724–26.

VAN DER CHIJS. Geschiedenis der Stichting van de Vereenigde O. I. Compagnie. By J. A. van der Chijs. 2nd edition. Leyden, 1857.

VAN DIJK. Zes Jaren uit het Leven van Wemmer van Berchem. By L. C. D. van Dijk. Amsterdam, 1858.

VAN LOON. The Fall of the Dutch Republic. By H. W. van Loon. London, 1913.

VAN TWIST. Generale Beschrijvinge van Indien. By J. van Twist. Amsterdam, 1648.

WHITEWAY. The Rise of the Portuguese Power in India. By R. S. Whiteway. London, 1899.

INDEX

THE END

BY THE SAME AUTHOR

8vo. 12s. *net*

INDIA
AT THE DEATH OF AKBAR
AN ECONOMIC STUDY

THE SPECTATOR.—"Mr. Moreland's excellent study of the condition of India in 1605, at the death of Akbar, shows how the subject should be approached. . . . Mr. Moreland writes dispassionately, citing all his authorities and giving his reasons for all his conclusions. He has thus produced a book of great historical interest."

THE TIMES.—"Mr. Moreland has set a standard of thoroughness, exactitude, and freedom from bias which provides a good model for Indian research students."

THE ASIATIC REVIEW.—"Mr. Moreland's economic study on India at the death of Akbar is valuable for many reasons. Not only is it brimful of instruction and suggestion, but it offers, almost for the first time, a coherent and consistent account of the condition of India at the period which may reasonably be taken to mark the beginning of the modern history of India."

THE JOURNAL OF THE ROYAL ASIATIC SOCIETY.—"The skilful way in which Mr. Moreland marshals his facts, and the interest he manages to impart to what might at first appear to be a dull subject, make most fascinating reading. A work of this kind was badly needed, and the want has been supplied in a manner that could not be improved upon."

LONDON: MACMILLAN AND CO., LTD.

NEW WORKS ON ECONOMICS

A TRACT ON MONEY AND THE EXCHANGES. By JOHN MAYNARD KEYNES, Author of "The Economic Consequences of the Peace," etc. 8vo.

An application of fundamental principles and reasoning to the chief monetary problems of the hour. A volume of unusual interest and value both to the financial world and to the students, with parts that will have an attraction for the general reader.

THE COLLECTED WORKS ON ECONOMICS OF PROFESSOR F. Y. EDGEWORTH. With Introductions to the various sections by the Author. Produced under the general supervision of the Author and J. M. KEYNES. 2 vols. Royal 8vo.

MONEY, CREDIT AND COMMERCE. By ALFRED MARSHALL. 8vo. 10s. net.

THE DISTRIBUTION OF INCOME. By the late WILLIAM SMART, M.A., D.Phil. New Edition. Crown 8vo. 7s. 6d. net.

PALGRAVE'S DICTIONARY OF POLITICAL ECONOMY. New Edition. 3 vols. Edited by HENRY HIGGS, C.B. Medium 8vo.

LONDON: MACMILLAN AND CO., LTD.